INDIA'S ECONOMIC CRISIS
Diagnosis and Treatment

INDIA'S ECONOMIC CRISIS

Diagnosis and Treatment

Editor
P.C. JAIN

CONCEPT PUBLISHING COMPANY, NEW DELHI 110059

ISBN 81-7022-393-8

First Published 1992

Published and Printed by
Ashok Kumar Mittal
Concept Publishing Company
A/15-16, Commercial Block, Mohan Garden
NEW DELHI 110059

Lasertypeset by
Microtech Advance Printing Systems (Pvt.) Ltd.
H-13, Bali Nagar
NEW DELHI 110015

Dedicated to

Late Professor V K R V Rao

CONTENTS

LIST OF CONTRIBUTORS

Agarwal, A.K., Reader and Head, Department of Economics, North Eastern Hill University, Mizoram Campus, Aizawal, Mizoram-796007.

Cauvery, R., Professor and Head, Department of Economics, Sri Sarada College, Salem-636016.

Chishti, Sumitra, Professor, School of International Studies, Jawaharlal Nehru University, New Delhi-110067.

Das Gupta, K.K., (formerly), Professor of Economics, Gokhale Institute of Politics and Economics, Pune, *at present*, UGC Emeritus Fellow.

Deb, Rajat, Department of Economics, Southern Methodist University, Dallas Texas 75275, United States of America (214) 692-4335.

Dholakia, J., Director, Development Research Centre, Ashram Road, Ahmedabad-380009.

Ferrantino, M.J., Department of Economics, Southern Methodist University, Dallas Texas 75275, United States of America (214) 692-4335.

Gandhi, P. Jegadish, Professor of Economics, Department of Economics, Voorhees College, Vellore-632201.

Giriappa, S., Professor, State Bank of India Chair in Rural Development, University of Manglore, University Campus, Mangalagangothri-574199.

Jain, P.C., Reader, Shri Ram College of Commerce, University of Delhi, Delhi-110007

Minocha, A.C., Professor and Head (retired), Department of Regional Planning and Economic Growth, Bhopal University, Bhopal, M.P.

Mohandas, M., Professor and Head, Department of Economics, Pondicherry University, Pondicherry-605003.

Mukherji, R., 2, Satrughna Ghosh Lane, Calcutta-700012.

Naidu, K. Munirathna, Professor and Head, Department of Economics, Sri Venkateswara University, Kurnool-518001.

Nayak, U.K. Sudha, Lecturer, Department of Economics, Sri Sarada College, Salem-636016.

Perumal, S. Velayudha, Reader in Economics, ICC&CE, Madurai-Kamraj University, Madurai-625021.

Pillai, G. Karunakaran, Professor of Economics, Department of Economics, University of Kerala, Thiruvananthapuram-695581.

Pushpalatha, Y., Ph.D. Scholar, Department of Economics, Osmania University, Hyderabad-500007.

Rao, S. Krishan, Professor and Chairman, Board of Studies, Osmania University, Hyderabad-500007.

Rao, J.S. Narayan, Professor of Economics, Department of Economics, Osmania University, Hyderabad-500007.

Reddy, D. Narasimha, Professor and Head, Department of Economics, University of Hyderabad-500007.

Reddy, K.N., Professor, National Institute of Public Finance and Policy, New Delhi-110067.

Selvaraju, V. Research Associate, National Institute of Public Finance and Policy, New Delhi-110067.

Shah, Maya, Professor of Economics, Department of Economics, M.S. University, Baroda-390002.

Shukla, Rohit, Professor of Economics, Sardar Patel Institute of Economic Change and Social Research, Thaltej Road, Ahmedabad-380054.

Singh, Ajit Kumar, Professor, Giri Institute of Development Studies, Lucknow-226020.

Sinha, R.K., Professor and Head, Department of Applied and Regional Economics, Rohilkhand University, Bareilly-243001.

Sinha, Rajeeva, Lecturer, Shri Ram College of Commerce, University of Delhi, Delhi-110007.

Vaidyanathan, A., Chairman, Madras Institute of Development Studies, Madras-600020.

INTRODUCTION

INDIAN ECONOMY is passing through a very difficult stage. There is a continued pressure on balance of payments, large budget deficits and double digit inflation. The problem persisted over the past few years but of late has reached proportions of a full blown crisis. India is virtually bust having drawn its reserves down below $ 1.8 billion lent by IMF in January 1991. Its total foreign debt of $ 71 billion is not in itself serious but its short-term debt of $ 6.5 billion and $ 10 billion in high-interest deposits collected from Indian residents overseas are causing concern. Worried about the possibility of India defaulting on its debt, bankers have cut off lines of short-term credit, and overseas Indians have started withdrawing their deposits. As a result Government of India had to go for double devaluation and airlifted 25 tonnes of gold to be parked in the vaults of the Bank of England.

Critical economical decisions need to be taken. Faced with apparently conflicting paradigms, the responsibility of economists is to identify the sources of differences in these paradigms. A failure to distinguish between the results of positive analysis and the role of normative considerations have bedevilled discussions of the merits of various paradigms. Unfortunately too many researchers, having undertaken positive analysis of some aspects of the working of a particular economy, have jumped too readily to sweeping 'policy conclusions', unwarranted by the coverage of their studies.

The papers presented in this book are an attempt to stand back from the heat of the debate. It is hoped that, by identifying the scope, strengths and weaknesses of existing knowledge, future research and teaching of the subject will be facilitated and better directed. It is a characteristic of the social sciences that a review of the accumulation of empirical evidence stemming from different sources or methodological approaches can reveal a consensus which is not apparent from the reading of individual contributions. Indeed, a number of papers in this volume reveal, that two opposing views, which are thought to stem from theoretical positions, often result from different assumptions about the magnitude of one or more critical parameters. These differences are often, in principle, testable.

The twenty-five papers selected are incisive and comprehensively researched papers reflecting on the present economic crisis. They are grouped under three sections. These are: (1) Economic Crisis: genesis, dimensions and acuteness; (2) Diagnosis: fiscal and monetary crisis, inflation, resource crunch, trade, balance of payments, structural adjustments, growth theory, polity and food subsidy; and (3) The Treatment: paradigm of growth, IMF recipe, liberalisation, economic policy etc.

Crisis

In the opening paper "Current Economic Crisis in India: Genesis, Dimensions and Salvage Strategy", **Prof. Pillai** traces its origin to large and persistent macro-economic imbalances and low productivity of investment, in particular the poor rate of return on past investments. He concludes his paper by suggesting that trade reforms, industrial policy and monetary and fiscal measures have to be looked at in their totality. This would require restructuring of the entire economy, effecting changes in agriculture, industry and trade to raise productivity and bring about technological upgradation.

Prof Mukherji in his paper "Indian Economic Crisis: Dimensions and Acuteness" hints that the crisis is looming large not only in the production base through industrial cost and price mechanism operative in the market but is also affecting both the private and public sectors, government budgetary operations, external debt servicing and, fiscal management. He sees India's economic crisis in the vortex of its old social order and imperialism, and discerns its solution in radical and substantial fundamental social change.

Prof Shah's paper "India's Economic Crisis: Invited but Unwanted Visitor" gives a cogent account of the economic scene in 1990-91, the economic policies of the new government and possible alternative policies and concludes that loan *melas*, loan waivers, corruption and tremendous waste are responsible for the present crisis.

Prof Agarwal in his paper "Growth Dimensions and Challenges of the Indian economy" describes the emerging socio-economic scenario in the country and concludes that the nation is confronted with a number of grim challenges posed by poverty, unemployment, inequality in income and wealth, unfavourable current account balances, foreign exchange difficulties, record budgetary deficits, severe resource crunch and an excessive dependence on borrowings propelling the economy towards a debt trap. He suggests the need to carry forward the advantages gained in the increased strength of the economy and to reinforce the infrastructure, both social and economic. He also suggests, that efforts will be required to increase the savings rate for improving the resource base, controlling wastages, making the best possible use of the basic resources like water, energy, minerals and environment.

Diagnosis

The economy is faced with a fiscal crisis. Government expenditure has outstripped revenue and the fiscal deficit in 1990-91 has reached 8.59 per cent of gross domestic product. Excesses in government spending, coupled with extraneous factors that led to the hike in prices of petrol and petroleum products, had a cascading effect on prices in general. The wholesale price index on a point-to-point basis is up 11 per cent. The average family has been hit even more because the index for primary articles has risen by 15 per cent, while that of manufactured products by only eight per cent.

To compound the problem, the country is faced with a balance of payments problem (The trade deficit has soared to a record Rs. 10,500 crores, as against Rs. 7,730 crores in the previous year). Foreign exchange reserves have depleted to around Rs. 2,500 crores. Only past year (in June 1990) the reserves were Rs. 5,800 crores. Thus, just within a year, the reserves have dwindled by over 50 per cent. This is despite the fact that India received $ 1.8 billion loan from IMF. Following paragraphs will diagnose in depth the various but related facets of present economic crisis.

Prof Sinha's paper, "The Fiscal Crisis: Wider Issues and Limited Policy Options" identifies the roots of the present economic crisis in macro-economic imbalances, and suggests a progressive reduction in the fiscal deficit of the Central Government. He also emphasises the need for a significant reduction of the revenue deficit as well as the current account deficit in the balance of payments to contain the exponential growth in internal and external debt.

Prof Naidu in his paper "Indian Economic Crisis: Imperatives of Fiscal Management, Needed Thought and Action" believes that the present crisis is not a sudden phenomenon but has been building up over the past ten years. To overcome the unprecedented fiscal crisis, he suggests measures to bring down the fiscal deficit to 1.5 per cent by 1994-95. The ministers, the bureaucrats, the administrators and government staff of all types should curtail their expenditure to the minimum by living within means, shedding all profigate living at the expense of government expenditure.

Prof Gandhi in his paper "The Deficit Dilemma in Development: A Trend Analysis" studies the financial deficit trends particularly since 1980 and its impact on the money supply and inflationary trends in the economy. One interesting conclusion that has emerged from the study is to design a price cut policy with an accent on more production of wage goods instead of luxury and semi-luxury commodities.

Prof Mohandas in his paper "Indian Economic Crisis: The Resource Crunch Trap" shows that the present crisis is essentially in the form of fiscal and liquidity crisis leading to a deficit-loan syndrome. According to him, the ultimate remedy lies in breaking the resource crunch trap by raising revenue, rationalisation of the tax system and improving the working of public administration, public sector enterprises, reduction of non-development expenditure and reducing the dependence on borrowed resources.

Prof Perumal in his paper "Structural Adjustment of the Indian Economy: Current Exercise" has analysed the implications of structural adjustment in an economy in the context of world trade and world capital flows. However, he concludes that the success of adjustment programmes depends much on the continuity in ideology, pattern of behaviour, and efficient economic administration which is lacking in India due to frequent changes of the party in power, civil administrators as well as economic administrators, and the members of the Planning and Finance Commissions.

Prof Reddy in his paper "Political Economy of Crisis in the Indian Economy" goes into the nature and causes of the present economic crisis and draws parallels with the experience of Latin American countries. He suggests that development should be understood from the perspective of the masses who are looking for better education, employment, health facilities and power to decide issues which affect their livelihood rather than on IMF package of liberalisation or globalisation.

Prof Rao in his paper "External Crisis, Sweeping Changes in Macroeconomic Policies and the Union Budget" examines the issues related to balance of payments, Fund-bank assistance, unemployment, poverty, devaluation, international trade, etc. and concludes that the recent changes in the macroeconomic policies and the budget proposals will do much damage to the Indian economy in general and to the bottom 40 per cent of the population in particular.

Prof Rao and **Pushpalatha** in their joint paper "X-crisis" examine the export crisis of the Indian economy and conclude that the Indian economy is in fact in a deep export-crisis. They suggest new avenues for exports.

Prof Sinha in his paper "Import Policy, Industrial Growth and Balance of Payments" takes a close look at the debate on import policy in the development literature. He argues that the relative merits and demerits of the two types of import regimes discussed is not the issue. There is a need to properly design an import regime. He suggests the difficult option of rationalising our imports and tackling structural contradictions in the domestic economy.

Prof Chishti in her paper "Economic Crisis in India and External Finance" believes that present crisis in Indian economy is due to external sector of the economy and suggests that the Government should retain its complete sovereignty to take all decisions affecting its economic and political destiny.

Prof Giriappa in his paper "Rural Energy Crisis" attributes the present energy crisis to the concentric effects of natural endowments and superfluous consumption patterns and suggests measures to manage it within the overall development perspective of the economy.

Prof Reddy and **Selvaraju** in their joint paper "Food Subsidy in the Context of Revenue Deficit and Treatment" describe the events that led to the governmental intervention in the distribution of foodgrains at subsidised rates and examine its role to the present economic crisis. They suggest a revaluation of the functioning of Food Corporation of India and target the food subsidies to the deserving classes only.

Treatment

The ongoing crisis requires a series of measures that make a clean break with past policies. The first task is to restore confidence of the international community in the quality of management of the Indian economy. There has to be new comprehensive economic policy statement. India has to take steps to join the global economic community. We seem to have got delinked from the global economy because of our inward looking policies during the past two decades.

Industrial licensing, import licensing, FERA and MRTP are some of the major restrictions on investment in India and their role needs re-examination. Banks and financial institutions need to be set up in the private sector to stimulate competition in the nationalised sectors. Serious thinking is needed in the areas of custom duties, patents, black money, etc. In the following paragraphs above issues and measures, taken by the Government in the recent past have been critically examined.

Prof Cauvery and **Nayak** in their joint paper "Coping with the Economic Crisis" examine a series of recent measures taken by the government to stimulate production, competition, exports and abolition of industrial licensing.

Prof Das Gupta in his paper 'The Crisis of Economic Deprivation in India and the Remedy' examines some critical dimensions of poverty and unemployment and suggests that transfer of income is an essential component of an 'affordable' social security which could be achieved through a voluntarist rather then a gradualist planned approach.

Prof Deb and **Ferrantino** in their joint paper "Foreign Exchange, Economic Reforms and Policy Freedom" study the relationship among economic development, exchange rate policy and policy freedom to understand the implications of recent changes in Indian economic policy to overcome the present crisis. They warn that if we fail to generate sufficiently positive incentives for attracting foreign exchange to the country we will be forced to return to the IMF with a more severe policy conditionalities.

Prof Dholakia in his paper "Indian Economic Crisis: Need for a New Paradigm of Growth" suggests that to be competitive in the international market, first we must be competitive within the national market. In order to bring about a new economic order we will have to alter fundamentally many of the behavioural parameters such as managerial autonomy and accountability, participatory production and work ethics, attitudes and norms of efficiency.

Prof Vaidyanathan in his paper "Emerging Issues in Policy Planning" argues for making change in the approach to rural development. The state should give overriding priority to rural development and the test of it would be in actual allocation of resources – for eradication of illiteracy, restructuring of education towards imparting skills and improvement in basic health facilities.

Prof Minocha in his paper "IMF Recipe for India's Balance of

Payment Crisis" analyses the factors which have contributed to the present crisis on the balance of payment front and examines critically the relevance of IMF recipe for overcoming the crisis in the context of Indian economy and suggests an alternative strategy. The alternative to IMF, according to him would be restricted imports as well as inflow of foreign capital, narrowing down of the fiscal deficit through a cut in subsidies to the rich, increase in direct taxation, economy in expenditure and change in the production structure.

Prof Singh in his paper "Liberalisation, Growth Strategy and the Present Economic Crisis" critically examines the nature of present crisis and suggests reorientation of our growth strategy towards a more balanced pattern of agricultural development, a greater concern for employment generation and focus on the production of wage goods.

Prof Shukla in his paper "Recent Changes in Economic Policy: Issues and Prospects" answers some of the moot questions of great relevance today: Is the world now headed towards a more promising future? Will all these policy changes like devaluation, opening up economy to the multinationals and others, etc., kindle new lamps in the huts and houses of millions of Indians? Will the new and emerging economic order usher in a just and harmonious comity of nations? Prof. Shukla sees a dim flicker of hope in maintaining peace and resolving conflicts by the Government. He argues that if the developed world start taking a more humane and helping approach, the debt of the developing world may be written off to some extent.

Prof Jain in his paper "Eighth Plan and Industrial Growth: Trends and Constraints" appraises the performance of Industrial growth during seventh plan and suggests some measures to boost the industrial growth during eighth plan period.

As editor of this volume, I am particularly grateful to the contributors who were willing to take pains to prepare original and thought provoking papers which have enabled us to go ahead with this publication. I should also like to thank Dr. D.C. Sancheti, Principal, Shri Ram College of Commerce for his perpetual enthusiasm for, and encouragement of, the enterprise. Finally, I owe a great deal to Shri Naurang Rai and Shri Ashok Kumar Mittal, my publishers, for their patience and support in dealing with a sometimes recalcitrant author.

University of Delhi
Delhi
November 14, 1991

P.C. JAIN
Shri Ram College of Commerce

1

CURRENT ECONOMIC CRISIS IN INDIA:
Genesis, Dimensions and Salvage Strategy

G. KARUNAKARAN PILLAI

INDIAN ECONOMY had been in the midst of an unprecedented crisis in the first half of 1991. Its origin can be traced to large and persistent macro-economic imbalances and low productivity of investment, in particular the poor rate of return on past investment. The combined impact of the imbalances in the internal and external sectors of the economy led the country to live with a mounting economic crisis. In the internal sector the macro-economic imbalances are characterized by high fiscal deficits and growing revenue deficits. Then is a long history of overspending by successive Governments that have lived beyond their means for more than a decade and borrowed huge amounts from public sector banks to meet their current consumption needs and finance investment in a public sector that obstinately refused to generate any returns worth the name. Despite its bourgeoning debt, the government sector was seriously short of resources, even for the core infrastructural sectors. Excesses in government spending led to the general rise in the price level and the country is in the grip of double-digit inflation.

The larger and persistent fiscal imbalances have strained the balance-of-payments position. The balance of payments which is characterized by a high current account deficit, a high debt service to export ratio and precariously low foreign exchange reserves, are assumed crisis proportions combined with the loss of exports to and remittances from West Asia owing to the Gulf crisis, there has been a sharp deterioration of balance of payments. Both the Gulf crisis and the domestic political developments affected the confidence abroad in the Indian economy. It became more difficult to borrow in the international capital market. Receipts under non-resident deposits also decelerated. All these led to a sharp decline in foreign exchange reserves. The immediate threat was that the nation would soon be bankrupt and have to default on foreign payments. The real solution to the problem, therefore, calls for urgent and effective measures to correct the structural imbalances which had led to the emergence of a chronic balance of payments problem in the first place. Immediately after assuming office, the Finance Minister, Dr. Manmohan Singh, introduced a package to pull the economy out of the mess that it was in. The structural changes effected within a short period consisted of: (a) a drastic downward adjustment in the external value of rupee, (b) radical change in foreign trade policy, (c) increase in the bank rate as well as in deposit and lending rates by banks and (d) liberalization of industrial policy.

In this paper an attempt will be made to examine the origin and dimensions of the macro-economic imbalances in the Indian economy and the appropriateness of the macro-economic stabilization programmes and the essential structural and policy reforms.

Growing Fiscal Deficits

The recent past of the Union budgets reveals a destabilizing trend in the Union finances as reflected in the staggering and unprecedentedly steep increases in deficit financing. It is interesting to note that the Central Budgets have recorded revenue surpluses in each year till 1978-79 but since then the structure of the Centre's revenue position has shifted from the traditional surplus to deficit. The Seventh Plan document reflected deep concern over the long-run disequilibrium in the budget. In the first two years of the Seventh Plan the gross fiscal deficit of the Centre (the gap between total government disbursement and revenue which is financed by borrowing, including from the RBI) was Rs. 21,857 crores and Rs. 26,342 crores respectively. In the succeeding year (1987-88) the fiscal deficit reached Rs. 27,044 crores, in 1988-89 it was Rs. 30,923 crores and in 1989-90 it was in the region of Rs. 35,630 crores. In 1990-91 the fiscal deficit was estimated to be Rs. 43,331 crores. The fiscal deficit during the past six years amounting to the staggering Rs. 48,000 crores underlines how we have been living far beyond our means. The fiscal deficit in 1990-91 accounted for 8.4 per cent of the GDP. The budgetary deficit as proportion of the GDP over the period has grown from 0.5 per cent of the GDP in 1970-71 to 1.3 per cent in 1980-81, to 1.8 per cent in 1984-85, to 3.3 per cent in 1988-89 and reached 3.5 per cent in 1990-91.

The trend in the budgetary deficit showed a disquieting picture of shortfalls in revenue while the expenditure continued to increase as budgeted. There was a structural shift in the pattern of financing the deficit after 1979-80, in the sense that deficit financing has been applied entirely to meet the worsening revenue account. On capital side the traditional deficits have turned into surpluses indicating that the Centre has been willing and able to borrow more than what it needs for its capital transactions with the surplus borrowing and the whole deficit financing being utilized to cover the revenue deficit. This anti-development practice of asset building resources – capital budget surplus – used to finance non-plan expenditure continued in the Central budgets since 1979-80.

As regards revenue mobilization much greater reliance has been placed on indirect taxes than on direct taxes. The Indian tax structure has become more and more regressive. The share of direct taxes in the total revenue structure has fallen from 36.9 per cent in 1950-51 to 23 per cent in 1974-75 and further to 15.8 per cent in 1987-88. The incremental taxation throughout the Five Year Plans, particularly the Seventh Five Year Plan, has been entirely from indirect taxation. Although equity, stability and the ushering in of an egalitarian society and the redistributive role of taxation has been much talked about, judging by the track record in this respect, the major thrust of our tax efforts has been to garner increased revenues for the exchequer from year to year. Concurrently restructuring of the income-tax rate schedule, wealth-tax and gift-tax concession and the abolition of estate duty have all contributed to a significant reduction in the progressivity as well as average incidence of the direct taxes on personal income and wealth. The lack of responsiveness of direct taxes due to increased rates has been due partly to evasion and partly to the plethora of concessions, and accordingly the base of the taxes has been severely eroded. However, as regards commodity taxes there has been a venitable boom during the past four decades, due to the expansion of the coverage of items subject to excise duties and Customs levies as well as an increase in production. Thus the dependence of the fiscal system on commodity taxation, which is regressive, has reached an unduly high proportions.

Deficit-borrowing Syndrome

Domestic borrowing as a share of the GDP which constituted 2.5 per cent in the early 1970s has risen to 4.3 per cent during 1976-80 and to 6 per cent in 1984-85. Internal public debt which was 19 per cent of the GDP in 1974-75 has doubled to 40 per cent in 1984-85. The bourgeoning size of the annual market borrowing at a high interest rate is the key reason for the spurt in the estimated annual interest liability. In 1980-87 the interest burden led to an increase in the overall budget deficit by 34 per cent, and in 1987-88 it was 87 per cent of the overall budget deficit. The budgetary deficit, the consolidated government and public sector borrowing requirements, and RBI credit to the Government has all increased in recent years as a proportion to the GDP. The strategy of financing the Central Government is a strategy in which deficits, borrowing and indirect taxation to meet the current account gap are resorted to. With an escalating trend in government borrowing, a sharp rise in the interest rates, further widening of the revenue deficit, large recourse to still higher levels of borrowing and deficit financing, is bound to occur and this is bound to retard the real rate of economic growth and distribution of income.

But the country was living beyond its means can be seen in the rising borrowing graph. A point-to-point comparison of India's indebtedness from March 1985 to March 1990, tells a revealing tale. India's external debt has risen from Rs. 34,000 crores in 1984-85 to Rs. 90,000 crores in 1989-90. The internal debt (the government dipping into bank and other accounts) had grown from Rs. 96,000 crores to Rs. 2,23,000 crores during the same period. Thus in five years the country's debt had grown by a whopping Rs. 208,000 crores, more than Rs. 40,000 crores per annum!

Gallcping Non-Plan Expenditure

The major components of non-development expenditure such as defence, interest payments, food subsidies, fertilizer subsidies and export subsidies account for 69.4 per cent of the Non-Plan expenditure. The three main Central subsidies account for Rs. 9,186 crores: subsidies on food Rs. 2,476 crores, fertilizer Rs. 4,601 crores and exports around 2,089 crores. However these amount to less than half the identifiable subsidies being doled out by the Centre and States. Almost an equal amount is given by the State governments as subsidies on power supply to agriculture, irrigation and State transport. To this should be added Rs. 4,500 to Rs. 5,000 crores of subsidies on higher education and 49 per cent of agricultural loans that are never repaid amounting to over Rs. 45,000 crores a year. In all, therefore, the identifiable subsidies are of the order of Rs. 30,000 crores which is one-fifth of the combined budgets of the Centre and States. Eliminating these subsidies can end the Government's fiscal and plan investment problems.

Most of the subsidies are open-ended. There has been no increase in fertilizer prices since July 1981. In these 10 years, procurement prices have doubled and the price of power has been halved in most States by populist-minded State governments. The hike in fertilizer prices hits only the larger farmers who have a surplus to sell. The budgetary subsidy to fertilizer industry was Rs. 3,650 crores in 1990-91. The support of the industry in the name of supplying fertilizers to the farmers at cheaper prices has only made the industry woefully less cost-concious and inefficient.

Following the recent devaluation of the rupee Cash Compensatory Scheme (CCS) has been discontinued. A reduction in export subsidy which should be aimed at closing our wasteful offices abroad, those that have not contributed any noticeable increase in our export trade.

The huge subsidy for public distribution is not so much for the consumer and the farmer as it is for the Food Corporation of India network. Public distribution should be limited to largest groups.

The subsidy on irrigation has led to the extravagant use of water and harmed the environment. Not even the maintenance cost of irrigation work is recovered. This subsidy may come to about Rs. 10,000 crores. Reducing the other subsidies will take time, political will and a considerable toning up of the State administration.

Interest Burden

The increasing level of non-plan expenditure, financed through borrowing, has led to an exponential increase in interest payments. In 1990-91 interest payment of Rs. 21,850 crores accounted for as much as 38 per cent of the net revenue receipts of the Central Government at the existing level of taxation. If the present trend continues, it is estimated that the interest payments would well account for more than 50 per cent of the net income receipts by 1994-95.

Loan Waiver

The Union Budget 1990-91 introduced a debt relief scheme under which outstanding loans up to Rs. 10,000 for the non-wilful defaulters engaged in agriculture and allied activities were waived by the Government. Of course this action increased the Government's financial liability and led to a much greater fiscal burden on the exchequer – Rs. 7,500 crores had been doled out in 1990-91. It was almost like handing a packet of cigarettes to a TB patient.

Double-digit Inflation

Recently prices have increased at an alarming rate. The Consumer Price Index (base year 1960=100) has risen annually by about 6 per cent during the 1960s, 8.5 per cent during the 1970s, and by about 9.8 per cent during the 1980s. However, in 1990-91 it has increased by about 11.6 per cent. The annual rate of inflation on the wholesale price index on a point-to-point basis works out to 12.1 per cent in 1990-91 as against 9.1 per cent in 1989-90. The inflation rate was the highest – 13.6 per cent – in 1970-91 as compared to only 6.6 per cent in 1989-90. The average family has been hit even more by because the index for primary articles has risen by 15 per cent. Inflation hurts every body, particularly the weaker sections, whose incomes are not indexed. The build-up in inflationary pressures in recent years is due to (a) fiscal imbalances, (b) supply and demand imbalances in several commodities and (c) inflationary expectations.

Worsening Balance of Payment

The balance of payment (BoP), which is characterized by a high current account deficit, a high debt service to export ratio and previously low foreign exchange reserves, has assumed crisis proportions. The Seventh Plan saw a widening of India's BoP. The ratio of current account deficit to the GDP averaged 2.2 per cent during 1985-90 which is far above the 1.6 per cent projected in the Seventh Plan. In 1990-91 it was 2.5 per cent of the GDP. The current account deficit averaged Rs. 7,771 crores ($ 5.5 billion) in the Seventh Plan as against Rs. 2,277 ($ 2.3 billion) during the Sixth Plan.

The BoP position has been under severe strain from August 1990 following the invasion of Kuwait by Iraq. As a result the oil import bill rose to 2.2 billion. The volume growth of exports which averaged around 10 per cent per annum during 1986-87 to 1989-90 came down substantially simultaneously. There was a severe loss of remittances from expatriates in that area. Further, there was a sharp decline in the invisible receipts from tourism due to disturbances in various regions in India. The inflow of non-resident Indian (NRIs) deposits in external account and commitment against commercial loans were much less in 1990-91 than in the previous years.

In the financing of this huge current account deficit in the BoP became a problem. During the Sixth Plan 50 per cent of the financing needs were met by external assistance, 28 per cent by way of IMF credits, 14 per cent by way of non-resident deposits and 8 per cent through other capital. During the Seventh Plan period the pattern of financing was the following: external assistance 29 per cent, commercial borrowing 24 per cent, non-resident deposits 23 per cent and resources drawn upon to the extent of 15 per cent. Thus with the current account deficit persisting year after year, external liabilities began to rise. The external indebtedness has been rising inevitably and the total stood at Rs. 97,966 crores, including NRI deposits of Rs. 17,831 crores, on March 31, 1990, and it has risen to Rs. 120,000 crores on March 31, 1991.

The problem was further aggravated by the sharp decline in foreign currency assets. The level of foreign currency assets declined from $ 3.4 billion in March 1990, to $ 2.2 billion in March 1991 despite the drawal of 1.8 billion SDRs from the IMF. The level of foreign currency assets declined further and stood at $ 1.2 billion at the end of March 1991.

The bourgeoning trade deficit during the 1980s had forced the nation to borrow recklessly from abroad. In the past bulk of the assistance consisted of official development assistance, or soft loans at lower interest rates. As soft loans diminished, we turned to commercial borrowing at higher interest rates. Thus the private commercial debt increased from $ 2 billion in 1980 to $ 18.6 billion in 1988. Interest payment rose from $ 503 million in 1980 to $ 2.6 billion in 1988. Our external debt servicing ratio increased from modest 9.3 per cent in 1980-81 to 26 per cent in 1990-91.

The immediate effect of the crisis was the drying up of two sources of finance, namely the NRI net inflow and loans from the commercial markets. The NRIs began to take out between Rs. 150 crores and Rs. 200 crores and the international banking institutions stopped lending to India. The short-term deficit had blown to an explosive position of $ 4 to 5 billion and a stage was reached when the NRIs could have withdrawn anytime their deposits of $ 11 billion in Indian banks between November 1990 and June 1991. During the seven months of 1991 foreign exchange resources have come down from Rs. 3,003 crores to Rs. 2,442 crores. The nation was forced to scrape the bottom to avoid default which was considered shameful. If the Government had not acted boldly in July 1991, India would have become an international defaulter whose consquences would have been unimaginable.

Appropriateness of Salvage Strategy

The current economic crisis provided a historic opportunity for Dr. Manmohan Singh, the Finance Minister, to reform the country's four-decade old economic policies. He has shown the courage to make the decisive break from the past and adopted a package of policies to restore India's solvency abroad. To overcome the grave economic crisis he adopted effective measures to control the BoP deficits as well as the fiscal deficits. He has thus set in motion a process of structural reforms and integration of the Indian economy with the rest of the world.

Macro-economic stabilization and fiscal adjustments alone cannot, however, suffice. They must be supported by essential reforms in the economic policy and economic management – reforms which would help to eliminate waste and inefficiency and impart a new element of dynamism to the growth process in economy. The thrust of the reform process should be to increase efficiency and international competitiveness of industrial production, to utilize for this purpose foreign investment and foreign technology, to improve the performance of the public sector and rapid modernization.

The macro-economic stabilization programme and the essential structural and policy reforms introduced so far consist of devaluation of the rupee, monetary policy measures, and reform of trade and industrial policies.

The devaluation of the rupee in two stages on July 1 and 3 by a total of 18 per cent against major foreign currencies was an integral part of the strategy to stimulate export promotion, to induce effective import substitution and to stop the flight of capital from India.

The devaluation has been followed by the announcement of certain monetary policy measures such as the increase in the bank rate (from 10 to 11 per cent) together with an increase in the scheduled commercial banks' deposit rates (raised across-the-board by one percentage point), lending rates (from 17 to 18.5 per cent, an increase of 1.5 percentage points) and the RBI's refinance rates. These measures come in the wake of devaluation, and aim at directly curtailing imports and reducing the aggregate demand in the economy.

Reform of Trade and Industrial Policies

The reform of trade and industrial policies announced on July 4 and July 24 was a bold and imaginative step and a major move towards restructuring the economy and particularly international trade. The past four decades have witnessed import substitution which has not always been efficient and was discriminate. Hence the new trade policy enables to expose the industry to competition from abroad in a phased manner. It aims at reduction in import licencing and vigorous export promotion and optimal import compression. It also liberalizes the policy regime for direct foreign investment.

The various measures such as trade reforms, industrial policy and monetary and fiscal measures had to be looked at in their totality. Correcting the macro-economic imbalances cannot be done in isolation. It necessitates the restructuring of the entire economy effecting changes in agriculture, industry, trade to raise productivity and bring about technological upgradation.

2

INDIAN ECONOMIC CRISIS:
Dimension and Acuteness

R. MUKHERJI

EXPANSION AND growth of industrial capital and market in general serve as the basis for recovery and high tension of production in different sectors of a country's economy. Industrial sector's contribution to the Gross Domestic Product (GDP) under the circumstances, grows at a faster rate over time. It influences other sectors and spheres of production which grow under its leadership and control, as suppliers and consumers in the house market. This marks a period of economic progress and prosperity.

Economic crisis is a quite opposite or antithesis to the orderly growth and expansion of an economy. It very much restricts and hampers especially growth and development of industrial capital in the factory sector and enterprises in other spheres of production and causes unemployment and misery in the society.

It thus seems logical and consistent that an overview of the characteristics and pattern of industrial development — or industrial capital's movement, activity and progress should centre the analysis of economic crisis, for the sake of locating the main factors of disturbance and disorder in the productive system of the economy. A proper insight to the characteristics, nature of composition and operation of the factory sector shows the sensitive spots, vulnerable points, fluctuations in production anomalies — and, in sum, the contradiction inherent in the capitalist system that itself engenders and precipitates the crisis. Furthermore, it reveals the inter-relation between the national and international capitals, growth of the factory sector and large-scale commodity production with the employment of wage-labour and their developments over time.

I. INTRODUCTION

A general enquiry and review of the factory sector is central and imperative to the analysis of the Indian economic crisis. A correct approach to the diagnosis of the crisis should proceed with the critical assessment of the growth and development of the factory sector proper — the basis of the advanced mode of production in the economy.

Economic development proceeds with the gradual and long-term expansion of large-scale commodity production and industrial development increasingly contributing to the growth of national income. Industrial development is the result of the sustained growth and development of large-scale commodity production with the employment of wage labour in a market economy. For, material production is centralised in the factory sector — the prime mover of industrial development. Factory sector hosts and absorbs the modern industry and its core function for industrialisation and progress of an economy. An analysis of the factory sector necessarily becomes of much more importance and great value to inquire about the characteristics and pattern of industrial development and locate the base and sphere of crisis. The advance of factory sector and its main characteristics which have progressed and developed during the past three decades, can be regarded as the factors constituting the basis structure, operation and growth of industries which influence the pattern of industrial development and growth of the country's economy.

II. THE FACTORY SECTOR AND ITS CHARACTERISTICS

The data in Table 2.1 show the developments of the factory sector in terms of number of factories, employment, fixed capital, grows output and value added during the period 1960 – 1984-85. It can be followed that the annual growth rates of fixed capital, gross output and value added were very high in comparison with that of employment. It largely follows the tendency of the centralisation and concentration of capital, and expansion of the process of capitalist production and contradiction between the labour and capital in the Indian situation.

It was found that the number of factories in 1982-83 through 1980-81 declined to 93,166 from 96,503 or by 3.5 per cent, but the factory sector has registered handsome rise over the long period. Their capital structure improved all through. Their fixed capital grew from

TABLE 2.1: India, Factory Sector, 1960 — 1984-85

(Amount in Crores of Rupees)

Year	Factories ('000s)	Employment ('000s)	Fixed Capital	Gross Output	Value Added
Main Characteristics:					
1960	40.5	3644	1450	3915	1017
1970-71	64.6	5216	87522	13768	3149
1978-79	88.1	7248	22886	44344	9554
1979-80	95.1	7673	26830	52258	10865
1980-81	96.5	7854	29900	61084	11929
1981-82	105.0	7894	34702	73630	14512
1982-83	93.2	8166	41006	86238	16674
1983-84	96.7	7994	48606	93537	20137
1984-85	96.9	7981	54642	105566	20887
Annual Growth (in per cent)					
1960	8.1	2.1	n.a	14.9	13.7
1970-71	7.3	3.7	10.2	14.2	13.4
1978-79	3.7	2.2	13.6	13.9	17.7
1979-80	8.0	5.9	17.2	17.8	13.7
1980-81	1.4	2.4	11.4	16.9	9.8
1981-82	8.8	0.5	16.1	20.6	22.0
1982-83	–11.2	3.4	18.2	17.1	14.0
1983-84	3.8	–2.1	18.5	8.5	20.8
1984-85	0.2	–0.2	12.8	12.9	3.7

Note: The data in this table and the next eight cover all factories employing 10 or more workers and using power and 20 or more workers not using power. Employment in this table includes persons engaged as working proprietors, unpaid family workers etc., but not in the subsequent eight tables.

Source: Statistical Outline of India, 1989-90, Tata Services Ltd., Department of Economics and Statistics, Bombay, p. 75.

Rs. 29,900 crores to 41,006 crores, productive capital from Rs. 43,120 crores to Rs. 57,326 crores and the invested capital from Rs. 46,381 crores to 62,992 crores during 1980-81 and 1982-83. The number of workers rose from 6047 thousand to 6313 thousand, employees from 7215 to 8010 thousand, and persons engaged from 7854 to 8166 thousand in 1982-83 through 1980-81. The value of total input of the Indian factory sector increased from Rs. 47,238 crores to Rs. 67,096 crores and gross output from the Rs. 61,084 to Rs. 86,238 crores during the same period. The amount of depreciation rose from Rs. 1,917crores to Rs. 2,467 crores. The net value added or value added, grew from

Rs. 11,929 crores to Rs. 16,674 crores, net fixed capital formation from Rs. 3,388 crores to Rs. 5,396 crores, while the net income rose from Rs. 9,030 to Rs. 12,400 crores. Wages to the workers increased from Rs. 3,945 to Rs. 5,148 crores, and total payment of emoluments rose from 6,096 crores to Rs. 8,046 crores during 1980-81 and 1982-83. Qualitatively, the increase of these characteristics in this period was as follows :

> Factories 3.5 per cent, fixed capital 37.1 per cent, productive capital 33 per cent, invested capital 34.4 per cent, workers 4.4 per cent, total inputs 42 per cent, gross output 41.2 per cent and net value added 39.8 per cent (Table 2.2).

Distribution[1] of the characteristics by capital-range of the factories in 1982-83 showed that, the factories with capital-range from below Rs. 1 lakh to Rs.7.5 lakhs in plant and machinery had 72.8 per cent of the factories, 3.5 per cent of fixed capital, 5.1 per cent of productive capital, 5.3 per cent of invested capital, 26.6 per cent of workers, 25 per cent of employees, 12.8 per cent of wages, 12.3 per cent of emoluments, 16.4 per cent of inputs, 15 per cent of gross output, 5.7 per cent of depreciation and 10.2 per cent of value added. Factories in the capital range of Rs. 7.5-20 lakhs accounted for 8.4 per cent of the factories, 2.4 per cent of fixed capital, 2.9 per cent of productive capital, 7.9 per cent of workers, 7.8 per cent of employees, 5.1 per cent of wages, 5.4 per cent of total emoluments, 7.6 per cent of total inputs, 7 per cent of gross output, 4.5 per cent of depreciation and 5.2 per cent of the value added. Factories unspecified capital range had 10.6, 0.2, 0.3, 0.3, 6.1, 5.2, 2.1, 2.6, 1.0, 1.0, 0.2 and 1.1 per cent of those characteristics respectively (Table 2.3).

Against this pattern, the units with capital range of above Rs. 20 lakhs reported 8.2 per cent of factories, 93.9 per cent of fixed capital, 91.1 per cent of productive capital, 91.1 per cent of invested capital, 59.4 per cent of workers, 62 per cent of employees, 80 per cent of wages to the workers, 79.7 per cent of emoluments, 75 per cent of total input, 77 gross output, 89.6 per cent of the depreciation and 83.5 per cent of value added in 1982-83 (Table 2.3). This trend of capital and production concentration[2] continued through 1984-85, when factories with capital range of above Rs. 20 lakhs numbered 9993 (10.3%) reported Rs. 51,940 crores worth of fixed capital (94.7%), gross output of Rs. 84,034 crores (79.6%), employment of 5222 thousand (66.3%)

and value added Rs. 17,421 crores (83.4%).

TABLE 2.2: Principal Characteristics — Factory Sector, India

Principal Characteristics	Unit	1980-81	1982-83	Percentage increase (+) or decrease (-) in 1982-83 over 1980-81
1. Factories	Number	96,503	93,166	–3.5
2. Capital Structure	Rs. Crores			
2.1 Fixed capital		29,900	41,006	37.1
2.2 Productive capital		43,120	57,326	33.0
2.3 Invested capital		46,381	62,992	34.4
3. Work from	Thousands			
3.1 Workers		6,047	6,313	4.4
3.2 Employees		7,215	8,010	11.0
3.3 Persons engaged		7,854	8,166	4.0
4. Wages to Workers	Rs. Crores	3,945	5,148	30.5
5. Emoluments		6,096	8,046	32.0
6. Total Inputs		47,238	67,096	42.0
7. Gross Output		61,084	86,238	41.2
8. Depreciation		1,917	2,467	28.7
9. New Value Added		11,929	16,674	39.8
10. New Fixed Capital Formation		3,338	5,396	61.6
11. Net Income		9,030	12,400	37.3

Source: Annual Survey of Industries — Factory Sector, p. 5 (Central Statistical Organisation, Government of India, New Delhi).

Factories employing 2000 persons and more numbered 521 (0.5%), absorbed 32.5 per cent of workforce, 62.3 per cent of fixed capital, 27 per cent of gross output and 36.1 per cent of value added in 1980-81. The number of such factories in this employment-range in 1984-85 dwindled to 436 (0.5%) but improved to 33 per cent of employment, 72.4 per cent of fixed capital, 30.2 per cent of gross output and 37.7 per cent of the value added. Factories with employment range of 500-1999 persons in 1980-81 numbered 1829 (1.9%) and accounted for 23.4 per cent of employment, 21.8 per cent of fixed capital, 28.2 per cent of gross output and 30 per cent of the value added. Their number

TABLE 2.3: Principal Characteristics, Factory Sector — Percentage Distribution 1982-83

Capital Range (Rs. Lakhs)	Factories	Fixed Capital	Productive Capital	Invested Capital	Workers	Employees	Wages to workers	Wages to workers	Total Input	Gross Output	Depreciation	Net Value Added
Up to Rs. 1	37.9	0.6	1.3	1.3	10.4	9.6	4.3	4.2	4.7	4.3	0.9	3.1
1.0 — 2.5	18.3	1.0	1.4	1.4	6.7	6.3	3.4	3.1	4.5	4.1	1.5	2.6
2.5 — 5	11.4	1.1	1.5	1.6	5.9	5.7	3.2	3.0	4.5	4.1	1.9	2.8
5.0 — 7.5	5.2	0.8	0.9	1.0	3.6	3.4	1.9	2.0	2.7	2.5	1.4	1.7
7.5 — 10	3.2	0.6	0.8	0.9	2.4	2.4	1.4	1.4	2.2	2.0	1.2	1.4
10 — 20	5.2	1.8	2.1	2.4	5.5	5.4	3.7	4.0	5.4	5.0	3.3	3.8
20 — 25	1.6	0.8	1.0	1.1	1.8	1.9	1.4	1.5	2.3	2.1	1.7	1.7
Above 25	6.6	93.1	90.7	90.0	57.6	60.1	78.6	78.2	72.7	74.9	87.9	81.8
Unspecified	10.6	0.2	0.3	0.3	6.1	5.2	2.1	2.6	1.0	1.0	0.2	1.1
Total	100.0	100.0	100.0	100.0	100.0	100.0	100.0	100.0	100.0	100.0	100.0	100.0

Source: Annual Survey of Industries, 1982-83, p. 12 (Central Statistical Organisation, Government of India, New Delhi).

TABLE 2.4: Principal Characteristics, Factory Sector, 1980-81 — 1984-85

Employment Range (Persons)	No. of Factories		Employment in Lakhs		Fixed Capital in Rs. Crores		Gross output in Rs. Crores		Value Added in Rs. Crores	
	1980-81	1984-85	1980-81	1984-85	1980-81	1984-85	1980-81	1984-85	1980-81	1984-85
Up to 99	85,883	86,552	17.6	18.9	2,107	3,996	13,006	20,898	1,676	2,865
100 — 499	8,270	8,085	16.4	16.6	2,663	5,806	14,487	22,203	2,393	4,272
500 — 1999	1,829	1,874	18.0	17.3	6,504	10,841	17,224	30,646	3,553	5,868
2000 & Above	521	436	25.1	25.9	18,626	34,199	16,367	31,819	4,307	7,882
Total	96,503	96,947	77.1	78.7	29,900	54,842	61,084	1,05,566	11,929	20,887
Percentage Distribution:										
Up to 99	89.0	89.3	22.3	24.0	7.0	7.3	21.3	19.8	14.0	13.7
100 — 499	8.6	8.3	21.2	21.0	8.9	10.6	23.7	21.0	20.1	20.5
500 — 1999	1.9	1.9	23.4	22.0	21.8	19.8	28.2	29.0	29.8	28.1
2000 & Above	0.5	0.5	32.6	33.0	62.3	62.3	26.8	30.2	36.1	37.7
Total	100.0	100.0	100.0	100.0	100.0	100.0	100.0	100.0	100.0	100.0

Source: Annual Survey of Industries, 1980-81 and 1984-85 — Factory Sector, p. 9. (Central Statistical Organisation, Government of India, New Delhi).

increased to 1874 (1.9%) in 1984-85 but their position appears to have declined in terms of employment, fixed capital and value added, although their gross output improved by 0.8 percentage point. Factories within the employment range up to 499 persons in 1980-81, numbered 94,153 (97.6%) engaged 44.0 per cent of the work force, and accounted for 15.9 per cent of fixed capital, 45.0 per cent of gross output and 34 per cent of the value added. Their number increased to 94,637 (97.6%) but had increased share in employment, fixed capital and gross output at 45, 17.9 and 40.8 per cent respectively in 1984-85. Their contribution to the gross output declined by 4.2 percentage point, while that of value added increased by 0.4 percentage point during 1980-81 and 1984-85. But while the factories in employment-range of 100-499 persons had actually increased their share in value added from 20.1 to 20.5 per cent, the share of the factories with employment range up to 99 persons, in the value added declined from 14 per cent to 13.7 per cent in the same period (Table 2.4).

On the whole, the variation and differentiation in the Indian factory sector and concentration of capital reached to such a high point that 2,350 factories (2.4%) belonging to both the public and private sectors and employing 500 and more persons and obviously with capital investment of Rs. 20 lakhs and above accounted for, on the average, nearly 83 per cent of fixed capital, 57 per cent of gross output and 65.8 per cent of the value added in the first half of 1980s. Capital makes and follows its own law of development peculiar to the society.

The ownership of India's factory sector is quite spatial and flexible, and it has undergone changes and transformation over the years. During 1981-82 and 1984-85, the total number of factories witnessed an absolute decline by some 8,084, while the number of public sector factories increased by 542, and joint sector factories by 105, and private sector factories decreased by 8,747. Employment in the public sector factories rose by 3.51 lakhs (16.6%), their fixed capital grew by Rs. 12,042 crores (52%), gross output by Rs. 11,041 crores (53.7 per cent) and value added by Rs. 1,358 crores (27.10%). Public sector factories represented 5.1 per cent of the total in 1981-82 and it improved to 6.1 per cent in 1984-85. Similarly, their share in the factory sector employment increased from 27.1 to 31.4 per cent and gross output from 27.8 to 29.9 per cent. Their fixed capital and value added, as a proportion, however, decreased from 66.7 to 64.1 per cent, and from 34.4 to 30.5 per cent respectively. Contribution of the joint sector factories increased in fixed capital from Rs. 2,509 crores to Rs.

4,511 crores or an increase of 79.8 per cent, gross output from Rs. 5,723 crores to Rs. 9,244 crores or by 61.4 per cent and value added from Rs. 1,011 crores to Rs. 2,120 crores or by 109.7 per cent during 1981-82 and 1984-85. But their employment of wage labour witnessed an absolute decline from 5.02 lakhs to 4.79 lakhs or by 4.6 per cent. In the private sector ownership of the factories, it was found that fixed capital grew by Rs. 6,096 crores (67.3%), gross output by Rs. 17,332 crores (36.6%) and value added by Rs. 3,866 (45.3%), but their wage labour employment declined from 51.6 lakhs to 49.3 lakhs or by 2.3 lakhs (4.5%). The share of the private sector factories in total factory employment decreased from 66.3 to 62.6 per cent, in gross output from 64.4 to 61.3 per cent, but, in fixed capital, it rose from 26.1 to 27.6 per cent and in value added from 58.6 to 59.4 per cent (Table 2.5).

Thus, while the relatively small number of public sector factories had improved in terms of employment provision and fixed capital, private sector factories contributed greater proportion of the gross output and value added during the same period. Industrial development is gradually becoming thorough and deep-rooted with the expansion and development of capitalism in the Indian economy.

Industry-wise distribution of employment, invested capital, gross output and value added showed that seven industries viz., food products, cotton textile, chemicals and chemical products, basic metals, electric machinery, electricity and transport equipment accounted for over 60 per cent of employment, gross output, and over 75 per cent of invested capital in the factory sector of the Indian economy during 1981-82 to 1984-85. But during this intervening period employment in these seven industries absolutely declined from 49.3 lakhs (63.4%) to 49.1 lakhs (62.4%) or by 0.2 lakhs. Further, the share of the seven industries in invested capital and gross output marginally declined but, for value added, it decreased by as much as 3.9 percentage points during 1981-82 and 1984-85. This speaks of a minor shift towards diversification of the industrial structure in the factory sector. Growth of invested capital, gross output and value added varied for these industries in the same period (Table 2.6).

It can be followed from the data on seven industries that the capital and intermediate goods industries had a much greater share in employment, invested capital, gross output and value added. Consumer goods industries comprising of food products and cotton textiles registered a drastic fall in employment, they recorded a moderate increase in the share of invested capital but had a reduced share in

TABLE 2.5: Factory Sector by Type of Ownership

	Factories (Number)		Employment ('000s)		Fixed Capital (Rs. Crores)		Gross output (Rs. Crores)		Value Added (Rs. Crores)	
	1981-82	1984-85	1981-82	1984-85	1981-82	1984-85	1981-82	1984-85	1981-82	1984-85
Public Sector	5,409	5,951	2,116	2,467	23,135	35,176	20,531	31,572	5,010	6,368
Joint Sector	1,707	1,822	502	479	2,509	4,511	5,723	9,244	1,012	2,120
Private Sector	97,921	89,174	5,160	4,926	9,059	15,155	47,418	64,750	8,533	12,399
Total	1,05,031	96,947	7,778	7,872	34,703	54,842	73,672	1,05,566	14,555	20,887
Percentage Distribution:										
Public Sector	5.1	6.1	27.2	31.4	66.7	64.2	27.8	29.9	34.4	30.4
Joint Sector	1.7	1.9	6.5	6.1	7.2	8.2	7.8	8.8	7.0	10.2
Private Sector	93.2	92.0	66.3	62.5	26.1	27.6	64.4	61.3	58.6	59.4
Total	100.0	100.0	100.0	100.0	100.0	100.0	100.0	100.0	100.0	100.0

Source: Statistical Outline of India, 1986-87 and 1989-90, pp.83 and 81, Tata Services Ltd., Bombay.

TABLE 2.6: Share of Major Industry Groups in Factory Sector (per cent)

Industry	Employment		Invested Capital		Gross Output		Value Added	
	1981-82	1984-85	1981-82	1984-85	1981-82	1984-85	1981-82	1984-85
Food Products	16.7	12.7	5.2	5.9	13.1	13.1	6.4	7.9
Cotton Textiles	13.1	12.1	4.5	4.4	7.3	6.7	8.3	6.5
Chemicals and Chemical Products	6.2	6.5	12.4	10.6	13.4	13.3	11.9	12.3
Basic Metals	7.6	8.5	15.5	14.8	12.5	12.2	12.1	8.9
Electrical Machinery	4.0	4.5	4.1	3.9	5.3	5.3	6.2	8.2
Electricity	9.4	11.5	29.8	31.0	7.5	8.2	15.5	12.9
Transport Equipment	6.4	6.6	5.7	5.7	5.8	5.5	7.6	7.4
Total of 7 Industries	63.4	62.4	77.2	75.7	64.9	64.3	68.0	64.1
Other Industries	36.6	37.6	22.8	24.3	35.1	35.7	32.0	35.9
Total of all Industries (per cent)	100.0	100.0	100.0	100.0	100.0	100.0	100.0	100.0
Total Amount (Rs. in crores)	77.8 (Lakhs)	78.7 (Lakhs)	53,991	80,502	73,672	1,05,566	14,555	20,887

Source: Statistical Outline of India 1986-87 and 1989-90, pp.82 & 80, Tata Services Ltd., Bombay.

gross output and value added during 1981-82 and 1984-85. The decline of the cotton textile industry has become quite perceptible in this period.

State-wise distribution of employment, invested capital, gross output and value added reveals a characteristic picture of regional production concentration of the industrial sector, Maharashtra, U.P. Tamil Nadu, West Bengal, Gujarat and M.P. together accounted for over 60 per cent of factory employment and invested capital, and over 65 per cent of gross output and value added in the factory sector until the first half of 1980s. Their shares had only marginally declined in 1984-85 compared to 1981-82. But even in these states, factories were located in a few selected districts. On the other hand, total of the shares of other states in percentage point increased during the intervening period as follows: employment 0.2, gross output 0.4 and value added 2.5. But their share in the total invested capital in the factory sector declined by 2.3 percentage points in the same period. All this confirms that industrial development in other states is very tardy and has still to go a long way in the process of development (Table 2.7). Consequently, uneven development has continued on and precipitated over the years. It operates as a law of capitalist development in the society.

Selected ratios of the factory sector indicate important and changing characteristic features. Factories with capital size up to Rs. 7.50 lakhs recorded an increase in the fixed capital per employee by 31.3 per cent, value added by 51.5 per cent during 1981-82 and 1984-85. The ratio of their fixed capital to gross output marginally decreased by 0.01 but the ratio of value added to the output improved by 0.03. Factories within capital-size of Rs. 7.50-20 lakhs had increased their fixed capital per employee by 37.6 and value added by 44 per cent. Ratio of their fixed capital to gross output marginally increased by 0.01 and that of value added to gross output by 0.02. Factories with capital size of above Rs. 20 lakhs showed that their fixed capital per employee rose by 87.4 per cent and value added per employee by 119.3 per cent. Ratio of their fixed capital to gross output improved by 0.24 and that of value added to gross output by 0.15. In the case of factories with unspecified capital structure, it was found that their fixed capital per employee grew by 762.5 per cent, and growth of value added per employee by 219 per cent. And the ratio of their fixed capital to gross output sharply rose by 0.12 but that of value added to gross output marginally decreased by 0.01 (Table 2.8).

TABLE 2.7: Share of Selected States in Factory Sector (per cent)

State	Employment		Invested Capital		Gross Output		Value Added	
	1981-82	1984-85	1981-82	1984-85	1981-82	1984-85	1981-82	1984-85
Maharashtra	16.9	16.9	17.8	17.4	23.0	22.3	23.3	22.8
U.P.	9.9	9.5	10.1	10.7	7.6	8.2	10.2	6.6
Tamil Nadu	10.6	11.2	8.8	8.1	10.8	10.5	9.8	11.3
West Bengal	11.9	11.7	9.0	7.9	9.2	8.1	9.9	8.8
Gujarat	8.7	8.7	8.4	9.2	11.3	11.4	8.7	10.2
M.P.	4.3	5.0	7.0	8.1	4.1	5.1	5.4	5.1
Six States	62.3	62.1	61.1	61.4	66.0	65.6	67.3	64.8
Others	37.7	37.9	38.9	38.6	34.0	34.4	32.7	35.2
Total	100.0	100.0	100.0	100.0	100.0	100.0	100.0	100.0

Source: Statistical Outline of India 1989-90 p. 79, the Tata Service Ltd., Bombay.

TABLE 2.8: Selected Ratios of Factory Sector, Capital – Size Class

Capital-size class (Rs. Lakhs)	Fixed Capital per employee (Rs.)		Value Added per employee (Rs.)		Fixed Capital/Gross Output Ratio		Value Added/Gross Output Ratio	
	1981-82	1984-85	1981-82	1984-85	1981-82	1984-85	1981-82	1984-85
Up to 1	3,147	3,347	5,784	8,402	0.07	0.07	0.13	0.18
1.0 – 2.5	6,533	8,223	7,816	11,488	0.11	0.10	0.13	0.14
2.5 – 5.0	9,586	12,105	9,643	13,951	0.13	0.13	0.14	0.15
5.0 – 7.5	10,925	15,980	9,894	16,501	0.15	0.15	0.13	0.16
7.5 – 10.0	12,746	16,470	11,255	16,584	0.14	0.15	0.13	0.15
10.0 – 20.0	14,231	21,249	14,105	19,941	0.15	0.17	0.15	0.16
Above 20	67,776	1,27,035	25,196	55,265	0.58	0.82	0.22	0.37
Unspecified	1,321	11,394	3,681	11,743	0.08	0.20	0.22	0.21
All Factories	44,617	69,670	18,713	26,534	0.47	0.52	0.20	0.20

Source: Statistical Outline of India 1986-87 and 1989-89, pp.80 & 78, The Tata Service Ltd., Bombay.

Looking into these characteristics according to the employment size-class for the Indian economy's factory sector it can be observed that in the case of factories with employment up to 99 persons, the amount of fixed capital per employee rose by 64.5 per cent and that of value added per employee by 50 per cent. But the ratio of their fixed capital to gross output on the average, fell by 0.03 indicating that, compared to capital investment, they depended more on labour power for production (Table 2.9). Similarly, the ratio of their value added to gross output declined by 0.02. Factories with employment size-class of 100-499 persons had increased their fixed capital per employee by 85.9 per cent and value added per employee by 65.3 per cent. The ratio of their fixed capital to gross output increased by 0.08, implying more investment in fixed capital. It can be stressed that it inexorably followed intensification and deepening of the process of capitalist development with all its pervasiveness. With increased fixed capital and consequently, more value added, the ratio of value added to gross output for the units of the factories with employment of 100-499 persons, improved by 0.04 within a short period of three years. Factories with employment range of 500-1999 persons had registered an increase in the fixed capital per employee by 67.7 per cent and value added per employee by 52.7 per cent. The ratio of their fixed capital to gross output rose by 0.03 confirming more amount of fixed capital investment, but the ratio of their value added to gross output remained constant during the intervening period. Factories employing 2000 persons and above had increased their fixed capital per employee by 29.2 per cent, and value added per employee by 21.2 per cent. But the ratio of their fixed capital to gross output on the average decreased by 0.04 and that of value added to gross output by 0.05 thereby indicating higher and faster growth rate of fixed capital investment and gross output in relation to the value added in the same period (Table 2.9). The symptom of lower capacity utilisation is also evident from these characteristics at large. It has implications for production in future.

Overall, in the entire factory sector, fixed capital grew by 50 per cent, gross output by 43.3 per cent and value added by 43.5 per cent during 1981-82 and 1984-85. The ratio of fixed capital to gross output decreased from 0.49 in 1980-81 to 0.47 in 1981-82, but moved upward to 0.52 in 1984-85. And the ratio of value added to gross output for the factory sector was 0.195, 0.198 and 0.198 in 1980-81, 1981-82 and 1984-85 respectively. The ratio of value added to fixed capital

TABLE 2.9: Selected Ratios of Factory Sector, Employment — Size Class

Employment Size (Persons)	Fixed Capital per employee (Rs.)		Value Added per employee (Rs.)		Fixed Capital/Gross Output Ratio		Value Added/Gross Output Ratio	
	1981-82	1984-85	1981-82	1984-85	1981-82	1984-85	1981-82	1984-85
0 — 49	13,077	22,686	9,995	15,043	0.16	0.20	0.12	0.13
50 — 99	12,032	18,629	10,035	15,322	0.16	0.18	0.13	0.15
100 — 199	15,397	32,017	12,720	20,817	0.19	0.27	0.15	0.18
200 — 499	21,806	37,156	17,586	29,270	0.19	0.26	0.16	0.20
500 — 999	38,161	58,066	22,390	34,703	0.33	0.34	0.19	0.20
1000 — 1999	36,842	67,691	22,082	33,214	0.32	0.37	0.19	0.18
2000 — 4999	31,667	52,388	21,157	29,963	0.35	0.35	0.24	0.20
5000 & above	1,48,735	1,80,757	28,730	30,619	1.77	1.70	0.34	0.29
All Factories	44,617	69,670	18,712	26,534	0.47	0.52	0.20	0.20

Source: Statistical Outline of India 1986-87 and 1989-89, p.80 & 78, Tata Service Ltd., Bombay.

improved from 0.398 in 1980-81 to 0.419 in 1981-82 but relatively declined to 0.380 in 1984-85.

During 1980-81 and 1982-83 value added in the factory sector of the Indian economy increased from Rs. 11,929 crores to Rs. 16,673 crores or by 39.8 per cent (Table 2.2). The average rate of labour exploitation[3] measured as a ratio of the difference (S) between the value added and emoluments paid to employees (V), or S/V was estimated at 95.7 per cent in 1980-81 and it rose to 107.2 per cent in 1982-83. Factories with employment-size class of 200-499 persons registered rate of labour exploitation at 139.8 per cent in 1980-81 but in marginally declined to 136 per cent in 1982-83. Factories with employment size-class of 500-999 persons operated at 133.7 per cent rate of exploitation in 1980-81 and it relatively decreased to 130 per cent in 1982-83. The rate of exploitation in the factories within the employment ranges of 1000-1999 and 2000-4999 persons remained somewhat unchanged around 80 per cent in the intervening period. But in the factories with employment size-class of 5,000 persons and more, the rate of labour exploitation increased from 58.8 per cent to 133 per cent during 1980-81 and 1982-83. But the generation of surplus value, its private appropriation and problem in exchange of commodities always engender and foment contradiction in the society.

The analytics of the parameters thus objectively present and idea of the trend and character of industrial development in India. The parameters or characteristics are inter-related and have been interlaced to weave the pattern of industrial development in the country over the years. The pattern is unmistakably capitalistic and it has been nurtured and developed through the past decades. It is still in the process of growth and evolution.

An regards ownership it is the public sector that matters very much in the factory sector. It leads and sets the pace of development. It has grown not only for itself. Joint sector and private sector have made vast strides under the leader-ship and guidance of the public sector. Private sector is characterized with the dominance of the big business houses or monopoly groups for whose growth and expansion, in India, the contribution of the public sector factories has been immense over the years.

Characteristics of capital-range and employment-range show classification and differentiation of the factory sector in terms of capital investment, employment of labour, as well as their contribution and relative importance in the gross output and value added in the factory sector. Ratios of the per capita fixed capital investment and value added in different employment size-classes of factories remarkably improved even in the short period under consideration. The ratios of fixed capital to gross output and value added to gross output according to capital and employment size-classes reveal differentiation of the factories as well as the strength and weakness of the mode of large-scale production of commodities in a growing capitalist market economy like India.

Factory sector in India no doubt has developed organised social production. It has expanded its area of operation in different parts of the country. Many industries operate in the factory sector but the major seven industries concentrated in a few centres of six states accounted for nearly two-thirds of employment, invested capital, gross output and value added in the first half of 1980s. The pattern of industrial development is invariably set to the grand process of generating surplus value with the employment of wage labour, accumulation, growth, centralisation and concentration of capital together with uneven development. It has developed a regime of commodity production with large wage labour employment, spearheading the even growing domination of capital with numerous foreign and international relations and collaborations. As evidence shows it has also developed many constraints and antagonism immanent in the system, leading to the crisis.

All this exposes the basic weaknesses and problems of an induced pattern of capitalist industrial development. A huge amount of foreign capital amounting over Rs. 50,000 crores has been invested in the factory sector and allied infrastructure in the form of direct foreign investment and loans over the last three decades. This means a big obligation of the Indian economy to the claims of the foreign investors. Certainly, this pattern of joint ownership of Indian and foreign capitals would be further extended and evolved with the investment of more capital under the new industrial policy in 1990 and 1991 of the Union Government and the official foreign investment policy being made more liberal and transparent in the 1990s. The Eighth Plan approach paper (1990) stressed that there will be no return "to the regime of direct, indiscriminate and detailed controls in industry" in the new plan, suggesting in its place "relatively simple, strategic and non-discretionary control mechanism"[4] with which to achieve rapid and sustainable industrialization. Units with higher capital range will surely get more concession and move faster, leading to more concentration and centralisation of capital. Consequently, the pattern of the factory sector and industrial development in India would be of more bureaucratic and monopolistic nature, and with complications of exogenous factors, it is developing its natural antipathy and sharp antagonism against the workers and toilers of the country. Actually, that is the result of the historical mission of capitalist development of the world economy.

Faced with the internal contradictions and open and anarchic world market, India economy has become more vulnerable and fallen in severe crisis. Interaction of the endogenous and exogenous forces is very complex and violent often leading to numerous difficulties and conflicts in the Indian economy. Commodity production does never provide a foal-proof system. Production based the wage labour and generation of surplus value more and more, relative decline of the market, reduction in the number of factories and employment, especially in the private sector, show the shrinking social base, great weakness and shadier side of the commodity production. The outcome is the general and permanent crisis in the present era of world monopoly capitalism. Indian economy can be of no exception to this since it is a part of the world market system. The entanglement of international finance capital is greatly responsible for the present difficulties of the country and it will precipitate the process of economic crisis in future.

III. CRISIS AND THE GOVERNMENT POLICY MEASURES

The above analysis of the factory sector of the Indian economy exposes the general contradiction and crisis of the Indian capitalist development in the contemporary period. Production system in the factory sector has been built up in such a socio-economic-system with large colonial characteristics and feudal vestiges in the economy, is bound to foment and aggravate the crisis. Production under certain Government guidelines, regulations and controls has certainly very much improved over time. But that has not at all solved the basic contradiction and crisis of the Indian economy. The crisis looms at large not only in the production base through industrial cost and price mechanism operative in the market, but it has also affected and engulfed both the private and public sectors, government budgetary operations, balance of payments problem, employment and price situation, external debt servicing and, moreover, fiscal deficit etc.

which broadly suggest the existence, dimension and acuteness of economic and financial crisis of the Indian economy. The fiscal deficit is a broad term that measures the gap between what the Government intends to spend, including the loan repayments and what it will earn from tax and non-tax revenue – for example dividends from pubic sector enterprises, foreign grants, interest on its own loans. The larger this gap, the more the Government becomes forced to borrow from internal and external markets or print money or both at a faster face of time. The anarchy in the mode of production, along with these adverse characteristic features – the attendant deteriorating critical parametres – actually measure the gravity and depth of the Indian economic crisis in the present times.

To cope with the aggravating economic crisis, the new Union Government, on the occasion of presenting the budget for 1991-92, in July 1991, largely liberalised[5] the industrial policy by abolishing licencing of all projects, except for a short list of industries, removing the asset limit for MRTP companies, raising the limit for foreign equity holdings from 40 per cent to 51 per cent and more and dismantling all bureaucratic controls to industrial growth.

Part disinvestment of holding in the public sector and reduction of products reserved for the public undertakings, throwing open more areas to the private sector are among the other features of the Government's new industrial policy. Automatic permission will be given to a foreign technology agreement in the high priority up to a sum of Rs.1 crore, 5 per cent royalty for domestic sale and 8 per cent for exports. Regarding exports, it would be subject to a total of 8 per cent of the sales over a ten-year period from the date of agreement or seven-years from the commencement of production.[6] Areas where security and strategic concerns predominate will continue to be reserved for public sectors and industries reserved for the small-scale sector will also continue to be reserved. "Government policy and procedures must be geared to assisting entrepreneurs in their efforts", the policy stated.

Regarding foreign investment, the new official policy states that in order to invite foreign investment in the high-priority industries, requiring large investments and advance technology it has been decided to provide approval for direct foreign investment up to 51 per cent foreign equity in such industries. "There shall be no bottlenecks of any kind in the process".[7] The new policy on foreign direct investments of up to 51 per cent equity in the high priority industries with include

34 broad areas such as metallurgy, electric equipment, transport, food processing, hotel and tourism industry. Clearance will be given if the foreign equity covers the foreign exchange requirement for imported capital goods. For this consequential amendments to the Foreign Exchange Regulations Act will be carried out.

Coming to the Monopolies and Restrictive Trade Practices Act, the policy states that the pre-entry scrutiny of investment decisions by the MRTP Companies will no longer be required. Instead, emphasis will be on controlling and regulation of monopolistic restriction and unfair trade practices rather than making it necessary for the monopoly houses to obtain prior approval of the centre for expansion, establishment of new undertakings, merger, amalgamation and takeover and appointment of certain directors. "The thrust of the policy will be more on controlling unfair or restrictive business practices".[8] Simultaneously, the new empowered MRTP Commission will be authorised to initiate investigations *suo motu* of all complaints from consumers regarding monopolistic and unfair trade practices.

In order to raise resources and encourage wider public participation, as part of the Government's share-holding in the public sector would be offered to mutual funds, financial institutions, the general public and the workers.

The new policy decisions of the Government are "a series of measures to unshackle the Indian industrial economy from the cobwebs of unnecessary bureaucratic controls".[9] These measures complement the other series of measures being taken by the Government in the areas of trade policy, exchange rate arrangement, fiscal policy, financial sector reform and overall macro-management, the official statement said.

The new industrial policy to meet the economic crisis is but an extension of 1990 industrial policy and a sequel to the 22 per cent depreciation or devaluation of the Indian rupee and IMF loan agreements, their stabilisation programme and conditionalities, and pragmatic current Union Budget – all presented in and made effective from July 1991. The IMF originally recommended as 20 per cent depreciation of the Indian currency and this was faithfully acceded to by the new Indian Government. With the depreciation or devaluation of Indian rupees by 22 per cent, foreign capitalists with the same unit of investment in dollar or pound starling will have more claims on the Indian assets in terms of rupees and that is more than the proportion of rupee devaluation. This obviously increases the load and change on the

Indian economy and leads to a greater economic and financial burden of the country.

To mitigate the crisis the budget for 1991-92 levied[10] direct and indirect taxes of Rs. 2,005 crores in the remaining nine-month period of the year 1991-92, leaving a total budgetary deficit for the current year at an estimated Rs. 7,719 crores, a large revenue deficit of Rs. 13,854 crores and a huge fiscal deficit of Rs. 37,727 crores. The highlights of the budget are an increase in the corporate tax by 5 per cent; limit to the depreciation on plant and machinery at 25 per cent; increase of petrol, LPG, aviation turbine fuel prices by 20 per cent; and other petroleum prices up by 10 per cent. The budget provides a tax concession for soft ware exports, tax concessions for export of processed foods and import duty on machines and spares is reduced by five per cent. Maximum rate of custom duty was reduced to 150 per cent. It has proposed a net revenue from direct taxes at Rs. 2,139 crores and government disinvestment upto 20 per cent in selected public sector undertakings. Excise duty on motor cars was raised from 50 to 60 per cent and on molasses by Rs. 150 per ton. Fertiliser prices were raised by 40 per cent and it will be compensated with increased procurement prices. Small and marginal farmers were granted some concessions on increase of fertiliser prices.

Exports subsidies have been abolished with effect from July 3, 1991. The export sector "is being adequately compensated through the adjustments" in the exchange rate and expansion of the replenishment licencing system which was started during the same period. The budget provided for an export subsidy of Rs. 1,224 crores as against Rs. 4,200 crores earlier estimated.

The Finance Minister in his budget speech acknowledged that the new Government "inherited an economy in deep crisis" and that "the crisis in the economy is both acute and deep".[11] As he elaborated: "There is no time to lose. Neither the Government nor the economy can live beyond its means year after year. The room for manoeuvre, to live on borrowed money or time, does not exist any more. Any further postponement of macro-economic adjustment, long overdue, would mean that the balance of payments situation, now exceedingly difficult, would become unmanageable and inflation, already high, would exceed limits of tolerance. For improving the management of the economy, the starting point and indeed the centre-price of our strategy, should be a credible fiscal adjustment and macro-economic stabilisation during the current financial year, to be followed by continued fiscal consolidation thereafter. This process would, inevitably, need at least three years, if not longer, to complete. But there can be no adjustment without pain. The people must be prepared to make necessary sacrifices to preserve our economic independence and restore the health of our economy".[12] The Government's objective would be to progressively reduce the fiscal deficit of the Central Government to move towards a significant reduction of the revenue deficit and to reduce the current account deficit in the balance of payments. Explaining the Government policy, the Finance Minister declared, "The time has come to expose Indian industry to competition from abroad in a phased manner".[13] As a first step in this direction, the Government has introduced changes in the export policy, aimed at a reduction of import licencing, vigorous export promotion and optimal import compression. The rupee devaluation of 1st and 3rd July, 1991 and enlargement and liberalisation of the replenishment system constitute the two major initial steps in the direction of trade policy reform.

The Finance Minister observed: "We are committed to adjustment with a human face. It will also be our endeavour that the adjustment process does not adversely affect the underlying growth impulses in our economy. We do not have time to postpone adjustment and stabilisation. We must act best and act boldly. If we do not introduce the needed correctives, the existing situation can only retard growth, induce recession and fuel inflation, which would hurt the economy further and impose a far grater burden on the poor".[14] He stressed that "Macro-economic stabilisation and fiscal adjustment alone cannot suffice. They must be supported by essential reforms and economic policy and economic management as an integral part of the adjustment process, reforms which would help to eliminate waste and inefficiency and impart a new element of dynamism to growth process in our economy. The thrust of the reform process would be to increase the efficiency and international competitiveness of industrial production, to utilise for this purpose foreign investment and foreign technology to a much greater degree than we have done in the past, to increase the productivity of investment, to ensure that India's financial sector is rapidly modernised and to improve the performance of the public sector, so that the key sectors of our economy are enable to attain an adequate technological and competitive edge in a fast changing global economy".[15] This broadly outlines the philosophy of the Indian ruling classes and their government. They want liberal import of foreign goods, exposition of industry to the foreign competition, more, foreign investment, macro-economic adjustment and also economic independence at the same time. No doubt, this guarantees the big business best in the present circumstances.

But whatever note of optimism played in the IMF – World Bank – India Government orchestra, India economic crisis is, indeed, very grave, fundamental and intractable in the country's existing socio-economic structure firmly strapped with innumerable steel wires and ropes of the international finance capital. The government resorted to large amount of borrowings from the IMF in July, 1990 and January, 1991 and there was a sharp reduction in the foreign exchange reserve of the country. Before the recent elections, both the Congress (I) and Janata Dal decided favourably to accept the handsome amount of IMF loan and its conditionalities to tide over the balance of payments problem. To maintain the country's international creditworthiness the Government of India had to lodge 49 tonnes of gold with the Bank of England in the first half of 1991 as security to earn confidence of the creditor countries and institutions. The nature and gravity of the Indian economy's crisis can be illustrated with the following sector's critical data of the more recent period (Table 2.10). The basic characteristics highlight the precarious condition of the public finance emanating out of the anarchy in the mode of production and crisis in the economy. Union government expenditure is expanding at an average annual rate of 13.2 per cent and much of the total expenditure is unproductive and whose share has been rising over time.

The Finance Minister's argument for increasing competitiveness of Indian industrial products in collaboration with the import and use of foreign capital more and more with the Indian capital and thereby to increase productivity of investment is to weak and unrealistic. Past experience of rupee devaluation and hosting foreign capital and technology suggest that they did not generally help increase Indian export, nor did they improve competitiveness of Indian products in the World market. Indeed it is very unlikely that they would lead to an export boom of Indian products in the world of big trade rivalry and earn adequate foreign exchange over the years. Previous surveys show that the import content of the export items of the joint ventures in India, was very high and therefore, generally uneconomic in relation to the value of export earnings. In many years, there were large net outflows of foreign exchange for the country. The collaborating Indian big business is quite dwarf to the international giants of multinational

TABLE 2.10: Indian Economy, Basic Characteristics

Sl. No.	Item	Unit	1986-87	1987-88	1988-89	1989-90	1990-91	1991-92 (Estimate)
1.	Revenue Deficit[1]	Rs. Thousand crores	7.77	9.13	10.51	11.91	17.58	13.85
2.	Budget Deficit[1]	"	8.26	5.81	5.64	10.59	10.77	7.72
3.	Fiscal Deficit[1]	"	26.34	27.04	30.92	35.63	43.33	37.72
4.	Total Foreign Debt	"	48.35	54.65	69.38	81.00	99.46	—
5.	Total Foreign Debt Service	"	4.55	6.00	6.81	8.10	9.63	—
6.	Foreign Trade Balance	"	–9.35	–6.57	–7.89	–7.73	–10.64	—
7.	Total Current Account Deficit	"	–5.83	–6.29	–10.41	–11.00[3]	–12.00[3]	—
8.	Foreign Debt Service as percentage of exports	%	36.5	38.0	33.6	30.0	27.0	—
9.	Industrial Production (1980-81 = 100)	—	155.1	166.4	180.9	196.0	214.0	—
10.	Industrial Security Prices (1980-81 = 100)	—	230.6	207.3	247.5	359.4	510.8	—
11.	Price Index (Wholesale) (1980-81 = 100)	—	132.7	143.6	154.3	165.7	190.8	—
12.	Unemployment[2]	Million	30.13	30.24	30.51	32.77	34.0[3]	—

Notes: 1. Refers to Union Govt. Budget only.
2. Number of persons on the Live Register of Employment Exchanges.
3. Estimate.

Source: Report on currency and finance 1989-90 (Vol. II), Reserve Bank of India, Bombay; ***Reserve Bank of India Bulletin***, June 1991; and Statistical Outline of India, Tata Service Ltd., Department of Economics and Statistics, Bombay.

corporations representing monopoly capital in the World economy. Naturally, the Indian business independently would not be actually able to compete and it is not the competitiveness of the Indian products and Indian capital that would develop; rather, on the contrary, it would actually, aid and increase tension among and revalry of the joint ventures, subsidiaries and branches of the international monopoly capitals and their contention in the world market.

The multinational corporations do not bring in their best technology in the third world countries like India but organise production based on imported ingredients and components from their principals and subsidiaries in other countries. So the possibility of competitiveness of Indian commodities would be elusive and of much remote nature. India will not be a net gainer in the coercive world trade and market dominated by international monopolies.

This point would be clarified from the ownership and transfer of patents and therefore of technology in the world economy that influence the socio-economic structure of the third world countries at large. During the 1970s, Surendra J. Patel[16] notes, there were about 3.5 million patents in existence. Of these, no more than six per cent (2 lakhs) were granted by the developing or less developed countries. An overwhelming majority of the patents – as high as 84 per cent – were owned by foreigners, mainly by the multinational or transnational corporations of the five major developed countries in the West. Over 95 per cent of these patents were not at all used in the production process in the less developed countries. The nationals of less developed countries together held no more than one per cent (30,000 in all) of the 3.5 million patents in the world. He therefore, writes to conclude, "The developing countries were thus plainly on the periphery of the world patent system. . . . The monopolistic privileges granted to the patentees impose heavy cost burdens on the patent-granting countries. They raise the sales prices of the patented products, thereby leading to a forced transfer of incomes from consumers to the producers. But these direct costs are only a tip of the iceberg for developing countries. The indirect or the hidden costs (transfer pricing, abusive practices, limiting possibilities of development of national manufacturing) are not figments of academicians' imagination. They are part and parcel of near universal acceptance nowadays".[17] The less developed countries are continually squeezed out in the process of the operation of the existing world royalty payments and technology transfer.

The Government of India is increasingly showing its eagerness and preference for foreign capital – oriented development of the country. Around 1960 only 506 companies were permitted to have foreign technical and financial collaborations. But thereafter, 'the number of such companies in the Indian economy, rapidly increased[18] to 2,477; 3,041 and 6,245 during 1961-70, 1970-80 and 1981-89. It is by this way and method, that the Government of India endeavours to improve "competitiveness and efficiency" of the Indian industry. But, ultimately, it goes to the service, interest and fortune of the international monopolies in the name of interdependence, competition and free world trade. Such a course of official policy actions obviously stifles indigenous development of the country's productive forces and converts it into a backyard and colonial market for commodities of the developed capital exporting countries – a continuous process, which along with the problem of debt service perpetuates the foreign dependence, economic and financial burden and crisis. This reality very much belies the official statement of "adjustment process with a human face".

IV. CONCLUSION

The new industrial policy and the so-called macro-economic stabilisation plan propounded and thrusted by the IMF-World Bank combine to the India Government is based on open world market, and harsh monetarism which has already failed in the West. But it is preferred very much by the developed capitalist countries and their cohort, IMF-World Bank combine insofar as this model keeps the economics of the less developed countries in constant surveillance and check to serve their own economic and political domination. "The grim truth is that while moves to dismantle external controls have virtually been forced down India's throat, the political mind-set remains attuned to past shibboleths".[19] The results of the IMF's stabilisation plans have become quite devastating to the less developed countries.

Mexico is a case in point of how the IMF – prescribed reforms[20] operate, for the 1.2 per cent growth rate of earnings per employee in the seventies fell to – 5.2 per cent in 1980-88. The country's GDP growth rate went down from 6.5 per cent in 1965-80 to 0.7 per cent in 1980-89, the average annual rate of inflation going up from 13 per cent in 1965-80 to 72.7 per cent in 1980-89, while its negative current account balance after official transfer rose from $ 1 billion, to $ 5.4 billion during 1980-89. The South Korean experience showed that the growth rate of earnings per employee shrank from 10 per cent to 5.9 per cent, while the GDP growth rate remained generally constant and the annual rate of inflation fell from 18.4 per cent to 5 per cent.

The IMF's stabilisation programme brought Chile a fall in per capita income of 12.7 per cent in 1975, and it had similar effect in Peru in 1977-78 (-3.9 and -4.6 per cent), in Zambia in 1977-79 (-7.4, -2.6 and -11.8 per cent) and in Turkey in 1979 - 1980 (-2.8 and -3.2 per cent). In Portugal in 1978 the IMF policies halved the economic growth even though the economy – in a favourable condition – was more export-oriented. The example of Argentina has shown how severely IMF deflationary policies particularly reduce domestic economic activity. At the end of a five-year stabilisation period from 1958-63 the country's GDP was slightly lower than its original level (-2%); industrial production which was largely oriented towards the domestic market dropped, while exports rose by more than a third. Fifteen years later (1976-78) two IMF programmes produced a similar trend: while exports achieved a significant growth rate of 15 per cent, industrial production in Argentina slumped – with only a slight change in the GDP – by 7.3 per cent.

It would be out of place to narrate the developments exhaustibly, but the hard facts in the representative countries speak for themselves and those can never be denied. "The contraction of the domestic economy imposed by the IMF leads to numerous dismissals and increases unemployment. Many companies go bankrupt, not only because they are hit by the contraction of the domestic economy but also because the liberalisation of foreign trade deprives them of protection against far more powerful world competition. The number of company bankruptcies in Latin America in a period of IMF – dictated stabilisation rose even more than in Portugal".[21]

Allaying fears about inherent risks in inviting multinationals with their equity investment of 51 per cent or more in India, Dr. Manmohan Singh in a press conference on 26th July, 1991 said the fears were valid 45 years ago when the country attained Independence, but now a new class of officers, industries and entrepreneurs had been created in the country. But what is their real character in the era of trade liberalisation and large-scale imports and exports of capital? What new social atmosphere the "new" class of officers, industries and entrepreneurs has created in our country? They have in reality, become more disposed of, and more compromising to the international capital. They even largely compete among themselves to collaborate with the foreign capital for protecting their narrow class interest, at the cost of the freedom and independence of the country. Their activity, actually saps self-confidence and self-respect of the nation and the country.

"Any such apprehension on allowing foreigners only displayed a lack of self-confidence",[22] Dr. Manmohan Singh said. But the government's historical alliance and firm compromise with foreign capital on an ever widening scale do not display self-confidence at all. With the constant crutch of foreign imperialist capital no country can ever enjoy self-respect and have self-confidence to make real national progress. The Government's compromising philosophy is the real cause of the lack of self-confidence and therefore unable to solve the national problems and economic crisis. The harsh situation in India, created by the troika of "corrupt businessman, corrupt bureaucrat and corrupt politician"[23] has reached to such a plateau of compradorship, that even the FICCI President, Mr. S.K. Birla concedes, it is "an unfortunate fact of life"[24] in India. In such a situation, black money is created "as fast as it is mopped up".[25] This black money is appropriated by the corrupt businessman, bureaucrat and politician together. The National Institute of Public Finance and Policy estimates the quantum of black money at 21 per cent[26] of the GDP, which means considerably more than Rs. 80,000 crores annually. Dr. Manmohan Singh, the Finance Minister, in 1991, allays fears about multinationals investment in the Indian economy. But some five years before in the second Zakir Hussian Memorial Lecture on May 1, 986 he rightly justified a cautions attitude to foreign commercial borrowing. Further, he said, "As regards concessional aid flows, one has to recognise that the international credit mechanism is increasingly seen as a political mechanism in which real politic though with a smile, represents the dominant concern of most donor countries. As such, it would be much too risky to count on larger flows of concessional assistance for financing our development".[27] But, now, he pleads for greater equity share for the multinational corporations working in the Indian economy. Will not the multinational corporations' greater role become too risky for financing our development and lifting Indian economy out of crisis? The risk element indeed is very great and critical form the viewpoint our national economic and political independence. Further, the entry of adequate amount of foreign capital and its ability to counter crisis are both controversial and doubtful owing to their big limitation, growing international credit crunch and strong negative impact of its exacting character on our economy.

Harry Magdoff in a recent illuminating article, noting the important difference between the past and the present on the Third World and its Debt, writes, "The extension of loans, combined with economic, political and military pressure, was used in the past to expand capitalism's terrain and bring the non-capitalist nations into the imperialist network. Now, in the era of decolonisation and wars of national liberation, the various forms of intervention are designed for the most part of prevent the separation of the peripheral nations from the core – to hinder delinking from the imperialist system".[28] He points out in the same vein that certain underlying similarities between the past and present still prevail. "The extension of loans does more than bring immediate profits to the lenders. It serves also as a door-opener and support for other forms of economic penetration: markets, investment opportunities, acquisition of natural resources. There is also the symbolic relation between the bankers and their state: loans are extended as instruments of diplomacy to widen the lending nation's sphere of influence; and the state acts, when needed, directly or through an international agency to assure collection of debt".[29] International finance capital always reaps tribute from the nations in diverse ways and means.

Stressing the historical development of capitalism and its present relationship with different Third World countries, Magdoff clarifies:

> "Typical of countries that sank into unending debt were those that were colonised or became informal outposts of the empire. There the long history of colonialism and economic penetration resulted in one-sided distorted socio-economic formations. As a rule, the landed aristrocrats retained control over tillable land as well as a good deal of political power, enabling them to stand in the way of the kind of agricultural revolution that has always been the precondition of successful capitalism. In these countries the patterns of economic growth – in natural resource extraction, industry, and foreign trade – *were and continue to be determined* by foreign investment and loans. The emerging business in this environment was one that fitted into the new patterns, and accordingly lacked the motive or strength to struggle for economic independence. This kind of capitalist class *works in tandem* with foreign investors and bankers for the sake of its own prosperity, and relies on co-operation with the landed aristocracy to keep the impoverished masses in land. Because of the high degree of

dependency on the technology, markets and investment of the advanced capitalist countries, there is frequent recourse to borrowing abroad. And that in turn reinforce the dependent relationship".[30]

What Harry Magdoff writes is very important and crucial to understand the reality of the present day world. In fact this is also, recognised and corroborated with the views of the highest level of the Indian defence staff. As Admiral J.G. Nadkarni asked in inaugural address at a seminar on March 6, 1990: Do we really believe that America, whose economic power has been steadily declining in relative terms, will not use the leverage of military power in the future to attain her economic and political objectives? In reply he was good enough to have pointed out "The unfortunate fact is that the perfect economic competition visualised by Adam Smith and David Ricardo, is *not* possible in today's world, as indeed it has *not* been possible any time in the past. Countries do not forge ahead economically only by working hard and raising productivity. The *do* also by cornering markets, cornering natural resources, restricting technology movements, fixing prices through cartels, weakening one's competitors, and also by using military, however, in deterrent and coercive model. We shall be doing ourselves a disservice if we believe that all conflicts of interests among nations are going to be settled in future on the basis of fair economic *competition* or through gentlemanly *negotiations* among diplomats. Power has been the *highest* priced coinage in international relations ever since nation states were formed. Power has many facts economic technological and military. All three are important and to *neglect* any would be courting *danger*".[31] The talented admiral rightly highlights the unity of the economics and politics in the present world dominated by the international monopolies and finance capital and this negates the thesis of "self confidence" of the present Union Government to invite Foreign capital and allow it to work at large.

It can be stressed that imports as percentage of value of total production for 594 surveyed companies under foreign collaboration in India increased 32 from 6 to 8.1 per cent for the minority capital participation companies, from 4.8 to 5.4 per cent for the subsidiaries and from 4.4 to 6.2 per cent for technical collaboration companies during 1977-78 to 1980-81. The value of exports for all these companies in 1980-81 was Rs. 513 crores while their imports accounted for Rs. 624.9 crores. During the four-year period ending 1980-81, their total exports figured Rs. 1647.4 crores but imports showed a higher amount of Rs. 1792.6 crores, leaving a deficit of Rs. 145.2 crores. The position has no doubt further worsened during the later period. Among the major economic powers of the world, the U.S.A. is passing through recession at present. Unemployment in U.K. and France rose to nearly 10 per cent of the working population. Germany is suffering severe indigestion after having very recently swallowed the whole of its eastern part. The U.K. is now in its worst recession in decades. Japan is prowling for the large market of the South-East Asia. With recession still on the somewhat chronic, will not the industrial countries fight more fiercely to control and capture more external market for their survival and interest? The rising right-wing trend in the Western politics demonstrates xenophobia and has again raised the fear of fascism. Suffice to say, India's competition to capture export market would be largely in effective and frustrated in the future.

In such an international economic and financial environment, the internal and external forces both work to influence the course of developments in countries like India. But the external force, i.e., imperialist finance capital is the principal and determinant to nurture the internal class forces according to its needs and creates conditions of markets and numerous collaborators to its own interest. Obviously, the factory and other sectors of India economy would be much more enmeshed and tied more firmly to the operation and manoeuvre of international finance capital. Agriculture will be increasingly subject to the whirlpool of world trade and market. The parametres revealing the Indian economic crisis will aggravate more with the Government's acceptance of a larger IMF loan ($ 7 billion) and stabilisation programme, declaration of a new industrial policy and consequent market contraction owing to the strict budgetory measures.

There is self-contradiction in the Government's policy to increase competitiveness of Indian industry. Its policy is practically reduced to the Indian Industry's walking with the crutches of foreign imperialist capital, leading to more instability, anarchy and perpetual foreign dependence and exploitation of the Indian economy. The success of the macro-economic policy action, as the experience of other less developed countries suggest, would be very doubtful and with all its harshness, lead to a general contraction of the market, more poverty and recessionary effects in the country. Opening of the Indian market to the foreign capital more and more actually means its conversion into a colonial market for exploitation and easy hunting ground of imperialisms. It will automatically lead to a declining and more subservient role of national capital and so the Indian economy will continue to lack the free development of its means of production. There is no way out beneficial to India in the existing social structure production. India has already not only fallen into a foreign imperialist debt trap, its economy from now on, will be sliding more fast into the deep gorge of neocolonialism. No law of the gasping India Parliamentary system or rule of the comprador ruling class can act as the panaccea to the social disease caused by the foreign imperialist capital, stop its ravage and really lift the Indian economy out of its crisis and social morass. True national feeling, national self-respect and national sovereignty have touched a benign low, thanks to the philosophy of the Indian ruling class and its international masters. India wails in crisis, as the comprador governments enchain her with more new laws of economic measures and administer new drugs at the behest of international finance capital. India's economic crisis is permanent in the vortex of its old social order and imperialism, and it will aggravate more in the future until the country undergoes a radical and sustained fundamental social change.

NOTES

1. Annual Survey of Industries — Factory Sector, 1982-83, C.S.O., p.12.
2. *Ibid.*, p.12 and Statistical Outline of India 1989-90, Tata Services Ltd., Bombay, p.76 and Table 2.4.
3. Calculated from the data in the Annual Survey of Industries — Factory Sector 1980-81 and 1982-83, pp.9 and pp.12, Central Statistical Organisation, Planning Commission, Government of India, New Delhi.
4. "Citation" from the editorial in the *Statesman*, Calcutta, 20th June, 1990, p.8. See also H.K. Paranjape, World Bank and India, *Mainstream*, New Delhi, March 29, 1986, pp.11-14 and pp.34 for an analysis of the earlier collaboration at the official staff level.
5. Press Statement, Government of India, *The Statesman*, Calcutta, 25th July, 1991, p.1.
6. *Ibid.*, p.1.
7. *Ibid.*, p.12.
8. *Ibid.*, p.12.
9. *Ibid.*, p.12.
10. Budget for 1991-92, Government of India, New Delhi, *Statesman*, Calcutta, 25th July, 1991, p.1 and p.4.
11. Budget Speech of the Union Finance Minister, Government of India, New Delhi, 1991; *Statesman*, Calcutta, 25th July, 1991, p.4.
12. *Ibid.*

13. *Statesman*, Calcutta, 25th July, 1991, p.4.
14. *Ibid.*
15. *Ibid.*
16. Surendra J. Patel, Trade Related Intellectual Property (TRIP) in Uruguay Round in GATT, *Mainstream*, New Delhi, March 17, 1990, p.42.
17. *Ibid.*, p.43.
18. Pradhan H. Prasad, Development and Employment Growth, *Mainstream*, New Delhi, March 17, 1990, p.13.
19. "Editorial" Down Mexican Way, the *Statesman*, Calcutta, July 23, 1991.
20. *Ibid.*
21. Peter Korner, Gero Maass, Thomas Siebold and Rainer Tetzlaff, The IMF and the Debt Crisis, Zed Books Ltd., London, 1987, p.130. For a detailed discussion see pp.128-134.
22. The *Statesman*, Calcutta, July 27, 1991, p.1 & 5.
23. Cf. "Editorial", Down Mexico Way, The *Statesman*, Calcutta, July 23, 1991.
24. *Ibid.*
25. Sunanda K. Datta – Roy, Not by Money Alone, The *Statesman*, Calcutta, July 28, 1991, p.6.
26. *Ibid.*
27. Manmohan Singh, "Development, Social Justice and Modernisation", *Mainstream*, May 10, 1986, p.16.
28. Harry Magdoff, Third World Debt : Past and Present, *Mainstream*, March 29, 1986, p.7.
29. *Ibid.*
30. *Ibid.*, p.8 (Italics added).
31. J.G. Nadkarni, Security and Integrated Response, Inaugural Address delivered at a seminar organised by the United Services Institute on "Foreign and Defence Policies for India in the 1990s" in New Delhi on March 6, 1990. See *Mainstream*, New Delhi, March 17, 1990, p.9, (Italics added).
32. Foreign collaboration in Indian Industry : Fourth Survey Report 1985, Reserve Bank of India, Bombay, pp.28-31. The Report notes, "A generally upward trend in imports as a percentage of production was noticed in all the three groups of companies, and the proportion was higher for the group of minority participation companies than the other two groups" (p.29).

3

INDIA'S ECONOMIC CRISIS: Invited but Unwanted Visitor

MAYA SHAH

WHAT IS a crisis? The *International Encyclopedia of Social Sciences* gives an explanation of what is a crisis: "Some scholars treat it as synonymous with a stress, panic, catastrophe, disaster. violence, or potential violence." Others, adhering to the medical connotation, regard it as a "turning point" between a fortunate and an unfortunate change in the state of an organism" (p.510). Crisis is accompanied by stress, panic, etc., and, therefore, it is not a welcome state of affairs. People would like to avoid a situation of crisis.

Crisis can be used as a "substantive" term or as a "procedural" term. "Substantive uses specify the content of a policy, problem, or situation. Procedural conceptions emphasize generic characteristics of situation without regard to whether a particular case involves, for example, an international crisis, a political crisis, or an individual crisis" (*Encyclopedia*, p.510).

A situation of crisis is not a chronic situation but is an acute situation, whose length is unspecified. Crisis is quite frequently relative and not absolute. It cannot last permanently, it is a visitor. Yet its visit is dreaded by all.

Out of the two uses of the term crisis, as used in the *Encyclopedia* which is more relevant for our purpose? To my understanding the more appropriate use of the term crisis is the "substantive" use in the present context. Hence in this article we will use the term circis in the sense of specification of the content of a policy, problem or situation in the economic life of our country. Keeping this usage in mind an attempt is made to observe the symptoms of crisis, the economic scene in the 1990-91, the economic policies of the new Government and possible alternative policies.

Is There a Crisis?

Is India really in deep crisis? If yes, then is the crisis all-prevading or there are some relieving features to this situation? It is now an accepted fact that India is in deep trouble. But, there are certain relieving features like residence of industrial growth to the existing crisis, consistently favourable weather conditions, agricultural production growing at a rate higher than the demographic growth rate resulting in a higher per capita availability of foodgrains, a positive and relatively higher rate of growth of the GNP (5%) in the presence of recession and slower rates of growth of the GNP for quite a large number of developed countries of the world. These are some of the features that make us feel optimistic in a pessimistic situation.

Even when weather has behaved well giving us a 3.8 per cent rate of growth in agriculture industries have shown fairly satisfactory growth rates, and the GNP has grown at a rate higher than the Hindu rate of 3.5 per cent why are we talking of crisis and are in a situation of panic? In other words what are the symptoms of crisis? The symptoms of an economic crisis are:

1. An acceleration in the inflation rate in the presence of a bumper harvest and satisfactory performance of the industrial sector. The per capita foodgrains production was 217 kg in 1990-91. As compared to this the per capita foodgrains production was lower at 209 kg in 1989-90. In spite of this, the wholesale price index for foodgrains exhibited an unbelievable rise of 23.9 per cent on a point-to-point basis between March 1990 and March 1991 (CMIE, June 1991, p.26). Compare this with a fall of 4.2 per cent between March 1989 and March 1990.
2. Existence of fiscal deficits that are unsustainable. A budgetary deficit of Rs 12,149 crores in 1989-90 (*Economic Survey, 1990-91*) is incapable of being sustained even over a short period of time.
3. The Balance of Payments (BoP) situation is precarious. Current account deficits have been increasing at an alarming speed since 1988-89 when it increased by about 65 per cent from Rs 6,293 crores in 1987-88 to Rs 10,410 crores in 1988-89. It stood at a high figure of Rs 15,500 crores in 1990-91 (*CMIE*, June, 1991).
4. Foreign exchange reserves have fallen to an extremely low level of Rs 2,152 crores in December 1990. These reserves were sufficient to finance only 20 days' imports. The foreign

exchange reserves exhibited a fall of 61 per cent from Rs 5,480 crores in August 1990, to Rs 2,152 crores in December 1990 (CMIE, June, 1991).

5. Accumulation of huge amounts of external debts resulted from the high as well as increasing levels of current account deficits. The total outstanding external debt of India was Rs 81,168 crores in 1989-90 resulting in a high debt service ratio of 21.6 per cent (CMIE, June, 1991).
6. An increasing proportion of commercial borrowing from the international capital market makes debt servicing even more difficult. Commercial borrowing increased from Rs 19,147 crores (i.e. 27.5 per cent of total outstanding external debt) in 1988-89 to Rs 24,500 crores in 1989-90 (i.e. 30.2 per cent of the total outstanding external debt) (CMIE, June, 1991).
7. Down-rating of India by international rating agencies made even commercial borrowing more difficult for us. India's credit rating was downgraded twice during the past year by Standard and Poor. India was put in the speculative grade by Standard and Poor. Moody also downgraded India's credit rating but did not put her in the speculative grade.

The above-mentioned are the major symptoms of the economic crisis faced by our country. It seems that on the growth side our performance was quite satisfactory and yet we face a severe economic crisis. What must have gone wrong? The pet scapegoat of our politicians is the gulf crisis. Does that mean that in the absence of the Gulf crisis we would have had no economic crisis? I doubt it. We have been mismanaging our external as well as internal resources. India is not a Resource Scarce economy, it is a Resource Waste economy, if I may say so. Now a quick look a the economic scene of 1990-91.

The 1990-91 Economic Scene

The *Economic Survey, 1990-91* paints a rather gloomy picture of our economy. During the Seventh Plan period the Indian economy exhibited an underlying strength which resulted in the Plan targets being exceeded in many fields. To get an idea about the change in the economic scene we give in Table 3.1 some interesting figures from the *Economic Survey, 1990-91* for the past six years. namely five years of the Seventh Plan and 1990-91.

TABLE 3.1: Selected economic indicators

(Percentage change over previous years)

Sl. No.	Economic indicators	1985-86	1986-87	1987-88	1988-98	1989-90 (P)	1990-91 (P)
1.	GNP (based on New Series at 1980-81 prices)	4.1	3.6	4.2	10.6	5.2	5.0*
2.	Agricultural Production	2.5	-3.7	-0.8	21.0	1.7	4.5*
3.	Industrial Production (base 1980-81 = 100)	8.7	9.1	7.3	8.7	8.6	8.4
4.	Electricity generated	8.6	10.2	7.6	9.5	10.8	7.1
5.	Wholesale Price Index (base 1981-82 = 100)	4.8	5.1	10.7	5.7	9.1	12.1
6.	Monetary Resources (M_3)	15.9	18.6	15.9	17.8	19.4	15.1
7.	Imports at Current Prices	14.7	2.2	10.7	26.9	25.4	21.9
8.	Exports at Current Prices	-7.2	14.3	25.9	29.1	36.8	17.5
9.	Foreign exchange reserves include foreign currency, SDR, gold at revalued October 17, 1990, prices (Rs. crores)	7820	8151	7687	7040	6251	11416
10.	Foreign Currency Reserves (Rs. crores)	7384	7645	7287	6605	5787	4388

Source: *Economic Survey, 1990-91*, *The Economic Times*, July 22, 1991, p.II, Table 1.1.
(P) = Provisional, * = Anticipated

Information given in Table 3.1 shows to certain disturbing features. Agricultural production is expected to be higher by 4.5 per cent in 1990-91 as compared to 1989-90 and growth in industrial production is marginally lower at 8.4 per cent in 1990-91 as compared to 8.6 per cent in 1989-90. Both these rates of growth are higher than the demographic growth rate of around 1.2 per cent. The growth in Money Supply, using the broad definition, i.e. M_3, has declined from 19.4 per cent in 1989-90 over 1988-89 to 15.1 per cent in 1990-91 over 1989-90. The GNP at constant prices is expected to grow at a slightly lower rate of 5.0 per cent in 1990-91 over 1989-90 as compared to a rate of 5.2 per cent for 1989-90 over 1988-89. These figures tell us that the prices are expected to come down. But in fact we are faced with a double digit inflation rate of 12.1 per cent in 1990-91 as compared to 9.1 per cent in 1989-90. We have seriously bungled with our growth performance.

Further the 12 per cent rate of increase in the wholesale price index is misleading. A little probing tells as that we had a record production of foodgrains, namley 177 million tonnes, in 1990-91. This record production was accompanied by two very disturbing features of 23.9 per cent increase in the wholesale prices of foodgrains in 1990-91 and a fall in the procurement of wheat in April-May 1991 to 7.5 million tonnes compared with 10 million tonnes in April-May 1990. Edible oils experienced the sharpest rise in prices of around 30 per cent. The *CMIE* (June, 1991 Economic Outlook) makes a very important observation: "Of the 12.2 per cent rise in the general price level between March 1990, and March 1991, primary articles group accounted for 46.6 per cent rise, fuel group 14.1 per cent and the manufactured products group 39.3 per cent increases" (*CMIE,* June , 1991, p.106). There were three main reasons for this double-digit inflation rate. These are: (a) Continuous increases in procurement/support prices, (b) Twenty five per cent Gulf surcharge on petroleum products since October 15, 1990 and (c) Excessive liquidity in the economy resulting from high rates of growth in money supply.

Why Higher and Higher Procurement Prices?

One really wonders at the wisdom of the Government in continuously offering higher and higher procurement prices for foodgrains. As agriculture has been subsidized in a number of ways one would expect a more imaginative policy of providing incentives to farmers who have marketable surpluses. All the inputs going in the agricultural production are highly subsidized. Fertilizer are subsidized, there is no agricultural income-tax, credit is available at subsidized rates (and one does not have to bother about repayment of loans either!), electricity is provided at subsidized rates (which are quite frequently not paid), etc. I am definitely not against the agricultural sector but I do feel that the Government owes responsibility to the general public in terms of passing over the benefits of agricultural development to the general mass of consumers, particularly in rural areas who do not have marketable surpluses and who have to buy food from the open market because they are left out by our public distribution system.

The infrastructure sector has exhibited a poor performance in 1990-91 as compared to earlier years. Given in Table 3.2 are some interesting figures relating to the performance of this sector.

TABLE 3.2: Performance of infrastructure sectors

(Percentage change)

Sl. No.	Item	1988-89 / 1987-88	1989-90 / 1988-89	1990-91 (P) / 1989-90
	Energy			
1.	Coal			
	(a) Production	8.3	3.2	5.4
2.	Electricity Generated (utilities only)	9.5	10.8	7.7
3.	Petroleum			
	(a) Crude Oil Production	5.5	6.4	-3.1
	(b) Refinery throughput	2.2	6.4	-0.3
	Transport & Communications			
	1. Railways Revenue Earning goods traffic	4.1	2.6	2.6
	2. Cargo handled at major ports	9.5	1.2	3.0
	3. Telecommunications New Telephone connections Provided	19.8	11.0	16.0

Source: Economic Survey, 1990, The Economic Times, 22 July 22, 1991, p.VIII, Table 4.1.

It is clear from the information given in Table 4.2 that the infrastructure sectors have let us down in our attempts at keeping the economic crisis out of our country. The Gulf war increased the price of petroleum products to an all-time high. Unfortunately this situation was accompanied by falling production of petroleum products at home.

The overall crude oil and petroleum products import bill increased from Rs 6,310 crores in 1989-90 to Rs 10,800 crores in 1990-91. This increase in the import bill was on account of the increase in the oil prices contributing 64 per cent of the increase in the import bill. Increase in the quantity of imports contributed another 22 per cent of the increase in the import bill in 1990-91. The share of domestic production in the total availability of petroleum fell from 31.3 per cent in 1988-89 to 23.4 per cent in 1990-91. The remaining 14 per cent of the increase was contributed by the depreciation of the Indian rupee.

The plan load factor (PLF) of the thermal plants was also much lower than the recommended PLF norm of 58 per cent by the Rajadhyaksha Committee. The PLF of the thermal plants was 56.5 per cent in 1989-90 which came down to 53.8 per cent in 1990-91. The Government should seriously think of formulating policies that can effectively improve the PLF. An improvement in the PLF should result in an improvement in the overall growth performance, other things remaining the same, as electricity is an extremely important input in all the branches of production.

Railways in Constant Trouble

The Railways also are in constant financial trouble with having to rely more and more on their own resources with the passage of time. Thus, the budgetary support from the Centre to the Railways declined from 45 per cent of the capital expenditure in 1985-86 to 34 per cent in 1990-91. The Railways, therefore, had to resort to borrowing from the open market. Such borrowings contributed about 23 per cent of the total development outlays of the Railways in 1989-90 and 1990-91. "Increasing dependence on market borrowings involves increase in debt service burden on the railways which to some extent has been made somewhat higher through the issunance of tax-free bonds" (*CMIE*, June, 1991, p.46).

In short, we have been having serious problems with our infrastructure sectors. The discussion in this section clearly indicates that there is something basically wrong with our economic policies as a result of which we end up having poor performance of infrastructure sectors and public sector units. Wherever the performance is quite satisfactory we have failed to pass on the benefits to consumers in terms of lower prices. Keeping this scenario in view let us see what the Narasimha Rao Government has to offer to us in terms of economic policies.

Economic Policies of the Rao Government

It is indeed too early to comment on the economic policies of the Rao regime. All the same whatever announcements are made in the form of trade policy and by the Finance Minister, Dr. Manmohan Singh, can always be analysed. The Budget is just being announced and it will take some time before all the details are known, comprehended and studied.

The Commerce Minister, Mr. P. Chidambaram, announced the new trade policy consisting of 13-point major trade reforms on July 4, 1991. These reforms are:

1. Suspension of the cash compensatory scheme (CCS) with effect from July 3, 1991. All imports actually effected until the midnight of July 2-3 will be entitled to the benefits of the CCS.
2. Replanishment licencing scheme (REP), to be called Exim Scrips, will be the principal instrument for export-related imports. These Exim Scrips will be freely tradeable.
3. All exports will have a uniform REP rate of 30 per cent of the f.o.b. value. Gems and jewellery, certain metal-based handicrafts and books and magazines will continue to have special rates.
4. Export having low import intensity like agricultural export will get maximum incentives under the new REP scheme.
5. All supplementary licences, with the exception of the small-scale sector and life-saving drugs/equipments, stand abolished. The small-scale sector and life-saving drugs equipments will be entitled to import under open general licence (OGL) or through supplementary licences.
6. All additional licences granted to export houses stand cancelled. These houses will be granted an additional REP of five per cent of value over and above the REP rate of 30 per cent of the f.o.b. value.
7. All items included in the limited permissible list are to be imported through the REP route.
8. All items under the category of unlisted OGL contained in the exim policy are to be imported only through the REP route.
9. The REP rate for advance licence exports is to be increased

from 10 per cent of net foreign exchange (NFE) to 20 per cent NFE.

10. Within a period of three years all import licencing for capital goods and raw materials, with the exception of a small "negative list", is to be removed.
11. Major changes in the entire canalization policy are to be announced shortly. All items except the essential once are to be decentralized.
12. Financial institutions will be allowed to trade in exim scrips which are to be replaced by foreign exchange certificates.
13. Within a period of three to five years Indian rupee will be made fully convertible on the trade account.

The Main Thrust

The major thrust of the new trade policy is to make export-related imports easier. The uniform REP rate of 30 per cent of the f.o.b value is a very imaginative policy measure that simplifies import and encourages exports of products with low import-intensity. So far so good. But, in the process we will be encouraging export of low-value agricultural products rather than high-value engineering products as these products have a higher import-intensity. Further, agricultural products do have a lower income elasticity of demand as compared to, say, electronics. One wonders at the wisdom of having a trade policy that shifts emphasis from export of high-value engineering products to low-value agricultural products. In India in spite of the Green Revolution and very good performance of the agricultural sector the cost structure in agriculture continues to remain high mainly on account of low productivity in comparison to most of the countries of the world. Is the new REP scheme expected to encourage productivity in agriculture which continues to be at the mercy of the Weather God? Another product with low import-intensity is textiles whose export will definitely be encouraged through the new trade policy. Unfortunately this and such items are subject to severe quota restrictions. On the whole I feel that the new trade policy will do more good than harm and is a step in the right direction.

No Loans without Conditionalities

Our Finance Minster, Dr. Manmohan Singh, has also made certain very important policy announcements. It is now an established fact that India faces a severe financial crisis and people are made to understand that we have to go in for huge IMF/World Bank loans. It is also known that IMF loans are never unconditional loans — rather strict conditionalities are usually attached to the IMF loan. As observed by Arun Ghosh, IMF package is a standard package consisting of "One, fiscal discipline; two, currency depreciation; and three, trade reform and import liberalization". The new trade policy has already been analysed above.

As far as fiscal discipline is concerned we all would agree to the proposal that such a discipline is welcome and has now become even essential, the IMF has recommended a reduction in the fiscal deficit from the existing level of around 8.5 per cent to 9 per cent of the GDP to a level of around 6.5 per cent. But a reduction in the fiscal deficit is not very easy to bring about. A reduction in government expenditure might result in recession and increasing levels of unemployment. If government expenditure is reduced by making public sector units more efficient or by reducing wastages in the economy is sure to benefit. But, if a reduction in government expenditure is achieved by reducing developmental or other expenditure geared towards alleviation of poverty and generation of employment then it will play havoc with our economic system and push us into a deeper crisis.

A reduction in he fiscal deficit may be achieved through raising the government revenue. If more revenue is earned by improving the tax compliance of the people, by making the government administration more effective in collecting taxes, curbing smuggling, etc., or by earning surpluses from the PSUs, then this increase in the revenue will have a healthy effect on the economy. It is quite likely that the government may raise its revenue by increasing the administrated prices, or by imposing more indirect taxes. If so then the economy is bound to suffer another setback.

Two Controversial Subsidies

Reduction in subsidies is another way of controlling government expenditure. The two most important and controversial subsidies are the fertilizer subsidy and the food subsidy. A reduction in both these subsidies is expected to raise the prices of agricultural products hitting the poorer sections of our population even harder. Subsidies to higher education usually are not discussed, may be education is a holy cow, as defence. Of course, defence is not subject to cuts, as education is whenever there is an economy drive.

Another string attached to the IMF loan is depreciation devaluation of currency. As expected, Indian rupee is devalued to the extent of 18 per cent. All the textbook advantages of devaluation are usually not reaped by the economy. Hence we also do not and should not expect export to rise substantially so that our net foreign exchange earnings increase remarkably resulting in relaxation of pressures on the BoP front. Devaluation will make imports costlier and exports cheaper but it cannot guarantee a reduction in imports and an increase in exports, particularly under Indian conditions. This is so because a large part of our imports are non-commercial imports on government account. Our fear is that under these circumstances, the government's import will rise substantially forcing it to borrow further or indulge in deficit financing. An increase in the fiscal deficit will not be acceptable to the IMF.

Increasing Import Costs Pro-inflationary

Further, increasing cost of imports will be pro-inflation, something our people will not be able to bear. If a very high price of imported inputs, particularly capital, discourages their import then there is a possibility of the index of industrial production falling leading to increasing levels of unemployment and lower rates of economic growth. It is also to be remembered that our net foreign exchange earnings are not very elastic with respect to the external value of the rupee. This is so because some of our important export items like textiles are subject to quota. In the case of exports, their price is not the main factor determining demands. Equally important, if not more, are other factors like quality, timely availability of products, honouring commitments, etc. Concentrating only on price via devaluation is, to say the least, inviting frustration when expected foreign exchange earnings are not realized.

It is accepted that we needed the IMF loan if we were not to default on loan repayment. It is also agreed that devaluation is a part of the IMF game and we had no alternative but to devalue our currency. It is now left to us to design policies that will make it possible to increase exports substantially, use the available resources productively and plan for the repayments of loans that are taken presently. I personally feel that it is not wrong to go to the IMF for loans whenever the need arises.

The New Industrial Policy of 1991-92 is a bold policy which has reduced the bureaucratic controls on the industry, and exposed the industries to international competition. This is a step towards freer market economy. It is feared that exposing Indian industries to foreign competition at this stage will force many of them to close down and generate more unemployment. To my mind Indian industries suffer more from the suffocating controls exercised on them in the form of permits and licences and other regulations than from competition. Foreign competition should make them more cost conscious and thereby make them more competitive internationally. But, the possibility of a large number of firms falling sick cannot be ruled out. Unfortunately, the New Industrial Policy is silent on the very important issue of industrial sickness.

A Real Boost for Industry

However to the extent there is debureaucratization in the field of industry, as the licence has been done away with, industries must get a real boost and this should promote industrial growth and generate more employment. Similarly, increasing the foreign participation by raising the maximum share in equity capital from the existing 40 per cent to 51 per cent is a welcome step and should make more foreign capital available to us. We really do not know at this stage what are the conditions imposed on foreign capital participation in terms of repatriation of dividends, etc. There should be conditions imposed on these so as to ensure that large amounts of foreign exchange do not to out in the form of dividends paid in foreign currencies.

The New Industrial Policy proposes to continue to keep the basic inputs in the public sector. Coal production, railways, armaments, atomic energy and the like key sectors will continue to be a the public sector. This is an understandable policy measure. It is to be hoped that the public sector units become more efficient. The New Industrial Policy proposes to divert 20 per cent of he share capital to financial institutions, mutual funds, employees and the general public. This cannot be a measure to raise government revenue in any substantial way. It appears that the idea behind this measure is to increase the participation of employees, general public along with financial institutions in the functioning of the PSUs, and thereby make the PSUs more accountable. Hope this dream of our policy makers is realized.

On the whole the new industrial policy is a step in the direction of more liberalization and a step consistent with the IMF conditionality. Indian industries did need a real shake-up and this policy is an attempt in this direction.

The Finance Minister has clearly expressed the inability of he Government to buy back the 20 tonnes of gold sold by the Chandra Shekhar Government. It is good to realize that our scarce resources are not being utilized for buying gold which is not productively used. Agreed that gold has a very high sentimental value for us, but I feel that we are too poor to be able to afford sentimentalism on a national scale.

A Bold Budget

The Budget for the year 1991-92 has just been presented and it is too early to make a studied comment on it. All the same, the Finance Minister, Dr. Manmohan Singh, deserves to be complimented for giving us a very imaginative, and a bold Budget. It makes an attempt at reducing the budget deficit to Rs 7,710 crores. A part of the reduction is on account of a reduction in fertilizer subsidy and elimination of subsidy on sugar. How much of this is the result of IMF pressure and how much of it is from the principles of sound economics needs to be seen. The price of some types of fertilizers has been increased by 40 per cent. This increase in the price of fertilizers is feared to increase the cost structure of agriculture and thereby raise prices of foodgrains and other agricultural products. This is bound to exert pressure on the prices which have already experienced a two-digit inflation. To pacify the producers of foodgrains the Finance Minister seems to have promised to raise the procurement price. We are again back to square one and hope that this does not force the Government to increase the deficit. If procurement prices are not raised *pari pasu* with an increase in fertilizer prices then agricultural production is likely to suffer. The choice is obviously between the devil and the deep sea.

Increasing the food subsidy is a step not consistent with the IMF conditionalities. But, in country like ours something has to be done to make food available at cheaper rates to majority of the poor people. I for one am not much satisfied with our food policy as it exists. This will be discussed in the next section.

It is to good know that the Finance Minister has decided to tax luxury items. He has further left the income-tax structure intact to the disappointment of many a salaried class person. The part of the salaried class that pays income-tax is a relatively better off section of our population and hence must bear a larger burden of economic development.

There is an imaginative step in the Budget to attract black money and use it for the benefit of the poor people. Forty per cent of the black money deposited in the housing bank is to be utilized for construction of houses for the poor.

There are also two proposals to attract the NRIs. The details of the proposals are not available and hence it is difficult to know whether these two schemes — one, of allowing the residents to accept tax-free gifts from abroad, two of selling the dollar bonds with a maturity of five years to the NRIs — are likely to benefit our country or not.

The Budget in all probability is going to be an inflationary budget though the claim of the Finance Minister is just the opposite. On the whole the Finance Minister has given us an imaginative, bold sensitive and a humane Budget.

Other Policy Recommendations

It has been agreed by one and all that fiscal deficits must be reduced. One of the ways of reducing fiscal deficits is by reducing food and fertilizer subsidies. The Finance Minister has already used fertilizer subsidy to reduce fiscal deficit.

After fertilizer subsidy comes food subsidy. The need for food subsidy arises because, on the one hand, our Government keeps on raising the procurement price, irrespective of production, and on the other it has to sell foodgrains at a price lower than the procurement price to a large section of the poor people who are unable to pay the ruling market price.

It is already observed earlier in this paper that we face a peculiar situation where foodgrains prices experience an inflation rate of around 23.9 per cent when we have bumper harvest in agriculture. Can the Government not keep the procurement price more or less constant and ask the farmers to contribute to the public levy only a fixed quantity of foodgrains required for the PDS? In a situation of a bumper harvest the farmers will benefits even when procurement price is not increased because they will be able to sale a larger percentage of their total production in the open market if hey have to contribute only a fixed quota as the levy portion. I am sure that nor raising the procurement price will not be a tremendous disincentive to agricultural production.

In the absence of agricultural income-tax, if the farmers with marketable surplus contribute a constant quantity at a constant price to the Government it is not too much to ask for as a contribution towards economic growth. Agriculture is a sector which is subsidized in a number of ways like fertilizer subsidy (now reduced) which mainly benefits large farmers, no agricultural income-tax, credit at subsidized rate, electricity at subsidized rate, no land revenue tax worth the name, no serious approach to water tariff, etc. If this sector is asked to pay a small price in the form of procurement price not being revised then I do not think we are being unfair to agriculture. True agriculture supports a large percentage of our population who are awfully poor. But, the policy of making procurement price a constant for a few years is going to affect only those farmers who have marketable surpluses. Small and marginal farmers with no marketable surplus are not going to be affected much.

Public Distribution System Needs District Change

The other aspect of our food policy is the Public Distribution System (PDS). This part of food policy needs to be changed substantially First, our PDS tries to cater to a much larger proportion of our population than what needs to be catered to. It will help to reduce the coverage of PDS and concentrate on a small well-defined target group. The PDS as in existence today mainly caters to the urban middle class whereas the people who are more in need of help are the rural poor. A large part of really very poor people are left out by our PDS. One of the reasons for this that those poor who seasonally migrate do not have a permanent address to get their rations from the fair price shops. Further, in order to get the ration the poor people have to sacrifice a day's wage so that they can wait in the long queue. Finally, even if they are ready to sacrifice a day's wage they may not have the wherewithal to buy a whole week's ration in one go. A more imaginative food policy is called for to tackle these problems. Instead of giving huge food subsidies what we need is a reduction in food subsidies and using the money thus saved to alleviate poverty of the bottom 15-20 pr cent of our population.

Since 1985 the Government of India has been borrowing from the international financial agencies huge sums of money. Unfortunately, not all the loans sanctioned are utilized and the country ends up paying a heavy price for this. India has not been able to utilize $12 billion worth of foreign loans and has to pay a huge sum of $30 million annually as the commitment charge. Can a poor and a resouce-scarce country like ours afford this luxury? A better utilization of loans is immediately called for.

Agricultural Sector Deserves Better Attention

A more imaginative handling of the agricultural sector is also called for. The Government should think of developing rental markets for tubewells and pumpsets. These are the markets that provide an access to water and energy resources to small and marginal farmers.

Another areas which remains quite neglected in government polices is water management. Large multi-purpose projects have their own role to play in the economic development but policies geared towards sustainable use of groundwater will also go a long way in developing Indian agriculture. In India publicly distributed water in command areas is looked upon a "public good: and, therefore, tends to be overutilized and wasted. Another way of saving rain water is to take care of siltation in dams, canals, reservoirs, rivers, etc.

The Government should come out with a policy that positively discourages time overruns. Time overruns escalate costs tremendously and make a mockery of our planning.

In the presence of law and order problems tourism is not likely to develop. No point building attractive five-star hotels, introducing new airlinks making civil aviation open to private sector when tourists are being kidnapped, tortured and killed. The recent case of Israeli tourists, for example is too shameful to be treated as a rare happening and expect the potential tourists to overlook it.

Scholarships for Poor Students

An area that needs a real hard shake-up is higher education. Nobody talks of subsidies to higher education. In a State like Gujarat education for girls is free at all levels of education. This is a ridiculous policy to say the least. Not only Indian girls in Gujarat pay no fees at the university level but even foreign girls are not required to pay any fees. Instead of using foreign students as a source of foreign exchange we take upon ourselves to impart education to them either free of charge (in case of girls) or ask the, to pay the fees that may equal at best their pocket expenses in terms of dollars. No country in the world will have such a ridiculous policy of higher education. Subsidies on higher education should be drastically reduced, if not totally eliminated, and fees should be raised substantially. Poor students can be given scholarships by having a policy of identifying occupations where majority of the poor people are concentrated and give real good scholarships to students coming from parents engaged in these occupations. This would relieve the Government of some financial burden.

These are some of the policies that our Government should at least attempt to formulate carefully and implement effectively.

Summary and Conclusion

It has been observed in the above discussion that ours is mainly a financial crisis. With an able economist like Dr. Manmohan Singh as the Finance Minister we are more or less confident of coming out of he present crisis.

But, why did we face the crisis? Crisis is a result or a combination of factors like lack of a co-ordinated approach to development, scarcity of resources, wastage of resources, uneconomic utilization of resources, etc. One of the important reasons for this crisis to my mind is the situation where economic decisions are politically taken. Take, for instance, the decision to waive loans. It is, a politically taken economic decision that played havoc with our banking system and aggravated problems of deficits. Such decisions force us to resort to external borrowing beyond our capacity to repay and we are forced to run to the IMF/World Bank for another distress borrowing. The tremendous, almost criminal, wastage that our politicians indulge in creates another financial crisis. How is a Minister going to control floods by flying over a flooded area in a helicopter or an Indian Air Force plane? Instead, if he refrains from rushing to the site and makes a careful study of the steps being taken to help the victims of flood and takes quick decisions it would help the economy by saving scarce petroleum products that we need to import. The Governmental should take steps to cut down important domestic and international visits of our leaders and bureaucrats and save resources for other alternative and more demanding uses.

To my mind the crisis is invited through loan melas, loan waivers, corruption, and tremendous wastage, Crisis as a visitor is neither welcome nor wanted in our houses. But, we extend an invitation to it knowingly or unknowingly, through our policies.

REFERENCES

Economic Outlook, June, 1991, Centre for Monitoring Indian Economy, 110-120, Kaliandas Udyog Bhavan, near Century Bazaar, Worli, Bombay-4000025.

Economic Survey 1990-91

Frontline, July 6-19, 1991, published by Messrs Kasturi & Sons Ltd., Madras-600002.

International Encyclopedia of the Social Sciences, David L. Sills (editor), The Macmillan Company and the Free Press, Vol. 3, 1968.

The Economic Times, recent issues from July 4 to July 25, 1991.

The Hindu, different issues from July 10 to July 25, 1991.

Report of the Indira Gandhi Institute of Development Research, Bombay.

4

GROWTH DIMENSIONS AND CHALLENGES OF THE INDIAN ECONOMY

A. K. AGRAWAL

THE INDIAN economy has witnessed reasonably good growth performance in the past few years. It witnessed a major break-through in the annual growth rate, which crossed the five per cent mark, after hovering around 3.5 per cent for three decades since 1951-52. It was made possible by sharp increases in foodgrains production despite droughts in many years and a sustained momentum of industrial growth. However, the emerging socio-economic scenario confirms that the nation is confronted with a number of challenges and a grave crisis posed by poverty, unemployment, inequality in income and wealth, on the one hand, and unfavourable current account balances, foreign exchange difficulties, record budgetary deficits due to severe resource crunches and an excessive dependence on borrowings pushing the economy almost in the debt trap, on the other. These together constitute the core of the challenges that the economy is facing along with the high price rise. The country would confront more challenges in the coming years also if the problems are left unsolved.

While the agricultural growth has been significant, it has been rather unbalanced. There has been a profound crisis of rising costs of cultivation, increasing dependence on expensive resources, glaring disparities in he regional distribution of agricultural growth, increasing discontent of the middle and small farmers and erratic crop yields. The diversified industrial sector has failed to impart dynamism to the economy. As a result the development efforts have remained ineffective in making a dent on the main problem of backwardness and diversification of the basic structure of the economy.

The decade of the eighties has shown a significantly higher growth rate. The growth rate (revised series of National Accounts) in the GDP was 3.81 per cent annum in the fifties, 3.49 per cent in the sixties, 3.43 per cent in the seventies and 5.23 per cent in the eighties. Even if the old series of National Accounts is considered, the growth rates would not be very significantly different. The long-term growth rate for the period 1950-51 to 1988-89 is 3.74 per cent which is due to the compound effect of a long period.

The GDP at factor cost at constant (1980-81) prices in 1989-90 registered a growth of 5.2 per cent as against the record growth rate of 10.4 per cent achieved during the previous year. Thus the average annual growth rate for the Seventh Plan works out to 5.6 per cent. At current prices, the GDP in 1989-90 is estimated to increase by 12.3 per cent during the year. However, the per capita income in real terms is estimated at Rs. 2,142 for 1989-90 as against Rs. 2,078 for 1988-89, registering an increase of 3.1 per cent during the year. The per capita income at current prices is estimated at Rs. 4,252 in 1989-90 as against Rs. 3,875 for 1988-89. The difference in the growth rate of the GDP and per capita income is due to population growth.

Remarkable Transformation of Economy

As a result of the planned process of growth and strategy of development adopted, there has been a remarkable transformation of the economy. Between 1980-81 and 1988-89, while the compound annual growth rate of agriculture and allied activities was 2.7 per cent, those of industry and services were 7.7 per cent and 6.4 per cent respectively. As against this, the growth rates had been 1.8 per cent, 4.8 per cent and 4.6 per cent respectively during the period 1970-71 to 1980-81. The share of agriculture and allied activities which was 30.0 per cent of the GDP in 1980-81 had declined to 32.6 per cent by 1988-89. This share was as high as 45.2 per cent in 1970-71. The share of the industrial sector which was 21.9 per cent in the total GDP in 1970-71 increased to 25.9 per cent in 1980-81 and to 28.1 per cent in 1988-89. The share of the services sector comprising transport, communication, trade, banking, insurance, public administration and other services, has gone fro 32.9 per cent in 1970-71 to 36.1 per cent in 1980-81 to 399.3 per cent in 1988-89.

Though the share of agriculture to the GDP has gone down over the years still its contribution is very large, i.e., about one-third. Out of over five per cent of the total growth during the eighties, one percentage point has come from agriculture, a little over 0.9 percentage point from registered manufacturing and 0.44 percentage point from unregistered manufacturing, making the total 1.36 percentage points from the manufacturing sector and more than the agriculture. Trade, hotels and restaurants and financial services are the next important contributors to growth. Another notable feature is the increasing proportion of services sector in the economic growth.

Of course, the developed countries have experienced much faster growth of the services sector than the commodity producing sectors and that is achieved by adopting resource saving technology through mechanization and automation. This resource saving technology also tends to be labour replacing technology largely. This is true of most of the material producing industries and this dilemma of high productivity, high production and reduced possibilities of labour absorption in materials producing sectors is resolved by absorption of labour force in the services sector. However, in the Indian context, we have to opt for labour intensive technology to absorb the expanding labour force along with mechanization and automation wherever necessary and feasible to compete in the international market for export. Here we should not forget that education, health care, extension work and research are all part of services and this contributes directly to the quality of life as well as productivity.

Declining Man-Land Ratio

The data thrown up by the Census 1991 points towards population of the country as 843.9 million (provisional) comprising 437.6 million males and 406.3 million females. The population has increased by 160.6 million (in absolute terms) during the decade 1981-91. It is almost equal to the increase in three decades 1931-61. As a matter of fact the declining land-man ratio has posed problems in many sub-regions, but, at the national level, the pressure of population will increasingly manifest itself in the strain on urban services and facilities.

Another notable point is high concentration of population in some pockets. For example, 63.73 per cent of the country's population lives in 31.45 per cent of the area. The phenomenal growth of population in urban areas is also due to migration from rural areas. The reasons may be many but it is placing severe strains on housing sanitation, transportation and educational facilities, which are proving woefully inadequate to meet the pressing demand.

The continuous unchecked growth of population will demand an additional expenditure on education, child health services and so on. Besides, pressure on resources will increase even more rapidly to allow backlogs to be cleared and quality to be upgraded. In the field of social services, the rising number of old persons, both the absolute and percentage terms, will require new initiatives in health care and social security. It may be noted here that the present measures for old persons are not at all adequate. Thanks to the social system of the young taking care of the old there are still no serious old-age-care problems but all the signals are there that we have to make more provisions for old persons in the near future, if not immediately.

The dominating feature of demographic development is the sharp rise in the number of persons in the working age-groups. The percentage of unemployment to the total labour force at the end of the First Plan period was 2.9, it want up to 3.6 at the end of the Second Plan and jumped to 4.5 at the end of the Third Plan. After the three Annual Plans it was 9.6 per cent. Subsequently, the average percentage of unemployment to the total labour force was estimated at 10.4.

Between 1972-73 and 1987-88, employment is estimated to have grown at 2.21 per cent per annum. However, the increase in overall employment growth rate decelerated from 2.82 per cent in 1972-73 to 1977-78 and to 1.55 per cent during 1982-83 and 1987-88. One per cent growth in the GDP had been accompanied by 0.6 per cent growth in employment during 1972-73 to 1977-78 period. This figure continued to be reasonably high at 0.55 during the next few years up to 1982-83, but declined steeply to 0.38 per cent during 1983-88.

The Seventh Plan visualized not more than a 3.99 per cent growth in employment per annum, manifesting the Micawberish attitude to the solution of the unemployment problem. At the beginning of the Plan 1980-85 (April 1985) the backlog of unemployment was estimated to be around 44 million persons. With the growth rate of population and the labour force at 2.48 and 2.54 per cent respectively, the economy has now to generate additional employment opportunities for a labour force of around 55 to 65 million persons.

There is widespread underemployment with regional variations in the levels of development in the country. There is a highly skewed distribution pattern of resource base in the form of land-holdings, productive assets and levels of technology adopted in villages. This is further supported by existing wide differences in the pattern of incomes, saving potential, investment capabilities, risk-taking entrepreneurial potentials, educational levels, and access to knowledge about improved agricultural factors.

Multi-pronged Strategy needed to Generation Jobs

The strategy for creating large employment opportunities has to be multi-pronged, since the organized sector absorbs at present on an average only half a million persons per year. The unorganized sector will continue to harbour the underemployed and the poor. Efforts will, therefore, have to be continued to improve the technology and income generation of the activities covered by the unorganized sector. Employment programmes linked to the creation of infrastructure and rural assets can also play an important rate in this process.

A determined effort will be required to generate new work opportunities in agriculture and related activities and in small and village industries. This will require a massive effort at skill formation and technological upgradation in rural areas and small towns, in farms, artisan households and small manufacturing units. Hence, it is now an economic necessity to promote quality improvements in education vocationalization, training and refresher programmes for workers and the re-orientation of the scientific and technological infrastructure to serve the needs of rural areas and the unorganized sector.

The potential of employment in non-agricultural rural economy should be fully explored in order to accommodate those who cannot find work in the land-based occupations. In urban areas unemployment problem can be tackled by making efforts to reduce the underutilization of the installed capacity in various industries to the minimum.

The rate of economic growth will depend on the resources available for investment and the efficiency with which all investments, old and new, are used to increase output. At the aggregate level the complex factors which determine this are summarized in the rate of savings and the incremental capital-output ratio (ICOR).

The gross domestic savings averaged about 9.5 per cent of the GDP during the period 1950-51 to 1954-55. Then the savings increased and remained around 13 per cent for a considerably longer period from 1955-56 to 1968-69. Then the period 1969-70 to 1978-79 saw a significantly rising trend in savings which went up from nearly 15 per cent in 1969-70 to 23.17 per cent in 1978-79. Since then there has been a little decline in the savings proportion. In recent years the average has been around 20 per cent and stood at 21.7 per cent of the GDP at market prices in 1989-90 as against 21.1 per cent of the GDP at market prices in 1989-90 as against 21.1 per cent in 1988-89. Thus the saving rate over the Plan period has fallen short by about 3 per cent than the target fixed.

During the period 1969-70 to 1980-81, higher savings came from both public sector and private sector and thereafter the share of both the sectors declined. In recent years there has been notable decline in the savings of the public sector. The household sector has shown signs of again making a better effort on savings during the recent years. The decline in the saving of the public sector is mainly due to large negative saving of the government administration which increased from Rs (-) 8,453 crores in 1988-89 to Rs (-) 12,208 crores in 1989-90. Another factor is the increase in the consumption of fixed capital. However, saving effort is reasonably good as a whole but still gives enough scope for raising domestic savings to that the saving rate can be raised to significantly higher levels by focusing on improving the financial performance of the public sector.

The gross capital formation as a percentage of domestic product has been around 23.9 per cent in 1988-89 which has gone up to 24.1 per cent in 1989-90. The rate of capital formation is higher than the rate of saving because of the substantial net capital inflow from abroad. This inflow from abroad constituted 2.4 per cent of the GDP at market prices although its share was 3.8 per net of the GDP in 1957-58 and hovered around 1-2 per cent of the GDP in most years of the eighties.

With incremental capital output ratio (ICOR) assumed at 4.43, growth of 5-6 per cent would necessitate a higher saving rate than at present. The relationship between growth rate and savings together showed altogether a different story. The growth rate had a tendency to decline a little over the three decades and then to rise to higher levels in the eighties, while the savings were also rising except during the eighties.

Prof. S.R. Hashim has calculated the ICOR from 1951-52 onwards taking into account five-year periods to 1989-90, the entire period divided into eight periods. The ICOR in the first period was the lowest, i.e. 2.9, in the second it increased to 3.40 and in the third (1961-65) it was 5.43. During the next period of 1966-71 there was a little decline but it improved in the two subsequent periods and reached a high of 6.7 during the period 1976-81. Thus during the three-decade period the ICOR has been almost constantly rising. But the period starting from 1981-82 shows a decline to 4.14 in the ICOR, and it remained above four during the Seventh Plan.

The decade of the eighties showing a significantly higher growth rate and a lower ICOR for the economy is due to the build-up of infrastructure and capabilities over the earlier three decades. Still there is a vast scope of utilization of resources already created particularly in the areas of irrigation, electricity and transport. If concerted effort is made to improve the utilization of our existing capabilities, the ICOR will decline further and the cost of production will also come down. Better resource use will certainly sustain higher growth in the long run.

Growth in the industrial production, on the average has been higher than agricultural production and has been responsible for the transformation of the economy. The average annual rate of growth in industrial production in the seventies had been only 4.4 per cent, but during 1980-81 to 1989-90 it increased to 7-8 per cent. The growth in the latter half of the eighties in particular was mainly concentrated in the manufacturing sector and electricity averaging about nine per cent. The growth in the mining sector was, however, lower at around 5.5 per cent. Another interesting feature of the industrial growth in the eighties was the marked increase in the output in the consumer durable industries, which increased by 14.7 per cent, though some of the fastest growing segments within the consumer durables sector are those where import content has been higher. Growth rate in the non-durable consumer goods was, however, much lower at 5.68 per cent. Basic goods and capital goods industries have grown at the rate of 8.09 per cent and 9.99 per cent respectively during the eighties. Expansion of consumer goods sector is necessary to meet the growing needs of goods and services as a result of injection of purchasing power to create employment, etc. Wage goods supply has to be streamlined to face effectively artificial inflation.

More Savings Needed for Developing Socio-economic Infrastructure

The growth in the private final consumption expenditure (PFCE) during the fifties was 3.36 per cent per annum, in the sixties 3.11 per cent and rose a little in the seventies to 3.54 per cent. But the significant step was achieved in the eighties when the growth rate became 4.84 per cent. In the case of per capita expenditure growth it just doubled during the eighties compared to the growth of 1.34 per cent during the seventies. This may be taken as an indicator of reduction in poverty as claimed by the Plan documents but certainly a part of it is at the cost of savings during the eighties. While the consumption may have a good short-term multiplier effect on growth in terms of creating demand for consumer goods but the savings and investments have a much higher growth potential creating an impact in the long run. Hence, further step-up in savings is desirable for building up the necessary economic and social infrastructure, needed more in rural areas.

The ratios of gross margin, gross profit to capital employed, etc. have remained steady during the past few years or so though there was a massive increase in the amount of the capital employed during the period. It need hardly be emphasized that if the overall management of an enterprise is streamlined and geared to its top level of efficiency and productivity, there is every reason to touch the dizzy heights to extraordinary performance by public enterprises. In fact, management is the crucial factor which ultimately decides the fate of an enterprise. This holds true for both private and public sector enterprises. However, in the latter, along with toning up of management side of performance, some other significant phenomena need to be taken care of.

Partial Privatization of Public Sector Needed

The Government should avoid getting involved in the day-to-day running of public enterprises. The monitoring of the unit should be to the extent functionally required. There should be professionalization of the board of directors of public enterprises. The Government is also expected to favour partial privatization of the public sector undertakings, particularly those which are chronically sick. It is also likely to ask for greater autonomy, more amalgamation to achieve viable units and gradual withdrawal of preferential treatment in regard to contracts and pricing. However, one crucial point has to be noted that the running of the public enterprises on business lines, though always emphasized, has never been practised. This has resulted in huge losses of enterprises which seeing to be nobody's concern.

What we really need today is a sector, private or public, committed to economic development in line with national priorities at minimum cost to the national exchequer. It is high time to provide ample opportunities to both private and public sectors to work together in areas such as roadways, waterways, communication, steel, coal, energy, banking and insurance. This can be done by jointly working either through specific allocation of work targets or through the formation of consortia to handle particular tasks. The public sector must concentrate on those things that only it can do well.

A source of major concern in the most recent period relates to the balance of payments situation. The formulation of all economic policies has been dominated by this concern. The overall balance of payments position deteriorated during the latter half of the eighties, as a result of the increasing volume of trade deficits (despite substantial pick-up in the export growth), a sharp decline in the role of invisibles, mainly inward remittances and earnings from tourism in financing trade deficits, increasing burden of debt servicing on account of the rising proportion of commercial and non-concessionary borrowings in the total external debt of the country. Besides, almost a plateau has reached in the indigenous production of crude oil, resulting in large imports of crude oil and petroleum products. The problem has been further aggravated with the Gulf crisis, forcing the Government to borrow from the IMF.

Trade deficits, which had been around Rs. 10 billion and much smaller till 1978-79, increased to Rs. 27.25 billion in 1979-80 and further to Rs. 58.38 billion in 1980-81. Since then they continued of around this level, going up to Rs. 87.63 billion in 1985-86, but declining thereafter. Although the increase in rupee terms is also partly due to the systematic depreciation of the rupee after 1985, even as percentage of the GNP (at market prices) the trade deficit in recent years has been high at between 1.8 and 4.3 during 1980-81 to 1989-90 against between 0.2 and 2.4 during 1970-71 to 1979-80, besides recording small trade surpluses in two years during the latter period.

Sharp Fall in Foreign Exchange Reserves

The continuing strain on the balance of payments is reflected in the steep decline of our foreign exchange reserves during the 1980s, specially since March 1987, when the reserves were worth four months' imports to Rs. 5787 crores ($3,364 million) at the end of March 1990, equal to two months' imports. During 1990-91, there was even a sharper fall in the foreign exchange reserves when, in December 1990, these had gone down to less than 15 days' imports. With the availability of an IMF loan, however, it had increased to one month's imports by January 1991. The external payments situation has forced the Government to take a number of measures which include devaluation of the rupee, borrowing against gold security from foreign banks, declaration of new Import-Export Policy restricting import of POL and other inessential items and boosting up exports in order to keep the balance of payments situation under control.

The balance of payments problem has to be addressed at two levels. First, during the next few years the current account deficit must be brought down to levels which can be sustained by normal capital flows. For this purpose, structural reform wherever necessary must be introduced. Second, in the immediate period, given the commitment to scrupulously honour all the external financial obligations, a substantial compression of imports has become unavoidable.

The need of the hour for India is to interest international institutions, multinational corporations and savings-rich countries who would look to India's medium- and long-term potential and arrange for foreign exchange resources to enable the country to tide over its short-term balance of payments problem. In return they can reap rich dividends in future, when the country emerges as a large and expanding market as also a sourcing arrangement for internationally competitive components and intermediates.

Rising Prices a Painful Problem

Continuous rise in prices year after year is a painful problem to cope up for everyone. The trend of continuous rise in prices leads to inflationary expectations in the country's economy. Because of continuity, these expectations will automatically get inbuilt into the various systems as if they are given exogenous variables thereby rendering controling of prices somewhat difficult. Rising budget deficits, increase in administered prices, faster monetary expansion compared to the growth of the economy, deficit in current account balance of payments, etc., contribute to a larger extent to the rise in prices apart from the imbalances in demand and supply conditions in the country.

We have had for many years now the phenomenon of deficits even on revenue account, owing to phenomenal increases in general administration, defence and social security services. Expenditure on unproductive activities does not produce goods and services for consumption, rather they create demand for consumable goods and services backed by easily available money supply, consequent to fiscal deficits or the inflationary rate.

After containing the rate of inflation to less than six per cent during the first two years of the Seventh Plan, the year 1987-88 witnessed a higher rate of 10.4 per cent as measured by the index of wholesale prices. This year the inflation rate has touched a new height of 12.1 per cent, of which it is estimated that 3 per cent is due to an increase in the administered prices of essential commodities.

The anti-inflationary strategy thus, consists of maintaining a balance between aggregate demand and supply the key to which lies in the prudent management of government finances. Increasing the productivity of large investments, introduction of fiscal incentives for improving inventory management, and encouraging the productive forces and competitive trends in the economy alone can contain the adverse impact of inflation. Reducing costs and improving product quality are the main planks of the strategy. Another element of the strategy to control inflation is to integrate agricultural sector to the whole economy. In this connection the scope of rural savings be widened for increasing the volume of funds available for investment.

A Time Frame Essential

The government is seized of these problems and is trying to address itself to them through a series of policy measures taken. What is needed is to carry forward the advantages gained in the increased strength of the economy and to build up the infrastructure, both social and economic. Besides, efforts will be required to increase the savings rate for improving the resource base, controlling wastages, making the best use of the basic resources like water, energy, minerals and environment. We must make sincere efforts to meet the growing essential needs in an acceptable time frame. Reduction in the rate of population growth, generation of productive employment opportunities on a much larger scale and efficient use of human resource development are other thrust areas which need specific attention. Further, it is necessary to effect an increase in productivity, reduction in costs in view of the resources constraints – both internal and external. Reduction in the external trade deficit is the crying need of the time to correct the balance of payments situation. Above all, there is a pressing need for better efficiency in the working of the system so that the gap between the performance and promise is narrowed.

5

THE FISCAL CRISIS:
Wider Issues and Limited Policy Options

R.K. SINHA

The important thing for a government is not to do things which individuals are doing already, and to do them a little better or a little worse; but to do those things which are at present not done at all.

— **John Maynard Keynes,**
"The End of Laissez Faire"

THE COUNTRY is in the midst of an economic crisis of unprecedented magnitude. This is because for a number of years it has been living beyond its means. If we do not solve the cluster of economic problems that confront us now, an economic charobyl may destroy all that has been built during last forty years. These developments are not an unfortunate coincidence, but arisen out of our shortcomings in the macro-manągement of the economy in the past. There has been an unsustainable increase in the government expenditure. Budgetary subsidies with questionable social and economic impact have been allowed to grow to an alarming extent. There has been poor returns on investment made in the public sector. Public Sector has not been managed in a manner so as to generate large investible surpluses. The excessive and indiscriminate protection frequently given to industry has weakened the incentive to develop a vibrant export sector. Such a situation has resulted in widening the gap between income and expenditure of the government and over all fiscal imbalance in the economy. Managing the economy in a free society is not only the concern of the government alone but all people must come forward with their suggestions and practice austerity in their life in the national endeavour of evolving a strategy for restoring the health of the economy.

While summing up the problems, the Economic Survey 1990-91 states that it is a difficult conjucture for the economy. The large fiscal imbalances persist; the balance of payments situation is fragile; and the inflationary pressures on the price level are considerable as people are faced with double digit inflation.[1] The unabated strains on public finances have continued to exacerbate a difficult balance of payment situation and fuelled high rates of liquidity growth with attendant inflationary consequences. The fiscal deficit stood at the staggering level of more than Rs. 43,000 crore at the end of 1990-91 while the budgetary deficit for the year has been estimated at Rs. 11,430 crore against Rs. 10,772 crore visualised in the interim budget. For many a years fiscal imbalances continue to be a major concern for the government and it has been regularly reminded that success in controlling the growth of governmental expenditure and increasing the surplus generation by public sector enterprises is sine-qua-non to bring about better balance in the fiscal position of the government but also for keeping inflation in check. Such advice has often been ignored. The Economic Survey 1987-88 has reminded the government that the continued rapid increase in government expenditures poses serious risks for inflation and our ability to attain public investment goals in real terms. Such a warning was given when the inflation rate was running at around 5 per cent. It is touching 13 per cent now and expected to get out of hand, if corrective measures are not taken immediately and effectively.

The management of balance of payments is another most important crucial tasks before the government and the nation. While presenting the election year budget in 1989 the then Finance Minister Mr. S.B. Chavan had reminded us that though it is not often appreciated, it must be recognised that high level of fiscal deficits tend to spill over and contribute to high current account deficits in the balance of payments. Our import bill for bulk items is increasing rapidly. The oil consumption has been rising at the rate of around 8 per cent in the recent past. There is no doubt that there has been huge outflow of foreign exchange on this account. Our foreign debt has been doubled during the last six years.

Thus, the root cause of the problem is the macro-economic imbalances. The fiscal deficits of the government have been met by borrowing at home and the current account deficit by borrowing from abroad. Consequently the burden of servicing the accumulated internal and external debt has now become onerous. A stage has come, where neither the government nor the economy can alive beyond it means for long. The soft options have been exhausted. There is no scope left for further manouvre. The nation has fully used its capacity to live on borrowed money.

For last several years deficits of the Central Government is worsening. They have gone from an average of about 5 per cent of GDP in the last half of the seventies to 6.5 per cent in the sixth plan period and to an average of over 8 per cent during the Seventh Plan period. It remained 8.3 per cent in 1990-91. The revenue deficit of the central government also widened significantly during the period. A large part of the market borrowing was used to finance the revenue deficit and some unremunerative expenditure. And what was left over for investment could not yield adequate return for a net income inflow to the government. However, the conventional budgetary deficit does not indicate the full measure of over all deficit and the government's draft on domestic savings and dependence on external savings. A fuller measure of the over all deficit, which is widely used, is the difference between government expenditure and net leading on the one hand and current revenue and grants on the other. Measured thus, the over all deficit of the central government increased from 6.1 per cent of GDP in 1980-81 to 8.2 per cent in 1988-89. This was met from the draft on domestic savings, which increased from 3.7 per cent of GDP in 1980-81 to 5.9 per cent in 1988-89, external borrowings and deficit financing. The net consequences of such pattern of budgetary financing has been a substantial increase in interest payments. It has gone up from 11.6 per cent of total expenditure in 1980-81 to 19.2 per cent in 1989-90 (B.E.) in the central budget. The more disturbing features has been the rise in net interest payments. It has gone up from 3.5 per cent in 1980-81 to 10.1 per cent in 1989-90 (B.E.). During the entire period of Seventh Five Year Plan BCR remained negative and further deteriorated to 1.2 per cent of GDP in 1989-90.

The net outcome of such pattern of financing has been the emergence of unsavoury budgetary imbalances during eighties. Increase in borrowings and deficit financing leads to rise in interest payments, liquidity growth and inflation and pushes expenditure further. Growth in expenditure, in turn, necessitates larger borrowings and deficit financing. In fact, the basic structural imbalance lies in the mismatch between revenue receipts and revenue expenditure. A sustainable fiscal system requires that revenue receipts should cover not just all revenue expenditure but also have a sufficient surplus at least to cover non-remunerative types of capital expenditure. Even this would not be sufficient if the capital investment do not earn adequate return. Thus, the correction of this fiscal imbalance is, perhaps, the most important step for raising the saving rate of the economy. Fiscal management in the immediate future must aim at correcting these imbalances to stem inflation, contain balance of payments pressures, and secure economic benefit, consistent with our national pride.

There has been upward movement in the inflationary situation during 1990-91. The wholesale price index at 12.1 per cent was higher than the rate of inflation at 9.1 per cent during 1989-90. The increase in consumer price Index was much higher at 13.6 per cent in 1990-91 compared with 6.6 per cent during 1989-90. The concentration of increase was much in essential commodities consumered by masses. In recent years the inflationary pressures have been influenced much by (i) fiscal imbalances resulting in a higher increase in money supply, liquidity overhang and thus effective demand, (ii) supply and demand imbalances in sensitive commodities mainly due to shortfall in domestic production and inability of the government to import desired quantity and (iii) consequent inflationary expectations. Thus a better fiscal balance, moderation in monetary growth and diversified agricultural growth will help to contain inflationary situation.

Our balance of payments situation remained under considerable pressure throughout the Seventh Plan despite a buoyant trend in exports. Exports in rupee terms increased by 25.9 per cent in 1987-88, 29.1 per cent in 1988-89 and 36.8 per cent in 1989-90. On the other hand, imports recorded an increase of 10.7 per cent in 1987-88, 26.9 per cent in 1988-89 and 25.4 per cent in 1989-90. However, the Gulf War turned the table by imposing an addition burden on import of POL import bill, a decline in exports as well as remittances from West Asia. In terms of rupees, exports registered a growth of 17.5 per cent in 1990-91 while import registered a growth of 21.9 per cent. Consequently, the trade deficit increased by 38 per cent. Thus the crux of the problem during recent years has been large and persistent trade deficit and the declining capacity of invisibles to finance the deficit. Net invisibles as a percentage of GDP declined from an average of 2.2 per cent during the Sixth Plan to one per cent during Seventh Plan, while trade deficit as percentage of GDP declined marginally from an average of 3.4 per cent to 3.2 per cent during the same period.

Consequently, the current account deficit which needs to be financed through capital receipts increased from an average of 1.3 per cent of GDP to 2.2 per cent of GDP during the same period. It is estimated to be more than 2.5 per cent of GDP in 1990-91.[2]

The government has to meet a monthly financing gap of yearly $ 400-430 million on balance of payments front during 1991-92. The financing gap in earlier years used to be almost the same but used to be met through commercial borrowings, NRI deposits on by drawing foreign exchange reserves. However, in recent months, the NRI deposits have completely dried up and the foreign exchange reserve on July 17, 1991 was Rs. 2,695 crore, do not allow much cushion to meet the financing gap. Given this scenario, the government has pledged 46.9 tonne gold from RBI reserve to the Bank of England for obtaining one month loan of $ 400 million. The recent policy changes, downward revision of exchange rate and IMF loan will surely improve the situation and bale us out from the balance of payments crisis.

The IMF loan provided us immediate relief. The balance of payments continued to be under severe strain. Since March 1991, the RBI have taken various measures for moderating import growth and protecting foreign exchange reserves. Important among such measures have been raising of the cash margins, deposit requirements for imports other than capital goods, import of capital goods only through lines of credit available with financial institutions, imposition of an incremental CRR at the rate of 10 per cent over the existing CRR of 15 per cent and the imposition of an interest surcharge on bank credits for imports. Also to improve the international competitiveness of our exports and to restrain demand for imports, RBI in two phases appreciated the value of major currencies in relation to rupee by 21 to 23.1 per cent. In a bid to curb imports and reduce aggregate demand in the economy on July 3, 1991, the RBI announced a package of monetary measures. The package included raising the bank rate from 10 to 11 per cent, an increase of one per cent in the scheduled commercial banks' deposit rates and lending rates. The government also announced major structural reforms in the area of trade policy on July 4, 1991. These include a uniform REP rate (to be called EXIM Scrip and to be freely tradeable) of 30 per cent of the FOB value of exports, abolition of all supplementary licences except in a few cash, suspension of cash compensatory support to name a few. Hence forth, REP would be the principal instrument for export-related imports.

With the announcement of the new Industrial Policy on July 24,

1991, the role of the government has changed from that of only exercising control over entrepreneurs to providing help by making procedure transparent and by eliminating delays. In its move to unshackle the industrial sector from the cobwebs of unnecessary controls, the government has done away with industrial licencing except for 18 specified cases, removed all restrictions on MRTP Companies, increased the foreign equity to 51 per cent in many high priority areas. The policy announcement has cleared the way for foreign trading houses and easier import of foreign technology. It has removed all registration and sharply circumscribed and redefined the role of the public sector.

Public Sector will only play its role in strengthening the economy and will not be used to control the commanding heights of the economy. Now fiscal and monetary instruments will be used for the purpose. The changes made in the industrial policy has opened a new chapter in our economic history.

The crisis in the economy is both acute and deep. We have not experienced any thing similar in the history of independent India. The root of the problem are traceable to the large and persistent macro-economic imbalances, and the low productivity of investment – particularly the poor rates of return of the past investment. There has been an unsustainable increase in the government expenditure. Budgetary subsidies, with questionable social and economic impact have been allowed to grow to an alarming extent in the past. The tax system has many loopholes. It lacks transparency to enable us to assess the impact of various concessions built in the structure. The public sector has not been managed in a manner so as to generate large invisible surpluses. The excessive and often indiscriminate protection provided to industry has weakened the incentive to develop a vibrant economy. Consequently, the disparities between income and wealth has been accentuated. And it has worked to the disadvantage of the rural economy. The challenge which we are facing is without precedent. Industrial revolution in the West did not face similar problems in its initial stages as the Western nations concentrated on the creation of Wealth, unmindful of the social misery and inequality developed in the process of transition. The democratization of the polity came much later. There is no doubt that the socialist experiment in chartering a new path of accelerated industrial transformation of undeveloped economy did achieve considerable success in developing technological and military capabilities, accumulation of capital for rapid industrial growth and human resource development, in countries such as USSR. However, recent developments have shown this approach too suffered from major weaknesses, specially in allocative efficiency, in the management of technological change, control of environmental degradation and in harnessings the vast latent energy and talents of individuals.

After independence we moved on the path of development under the leadership of Pandit Jawaharlal Nehru and designed our strategy by uniting the strengths and merits of different approaches to accelerate development. No doubt, we have achieved considerable success in the field of development, modernisation and social equity. Yet we have miles to go to achieve our objectives. For realising our goals we have to restore the creation of wealth to its proper place. For, without it, neither poverty can be removed nor employment can be generated. The task before ıs is to suggest the ways as to how creation of wealth is not tempered by equity and justice but is harnessed to the goal of removal of poverty. For creation of Wealth, we must encourage accumulation of capital and as said earlier practice austerity. The task before us is how to remove the stumbling blocks from the path of those who are creating wealth. In fact, there need be to develop a new attitude towards Wealth.

As has been pointed out by the Finance Minister Dr. Manmohan Singh in his budget speech that the beginning of any attempt to correct the fiscal imbalance in the economy must be directed at a reduction in expenditure and an increase in the income of the government, so as to reduce the fiscal deficit. This is our immediate task. However, in the medium term, our fiscal system would be sustainable only if revenue receipts not only meet revenue expenditure but also provide a sufficient surplus to finance capital expenditure that do not yield economic return as such as in defence or in social sectors. In fact, the elimination of structural imbalances in our fiscal system would require a reduction in both the fiscal deficit and revenue deficit as a proportion of GDP. It is heartening to note that a beginning has been made in the Union Budget for 1991-92. Although it is a stupendous task to reduce fiscal deficit, yet the Finance Minister has succeeded in reducing fiscal deficit to 6.5 per cent of GDP at Rs. 37,727 crore by raising revenue and curtailing expenditure. In fact an attempt has been made to attain our old goals of growth and social justice but by using very different means which have proved their superiority world over in the last few decades. Instead of command socialism we have opted for a market friendly, outward looking approach.

Our past experiences indicate that macro-economic stability is necessary for sustainable growth. Sound fiscal and monetary policies create a hospitable climate for private investment and thus promote growth. It is certainly true that macro-economic stability by itself does not lead to development but at the same time it is equality true that without it all other efforts are likely to be in vain. Nations often experience external or internal macro-economic shocks. Flexibility in adjusting quickly to the fiscal and monetary problems caused by such shocks is crucial if growth is to be sustained. Lack of adjustment may result in high inflation, an over valued exchange rate and a balance of payments crisis. This in turn lead to low investment and slow growth. For a country like ours experiencing significant domestic and external imbalances, a credible reduction in the fiscal deficit is almost always necessary to reduce inflation and an appropriate exchange rate is needed to reduce the balance of payments deficit. Though these prescriptions seem to be straight forward, putting them into practice is not so simple. The pace and sequencing of macro-economic stabilisation policies are difficult issues in their own right. The task is all the more demanding when macro-economic reform is merely an element of a broader programme of economic reform. In view of the broader perspectives, potential conflicts among various reforms need to be minimised and complementaries need to be taken advantage of.

A prudent fiscal policy is the foundation of a stable macro economy. Taxes and public spending affect resource allocation and fiscal deficits affect both the balance of payments and depending how they are financed, the rate of inflation. Monetary policy largely follow fiscal policy. The degree of the autonomy of the RBI may affect the conduct of monetary policy. In recent years money creation has become the residual source of financing. And if RBI is obliged (which it has to in the absence of needed autonomy) to finance a big deficit, it may be unable to implement a restrictive monetary policy targeted at controlling inflation. The mode of deficit financing is important in understanding the problem and searching the solutions. When a deficit is financed by printing more notes than the people wants to hold, prices will rise. Inflation often bring a reduction in private wealth in so far as the value of financial assets may be eroded. However, if real tax revenues also fall with inflation because of delays in collection, the deficit will widen; resulting in faster money creation and even high inflation. When budget deficits are financed by excessive borrowing, that can lead to higher interest rates that crowed out the private sector. There are limits to a rapid accumulation of domestic debt. Beyond a point, the public will be unwilling to hold more debt or will do so only at a higher interest rates, further increasing the cost of debt service.

High and unstable inflation often reduce growth by creating an unstable climate, causing distortions in relative prices and absorbing resources. Such situation lead to diversion in entrepreneurial effort from production and investment decisions to short-term financial matters. Distortions in key prices and real exchange rate are also likely to hamper growth. Corrective inflation can be more efficiently achieved when inflation is low and is expected to remain that way. Inflation worsen the distribution of income by harming the poor most.

In 1980s many countries embarked on programmes of stabilisation and structural reform. Stabilisation policies work mainly on the demand side to reduce inflation and external deficit, structural policies are concerned with the supply side. Such policies address the efficiency of resource use, emphasizing reforms in sectors like trade, finance and industry. One can postponed structural reforms during stabilisation, but the opposite is rarely true. Structural reforms are unlikely to succeed unless they are preceded or accompanied by stabilisation. Similarly, stabilisation is unlikely to be sustainable without structural reforms. Adjustment programmes needed in the process of structural reform very often include the measures to reduce fiscal deficit and fiscal reforms involves difficult tradeoffs. Reducing capital spending may create less political resistance than cutting current spending. Abolishing inefficient investment projects is fine, but curtailment in productive investment in sectors like infrastructure and education are likely to hurt long term growth. All types of spending should be reviewed; dispensing with undesirable programmes. On the revenue side tax reform has a role to play. Exemptions, inefficient tax collection, narrow bases and low compliance mean that high tax rates are needed to raise relatively little revenue. This great nation has embarked on to the path of supply-side economics and no one can minimise the difficulties that lie ahead on the long and ardous journey.

In the macro-management of the economy, over the medium-term, it should be our objective to progressively reduce the fiscal deficit of the central government and to move towards a significant reduction of the revenue deficit as well as the current account deficit in the balance of payments. It is only such a prudent management would enable the nation to curb the exponential growth in internal and external debt and limit the burden on debt serving, for the government and the country to manageable levels. However, it must be the endeavor of the government that the process of adjustment do not adversely affect the underlaying growth impulses of the economy. Dr. Manmohan Singh is quite right while observing that we do not have time to postpone adjustment and stabilisation. We must act fast and boldly.

If the intended reform which has been partially introduced in the budget and other policy measures is to succeed, investment must respond. The private sector may not respond as quickly as intended and they may choose wait and see. And if longer period than the intended is taken to restore the confidence and investment, we may not succeed alone for this reason. However, based on the credibility of the reform, additional transfers of resources from abroad may raise confidence and fuel an even greater investment recovery than intended. There is no doubt that our credibility can be improved largely by achieving macro-economic stability. Low inflation is an essential element of macro-economic stability. It is vital not just because it makes the intended programme more credible, but without it other elements of the programme will be directly undermined. Expansionary fiscal and monetary policies are the single obstacle to such reform. Macro-economic stability makes reform of financial sector more likely to succeed, and thereby supports the development of capital market which may foster private investment. Economic and political crisis are opportunities for radical change. We have got the opportunity and have embarked on to the path of reform. We have now to decide the speed. Should reform be gradual or "shock therapy"? In most cases gradualism in implementing reform is defined that it should be spread out over more than two years. Whereas shock therapy implies that reforms are implemented quickly in a concentrated period lasting less than two years. Gradualism may some times be justified when reform faces large economic uncertainties. In general the analytical case for speed is strong as swift actions brings the benefit of reform more quickly. Gradualism may not be feasible for a country in acute economic crisis or for government with limited credibility. If the political opportunity for reform is unlikely to last, speed of reform acquire added significance. Realising fully that the crisis in the economy is both acute and deep and we must act fast and boldly, we are not intending to move on to the path of reform with the desired speed. To quote the Finance Minister "This process would, inevitably, need three years if not longer, to complete". The nature of the economic crisis which our nation is facing needs "shock therapy" and not gradual reform.

The economies which have followed the path of reform prescribed by the experts have often been succeeded and those who have not failed. There is no uniform path of reform to be followed everywhere to ease the economic crisis. The path of reform varies from country to country depending upon the nature and gravity of the crisis. Some urgently need to nationalise prices and incentives others need to privatise state owned enterprises or investment for human resource development and infrastructure. Everywhere such measures need to be grounded in macro-economic stability. Experience shows that the surest path to development is to improve policies in all these respects.[3] But how are such diverse elements to be combined? In what order should reforms be undertaken and with what speed? There are few hard fuels but history does suggest some general principles.[4]

Reforms have to deal with trade-offs among policies -- as for example, reform of the financial sector often calls for distressed financial institutions to be restructured; in the short-run, this may raise public spending and make it harder to cut the budget deficit. And adopting positive real interest fates will lower the burden of credit subsidies but increase the cost of serving the cost of internal debt. Lower tariffs may initially reduce government revenues as in case of Mexico and Morocco, whereas shifting from quantitative restrictions to tariffs will invariably raise them as has happened in Indonesia and Peru, the net effect may be a bigger fiscal deficit. In fact, these trade-offs make it harder for a government to adopt programmes which, taken as a whole, appear to add up fiscal deficit. Yet it is essential that programmes not merely add up, but are sure to do so.[5]

There is no denying the fact that many reforms have successfully dealt with conflicts and trade-offs. But there are countries where reforms have failed as in 1977 in Tanzania and in 1985 in Zambia. In the aftermath of coffee boom, import controls and foreign exchange licencing were removed in Tanzania without complementary changes in exchange rate and macro-economic policy. Within months, the balance of payments turned sharply negative and the country lost most of its foreign exchange reserves. These reforms were abandoned, leaving the external sector more restrictive than before Zambia too adopted an ambitious programme to cut public expenditure, auction foreign exchange and reduce subsidies to urban consumers amid significant internal political opposition with in the government. Within a year export fall sharply and fiscal and monetary situation deteriorated. Consumer subsidies on some food stuples were removed overnight. Consequently, urban unrest followed and a government depending on their votes, reversed the reforms.

The agenda of reforms that has emerged from policy pronouncements and budgetary papers calls for the government to intervene less in certain areas and more in others for the state to let markets work where they can, and to step in promptly and effectively where they can not. History suggests that this is the surest path to faster growth in productivity, rising incomes, and sustained economic development. In the past decade of the twentieth century, India stands at the cross roads. The Finance Minister has reminded us at the right time that our decision at this juncture will determine the shape of things to come for quite sometime. For India to survive, there is no other option available for India except to expand the scope and the area for the operation of market forces. But as Victor Hugo once said, "no power on earth can stop an idea whose time has come". The time has come for the emergence of India as a major economic power and the surest path of success is friendly market approach.

India has moved on to this path. It can move well on to the path if backed by a spirit of high idealism, self sacrifice dedication and the needed political will. But the way the political leadership have reached to the abolition of fertilizer subsidy and raising of its prices and forced the Finance Minister to give some concession, do not speak well of the future. We have miles to go to pick up the sustainable speed for safe movement on the path of reform.

I have may own reservations, because of limited speed of our reform, we may not be able to achieve for which reforms are being introduced. May be because of political compulsions, the needed speed is not picking up. No one will wait for us in the race because we are driving at a slower speed and guided by our age old philosophy that "Slow and Steady Wins the race". In the age of science and technology, the fastness of the speed matter most. Perhaps our political leadership has yet to realise fully the gravity of the situation, and the required speed of reform which the experts have prescribed.

NOTES

1. Government of India, *Economic Survey 1990-91*, p.181.
2. *Ibid.* p.99.
3. *World Development Report 1991*, p.115.
4. *Ibid.*, p.115.
5. *Ibid.*

6

INDIAN ECONOMIC CRISIS:
Imperatives of Fiscal Management, Needed Thought and Action

K. MUNIRATHNA NAIDU

INDIA'S ECONOMIC crisis has not developed suddenly, but has been building up over the last ten years.[1] Previously there was a revenue surplus, an outcome of revenue income and revenue expenditure, which had been invested. This surplus started diminishing and finally the revenue expenditure was greater than the revenue income. It means that even for daily expenses, India had to resort to loans, not to think of investment. India slowly moved into a situation where it had no savings to invest. Though India depended mostly on internal borrowing, yet it incorporates foreign exchange expenditure which increased to a big size beyond India's frame. In 1986 itself the finance ministry at the centre had the knowledge of deep financial crisis India would land into in 1990 or 1991 because of the ever increasing gap between revenue income and revenue expenditure and last of savings for investment. India should have applied sufficient brakes since 1986 to avert the accident in terms of the present economic crisis. The article essentially deals with the fiscal crisis responsible for the overall economic crisis into which India is trapped and the needed options to overcome it. The government's thought and action are still apart due to the soft options tried to be followed for making India strong to over come the economic crisis. How it would realise the goal to come out of the crisis is anybody's guess, but only strong and severe action from all sections of people could save India and put on strong road of development.

India is led into in a serious fiscal crisis of huge magnitude due to its action of "living beyond its means" since 1980s. The fiscal deficit of the Central Government, measured in terms of the difference between revenue receipts and total expenditure, is estimated at more than 84 per cent of gross domestic product (GDP) in 1990-91, as compared with 6 per cent at the beginning of the 1980s and 4 per cent in the mid 1970s.[2] Budgetary deficit or fiscal deficit was unknown until 1970 due to dislike to it by Finance and Prime Ministers. The budgetary deficit increased from 0.12 per cent of GDP in 1969-70 to 1.07 per cent in 1970-71 and 1.75 per cent in 1971-72.[3] But in 1975, in spite of serve death blow to "Garibi Hataoism" due to oil shock of October 1973 (the grants on central plan schemes was maintained at 4.78 per cent of revenue expenditure in 1973-74), Indira Gandhi courageously inaugurated a phase of fiscal contraction. Hence the budgetary deficit was brought down to 0.49 of GDP in 1975-76 and 0.18 per cent in 1976-77. The outcome of this rational fiscal action was total political defeat in 1977 elections which was a serious lesson to Mrs. Gandhi. The Janata Party that came to power took it as a mandate for fiscal expansion. Due to sharp rise in grants for central plan schemes the budget deficit once again was beyond control. The second oil shock of 1979 further encouraged this expansion. Looking into the wealth of data in the 1991-92 prebudget economic surveys statistical appendix it is to be inferred that the origins of the present problems is to be traced to the aftermath of the Second oil crisis in 1979, when India succumbed to the sure of debt-financed solution rather arrange adjustments independently. The IMF then played a different role; it gave a large credit without harsh conditionalities. It turned out to be the bait with a strong hook of liberalisation and external indebtedness which the country swallowed eagerly. We could have given up the IMF loan at that period, but India's international borrowing began on a large scale relying mostly on commercial credit including the risky short term loans. This was done on the advice of new economic advisers inducted from the World Bank and continuing in prominent positions to-day. They said that the country had missed the bus because it had failed to take bold recourse to international finance. On this advice the domestic fiscal policy prudent up to 1979, became irresponsible and wildly expansionary. Hence the Government which managed to generate positive savings, became a dissaver, depending heavily on borrowings even to meet current expenditure. Thus the combination of an internal fiscal imbalance and growing external debt is the economic crisis (tiger) the country has been riding (living) for the last one decade with hardships to middle classes and poorer sections. India began to chase shadows rather than face reality which cost fall off the dangerous steed into the mouth of IMF. Coming back to power in 1980, she became doubly wise with retrospective wisdom of her experiments with fiscal expansion and contraction. She gave more weightage to political stability by under writing high levels of public spending. She again inaugurated a new fiscal policy in 1980 and public sector outlays have steadily grown from around 30 per cent to 40 per cent in 1991-92.[4] The revenue gap increased enormously which was made good through massive internal borrowings. Even then large portion left uncovered which has been met through deficit financing. The budgetary deficit in 1980s went below 1.5 per cent of GDP in only three years, but in 1970s it was more than this figure in only three years. Sri Rajiv Gandhi without properly knowing the implications gave further fillip to this trend and the National Front government and its successor government also followed the policy of excessive deficit spending landing India into an unprecedented fiscal deficit requiring immediate expert management.

Magnitude

The interim budget presented to Parliament in March 1991 estimated the fiscal budget at Rs. 38,475 crores. The postponement of regular budget, no effort at fiscal correction with revenue and expenditure, the fiscal deficit during 1991-92 could reach Rs. 52,000 crores. The difference between the two types of figures also provide the real measure of fiscal correction needed during 1991-92.[5]

Management of Deficit

Reduction in the fiscal deficit during 1991-92 is a stupendous task and needs immediate serious attention. Whoever is responsible in whatever manner, during what period and for any reason – all these are questions for calm brooding over, like a resting bull over a road, but what required is, overcoming the crisis and putting the economy on the normal path.

Issues

1. Immediate step of raising a large loan – either from IMF or some other government or private source to meet. India's credibility problem. Any other alternative way is to be seen.

2. How to tackle the serious balance of payments problem touching upon fiscal deficit.
3. How to increase exports and reduce imports to the minimum essential.
4. Cut down non-development expenditure like defence, petrol imports, subsidies on food, fertiliser exports etc.
5. Increase tax revenue – from direct taxes, indirect taxes, earnings from pubic enterprises, sale of inefficient and chronic loss making unit etc.
6. Live within means for the period – 3 to 5 years – avoid profligate lift.

Policy Action

Immediate short-term needs of external payments (like BoP interest etc.) have to be met by securing a loan of $ 5 billion or some such amount from IMF. The exact figure is known to government as they keep all facts to themselves regarding IMF conditionalities, loan needs etc. So far long term loans are concerned, it is better to get approval from Parliament, but its usage must be phased depending upon the improvement in export, import and other sectors.

Exports

In 1990-91 exports were Rs. 32,527 crores and imports 43,170 crores, leaving a gap of Rs. 10,643 crores. This gap must be reduced to Rs. 5000 to Rs. 6000 crores within two to three months by effecting stringent economic on imports and encouraging exports by all ways. The exports must became competitive, (through quality and price levels) and accepted in international markets. The protective measures adopted by developed countries like U.S.A. (Super 301 measure), Japan etc., have to be abolished on appeal from India for economic reasons.

Imports

Imports of fertilizers must be fully stopped as well as food imports (exempting those that are meant for poorer sections). Petroleum imports have to be reduced to half, meanwhile making efforts to increase indigenous production of capital stock like machinery, skills, raw materials etc., if not helping export sector, must be slashed to the minimum. Imports, for richer sections and luxurious goods have to stopped immediately.

Subsidies

This is one area of over spending by Government of India. There are three types of subsidies – Export subsidy, fertilizer subsidy and food subsidy. Luckily due to devaluation government abolished export subsidy (Rs. 2,700 crores in 1990-91) substantially by way of removing cash compensatory support scheme since the exporters have been compensated by the rupee devaluation. But the real problem areas are food and fertilizer subsidy.

Food subsidy touching valuable sections of poor and very poor category particularly in rural areas cannot be removed. Perhaps to avoid leakages better targeting and restructuring and efficient management of public distribution system (ration shops etc.) has to be followed strictly. Introduction of income criteria would eliminate a large percentage of beneficiaries especially in urban areas. These measures would bring down the food subsidy (Rs. 2,450 crores in 1990-91) considerably.

Fertiliser subsidy (Rs. 4,400 crores in 1990-91) has been abolished by Dr. Manmohan Singh in the budget of 1991-92. It is a right step which should have been taken five years back. This subsidy is enjoyed mostly by rich farmers (intensive cultivation in green revolution areas and other irrigatied areas), manufacturers and intermediaries like agents and dealers, and not benefiting the 90 per cent of cultivators owning 30 per cent of cultivated area (marginal and small farmers). The only thing the government has to do is to device measures, in consultation with farmers and their representatives, to compensate the farmers to face higher fertilizer prices (foodgrain prices by enhanced marginally to offset the removal of fertilizer subsidy). The marginal and small farmers, however, be supplied the needed fertilizers at the low prices by government distribution agencies.

Non-Plan Expenditure

The non-plan expenditures are mostly outlays towards defence, interest payments and subsidies. The revised estimate for total non-plan expenditure in 1990-91 was Rs. 76,761 crores (71.5 per cent of total expenditure) and would have increased to Rs. 89,000 crores in 1991-92, but estimated to reach by Finance Minister to Rs. 79,679 crores in 1991-92, that means reduced by 10 per cent in the current financial year. As it deals with sovereignty, protection of borders as well as international competitiveness of Indian armed forces, defence experts should be involved in reducing the expenditure on this head. It means there is little chance of reducing the outlay on defence.

Interest Payments

This is the largest component of non-plan expenditure. India has to bear Rs. 35,000 crores in 1991-92 by way of interest payment even if drastic reduction in government borrowing is ensured by Central Government. According to Union Finance Minister, in view of large debts already made requiring periodical repayments, the exponential increase in interest payments can be brought under some measure of control only in 1994-95 i.e., after four years.[6] This is possible only through a strict discipline on government borrowing for three years i.e., up to 1993-94. Here also we have little manoevurability.

Subsidies

On this comments have been made earlier.

Positive Actions

The above comments relate to slashing of expenditure. However to reduce fiscal deficits from 8.4 per cent in 1990-91 to 6.5 per cent in 1991-92 and thereafter to 3.4 per cent in the subsequent years, we have to exhibit generosity to collect more revenues by undergoing austere measures. If government of India wants the loan/loans (short-term and long term) from IMF, it has to create resources to the extent of Rs. 17,000 crores and for which Union Finance Minister is making efforts in his 1991-92 budget.[7] The ways are: Taxation, partial or full privatisation of public sector units, earnings from Public sector, etc.

Taxation

All possible ways of raising revenue from direct and indirect taxes must be explored covering all sections of people, leaving out the poor, poorest and the vulnerable sections. Though during 1991-92, the

Finance Minister is satisfied with soft options in collecting revenues. Yet I am sure in the future, more harsh measures are likely to be implemented by him to reduce the fiscal deficit to 3.4 per cent. All the political parties have to cooperate with him more so the ruling Congress Party, by containing the noisy and louder elements.

Privatisation

All sick and chronic loss making units should be privatised which if done is likely to net in (estimated) nearly Rs. 25,000 to Rs. 40,000 crores. As a first step the expert economist Finance Minister on the advice of intelligent, highly educated, experienced and worldlywise Prime Minister (Sri P.V. Narasimha Rao) proposed in the budget 20 per cent of disinvestment in selected public sector units which may fetch the exchequer Rs. 2,500 crores. If 40 per cent of shares in selected 40 public sector units are disinvested, the government could secure Rs. 7,000 to Rs. 8,000 crores.

Public Enterprises

The efficient public sector units should be given targets to earn a profit between 20-40 per cent every year by raking in nearly Rs. 3,000 crores per year; otherwise they must be sold to workers of the units for better management and revenue earning achievement.

Conclusion

All said and done, to overcome the unprecedented fiscal crisis being faced by India in 1991-92, there are no soft options, but only harsh and severe measures to be followed. Revenues must be hiked to the maximum slashing expenditure to the minimum so as to bring down the fiscal deficit to 6.5 per cent in 1991-92 and to 3.4 per cent by 1993-94 and to 1.5 per cent (ideal size) by 1994-95. The Ministers, the bureaucrats, the administrators and government staff of all types should curtail their expenditure to the minimum by living within means, shedding all pronfigate living at the expense of government expenditure. The people of all classes, except the poor and poorest, should contribute their full might for revenue raising efforts of the government in a serious and committed way. This is not one day, one month and one year affair but a long drawnout strategy in which all sections must cooperate to save the honour of India, by upholding its international credibility and creditability at all times Fiscal (deficit) Management is easy, if monetary management is supplement with man management of his financial traits of save more and spend less, earning maximum income through achieving highest productivity and production in all sectors of the economy. India can overcome its serious financial problem, as in earlier in 1970s by the willing cooperation of all sections of people to the fullest extent.

NOTES

1. It is now clear to everybody that the current crisis is not primarily the outcome of policy feelings of the past two recent non-Congress governments, but the result of the imbalances which developed in 1980s up to 1989 and exacerbated in 1990 by developments largely beyond the control of any government (Abhijit Sen: "Balanced document, The Economic Survey and the Budget", *Frontline*, August 13-16, 1991, p.7.
2. Dr. Manmohan Singh, Union Finance Minister, Government of India: Union Budget for 1991-92 presented to Lok Sabha on 24 July, 1991.
3. S.M. Menon, "Consent to Coercion — behind the mess" in *Frontline*, July 20-August, 1991, p.15.
4. *Ibid*., pp.14-15.
5. Central Budget for 1991-92.
6. Union Budget for 1991-92.
7. Ashok Mukherjee, "Austere days are ahead" in *The Hindu*, July 21, 1991, p.17.

7

THE DEFICITS DILEMMA IN DEVELOPMENT: A Trend Analysis

P. JEGADISH GANDHI

FROM THE "Quite crisis" of the sixties, the Indian economy has entered into the open crisis in the beginning of 1990s. Even after 44 years of planned path of development, we are still saddled with self-coiled problems. Especially, the present macro-economic imbalances are not a sudden development, but a short circuited effect of budgetary and fiscal deficits and balance of payments gap due to the mismanagement of economic forces for the past ten years. The present open crisis is most serious and severe in terms of its simmering effect on the fiscal and foreign trade sectors and on the general price situation in the country. The prime purpose of this paper is to focus the financial deficit trends particularly since 1980 and to particularise its impact on the enlargement of money supply and elongation of inflationary trends in the economy.

I

In a developing country like India, there is need to accelerate investment in order to generate rapid growth of production and employment. If the resources raised both from internal and external sources are not sufficient to finance all the development programmes and projects, the gap is to be covered by "deficit financing" (DF). In this context, it is better to comprehend the conceptual clarity of the various facets of financial usage in the Indian fiscal framework. The accounts of the central and state governments are divided into two parts: Revenue Account and Capital Account. Each account has two sides: receipts and expenditure. Expenditure is further classified into two categories: development and non-development. Broadly speaking, non-development expenditure relates to expenditure incurred on maintenance of existing levels of economic services and is or should be normally be met from tax and non-tax revenues. It is also expected that should be a surplus over expenditure and this should be utilised for the purpose of development, that is, the expansion of the current level of services. This forms part of the capital account. The government also differentiates between plan and non-plan expenditure but broadly speaking it can be assumed that the entire capital expenditure (known also as capital disbursement in government accounts) is used for the purposes of development and is financed by surplus from revenue account and by capital receipts, which are borrowings or loans of various categories, both internal and external, including borrowings from the Reserve Bank.

A budgetary deficit may be caused either by a deficit in the revenue account or in the capital account or by both. The strategy of the Finance Ministers and the planners of India was to get as much surplus as possible in the revenue account so that it would fill part of the deficit in the capital account. Deficit financing was clearly intended to assist the capital budget which would allocate investments for productive and employment-oriented development.

Before the eighties, the capital disbursements were much higher than receipts. Thus assets were created out of capital receipts (mainly borrowed funds) which were supplemented by revenue surplus and deficit financing. This practice was consistent with the basic principles of fiscal management. The balance from current revenue had to be positive and capital expenditure had to be finance, to some extend by the revenue surplus. The revenue surplus which was Rs. 59 crores in 1950-51 rose to Rs. 887 crores by 1975-76. (Table 7.1). During this period, barring a few cases, the capital accounts normally showed deficits.

A clumsy appendix chapter was added deliberately to the fiscal history of India in 1980. Since 1979-80, the Government started incurring *a deficit on the revenue accounts*. This means that its revenue receipts from tax and non-tax income was less than its revenue. The revenue deficit has ranged from Rs. 175 crores (1980-81) to Rs. 17,585 crores (1990-91) thereby registering a more than ten times increase. Capital deficits were shown continuously for three years from 1980-81 and later in 1986-87. On the other hand, the revenue expenditure has ranged from Rs. 14,411 crores (1980-81) to Rs. 74,966 crores (1990-91) thereby recording a more than five times increase. It is to be noted that actually there were deficits under both accounts in 1979-80 but that year was peculiar with the Lok Sabha dissolution for about six months sandwiched between two governments of different political parties.

TABLE 7.1: Trends in Surplus/Deficit of Union Budgets

(in crores of rupees)

Year	Revenue Account	Capital Account	Overall Budgetary
1950-51	+59	–78	–21
1955-60	+41	–182	–141
1960-61	+51	+127	+178
1965-66	+320	–493	–173
1970-71	+163	–448	–285
1975-76	+887	–1253	–366
1980-81	–1715	–862	–2577
1985-86	–5889	+574	–5315
1988-89	–10515	+4873	–5642
1989-90	–11912	+1320	–10592
1990-91 (RE)	–17585	+6813	–10772
1991-92 (BE)	–15859	+6135	–9724

Source: Commerce Research Bureau "Basic Statistics of Indian Economy" and Government of India "Receipts Budget" 1990-91 & 1991-92.

Above all, what is important is the overall resources gap that the government confronting, that is, *the fiscal deficit* (FD). For the first time in India's fiscal history, the 1991-92 Budget interim and final-incorporates this concept and gives the relevant figures. FD is "the broadest concept which measures the total resources gap in terms of excess of aggregate disbursement over revenue receipts including grants and which reflects the impact of fiscal operations on the indebted of the Central Government". In short, it underlines the structural imbalance in government's finance. The FD has been growing in absolute magnitude from Rs. 8,299 crore in 1980-81 to Rs. 43,331 crore in 1990-91. As a proportion of the gross domestic product at market prices it has been fluctuating from 6.11 per cent of the GDP in 1980-81, to a high of 8.98 per cent in 1986-87 and thereafter declining to 8.36 per cent in 1990-91. The conventional budgetary deficit, on the other hand, rose from 1.82 per cent to 2.82 per cent and thereafter declined to 2.07 per cent in a similar time frame. The FD was 9.2 times the conventional budgetary deficit in 1983-84, in 1988-89, 5.5 times and for 1991-92, it is projected at 4.9 times. The Government has to contain the FD to 6.5 per cent of GDP as per its promise to the IMF. It has only two options left before it. One, it imposes more taxes to generate more revenue to bring down the FD to 6.5 per cent. Two, it cuts expenditure so that the FD does not exceed the targeted level.

It is stunning to study that the total annual wage bill of the Union Government is 40 times the Plan outlay on health for the current year, 45 times more than the combined Plan expenditure on science and technology and scientific and industrial research, 15.5 times the Plan outlay on family welfare, 12 times that on education and 11.5 times that on agriculture and cooperation. Even more interesting is the fact that the wage bill is 3.3 times larger than the outlay on rural development. The wage bill in 1991-92 is equal to about 35 per cent of the total Annual Plan outlay for the year of Rs. 33,724.87 crores. In 1991-92, the Union Government's wage bill was equal to 34 per cent of the Plan outlay for the year, indicating that Government salaries and allowances are rising faster than development expenditure. The salvation of the sagging economy lies more in terms of a subsided level of Government expenditure for a period of two years (1991-93).

II

Apart from keeping a Constant Vigil on the fiscal deficit front, *budgetary deficit* zone should also be checked every year. The phrase "deficit financing" is used to "describe the financing of a deliberately created gap between public revenue and public revenue or a budgetary deficit, the method of financing resorted to being borrowing of a type that results in a net addition to national outlay or aggregative expenditure." In India, the budgetary deficit is normally covered by (1) withdrawal from cash balances, (2) borrowing from the Reserve Bank of India and (3) issue of notes. When the Government borrows from the Reserve Bank, the latter which is the note-issuing authority simply issues more notes. In the final analysis, deficit financing means issuing of more new notes. DF is more generally regarded as an inflationary way of financing development. The immediate result of DF is to increase the money supply, which is associated with the time lag, with a decline in the availability of consumer goods. The combined effect of these is frequently the generation of inflation in the economy. After a stage, in the race between costs and prices, the economy gets into the grip of spiral inflation.

Deficit financing is like a drastic drug, which should be administered only sparingly. But our experience shows that it has become a regular therapy in our country with more than the prescribed amount in the Five-year Plans. Since the Third Plan, it has registered two-fold increase over the estimated plan outlays and even , a three-fold increase in Fifth and Sixth Plans. The story of a two-fold increase in deficits over the original target has been repeated during the Seventh Plan (1985-90) period. Insofar as its share in GDP is concerned, it went up from 1.2 per cent in the Sixth Plan to 2.1 per cent in the Seventh Plan. The spread effect of the Gulf crisis in oil prices and the crippling effect of the balance of payments problem have already widened the budgetary gap in 1990-91. The Planning Commission has recently decided to peg DF during the Eighth Plan period 1992-97 at Rs. 37,000 crores. This would mean average DF of Rs. 7,400 crores over the five-year period. The 1991-92 Budget has provided for DF of Rs. 7,719 crores against the actual Budget deficit of Rs. 10,772 crores in 1990-91 and Rs. 10,592 crores in 1989-90. If past experience is any pointer, the actual level of deficit finance never conformed to the budgetary estimates in recent years. Thus Rs. 10,000 crores of actual deficit finance seems to be the "floor level"!

III

The Indian money history is replete with facts and figures which shows that money supply is really responsible for fanning the flames of rise in prices. To quote Dr. C. Rangarajan, former Deputy Governor of RBI: "Broad money (M_3) increased from Rs. 10,958 crores in March 1971 to Rs. 1,18,338 crores in March 1986. The wholesale price index rose from 100.4 (Base 1970-71 = 100) to 359.8 during the same period. In comparison between March 1971 and March 1986, the increase was 17.2 per cent in M_3 and 8.9 per cent in the wholesale price index on an annual average basis." According to an other estimate, M_3 would have risen on a trend basis at 16.12 per cent, the wholesale prices at 6.33 per cent, the cost of living (industrial) index at 8.18 per cent and agricultural labour's index at 7.2 per cent between 1981-82 and 1988-89. As per the *Economic Survey* 1990-91, while broad money has increased during the last five years (1985-90) by an average rate of

17.6 per cent per annum and net RBI credit to Central Government has increased by 17.8 per cent per annum, the GNP recorded an average growth rate of 5.7 per cent.

It is thus seen that there is always a correlation between the contents of money supply and convulsions in price levels in the Indian economy. Also it is equally true that there is a retreat of inflation since 1981. But this is made possible only by actively pursuing a tight money policy. As can be understood from Table 7.2 there is a direct relationship between the restricted money flows and the reversed inflationary trends between 1981-82 and 1988-89. The WPI has declined from a high level of 16.7 per cent in 1981-82 to 5.1 per cent in 1988-89 whereas the flow of money resources has come down from 18 per cent to 13 per cent in the same period. As Prof. P.R. Brahmananda observed: "It is only by reducing the M_3 growth rate to eight per cent and M_1 growth rate to 5-6 percent, the price stability can be obtained. Two major requirements in the direction are: getting rid of the Central deficit and obtaining strict RBI control over the monetary system."

TABLE 7.2: Macro-economic Indicators

(in percentage)

Year	Monetary resources (M_3)	Wholesale prices (on point — to — point)	Gross National Product (GNP) (at 1980-81 prices)
1980-81	18.1	16.7	7.4
1981-82	12.5	2.4	5.9
1982-83	16.1	7.3	2.6
1983-84	18.1	8.2	7.7
1984-85	18.9	7.6	3.1
1985-86	15.9	3.8	4.1
1986-87	18.6	5.3	3.6
1987-88	15.9	10.6	4.2
1988-89	17.8	5.7	10.6
1989-90	19.4	9.1	5.2

Source: *Economic Survey*, 1990-91.

Disinflationary Phase

The monetary analysis found the inadequacy of the two much-used terms "inflation" and "deflation" to explain the new monetary experiences especially in the post-war years. Terms like "reflation", "disinflation", and "stagflation" have been coined to interpret the emerging monetary phenomena both in the developed and developing economics. It is not any fall in prices which presupposes the deflationary period in an economy. On the other hand, the process which brings down the inflationary trend in prices from high level without causing unemployment or reducing output is called "disinflation."

It is really a disinflationary phase in India? As seen from Table 7.3 the trends in employment and output do not indicate stable prices. The backlog of unemployed at the beginning of March 1985 was estimated at 9.2 million for the age-group of 5-plus at 8.7 million for the age-groups of 15-plus and at 8.6 million for the age group of 15-59. The number of job-seekers on the Register of Employment Exchanges throughout the country has increased by 170 per cent from 178.38 lakhs in 1981 to 301.31 lakhs in 1986 and to 304.95 lakhs in 1987 – whereas the vacancies notified declined by 70 per cent from 897,000 in 1981 to 703,000 in 1983 and further to 623,000 in 1986 and still further — to 543,300 in 1988. Also there is a wide gap between the number of registrations and placements of job seekers between 1981 and 1988.

TABLE 7.3: Trends in Employment

Year	@ Registrations	@ Applicants placed in employment	*Public sector industry*	*Private sector industry*
				(in lakhs)
1981	62.76	5.04	154.84	73.95
1982	58.62	4.73	159.46	75.47
1983	67.55	4.85	164.56	75.52
1984	62.19	4.07	168.49	73.45
1985	58.21	3.88	172.69	73.09
1986	55.35	3.51	176.83	73.73
1987	60.11	3.34	180.25	73.64
1988	59.63	3.28	183.20	73.91

Source: @ India 1988 — 89 A Reference Annual, Govt. of India p. 591
* *Economic Survey*, 1990-91.

With a population growth of 2.4 per cent a year, it is essential that employment increased at a rapid rate. This, however, does not seem to be happening, except to a small extent in the public sector. According to the *Economic Survey*, 1990-91, employment in the public sector increased by 30.32 lakhs between 1981 and 1989 whereas in the private sector it is stagnant at 73 lakhs except in 1982, 1983 and 1989. It should be borne in mind that the share of private sector investment has actually gone up from 47.1 per cent in the Sixth Plan (1980-85) to 52.2 per cent in the Seventh Plan (1985-90) period. Liberalisation may have led to growth in the private sector during these years, but it does not manifest itself in employment generation. It is to be noted that in the size of Eighth Plan (1992-97), the gross public investment has been set at Rs. 3,42,000 crores (43.18 percent) while the private sector investment has been pegged at Rs. 4,50,000 crores (56.82 per cent).

Double Digit Inflation

The annual rate of inflation in India has touched again the 10 per cent double-digit mark with official WPI for all commodities (1981-82 = 100) scale up 184.3 during the week ended November 10, 1990. The pressure on the price front continued unabated with WPI went up to 209.2 during the week ended September 14, 1991. The rentless rise in the inflation rate since the Budget 1991-92 witnessed a let up with the rate remaining at 15.7 per cent. The recrudence of the current deficits-induced double-digit inflation is not entirely a new phenomenon in our economy. Inflation springs significantly from prolonged monetary expansion. There may be other contributory factors, but they cannot sustain the spiral of rising prices in the absence of increasing growth in the money supply.

The popular proposition is that we can rule out the possibility of emerging inflationary potential under excess capacity and unutilised resources in a developing country like India. Then how do we account for the current inflation in the economy? Apart from the seasonal and speculative factors connected with certain essential commodities, the percolation of newly created money in both urban and rural sectors has stoked the fires of price rise of all commodities. In general, inflation due to demand pulls has resulted in a negative income effect for a vast majority of people in our society. The purchasing power of the rupee has dwarfed to 15 paise in 1989-90 from its 99 paise value in 1949-50. During the 40-year span of economic development, the value has dwindled to one-sixth of the rupee. The pathology of the fall in the value of the rupee since 1950 shows the presence of large germs of deficit financing.

Further, we need to recognise the nature of price phenomena in

India-in particular, the absence of downward flexibility, feed-forward effects of indexing agricultural procurement prices with overall inflation, price-wage-fiscal deficit nexus, high price sensitivity to supply-demand imbalance of certain basic consumer goods and the role of administered prices. Viewed against this background and allowing for lagged effects of high monetary expansion of recent years, annual inflation for 1991-92 could be as high as 18 per cent. However, if the benefits of devaluation are not to be neutralised it is imperative that inflation is contained at all costs.

IV

Income Trends

The GNP and its distribution mirrors the macro flow of goods and services and the economic structure of the economy. The GNP in India has actually declined from a high level of 7.4 per cent in 1980-81 to 2.6 per cent in 1982-83 and reached a high level of 7.7 per cent in 1983-84. Since then it shows only nose-diving trends. It took off to a level of 10.6 per cent in 1988-89, but again it turned a somersault of 5.2 per cent in 1989-90. A study made by the Central Statistical Organisation (CSO) has revealed that as much as 76 per cent of the increase in incomes has accrued to 30 per cent of the population engaged in non-agricultural pursuits while only 24 per cent has gone to the 70 per cent population engaged in activities like agriculture and fisheries. Thus income distribution continues to remain highly skewed and consumption of affluent sections of the population has put pressure on the elitist production segment of economy. Coupled with this phenomena is the cancerous growth of black money in the economy. According to the estimates of the Institute of Public Finance and Policy, the black money generation is of the order of Rs. 40,000 crores. It excludes that generated through smuggling activities. This parallel money has actually put the economy on the mat.

According to the Centre for Monitoring Indian Economy (CMID), the long term growth of agricultural production for 1977-78 to 1988-89 continued to be at 2.3 per cent per annum against 2.5 per cent during 1967-68 to 1977-78, the first phase of the Green Revolution. No doubt, there are uptrends in the production of industrial goods since the Eighties, but only at the cost of the output of wage goods. For instance, the output of consumer durables to satisfy the demand of a small section of the elite, increased by no less than 21.6 per cent in 1984-85, by 18.7 per cent in 1985.86 and 19.5 per cent in 1987-88. This was more than double the overall growth of the industry. Thus the economy does not possess adequate stocks of wage goods to meet the flow demands governed by aggregate employment and the wage-pattern or wage-income hierarchy. It seems that in the past few years we have been trying to meet the commodity effects of a higher targetted growth rate, primarily, by tilting domestic distribution to make it more unequal and also by somehow obtaining foreign exchange without taking care of the consequences. The beneficial effects of the recent structural reformatory steps like devaluation, desubsidisation, deregulation, opening of the economy to allow large direct foreign investment and greater latitude to multinational companies will peter out in the absence of a proper stability of price trends in the domestic economy.

V

Policy Programmes

In the light of the past experiences, the proper policy in stabilising prices should be in the direction of (1) fixing a ceiling on the growth of money supply during a period, (2) strengthening and reorientation of our agricultural programme, (3) remodelling of the procurement and public distribution systems, (4) showing greater selectivity in development of credit than in the past so as to reduce the dependence of commercial banks on the Reserve Bank, (5) applying budgetary gadgets to mop up the excessive purchasing power in the hands of people, (6) slashing the non-developmental expenditure to an irreducible minimum during the particular period, (7) providing proper incentives to the expert-oriented industries so as to earn the necessary foreign exchange to compensate our losses at the time of deficits and difficulties, (8) creating a favourable climate for small entrepreneurs to contribute to the industrial production, (9) supervising the fuller and quick utilization of international aid funds, (10) recognizing the merits of internal technical know-how so as to ward off the flight of this skills to foreign countries, (11) intensifying further the operations against smugglers, hoarders, tax evaders and black-marketeers, (12) a moratorium on wage revisions for a certain period and (13) a better management of Government finances.

If the trade and industry are genuinely interested in holding the price line and in wiping out recessionary symptoms in some sectors, it should adopt a price-cut policy with an accent on more production of wage goods, instead of luxury and semiluxury commodities. The common man is not concerned with the calculus of price indices, but he is more confounded by the highly fluctuating prices in daily purchases. It has thus become imperative on the part of the Government to reduce the yawning gap of budgetary deficits.

REFERENCES

Brahmananda, P.R., Growthless Inflation by means of stockless money: New Classical Treatise on Rising Prices, Himalayas, Bombay 1980.

———, "Curb money supply Growth," *The Business & Political Observer*, June 7, 1991.

Dubashi, Jay, Is India going bankrupt? A publication of the Project for Economic Education, Bombay 1989.

Gandhi, Jegadish P., "The Anatomy of Inflation, " *Southern Economist* (SE) May 1, 1975.

———, "Price Stability: An Analysis of Government's anti-inflationary policy, SE, August 15, 1976.

———, "Flare-up on the Price Front," *Indian Banking Today & Tomorrow*, March 1977.

———, "Budget; what it should mean this time." *Indian Express*. February 13, 1978.

———, "Inflationary Potential of Sixth Plan," SE, April 15, 1978.

———, Deficit Financing, *Indian Express*, October 24, 1978.

———, "Challenge on the Price Front," *Indian Banking Today & Tomorrow*, June, 1980.

———, "Invitation to another Bout of inflation," SE, March 1981.

———, "Will the Budget help in bringing down prices," SE, March 15, 1983.

———, "No attempt to curb money supply," SE, March 15, 1984.

———, "Budget leads to high cost economy," SE, March 15, 1989.

———, "Disinflationary Phase in India?", *The Hindu*, July 18, 1989.

———, Indian Economy — Some Issues, Institute for Social Sciences & Research, Vellore 1982.

——— (Ed.), India Economic Issues, Part I, Pointer Publishers, Jaipur, 1989.

Jalan, Bimal, India's Economic crisis — The way Ahead, Oxford University Press, New Delhi 1991.

Nambiar, K.V., "Economic crisis: A fall-out of past policies," *Financial Express* (FE), September 15, 1991.

Ramachandran, K.S. and Vaidyanathan, P., "Towards Conceptual Clarity," *FE*, September 4, 1991.

———, "Bridging a widening gap," *FE*, September 12, 1991.

———, "More on diversion of capital receipts," *FE*, September 19, 1991.

Rao, VKRV, "Deficit Financing, capital formation & Price Behaviour in an underdeveloped economy," *Indian Economic Review*, February 1953.

Sethi, J.D., "Indian Economy under siege, (forthcoming) Vikas Publishing House PVT. Ltd., New Delhi, 1991.

Sezhiyan, Era, "Budget Deficits — Precept & Practice," *The Hindu*, September 5, 1991.

Sharma, P.D. et al, "Indian Economic Outlook, 1990-92," A paper, presented at the National Academy of Sciences, Moscow, USSR, September 23-27, 1991.

Vijayaraghavan, R., "Cutting the fat in Government," *The Hindu*, October 1, 1991.

The Economy — Crisis and Adjustment, A Debate; observer Research Foundation, New Delhi, July 1991.

Economic Survey, 1990-91 & Union Budget, 1991-92, Government of India.

8

INDIAN ECONOMIC CRISIS: The Resource Crunch Trap

M. MOHANDAS

Introduction

THE INDIAN economy was steadily heading towards a financial crisis which has presently taken the shape of fiscal and balance of payments crisis. The economy is passing through a very difficult stage due to continued pressure on balance of payments, large scale budget and fiscal deficits and double digit inflation. These problems have been gathering momentum for quite some time, but got aggravated by the gulf crisis and political uncertainty during the last year and a half. Recently the Government of India initiated a package of measured including two successive doses of devaluation of the rupee and liberalisation of industrial and trade policies, apart from pledging gold in Bank of England. These measures were primarily intended to boost exports, reduce merchandise imports as also to send right signals to outside agencies like IMF, World Bank, Aid India Consortium and the Non-Resident Indians for attracting foreign assistance and capital inflow.

These signals have worked in a limited way as the IMF has already sanctioned an aggregate amount of \$ 635 million under the Compensatory Contingency Financing Facility and Aid India Consortium has also pledged \$ 6.7 billion. Similarly Japan and Germany have made certain commitments already. The response of Non-Resident Indians is not yet fully clear. Apparently the Government seems to have averted the balance of payments (BoP) crisis temporarily. But the basic issues which led to such an un-enviable situation persists for long-term remedy.

At the outset it may be noted that the fiscal crisis and the BoP crisis are merely symptoms rather than the disease proper. They are only manifestations of certain deep-rooted problems associated with our development policy and development strategy, which are examined in section 3 of this paper. The present crisis appears to be more a "fiscal" and "liquidity" crisis. Though it is true that there is no serious "economic crisis" in the sense of a breakdown of the production or distribution system, the present "fiscal" and "liquidity" crisis have the inherent potential of creating distortions and shocks in the economic system which may traverse towards an impending economic crisis in the not too distant future, if left unchecked.

The paper is divided into four parts. The extent and nature of the present crisis is discussed in Section I. The interlocking resource crunch trap is examined in Section II and the analysis of the development policy and development strategy which had led to the present crisis is examined in third section. Finally conclusions are given in Section IV.

I

Fiscal Imbalance

The fiscal imbalance in the economy is reflected in (1) widening revenue deficits; (2) widening budgetary and fiscal deficits and (3) mounting internal and external debts and rising debt service obligation. It may be noted that up to 1978-79, there was no revenue deficit for the Government of India. In fact the average annual revenue surplus during 1974-79 period was Rs. 534 crores. The revenue deficit appeared for the first time during 1979-80 and the average annual revenue deficit went on mounting from Rs. 1449 crores during 1979-84 to Rs. 13726 crores during 1988-89 to 1991-92.

The revenue account deficit has gone up steadily from 0.6 per cent of G.N.P. in 1980-81 to 1.5 per cent in 1984-85 and 2.1 per cent in 1985-86, which was stagnant at 2.7 per cent during the period 1986-87 to 1989-90. But it went up further to 3.4 per cent during 1990-91 (see Table 8.1). As a consequence, the budget deficit also went up from 1.9 per cent of GDP in 1985-86 to 2.7 per cent in 1989-90 which declined slightly to 2.3 per cent in 1990-91. The monetised deficit however was higher in most of the years which declined from 2.6 per cent of GDP to 1.7 per cent. The corresponding overall deficit which broadly reflects the fiscal deficit also went up from 6.1 per cent of GDP in 1980-81 to

8.9 per cent in 1985-86 and remained stagnant up to 1989-90. But in 1990-91 it further went up to 9.5 per cent.

TABLE 8.1: Centre's Revenue Receipts and Revenue Expenditure

(as percentage of GDP)

	1980-81	1985-86	1989-90	1990-91 R.E
1. Tax Revenue (Net of State's Share)	6.9	8.1	8.7	8.6
2. Non-tax revenue	2.5	3.1	3.5	2.9
3. Total Current Revenue (1+2)	9.4	11.2	12.2	11.5
4. Total Current Expenditure	10.0	13.3	14.9	14.9
a. Interest payments	2.0	2.9	4.0	4.3
b. Subsidies	1.2	1.8	2.5	1.8
c. Defence Expenditure	2.6	2.9	2.7	2.4
d. Grants to States & UTs	2.1	2.7	2.0	2.2
e. Others	2.2	3.0	3.8	4.2
Total expenditure on interest, subsidies and defence (a+b+c)	5.8	7.6	9.2	8.5
5. Revenue Surplus + or Deficit (-) (3-4)	-0.6	-2.1	-2.7	-3.4
6. Budget Deficit	1.9	1.9	2.7	2.3
7. Overall Deficit	6.1	8.9	8.2	9.5

Source: *Economic Survey*, 1990-91 pp 102 and 110 and Budget for 1991-92.

Although the Centre's current revenue receipts had grown from 9.4 per cent to 11.5 per cent of GDP during the period 1980-81 to 1990-91, the current revenue expenditure had grown at a faster rate from 10 per cent to 14.9 per cent leaving the revenue deficit wider during the period from 0.6 per cent to 3.4 per cent. In other words, the revenue deficit as a proportion of revenue receipts went up sharply from 20.7 per cent to 30.7 per cent during this period.

This has caused the fiscal deficit also to move up from 36.4 per cent of the total budgetary expenses in 1980-81 to 40.6 per cent in 1990-91 (RE) (see Table 8.2). The corresponding figure for 1991-92 is shown to be lower in the budget based on a very conservative estimate. The actual figure for the year will be likely to be made higher judged by past experience.

The main factor leading to the widening gap between revenue and expenses is the mounting non-development expenses. Interest payments, subsidies and defence expenses together consume little below four-fifths of the revenue receipts according to the budget for

1991-92. In 1987-88 their total share came to 78 per cent of the revenue receipts. In 1991-92, B.E., interest liabilities alone take away 42 per cent of the revenue receipts of the centre which made the Finance Minister to warn that at this rate, the interest obligations would cross 50 per cent of the revenue receipts by 1994-95. This is an alarming situation in which very little money is left for development purposes.

TABLE 8.2: Revenue Receipts and Expenditures of the Government of India

	1980-81	1985-86	1988-89 R.E.	1990-91 R.E.	1991-92 B.E.
Revenue receipts (Rs. crores)	11937	27112	42424	57381	67529
Revenue deficit (Rs. crores)	2473	6049	11030	17585	13854
Revenue deficit as proportion of revenue receipts (%)	20.7	22.1	25.6	30.7	20.5
Direct taxes as percentage of total tax revenue	22.1	19.4	20.7	18.9	19.6
Fiscal deficit as percentage of total budgetary expenditure	36.4	39.0	37.9	40.6	33.3
Plan outlay as percentage of total budgetary expenditure	40.8	40.1	35.5	28.1	29.7
Expenditure on Interest, defence and subsidies	37.3	41.0	46.4	41.0	42.0
(a) Interest	11.8	15.1	18.7	18.0	21.0
(b) Defence	16.3	16.1	17.4	14.0	13.0
(c) Subsidies	9.2	9.9	10.3	9.0	8.0

Alternatively 42 per cent of the budgetary expenses are incurred on these three items in 1991-92 B.E. which was only 40.1 per cent in 1985-86. The figure for 1991-92 is likely to be higher due to relaxation of certain provisions in respect of fertiliser subsidy and higher defence outlay (see Table 8.2). One very interesting observation is that the size of the aggregate budgetary deficit (fiscal deficit) and the total expenditure on these three items are rather very close which reflects the causal relationship between the two. While the expenditure on interest, subsidy and defence went up from 5.8 per cent of GDP in 1980-81, to 7.6 in 1985-86 and 8.5 per cent in 1990-91 the corresponding proportion of fiscal deficit had increased from 6.1 per cent in 1980-81 to 8.9 per cent in 1985-86 and further to 9.5 per cent in 1990-91 (see Table 8.1). In certain years like 1989-90, the expense on these items had even exceeded the overall budgetary deficit. Thus, it is evident that interest and subsidies are mainly instrumental for the present fiscal crisis.

The mounting non-development expenditure had generated two types of unfavourable impacts in the Indian economy: (1) one is the deleterious effects on the public sectors contribution towards savings and capital formation and (2) the second is the mounting debt burden and the vicious circle of deficits and loans. The public sector savings which had reached 4.6 per cent of the GDP in 1978-79 (the year previous to the appearance of revenue deficit) registered continuous decline to 1.7 per cent in 1989-90 mainly due to dissavings by the central governments in the form of steadily rising revenue deficits. As a consequence, the public sectors' share in aggregate domestic savings declined from 16 per cent in 1980-81 to 7.7 per cent in 1988-89. The decline was on account of deterioration in savings by government departments. As a result, the share of departmental enterprises (DEs) and non-departmental enterprises (NDEs) in aggregate savings increased from 7.3 per cent in 1980-81 to 18.3 per cent in 1988-89.[1] But these shares compare poorly with their share in investment which came approximately one-third of aggregate investment and three-fourth of the public sector investment. Nevertheless, there has been increased provision for depreciation from Rs. 4131 crores in 1980-81 to Rs. 12312 crores in 1987-88, which accounted for 97.5 per cent of the gross savings in the latter year indicating the meagre net profits (retained) generated by public enterprises.[2]

The main consequence of the poor performance of the public enterprises is the persistence of wide resource gap. For example, investments in DEs and NDEs together increased from 7.87 per cent of the GDP in 1980-81 to 8.2 per cent in 1987-88 while their share in savings was only 2.98 and 3.70 of GNP, which left a resource gap of 6.36 and 4.40 per cent respectively.[3] For the public sector as a whole the gap between savings and capital formation has widened from 6.2 per cent of GDP in 1970-71 to 7.5 per cent in 1980-81 and further to 9.3 per cent in 1989-90 (see Table 8.3). This unenviable situation has emerged due to the fall in savings by Government administration from a negative 0.2 per cent in 1985-86 to a negative 2.6 per cent in 1989-90. While the savings by departmental enterprise varied around 0.5 per cent of GDP only, savings by the non-departmental enterprises increased from 2.6 per cent to 3.8 per cent leaving a net savings of 1.5 per cent (provisional) of the Government Sector.[4] Hence in order to maintain the level of capital formation the dependence on external savings increased from 2.4 per cent in 1985-86 to 2.9 per cent in 1988-89.[5]

TABLE 8.3: **Sector-wise Aggregate Savings and Capital Formation**
(as per cent of GDP at current prices)

Year	Gross Domestic Savings				Gross Domestic Capital formation		
	House-sector	Private corporate sector	Public sector	Total 1+2+3	Private Sector	Public Sector	Total (5+6)
	1	2	3	4	5	6	7
1970-71	11.3	1.5	2.9	15.7	5.5	9.1	14.6
1978-79	17.0	1.5	4.6	23.2	8.0	10.1	18.1
1980-81	16.1	1.7	3.4	21.2	8.6	10.7	19.3
1985-86	14.5	2.0	3.2	19.7	10.5	10.2	20.7
1986-87	13.9	1.7	2.7	18.4	11.4	9.6	21.0
1987-88	16.5	1.7	2.2	20.3	10.4	10.9	21.3
1988-89	17.1	2.1	2.0	21.1	10.0	11.1	21.1
1989-90	17.8	2.1	1.7	21.7	10.4	11.0	21.4

Source: *Economic Survey*, 1990-91, p. 5-8

Mounting Debt Burden and Debt Service Obligations

The latest Economic Survey (1990-91) shows that the outstanding interval liabilities of the Central Government has gone up from Rs. 48451 crores in 1980-81 to Rs. 2,79,528 crores in 1990-91 (RE).[6] As proportion of GDP it had appreciated sharply from 35.6 per cent to 54.4 per cent during the 11-year period. Here again the major component was market borrowings which had increased from Rs. 15,676 crores (32.35%) to Rs. 70,575 crores (25.24%). Other internal liabilities in the form of small savings, provident funds, reserve funds and deposits have gone up from 12.9 per cent of GDP to 25 per cent of GDP. This relative appreciation in the share of long-term liabilities of the Government of India will be a significant constraint which will limit the future growth potential of the economy due to mounting debt service obligations. The interest liabilities have already reached 42 per cent of revenue receipts and 21 per cent of the budget outlay which is likely to go up substantially in the coming years.

Foreign Exchange Crisis

India is also facing a liquidity problem in the form of a foreign exchange crisis. This is the combined effect of (a) a yawning trade gap of Rs. 10,644 crores. (b) Fall in foreign exchange reserves. (c) Rise in debt service payments from 46.56 per cent of the gross disbursed external assistance in 1985-86 to 65.32 per cent in 1990-91. The debt service ratio had doubled in the case of external commercial borrowings from 65.31 per cent of gross disbursals to 131.34 per cent in 1990-91 resulting a net-outflow of foreign exchange (see Table 8.4). Here again interest payments have gone up to almost half the debt service obligations. (d) The emerging foreign exchange crisis has been aggravated by gulf crisis which is estimated to have created a total impact on foreign exchange to the tune of Rs. 5180 crores of which Rs. 3625 was the additional POL import bill. Other components of the loss were: (1) export loss to West Asia (Rs. 500 crores); (2) non-realisation of other export dues from Iraq (Rs. 205 crores); (3) loss of remittance from Iraq and Kuwait (Rs. 490 crores) and (4) foreign exchange costs of emergency repatriation (Rs. 360 crores).[7] (e) Rise in the proportion of commercial borrowings from 16.6 per cent in 1984-85 to 22.4 per cent in 1989-90 which carry higher rates of interest and shorter period of repayment. (f) NRI deposits leave substantially increased from 7.4 per cent to 18.2 per cent during this period.

II

Vicious Circle of Deficits and Loans

The Indian economy has thus entered into a nasty circle of deficits and loans which entraps the economy into a resource and liquidity crunch. (See Fig. 8.1).

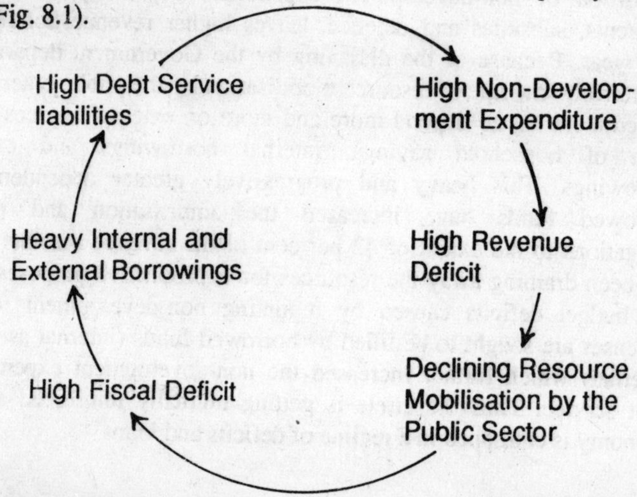

TABLE 8.4: Flow of External Assistance and Commercial Borrowings

(in Rs. crores)

	External assistance			Commercial Borrowings		
	1985-86	1989-90	1990-91 (P)	1985-86	1989-90	1990-91 (P)
1. Authorisation	5650	10826	6252	1700	5479	3414
2. Gross Disburse-ment	2936	5802	6660	1790	4196	3050
3. Debt Service payments	1367 (46.56)	3686 (63.52)	4350 (65.32)	1175 (65.31)	3041 (72.47)	4006 (137.34)
(a) Amort-isation	776	1987	2395	565	1455	2137
(b) Interest payments	591 (20.13)	1699 (29.28)	1955 (29.35)	610 (33.91)	1586 (37.80)	1869 (61.28)
4. Net Capital Inflow (2-3a)	2160	3815	4265	1234	2741	913
5. Net Capital Transfer (2-3)	1569 (53.44)	2116 (36.48)	2310 (34.68)	624	1155	-956

Figures in brackets are percentages of gross disbursement.

Note: These figures do not include supplier's credit and IMF credits other than Trust Fund loans.

Source: RBI, *Economic Survey 1990-91*, pp. 165-66.

Given the revenue receipts of the Government of India, high proportion of non-development expenditure especially for interest payments, subsidies and defence, leaves higher revenue deficit year after year. Because of the dissaving by the Government departments and terribly low rate of resource mobilisation by the public enterprises, Government has to depend more and more on external sources in the form of household savings, internal borrowings and external borrowings. This heavy and progressively greater dependence on borrowed funds have increased the amortisation and interest obligations to the extent of 42 per cent of the revenue receipts which has been draining away the resources for unproductive purposes. Thus the budget deficits caused by mounting non-development revenue expenses are sought to be filled by borrowed funds (internal as well as external) which further increased the non-development expenses for debt service. Thus the circle is getting mutually reinforced and the economy is entrapped in a regime of deficits and loans.

TABLE 8.5: External Debt (Outstanding) in Rs. crores (LT, MT and ST)

	1984-85	1988-89	1989-90
A. *Medium and Long Term*			
i. External Assistance			
a. On Government Account	24004	46838	54095
	(62.2)	(56.4)	(55.2)
b. On Non-Governmental Account	758	1164	1763
	(0.2)	(1.4)	(1.8)
ii. Commercial Borrowing	6413	17482	21912
	(16.6)	(21.1)	(22.4)
iii. IMF Credit	4550	3347	2362
	(11.8)	(4.0)	(2.4)
Total: MT and LT	35725	68813	80132
	(92.6)	(82.9)	(81.8)
B. NRI Deposits	2847	14154	17831
	(7.4)	(17.1)	(18.2)
Total (A+B)	38572	82985	97963
	(100)	(100)	(100)

Figures in brackets are percentages to the total.

Resource Crunch Trap

From this vicious circle (Fig. 8.1) "a resource crunch trap" has emerged which is squeezing the future development potential of the economy. The "resource crunch trap" is a closely interwooven system which has five interlocking and mutually interdependent components, viz.,- rising revenue deficit, increasing share of non development expenditure, rising fiscal deficit increasing share of non-development expenditure, rising fiscal deficit, increasing domestic debt and external debt. Figure 8.2 shows the interlocking mechanism of the system where the arrows show the nature of interdependence between each component. It shows 20 possible ways of inter-dependence between items. It is thus clear that the crisis is deep rooted in the system itself which is getting reinforced in successive rounds of fiscal operations. Hence the remedy lies in consciously reversing this process through appropriate policy measures to reduce the revenue deficit and fiscal deficit by cutting the prohibitively high level of non-development expenses, and by raising the revenue receipts of the Government by rationalising and widening the tax structure and by enhancing the resource mobilisation by the Public Sector. These structural improvements will certainly necessitates radical restructuring of economic policies especially in the field of industry, agriculture, technology development, energy, public sector and export and import. These issues are examined in detail in the following section.

RESOURCE CRUNCH TRAP

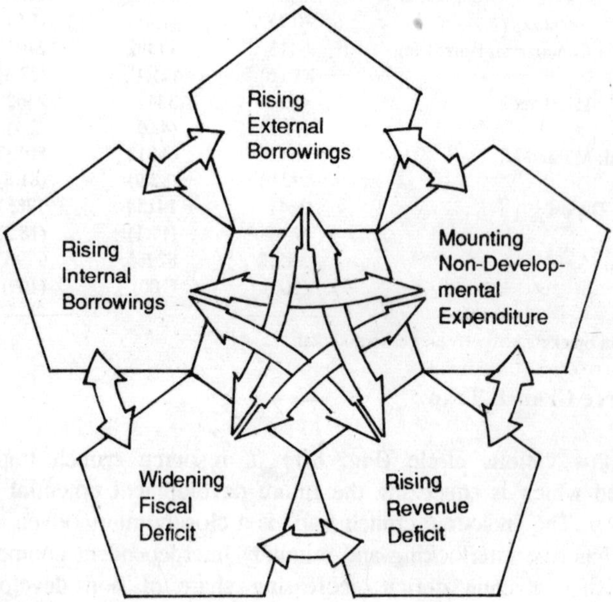

FIG 8.2: Resource Crunch Trap

III

Genesis of the Crisis

The roots of the present crisis lie partly in the past development policy and partly in the development strategy. The self reliance goal of the earlier plans have no doubt created substantial infrastructure in the form of basic and heavy industries. But most of them especially in the public sector continues to be inefficient and sterile due to lack of periodical technology upgradation, highly protected markets, lack of professional management, over-capitalisation due to cost over-run, and lower capacity utilisation. But later policy of liberalisation with excessive reliance on imported technology and components acted as a further disincentive for the promotion of Research and Development (R&D) for technology generation and development. The drive towards self-reliance was short-circuited by the efforts to attain self-reliance in consumer goods and durable consumer goods by import of screw driver technology and production components.

The deepening crisis was the consequence of the package of economic policy measures pursued by the country for quite some time which encompasses: (a) industrial policy; (b) technology and energy policy; (c) export-import policy; (d) public sector policy; (e) agricultural development and (f) public investment and expenditure policy.

Industrial Policy

One of the main factors contributing to the foreign exchange crisis and the wide trade gap is the liberalised industrial policy pursued since late seventies which was further liberalised since mid eighties. The late eighties have witnessed rapid growth in the consumer goods industries, electronic industry and light automobiles with imported machineries. These grew at the rate of 8.3 per cent and 8.5 per cent respectively during 1989-90 and 1990-91. Capital goods sector grew at the rate of 24.9 and 21.9 per cent respectively. Consumer durable goods sector has also shown higher rates of growth during this period.[8]

This shift in emphasis is very much reflected in the changing composition of imports as well. Imports of capital items have gone up from 18.5 per cent in 1984-85 to 32.3 per cent in 1986-87. But in the following three years it varied between 24-25 per cent.[9] Similarly export related imports have also gone up from 11.9 per cent to 18.2 per cent of the imports during the period 1984-85 to 1986-87. The exact share of these items for later years is not known. But imports of pearls, precious stones and chemicals together shared 19.78 per cent of aggregate imports in 1988-89 and 16.16 per cent in 1990-91.[10] Thus the import of capital equipments, technology, product component and export related raw materials and components constituted approximately little below half the imports during the late eighties. The recent liberalisation of industrial and trade policy is likely to aggravate the situation by huge import of technology and components in the wake of larger foreign investments and industrial collaborations.

As already seen, the massive investments in the public sector has widened their resource gap during the Seventh Five Year Plan. Two major factors responsible for this were (1) declining share of public enterprises and the public sector in gross domestic savings and (2) rise in capital-out ratio. The first phenomenon has been already examined in part I of the paper. The Capital/Out-put ratio (C.O.R.) has gone up both in agricultural and industrial sector as shown in Table 8.6.

The average capital out-put ratio at 1960-61 prices had gone up from 2.46 in 1951-52 to 2.89 in 1961-62, 3.70 in 1971-72 and 4.58 in 1979-80.[11] Two factors seem to have contributed to the rise in C.O.R.: (1) The first is the over capitalisation caused by cost overrun arising from inordinate delay in the execution of public sector projects. For instance it was Reported by the Government in the parliament that the cost overrun of 152 central sector projects (each with an investment of Rs. 20 crores) up to 30.6.1987 came to a colossal figure of Rs. 18,900 crores. Another typical case is the investment expenditure in the river valley projects. The aggregate original estimate of 11 major irrigation projects under construction in Kerala was only Rs. 93.04 crores. Even after spending Rs. 698 crores up to 31st March, 1989, none of them have been completed. The revised estimate in 1989 came to Rs. 957.02 crores[12] which was more than 10 times the original project outlay. Now it is estimated that another 400-500 crores may be additionally required for their completion.

TABLE 8.6: Capital out-put Ratio over the Plans

Plan	Agriculture	Industries
First Plan	2.48	5.52
Second Plan	2.51	7.49
Third Plan	4.37	6.67
Fourth Plan	3.63	11.46
Fifth Plan	3.35	8.73
Sixth Plan	4.75	6.96
Seventh Plan	6.56	7.63

Source: B.N. Ghosh (1990). *Political Economy of Rural Poverty in India*, Deep and Deep Publishers, New Delhi, p.45.

The second factor is the lower capacity utilisation in especially in the basic industries sector and infrastructure. For example the plan load factor of thermal power plants which contribute about 70 per cent of the power generation was only 53.8 per cent during 1990-91.[13] Here again the plant load factor of state electricity boards was only 51.6 per cent during 1988-89.[14] The highest plant load factor of the thermal power plants were achieved during 1987-88 and 1989-90, when it had reached 56.5 per cent.[15] The same pattern holds goods in the case of a number of industries as well.

Another area of serious concern is the growing sickness in industry over the years. At the end of December 1988, there were more than 2.4 lakh identified sick industrial units including the weak units on the rolls of All India Financial Institutions and commercial banks involving as outstanding credit of Rs. 7705 crores which came to one-tenth (9.8%) of the total outstanding bank credit. Between December end 1987 and 1988, the number of sick units went up by 17.7 per cent and outstanding bank credit by 23.2 per cent.[16] What is more disturbing is the fact that 93 per cent of the sick SSI units involving an outstanding bank credit of Rs. 1551 crores and 44 per cent of non-SSI sick and weak units involving an outstanding bank credit of Rs. 1867 crores were not potentially viable for revival.

Moreover, the Indian industry was complacent and indifferent towards technology upgradation, productivity and consumer preferences due to high degree of protection which insulated them from foreign competition. In this context opening up of the industrial sector to foreign firms and foreign capital may have desirable effects. But given the present fragile structure of technology and capital base, the outcome is more likely to be unfavourable rather than favourable. Large scale closure of small and medium units may be the immediate consequence unless the entry of foreign firms and foreign technology are consciously channallised to new avenues and more essential products.

Lack of Technology Policy

One of the basic factors which have contributed to the present plight of the economy is the excessive reliance on imported technology for the development of industries and infrastructure. The heavy capital investments made by a capital poor country for building world's third biggest scientific stock and prestigious science and technology institutions have thus turned to be grossly under utilised and unproductive. The growing dependence on foreign technology has left the indigenous R and D without adequate linkage with the industry, which is an essential pre-requisite for technology innovation and development.

The technology development in India has been hampered by the policy to set an industrial base instead of a technological base, with foreign "knowhow". The crucial difference between the two is that the technology base is "self-generating" which can be transferred from one sector to another and reduces continued dependence on others for upgradation. It naturally leads to self-reliance. In contrast, industrial base continues to depend on fresh import of "knowhow" for each stage of upgradation.[17] Without a technology base which involves understanding of the underlying scientific, technical, engineering, design principles, we cannot convert the imported production "knowhow" into technological "know-why"[18]. The inadequate attention given for technology development is evident from the negligible per capita R & D expenditure spent by India ($ 3) compared to more than $100 incurred by developed countries.[19]

The easy facility for technology import motivated the Indian industry to short-circuit technology innovation, development and indigensation. The experience of other countries like USA, and Japan clearly demonstrate that technological self-reliance comes not by Government but by those made by the industry. For instance in Japan, 70 per cent of the R & D investment was made by the high technology industry whereas Government expenditure was only 30 per cent of which 10 per cent came from the University system. The average investment was 1.6 billion US dollars for the top 10 industries, consisting of 4 to 10 per cent of the sales turnover with an average of seven per cent. The corresponding proportion spent by Indian industry was only one-tenth of this proportion in 1986-87. which came to Rs. 555 crores (20%) compared to Rs. 2865 crores (80%) spent by the Government.[20]

It is also significant to note that the industrial success depends not so much in innovation *per se*, as on further development. Japan, Korea, Taiwan and East Asian countries have prospered on innovations made elsewhere. Therefore, it may be better for us to concentrate on these aspects immediately and to initiate technological innovations and development based on this experience and expertise.[21] Nevertheless, progressive reduction in technology import and component imports and promotion of indigenous R & D for technology development are the pre requisites for a long-term sustained industrial development free from foreign exchange crisis.

Energy Policy

Besides, the development strategy pursued by the country is not eminently suitable to the resource base and the physical environment in the country. We had tried to imitate the urban-metropolitan model of development, suitable for the small urban states of Europe. These contrasts are more pronounced in the case of transport, energy and communication. The BoP crisis in India has always been accompanied by the oil crisis. The first and second oil shocks had created b.o.p. crisis earlier and of late the gulf war also created a temporary crisis. As a result the cost of POL import went up by 44 per cent and 72.5 per cent respectively during 1989-90 and 1990-91.[22] This was the single largest item of import which cost India Rs. 10820 crores out of the total import bill of Rs. 43171 crores in 1990-91. The average annual growth in POL consumption during the seventh plan was 6.7 per cent compared to 5.4 per cent during the sixth plan.[23] At the same time the liberalisation of industrial policy has led to substantial annual addition of light vehicles especially two-wheelers which not only nullifies our efforts to reduce petroleum consumption but generates substantial net additional demand. Instead the policy should have been to strengthen, expand and modernise the public transport system effectively, to progressively satisfy the transport requirements of the people thereby reducing the necessity for own vehicles, by provision of cheap and efficient transport. While making all efforts for stepping up domestic production of petroleum products, the demand should be managed on a self-sustainable basis so as to avoid any permanent strain on the economy.

One of the important factors influencing the present industrial pattern with imported technology and production components is the growing consumerism in different parts of the country, thanks to the extensive advertisement campaigns through TV network and the media and through aggressive salesmanship. Even a small state like Kerala with less than four per cent of the population in the country is seen to consume 15 to 20 per cent of the different consumer items like tooth pastes, cosmetics, cigarettes and consumer durables. No wonder, the large scale use of electrical and electronic gadgets have made Kerala a deficit state in electricity eventhough no new industry has been started in the state over the last one decade. Of late the consumerism is gradually spreading to other parts of the country thanks to the aggressive marketing efforts of multi-national companies which are moulding the consumption pattern of the rural folk in favour of fancy and less essential items produced out of imported technology and production components resulting in substantial drainage of the scarce foreign exchange. The TV network which receives only Rs. 350 crores through advertisement is in effect spreading the message of consumerism far and wide with disastrous consequences for the economy.

Hence, it is essential to have a thorough critical review of the development strategies pursued in each sector of the economy so as to restructure them, to make them self sustainable and most suitable for the natural environment, resource endowments and needs and requirements of the population. The production technology, transport system, building technology and energy policy need to be closely reviewed for this purpose to minimise external assistance and to have maximum self-reliance without anyway affecting productivity, efficiency and economy. In a tropical country the potentialities of solar energy wind energy and tidal energy have not yet been adequately explored. The urban-metropolitan garbage can very will be utilised for the production of bio-gas and for the organic manure which can be used to prevent the reduction of fertility of the soil as also be reduce the requirements of the high cost of imported fertilizers or fertilizer subsidy.

There is, therefore wide scope for structural and policy change in the development pattern which can bring down the use of certain scarce resources perceptibly while satisfying the present levels of demand. It also calls for conscious efforts to build up indigenous technology which employs locally available resources without having foreign exchange components and at the same time improving the quality of life perceptibly by recycling the resources and employing renewable energy sources wherever is feasible. A long-term solution to the emerging crisis lies in restructuring the development strategy to make it viable and sustainable in terms of resources, energy and ecology and appropriate to the natural, physical and socio-economic environment of the country.

Public Sector Policy

As already seen, despite heavy investments, public sector in India has failed to generate adequate profits and internal resources which has led to a widening of the resources gap. Over capitalisation and cost-overrun due to inordinate delay in project execution, high COR, low capacity utilisation, and lack of professional management make most of them incapable of survival not to say dynamic growth. Above all, much of the bad name for the public sector can be attributed to the takeover of sick and non-viable units under political or trade Union pressure. Under such circumstances the remedy lies in the creation of a self-liquidating corpus for rehabilitating or compensating the labour of sick or closed units both in private and public sectors which can be created by nominal contribution out of the gross profits of the running enterprises on a regular basis. This can also be linked with a supplementary scheme for un-employment insurance of the labour at a very nominal premium. These schemes should essentially relieve the Government both from take over of sick units as also from providing budgetary support, the modalities of which can be worked out by an Expert Committee on Labour Rehabilitation.

Moreover, the public sector needs to be reconstituted and rationalised by limiting the public ownership to 51 per cent of the equity. In order to ensure genuine workers participation, 20 per cent of the shares are to be offered to the workers, 10 per cent of the financing institutions and 20 per cent to the investing public (other than corporate bodies). The accountability and efficiency should be enhanced by introduction of scientific and professional management. As a part of the total overhauling of the public sector those establishments which have been making losses for over 8-10 years consecutively should be either denationalised or closed in due course utilising the self-liquidating corpus recommended in the previous paragraph. A suitable price policy also should be pursued for preventing colossal losses of electricity boards and Transport Corporations.

Cut Subsidies

The mounting subsidies have also been draining the exchequer very heavily, acting as a drag on government finances which were severely limiting the potentialities of future development. Subsidies of public sector enterprises (through budgetary support) added up to as much as Rs. 15080 crores in 1987-88[24] accounting for 4.5 per cent of GDP. These are not even reckoned as subsidies. A recent study on subsidies by Sudipto Mundale and Govinda Rao at the National Institute of

Public Finance and Policy estimated the volume of subsidies in 1987-88 at Rs. 42,324 crores which constituted 14.38 per cent of GDP. The study infact covered only part of the implicit subsidies of which the centre's share was Rs. 16065 crores (37.96 per cent of the total subsidy) and that of 14 major states Rs. 26,259 crores (62.04%).[25] What is more disturbing is the fact that subsidy on economic services contributed 60.49 per cent of the total while social services accounted for only 39.60 per cent. Thus it is evident that substantial part of the public resources are wasted for not so necessary items of subsidies and there is tremendous scope for reduction of non-development expenditure due to mounting subsidies.

Reduction of Instability in Agricultural Sector

Though the agricultural sector has exhibited much more resilence in recent years, it still suffers from instability created by periodical droughts. Empirical data show that years of drought and agricultural instability were also the years of low growth rates of negative rate in GNP. For instance 1979-80 was a drought year in which production of all major crops declined. While agricultural production declined by 15.2 per cent foodgrains production declined by 16.8 per cent. As a consequence there was a fall in GNP by 4.9 per cent. In 1982-83 agricultural production and foodgrains production declined by 3.8 per cent and 2.9 per cent respectively resulting in lowest rate of growth in GNP in the eighties (2.6%).[26] Similarly, during 1984-85, 1986-87 and 1987-88 which were the other three years with lower growth rates in GNP, both agricultural production and food grains production were negative.

One of the main factors responsible for the persistence of this instability is the inadequate coverage of irrigation facilities which can minimise the vagaries of the fluctuations in rain fall and weather conditions. The pre-eminence given to major and medium irrigation projects have raised the cost of irrigation per hectare to an astronomical level of Rs. 55,000 compared to just Rs. 3,000-4,000 for minor irrigation. So more attention needs to be bestowed on greater coverage of irrigation and for reducing the variability in output levels to minimise the shocks on the economic system which is essential for reducing budgetary allocations for subsidies, food import, debt relief and preventing reduction in export earnings and revenues.

There are other similar areas which need immediate corrective action, all of which cannot be discussed in a small paper. But one important area which needs immediate consideration is the need for organic linkage between small and big industries through ancilliarisation and anxiliarisation and modernisation of small sector with labour productivity augmenting technology and devices.

IV

Conclusion

The foregoing analysis shows that the present crisis is essentially in the form of "fiscal" and "liquidity" crisis which is engulfing the economy into a deficit-loan syndrome. The fiscal and the BoP crisis are mutually inter related problems which have their genesis in the past development pattern. The progressive deviation from the policy of self-reliance from 1978-79 through successive stages of liberalisation resulting in increased reliance on foreign capital and technology has landed as in doldrums. The major components of economic policy like fiscal and monetary policy, industrial and agricultural strategies, technology and energy policies, public sector and pubic investment policy need to be comprehensively reviewed in the light of past experience to make them appropriate and relevant for this resource potential and physical, natural and the socio-economic environment of the country. The ultimate remedy lies in breaking the resource-crunch trap by a multi-dimensional policy management for raising revenue by rationalisation of the tax system and improving the working of the public administration and public sector enterprises, reduction of non-development expenditure and consequently reducing the dependence for borrowed sources of finance.

NOTES

1. Kalyan Raipura (1991) "Resources Mobilisation for Public Sector Development", *Economic and Political Weekly*, Vol. XXVI, No. 3, January 19, p. 123.
2. *Ibid.*
3. *Ibid.*, p. 125.
4. Arun Ghosh (1991) "IMF Borrowings: Some Myths Exposed", *Economic and Political Weekly*, Vol. XXVI, No. 29, July 20, p. 174.
5. Arun Ghosh (1991) "Eighth Plan: Challenges and Opportunities XIV, Financing the Plan", *Economic and Political Weekly*, Vol. XXIV, No.18, May 4, p. 1133.
6. Reserve Bank of India, *Economic Survey*, 1990-91, p. 111.
7. *Ibid.*, p. 156.

8. *Ibid.*, p. 41.
9. *Ibid.*, p. 159.
10. *Ibid.*, p. 159.
11. Rao, V.K.R.V. (1983). *India's National Income 1950-1980*, Sage Publications, p. 158..
12. Government of Kerala, *Economic Review 1990*, p. A-40.
13. RBI, 1990-91, p. 57.
14. C.M.I.E. (1990). *Basic Statistics Relating to the Indian Economy*, Vol.I, All India, August Table 4.25.
15. *Ibid.*
16. RBI, 1990-91, p. 52.
17. S.R. Valluri "Technological Self-Reliance: Need for a New Approach" *Yojana*, Vol.35, Nos. 1&2 January 26, 1991, p. 32.
18. *Ibid.*
19. *Ibid* p. 4 34.
20. *Ibid*, p. 34.
21. P.V. Indiresan (1991). "Self-Reliance in Industrial Technology" *Yojana*, Vol.35, Nos, 1&2 January 26, p. 52.
22. RBI, 1990-91 p. 159.
23. *Ibid*, p. 153.
24. Sudipto Mundale and Govinda Rao (1991). "Volume and Composition of Government Subsidies in India 1987-88" *Economic and Political Weekly*, Vol. XXVI No.18, May 4, p. 1136.
25. *Ibid*, p. 1160.
26. RBI, 1990-91, pp. 1, 17 and S.23.

9

STRUCTURAL ADJUSTMENT OF THE INDIAN ECONOMY: The Current Exercise

S. VELAYUDHA PERUMAL

THE ESSENCE of development is structural adjustment: from country to town, from agriculture to industry, from production for household consumption to production for markets, from largely domestic trade to a higher ratio of foreign trade. While the advanced industrial countries also have to adjust to a changing world and to new technologies, their structures are more stable and less subject to change. In the pursuit of their development objectives – growth, equity, poverty eradication, self-reliance, environmental protection, cultural values – developing countries are faced with major disruptions to which they have to adjust.

The main issues to be analysed are the implications of structural adjustment in an economy in the context of world trade and world capital flows. Structural changes or shocks originating within the country also have repercussions on the balance of payments and require correctives and adjustments. A special case is adjustment from a set of wrong policies to better policies which comprises adjustments both for a given set of objectives and for a particular set of course of action.

The balance of payments of a developing country reflects attempts of domestic adjustments and imposes the need for domestic adjustments to changes in the rest of the world. Thus, a changeover to an export-oriented strategy, an attempt to increase food production, land reforms, tax reforms and redistribution of income may lead to a temporary balance of payments deficit. But certain external shocks which inflict deeper wounds in their economies make the developing countries go in for specific objectives of structural adjustment. The objectives are: (i) Reduction or elimination of a balance of payments deficit and (ii) Resumption of higher rates of economic growth and achievement of structural changes that would prevent future payments and stabilization problems. There are also more fundamental objectives such as the elimination of hunger and malnutrition or the alleviation of poverty or cultural autonomy, or self-reliance or greater national strength and military power.

But, at present, the structural adjustment requirement of the developing countries is due to certain global events. They are: two global inflations during 1971-73 and 1977-78; primary commodity booms and busts during 1972-73 and 1978-82; stagflationary impacts of the three oil shocks during 1973-74, 1979-80 and 1990 due to the Gulf crisis; huge current account deficits; cycling and recycling of petro-dollars; the change in the structure of international debt; deflationary arrangements in countries where recycling failed; drastic changes in the sources of international liquidity; continuation of inflationary pressures throughout the 1970s; and policy of disinflation during the 1980s. These events indicate how the international financial system operates and how the inter-dependence between the OPEC, other developing countries and the West has grown over the past few years. It has led to the collapse of the rule-based trade and monetary orders. The lack of international control over liquidity, composition of reserves, variation of exchange rates and new protectionism have all deepened the crisis.

All these have brought about the global debt crisis. The trends and development of the debt crisis were: (a) oil price increases led to the balance of payments difficulties for many developing countries and enormous surpluses for a handful of oil producers; (b) placement of a large part of these surpluses in banks for on-lending and recycling; (c) great propensity to borrow by developing countries buoyed by negative real interest rates during the latter part of the 1970s; (d) use or misuse of borrowed resources by many debtor countries to buttress consumption, delay adjustment, or invest in projects with low rates of return; (e) deterioration in the terms of trade of borrowing counties during the 1980s; and (f) financial and economic policies of the industrial countries which adopted measures which reduced their economic growth and sharply raised interest rates further jeopardizing the ability of the developing countries to service their debt. Hence the resulting adjustment, though thought as temporary, initially, became painful.

Structural Adjustment

To overcome these difficulties both the IMF and the IBRD insisted on a structural adjustment and stabilization of the economy as a precondition for providing assistance and help to negotiate loans. The structural adjustment was insisted on due the belief in the superiority of a market-oriented and outward-oriented development strategy. Structural adjustment involves: (a) changes in trade policy – tariff reforms, import liberalization, removal of quotas, tariff cuts, export incentives and improved institutional support; (b) resource mobilization – budget policy, interest rate policy, strengthening institutional capacity for external borrowing and public enterprises financial performance; (c) efficient use of resources public investment programme, revision and review of structural prices, review of agricultural prices, revision of energy prices, development of indigenous energy sources and industry-wise incentive system; and (d) institutional reforms – strengthening the capacity to formulate and implement public investment programme, institutional efficiency of public sector enterprises, improved institutional support to agricultural development and institutional improvements in industrial and sub-sector programmes. In addition, devaluation of the currency is insisted as a supply side measure on the basis that it encourages the supply of exports and import substitutes. Overall policy of liberatization and privatization of the economy are also advocated.

India's Balance of Payments Position – A Review

All the above consequences were faced by India along with other developing countries. The result is the present external debt crisis and chronic deficit in the balance of payments position.

The entire expansion of external debt during the First Plan was met by dollar loans. In the course of the Second and Third Plans external debt reached the levels of Rs. 643 crores (462%) and Rs. 2,611 crores (234%) respectively, which escalated further to the level of Rs. 25,000 crores in 1985 and to Rs. 55,000 crores in 1988-89, as per the pre-Budget survey of the Indian Economy of 1989. The level of debt-service – interest and amortization – during 1988-89 was around 24 per cent. The World Bank estimated in 1986 that even if India achieves 4.8 per cent of export growth, it will have to borrow an additional $ 6.1 billion in which case the debt service ratio will rise and put a heavy strain on the resources in the years ahead. Table 9.1 shows an estimate of projections of foreign debt liabilities on the IMF and non-IMF loans.

TABLE 9.1: An estimate of projections of foreign debt liabilities

(Rs. in crores)

Year	Repayments	Interest	Total
1991-92	1326	608	1934
1992-93	1196	543	1739
1993-94	1046	517	1563
1994-95	969	478	1447
Total	4537	2146	6683

This was an old projection. According to the latest World Debt Tables, India's debt service obligations have increased to Rs. 1,62,000 crores from Rs. 1,31,000 crores as a result of the recent downward revision of the rupee value.

The external debt as a proportion of national income has risen from 38 to 47 per cent which could have serious implications for the debt servicing obligations over the next few years. Debt service commitments have been growing at an annual rate of about seven per cent since 1985. Assuming that this rate still applies without considering devaluation content, repayments of interest and principal this year would be around $ 7,300 million. At the exchange rate prevailing prior to July 1991, this would have amounted to about 47 per cent of India's total merchandise exports for 1991-92. However, at the current exchange rates, this would amount to over 58 per cent of the total merchandise exports.

Another disquieting feature is that India's external commercial borrowings are on the increase (Table 9.2).

All these indicate that the malady is structural and deep-rooted in character. The country's resources are inherently limited by its low per capita income with claims from the social sectors and poverty alleviation programmes. Hence continued inflow of external resources will be needed to maintain growth. The pertinent question is whether the country is faced with a bigger resource gap or a trade gap. There is an opinion that since the time of the Third Five Year Plan, India faces a dominant trade gap. Hence exports would have to grow at a faster rate to keep the debt service ratio at the current level. But three basic features are against this. They are stiffness of terms in borrowing, export failures and import excesses.

TABLE 9.2: External commercial borrowings

(Rs. in crores)

	1988-89	1989-90	1990-91
Authorizations	4314	5479	3414
Gross disbursements	4069	4196	3050
Debt service payments			
a. Amortization	1103	1455	2137
b. Interest	1121	1586	1869
Net capital inflow	2966	2741	913

It is against this background that the proposed changes in the economy envisaged and their long-term impacts have to assessed.

Key Indicators of the Economic Survey

The pre-budget Economic Survey of the Indian Economy for 1990-91 indicates the following:

(a) *Agriculture*

Foodgrains production continues to increase. Rice output has grown to 75 million tonnes and wheat to 54.6 million tonnes. Coarse cereals declined marginally while pulses output was higher by 1.6 million tonnes.

(b) *Industries*

The growth of industrial production has been stagnating between 8.4 and 8.7 per cent during the past three years. Basic goods' growth has more than halved from 9.9 per cent in 1988-89 to 4.3 per cent in 1990-91, while that of capital goods has more than trebled in the period. Consumer durables declined sharply in 1989-90 and bounced back to a 10.9 per cent rate in 1990-91 but this is still lower than the achievement in 1988-89. Consumer non-durables showed an upswing from three years but dropped last year to 5.2 per cent. The growth rate of intermediates dropped by nearly half though there was some improvement in 1990-91 (Table 9.3).

TABLE 9.3: Growth rates of industrial groups

(in percentage)

Industry group	1988-89	1989-90	1990-91
Basic goods	9.9	5.4	4.3
Capital goods	7.0	22.4	21.9
Intermediates	11.5	4.3	5.6
Consumer durables	12.0	1.7	10.9
Consumer non-durables	2.5	7.5	5.2

(c) *Investment Climate*

While disbursements and sanctions of the all-India financial institutions kept rising substantially in the past three years, consents for capital issues flattened out, increasing only by Rs. 556 crores in 1990-91. Approvals for capital goods imports dropped by nearly half while registrations of units also dropped considerably (Table 9.4).

TABLE 9.4: Industrial approvals/sanctions

	1988-89	1989-90	1990-91
Foreign collaborations/approvals	636	595	640
DGTD registrations	651	543	404
			(approvals in crores of rupees)
Capital issues	8235	12076	12632
Import of capital	1037	1633	854
FI sanctions	13564	15035	19385
FI disbursements	8375	9102	11643

(d) *Core Sectors*

The infrastructure industries have been performing creditably, except for crude oil and petroleum products. Coal production and electricity generation – hydel, thermal and nuclear – have continued to grow steadily and substantially each year since 1988-89. The same has been the case with revenue earning freight traffic of the railways and cargo handling at major ports though the growth rate is not as impressive as in coal and power. Crude oil output and refinery output throughout have stagnate (Table 9.5).

TABLE 9.5: Performance of infrastructure industries — 1988-91

	1988-89	1989-90	1990-91
Coal production (million tonnes)	194.60	200.89	211.73
Electricity generation (billion kWh)	221.4	245.4	264.2
Crude production (million tonnes)	32.04	34.09	33.03
Refinery (million tonnes)	48.80	51.94	51.77
Railway goods traffic (million tonnes)	302.05	309.97	318.02
Cargo handling at ports (million tonnes)	146.43	148.14	152.55

Steps taken for Structural Adjustment

The Budget for 1991-92 has many strange features. First, it speaks frankly about the past mistakes very boldly. Then its advocacy of liberalizing the economy and resort to foreign assistance is straight. The Budget seeks to reform the economy through sweeping changes proposed.

The Budget puts the blame for the present situation to large and persistent macro-economic imbalances and the low productivity of investment. It admitted that there were unsustainable increases in public expenditure and budgetary subsidies with questionable social and economic impacts have been allowed to grow to an alarming extent. The tax system has many loop-holes and lacks transparency so that it is not easy to assess the social and economic impact of various concessions built into its structure. The public sector has not been managed in a manner so as to generate large investible surpluses. The excessive and often indiscriminate protection provided to industry has weakened the incentive to develop a vibrant export sector. It has also accentuated disparities in income and wealth. It has worked to the disadvantage of the rural economy. Due to the Gulf crisis, the balance of payments which has already deteriorated has lurched from one liquidity crisis to another. The price situation poses a serious problem with inflation reaching a double-digit level. By the end of March 1991, the wholesale price index registered an increase of 12.1 per cent, while the consumer price index 13.6 per cent. The cause of concern is that it was in essential commodities.

Under the circumstances, the centrepiece of the strategy should be a credible fiscal adjustment and macro-economic stabilization which includes progressive reduction of the fiscal deficit, a significant reduction of the revenue deficit and reduction of the current account deficit of the balance of payments. These must be supported by essential reforms in economic policy and management. The thrust of the reform process would be to increase the efficiency and international competitiveness of industrial production, to utilize for the purpose foreign investment and technology to a much greater degree than in the past, to increase the productivity of investment, to ensure that India's financial sector is rapidly modernized and to improve the performance of the public sector, so that the key sectors of the economy are enabled to attain an adequate technological and competitive edge in a fast-changing global economy.

Budget Proposals

A large-scale fiscal adjustment is needed the poor should be protected from the burden of adjustment. For one thing, the budget makes a major shift in revenue raising from indirect to direct taxes and should result in equity. Even within the indirect taxes luxury items are to bear a significantly heavier burden. Even in the sphere of expenditure, while producers' subsidies including export subsidies and fertilizer subsidies have been virtually done away with, the food subsidy which benefits the poor has been marginally increased.

The magnitude of the adjustment is reflected in the substantial reduction of the budget deficit to a level that, for the first time, in recent years, seems reasonable. Major efforts on both expenditure and revenue sides have contributed to this reduction even as the Plan expenditure has been raised. Non-plan expenditure including interest payments has been cut by 4.9 per cent, a significant achievement in itself. With the Government itself at last getting down to some drastic pruning of its expenditure, the tax payers have much less room to complain.

In the sphere of direct taxes, personal and wealth taxes are not touched. There is a minor concession on long-term capital gains aiming at giving a boost to the share markets. Dealing with black money, the Government came with two new schemes. The first is to draw out black money for slum clearance and low-cost housing. The amnesty scheme for income-tax evaders and the softer settlement provisions are in the expectation that the liberalized trade and industrial policies would mitigate the impact.

In indirect taxes, the Government is against mindless consumerism of the Western type and hence luxurious items have been hit harder.

While previous budgets have talked of the need to rationalize the extraordinary high rates of Customs duties, this budget has made a beginning in that direction. The cut in the high rate of import duty from 300 to 150 per cent was long overdue and was indeed rendered imperative by the devaluation of the rupee and the rising premium on REPs which have pushed up import costs. On the expenditure side, there are two surprise elements: increase in defence expenditure and food subsidies. The Government's claim that the fiscal adjustment would not affect the growth impulses seems valid except in two aspects, namely, the increase in fertilizer prices and the substantial new burden on the corporate sector.

The New Industrial Policy

This is the outcome of careful exercise after taking into account various considerations and safeguarding national interests even while throwing open select areas for foreign investment through majority participation. The role of the public sector enterprises also came in for considerable discussion for ensuring a reasonable return on the huge investment already incurred.

The policy outlines that since the acute scarcity of rupee and foreign exchange resources, the latter particularly, has been posing serious problems and the large industrial bases created in the 1980s had to be advantageously integrated, the opportunity has been utilized for harnessing the pace of industrial growth with provision for new facilities to those with entrepreneurial and technical skills and who can also mobilize the needed resources.

Industrial licencing is being abolished to make sure that there is no net outflow of foreign exchange due to payments towards dividends, royalties and imports of raw materials and components. MRTP companies are free to implement expansion and new schemes apart from attempting mergers and takeovers. The fears about free entry of foreign investment having a discouraging effect have been set at rest as it will be allowed only in areas involving high technology and where it is necessary to raise the output of electrical and communication sectors.

The role of public sector enterprises has not been undermined since it will be functioning in vital areas having strategic implications and requiring judicious use of mineral resources. However, certain areas are to be thrown open to entrepreneurs in the private sector where they are already functioning on a competitive basis. The new approach of the Government would have a far-reaching significance if there is a careful allocation of responsibilities and coordinated industrial development by the public and private sectors and foreign interests.

No doubt, the budget and the new industrial policy resolutions aim at a thorough structural adjustment and stabilization of the Indian economy. But doubts of very serious nature have been expressed at different quarters as to the viability and resultant benefits of these structural attempts.

IMF Loans

The first criticism relates to the IMF conditionalities and the humiliations which a nation has to undergo in its efforts to obtain financial assistance. There are criticisms that the budget is prepared to please the IMF and the national sovereignity is pledged to the West. The examples of the humiliations and difficulties of the nations are cited in support of this contention. Britain's experience in 1976, Zambia's in 1977, Dominican Republic's in 1964, Ghana's in 1972 and Chile's in 1976 are cited. But it should not be forgotten that the IMF's role was praiseworthy during the 1982 debt crisis in rescuing the Latin American countries. Another thing is that the IMF's financial assistance is not meant to meet the growing demand of developing countries, instead it is meant only for meeting the temporary setbacks in the balance of payments deficits of the countries.

It is also to be justified that the IMF must satisfy itself that the assisted country is being managed reasonably well, so that in a relatively short period it not only arrests the deficit in its balance of payments but also produces a surplus to meet non-IMF obligations. It requires growth, stale prices and balance of payments, expansion of employment opportunities and social justice. The IMF is dominated by market-oriented economies and as such some ideological bias is inevitable. The performance of developing countries was given the benefit of the doubt for two decades but the performance was disappointing. The IMF stands for liberal trade and the East European countries' efforts to restructure their economies towards market orientation should be taken note of before any criticism is made.

Devaluation

Devaluation is criticized as it will retard the modernization of Indian industry since the higher price of imported capital goods will tempt entrepreneurs to postpone modernization or look for second-hand machinery which is always obsolete in relation to the world market. It will deter the growth of industries that depend heavily on imported raw materials and components.

Devaluation has also made it imperative to overhaul the tax system by replacing excise duties with VAT and the present Customs regime which consists of import restrictions, *ad valorem* and specific Customs duties. Since devaluation has made it far more difficult to cut expenditure, the Government must rely perforce on increasing its tax revenue in real terms. The reform should reduce evasion and bring money back from the parallel economy. But the structure of the economy is such that devaluation will only push up imports and the trade gap will widen.

Abolition of Subsidies

Currently the total amount of subsidies that are given to various sectors is Rs. 12,000 crores per annum. The focus on removing or reducing fertilizer, food and export subsidies in order to reduce fiscal deficits without removing many other subsidies hidden or otherwise may bring more damage than benefits. These three subsidies which served some economic goals constitute less than 20 per cent of the budget. Another 20 per cent goes in the form of open or hidden subsidies to the middle and upper classes which have vested interest in structural rigidities and exploitation.

Flight of Capital

The structural links between the balance ot payments and fiscal deficits are such that even if devaluation is successful in reducing imports, it may hurt industrial growth. The domestic supplies for the production of exportables may be inadequate. Another factor is that the group of exporters who subsist on cash compensatory allowance are not the producers. They will turn into speculators. This will be all the mere difficult if REP is subjected to a restricted list. The trade reforms now introduced should have come earlier in which case the need for a 20 per cent devaluation would not have come Almost half of the Indian external debt is matched by legal or illegal flight of capital from India. So it would be rash to believe that this capital flight will disappear if the rupee is totally convertible. Even if all the restrictions on the transfer of capital are removed, black money in the country will always need external outlets.

Industrial Production

For decades the structure and pattern of industrial production have ceased to be conducive either to export orientation or to production of labour-intensive goods where the country has had a vast comparative advantage. For example, the rate of growth of consumer durables which are highly capital- and import-intensive can make very little contribution to exports, and may further be stimulated because of the promised duty-free import of capital goods in the future. Ultimately the labour-intensive small sector will suffer.

The domestic capital goods industries hitherto enjoying great protection will face such stiff competition that their survival will be difficult. So long as the Indian industrialization is subjected to unlimited collaboration agreements without commitment to technical upgradation and innovation, India's competitiveness in the world market would remain in jeopardy. In the short-term the adjustments are bound to be painful for the import-dependent industrial units.

Privatization

Privatization is advocated in the new industrial policy on grounds of equity in ownership, increase in efficiency and productivity, comparative cost advantage, mobilization of resources, economic pragmatism, technical and financial gains and so on. But privatization need not be the right step to liberate the kind of economy in India from slow growth or stagnation due to a weak public sector. Privatization in the long run introduces private monopoly. Certainly state monopoly is more tolerable than private monopoly. There is little or no advantage in transferring a public sector monopoly, no matter how inefficient. Private sector would become a private monopoly which is not advantageous to society at large.

The limited goals of resources of private individuals cannot meet some of the important tasks which change the very character of the economy. The private sector is incapable of becoming the leading force in economic development. In the long run there is no guarantee that the free and larger role for the private sector would improve the performance, growth, and employment potential of a developing economy. Privatization has nothing to do with goals like removal of poverty, raising the levels of income, meeting the basic needs of people and preserving ecological and environmental aspects in a developing country. Hence the appeal does not seem to be universal and it remains to be seen whether the country is really going to be benefited.

Inefficient Administration

The new policies are subject to the severe constraint of efficient administration. The country began with a large proportion of civil servants of the colonial administration. Today the individual civil servants exert considerable influence on policy formation and work against radical agents. With the administrative machinery also saturated by caste, complaints are on the increase about the aloofness of officials in their dealings with the public and about their notions of status and accumulation of wealth.

Hence, all social and political mechanisms in India operate mainly in accord with the power structure. The country is ruled by compromises and accommodations within and between the upper class and various groups. In the background are powerful big business interests who provide the necessary funds for political activity. These manifestations tend to widen the gulf between the rulers and the ruled and to divert official attention from the urgent need for drastic changes in the economy and the society. Political independence and parliamentary democracy of the kind in India have done nothing more than displace a foreign colonial-minded group with native privileged group.

Rural and Urban Differences

One thing that strikes glaringly in Indian economic growth is that when it comes to inter-sectoral balances, seldom we come across the recognition of the need for rural-urban balance as an important criterion in the process of development. There is a marked imbalance between urban and rural areas with regard to infrastructural facilities. This has created one India of a sea of poverty and lack of basic necessities. Hence a majority of the rural population remains unhealthy, unskilled and consequently, only marginally productive. But the other India represents one of high technology centred in defence and its space programmes with scientific and technological potential.

This rural-urban imbalance is increasing which is the result of the machinations of the urban power club comprising politicians, civil servants, academicians, businessmen, trade unionists and rich farmers who are in the centre of the power struggle in the Government. Unless some effective steps are taken and implemented faithfully this rural-urban imbalance alone can retard the growth of the economy.

Conclusion

Structural adjustment of a developing economy is a long-term process. The success of adjustment programmes depends much on the continuity in ideology, pattern of behaviour, and efficient economic administration. Those who are at the helm of affairs should have a commitment to the schemes and must be ready to shoulder the responsibility to carry out the schemes. The administration should be single-minded and the political leaders should have a perspective plan for running the country. Under the present circumstances, when Governments are frequently changes with no clear majority for a single national political party, these adjustment programmes suffer. Frequent changes of the party in power, civil administrators as well as economic administrators, members of the Planning and Finance Commissions are against the very concept of bringing structural changes in the Indian economy.

10

POLITICAL ECONOMY OF CRISIS IN THE INDIAN ECONOMY*

D. NARASIMHA REDDY

NEVER DID an economic problem draw as much attention during the past two decades as the present crisis. The magnitude of the crisis is well documented. Though an effort is made here to minimise the repetition, for the sake of capitulative of the problem a certain unavoidable repetition becomes inevitable. This paper is divided into three sections. The first section deals with the nature and causes of the present economic crisis. The second refers to the alternative solutions with particular attention to the officially chosen policy options and the possible consequences. The third part tries to draw certain conclusions based on the experience in other countries.

II

The Economy in 1980s

What apparently strikes paradoxical about the present economic crisis is the reasonably satisfactory decade of economic performance that immediately preceded it. At the end of the Seventh Plan there was a kind of euphoria that the Indian economy after decades of relatively slow growth, broke out of the Hindu.

There was even reference to the industrial growth becoming autonomous of agricultural performance and agricultural growth

* An earlier version of the paper was presented at IEA Trust sponsored Seminar on 'Fiscal Crisis in the Indian Economy' held on August 9, 1991 at the Centre for Economic and Social Studies, Hyderabad.

showing resilience to whether the worst kind of droughts and other natural calamities. The performance of the economy during the second half of the 1980s was considered to be much better. Particularly, the performance of the Seventh Plan was widely applauded since man of its targets were exceeded. The annual growth rate during the plan was 5.6 per cent against the targeted 5 per cent. Despite poor monsoon, the agricultural production increased at 4.1 per cent per annum against the target of 4 per cent. Though there was a marginal short fall in the annual overall industrial growth rate from 8.7 to 8.5 per cent, the manufacturing sector did exceed the target growth rate of 8 per cent to achieve 8.8 per cent. The ratio of gross domestic savings to GDP which declined from 21.6 per cent in 1979-80 to 18.2 per cent in 1984-85, increased to 21.7 per cent by 1989-90. The ratio of average domestic savings to GDP was 20.2 per cent in the Seventh Plan compared to 19.6 per cent in the Sixth Plan and the ratio of gross investment to GDP increased from 19.6 per cent in 1984-85 to 24.1 per cent in 1989-90. The average gross investment ratio to GDP was 22.6 per cent in the Seventh Plan compared to 21.1 per cent in the Sixth Plan.

Paradoxically the very same decade of 1980s, which was proclaimed as the one that hitched the Indian economy to the high growth path, also witnessed the seeds of fiscal imbalance taking strong roots. It was a decade of slow but consistent movement towards 'liberalisation'. The lack of fiscal discipline and liberalisation together have grown into a proportion where all the much trumpeted growth performance is being threatened with serious instability as it has emerged into serious fiscal and payments crises. It may be necessary here to pay attention to the fact that while the role of the State in the better growth performance is doubtful, it is certain that fiscal and payments crises are directly the consequences of the policies and practices of the State. Needless to say that the State is essentially a political creature and its policies, even apparently economic, are political in nature. To describe increasing fiscal deficits as a consequence of additional loans to the states (about Rs. 90,000 crores presently), higher interest payments, rural debt relief provision, higher burden on the account of fertilizer and food subsidies and shortfall in revenues, may be an economic glossing over but certainly is a question begging description. Why does the State get into these additional commitments. Aren't these 'commitments' of the State due to its own strategies of legitimisation and perpetuation of the rule of dominant classes whose interests, though conflicting thus needing compensatory rewards, ultimately find in the unity of the objective of survival in political power. Whether it is a salary hike of government employees, food subsidies or fertilizer subsidies, these are political decisions linked to the political objectives and not merely acts of economic intervention. If this perspective is lost we may not make much headway in unravelling the present crisis.

The Fiscal Crisis

Let us consider the nature of the fiscal and balance of payments crises. First, the fiscal crisis. The process of 'living beyond the means' could be seen as perpetuated continuously beginning with 1979-80 when the revenue receipts of the Centre fell short of revenue expenditure by an amount equivalent to 0.61 per cent of the GDP. Since then there has been growing revenue deficit, reaching 2.6 per cent of GDP in 1990-91. It is normally expected that the revenue receipts not only meet the revenue expenditure but also leave a surplus for financing the plan. What has been happening is quite the contrary. The centre has to borrow increasingly not only to finance plan expenditure but also non-plan revenue expenditure. The deficits could no longer be covered by budgetary deficit financing through treasury bills or drawing down the reserve bank, or market borrowings or foreign assistance. There has been growing reliance on other internal liabilities like small savings, Provident Fund contributions etc. The growing diversity of financing deficit has rendered the very concept of 'budgetary deficit' not much of use in assessing the fiscal health of the economy (K.S. Gill, 1991). Conventional 'budgetary deficit' is a narrow concept since it accounts for only the difference between all receipts and expenditure, both revenue and capital. It doesn't indicate the Government's draft on domestic savings and dependence on external borrowings. A more comprehensive concept, viz., 'fiscal deficit', globally used, is found to be more appropriate for India (Perhaps as a first step in the process of globalisation). The fiscal deficit' which was about 4 per cent of the GDP in the mid-seventies increased to an average of 6.3 per cent in the Sixth Plan, 8.2 per cent in the Seventh Plan and was Rs. 43,331 crores or 8.4 per cent of GDP in 1990-91. The pattern of financing fiscal deficit also changed in 1980s from conventional but relatively less expensive sources like the Reserve Bank, market borrowings and foreign assistance to more captive, less conspicuous but more expensive sources like the small savings, Provident Fund contributions. While conventional sources like the 'budgetary deficit', market borrowings and external assistance together declined from 73.1 per cent of financing fiscal deficit in 1980-82 to 52.5 per cent in 1990-91, the share of 'other internal liabilities' like small savings and Provident Fund increased from 26.9 per cent in 1980-81 to 47.5 per cent in 1990-91. Since the interest charges on the latter are much higher than the former, the change in the composition of financing the fiscal deficit raised the average interest charges from about 8.8 per cent to about 11.5 per cent. What is more disquiting is that much of its has gone to finance the current expenditure of the government. The result is unprecedented growth in debt burden during 1980s. The total internal debt of the Government of India increased from Rs. 48,451 crores or 35.6 per cent of GDP in 1980-81 to Rs. 2,79,528 crores or 54.5 per cent of GDP in 1990-91. Along with an external debt (official long-term only), which increased from Rs. 11,298 crores in 1980-81 to Rs. 31,831 crores in 1990-91, the total debt of the Central Government stood at Rs. 3,11,359 crores or 60.6 percent of GDP in 1990-91. The gross interest payments on the debt amounted to Rs. 21,850 crores or 21.4 per cent of GDP in 1990-91. This does not include an other innovation of 1980s viz. allowing public sector undertakings like NTPC, ITI, Railways to raise their own 'deposits' or loans. To the extent these establishments succeed in mobilising their own resources, fiscal deficit will appear to be lower.

In 1980s there was unbriddled growth of non-plan expenditure at an annual rate of 19.4 per cent compared to 12.8 per cent in plan expenditure. The share of plan expenditure declined from over 40 per cent in 1980-81 to less than 30 per cent in 1990-91. Within the non-plan expenditure there was faster growth of 'charged' expenditure, which is largely 'non-developmental' and administrative, while developmental expenditure like education and health showed a declining proportion. The three items which accounted for more than fifty per cent of the non-plan expenditure viz., the interest charges, subsidies and the defence expenditure, increased by annual growth rate of 23.7, 19.6 and 15.9 per cent respectively during 1980s. Needless to say that there was no concerted measure to curb any of these items of expenditure. In contrast there was a steady decline of the share of capital formation in the centre's expenditure. The proportion of expenditure on capital formation declined from 40 per cent in the mid-1980s to 32.7 per cent in 1990-91.

On the revenue side, the reluctance to tax the rich is matched only by the eagerness to borrow. The direct taxes-GDP ratio has remained at about 2.5 ever since 1950-51 while indirect taxes — GDP ratio increased from 4.23 in 1950-51 to 14.62 in 1988-89. In India the direct tax-GDP ratio may not be meaningful for two reasons. First, the extensive and all pervasive parallel economy or black money which reduces the official GDP into an underestimate and tax ratios, over estimates. Second, the inclusion of agricultural income, which is not in the purview of central direct taxes. If we look at direct taxes as a proportion of total non-agricultural income, it has declined drastically because of steep rise in the share of non-agricultural incomes in the GDP from less than 50 per cent to very nearly 70 per cent by 1990-91 and the growth of national income by an annual average of more than 5 per cent in the 1980s.

Etatism in fact lies in using the State to squeeze the surplus for private gain by the dominant classes. State's own activities become sources of implicit gain like low or no power charges, communications, low-irrigation charges, besides explicit subsidies like fertilizer or export subsidies. This, not taking account of State aiding the generation and retention of black money in activities like excise contracts, public works contracts etc. The very nature of the measures of schemes introduced in the name of unearthing 'black money' betray the connivance of the State. It is everybody's knowledge that much of black money is a 'flow'. If it has to be tapped or curbed, the measures deviced should be the ones that would deal with the flow. If one is a professional, a black-marketeer, or a bureaucrat who has access to illegal income, the introduction of a scheme of declaration, which incorporates a 'stock' notion of black money, can hardly serve the purpose. With the growing non-plan, non-developmental expenditure, and with an inability to raise more revenues by taking those who profiteer on the direct and indirect investment the State, the economy is at a crisis out of which only political action can retrieve it. The *Etatist* State has got into this fiscal quagnise and the logical direction seems to be towards increasing accommodation of the 'global, interests.

The Balance of Payments Crisis

The balance of payments crisis makes it much more explicit. The average ratio of exports to GDP was around 5 per cent in the Sixth Plan while it marginally increased to 5.1 per cent during the Seventh Plan. The imports were persistently about 8.4 of GDP in the Sixth Plan and 8.3 per cent during the Seventh Plan. The average current account deficit, however, was much less in the Sixth Plan around 1.3 per cent of the GDP while it worsened to 2.2 per cent in the Seventh Plan. Besides certain fortutious circumstances regarding the international oil prices and growth in domestic oil production, the balance of payments position was well within manageable limits. But the Seventh Plan witnessed certain policy measures of the State along with the dwindling invisibles, largely in the form of remittances, because of which the country ran into a serious payments crisis. In 1990-91 the rupee value of exports increased by 17.5 per cent and imports by 21.9 per cent. While the trade deficit increased by 38 per cent from Rs. 7735 crores in 1989-90 to Rs. 10,644 crores in 1990-91. The invisibles declined. While the inflow under FCNRA scheme declined from Rs. 2179 crores in 1989-90 to only Rs. 255 crores, in 1990-91, there was net outflow of Rs. 54 cores under NRER deposits during 1990-91. Much of the crisis in balance of payments during the year was blamed on the events as fall out of the Gulf Crisis. Truem Gulf Crisis did increase the oil bill by Rs. 4420 crores, from Rs. 6400 crores in 1989-90 to Rs. 10,820 crores in 1990-91. Added to this there was loss of remittances and loss of export earnings from Kuwait and Iraq which together meant a decline of foreign exchange of Rs. 965 crores. The foreign exchange reserves declined from Rs. 5,050 crores in Aug. 1990 to Rs. 2,500 in April 1991. Besides, there was steep decline the credit rating of India which resulted in difficulties in borrowing commercially. While certain unforeseen events like Gulf Crisis did contribute to the problem, the roots of the crisis line in the kind of euphoric import liberalisation strategy adopted during the Seventh Plan period. Carried away by the expansion of domestic oil production from 10 mt to 30 mt during the Sixth Plan and the decline in the world oil prices during the same period, there was indiscriminate liberalisation of imports of "capita goods" which increased from Rs. 1910 crores in 1980-81 to Rs. 8831 crores in 1989-90. Similarly more lasting damage was done, in their eagerness to demonstrate that India as moving closer to self-sufficiency in oil, by over exploiting some oil wells in the Bombay High which caved in and the supplies are permanently lost. Under this account alone it is estimated the country stands to lose annually Rs. 2000 crores. (Aspects 2) Further, there was no effort to exploit fully the natural gas, which is flared to the tune of Rs. 1500 crores annually. These measures together would have brought much savings of the foreign exchange resources. Much of the liberalisation of capital and intermediate goods imports may prove irreversible and to that extent cow-tow the Indian industry to imports. The payments crisis during the last half of 1980s landed the country in serious external debt. The external debt of India consisting of external assistance on government and non-government accounts, external commercial borrowings and IMF liabilities amounted to Rs. 80,135 crores (about 18 per cent of GDP) at the end of 1989-90. If we add NRI deposits the aggregate debt of the country at the end of 1989-90 stood at Rs. 97,000 crores accounting for 22 per cent of GDP. By the end of March 1991 it was Rs. 1,20,000 crores. In June 1991 it was estimated at Rs. 1,31,000 crores and thanks to devaluation the same increased to Rs. 1,62,000 crores in July 1991. There are no single comprehensive source of information foreign debt. The OECD estimates for 1989 shows a total foreign debt of India as $ 71.3 billion of which long-term debt was $ 63.47b and short-term $6.26b. Added to the growing magnitude, there has also been changing composition of the debt with a tendency towards a rise in the share of higher interest bearing loans during the 1980s. The external assistance which constituted almost 90 per cent of debt stock in 1980-81, declined to less than 70 per cent in 1989-90 and external commercial borrowings increased to 27 per cent of debt stock during the period. The declining share of external assistance, combined with commercial borrowings contributed to a bulge in debt service payments in the late 1980s. The debt service ratio, measured as the proportion of amortisation and interest payments to exports and gross invisibles, which stood at 9.4 per cent in 1981 reached 23.3 per cent in 1987-88 and after a marginal decline, it is estimated that it may hit anywhere between 50 to 58 per cent in the 1990s.

II

To enable the Indian economy to overcome the fiscal and payments crises a number of strategies are suggested, or which we may consider the two that received wide attention. One is the 'globalisation' package as a part of the IMF and World Bank conditionalities for helping the country with short-run and medium-term loans to meet the payments and structural adjustment needs. The other is from a group of Economists which emphasises 'self-reliance' strategy by curbing unproductive state expenditure, reducing import content of internal industry by placing appropriate restriction and imports, mobilisation of more resources by widening the direct tax base, decentralised planning and development process so as to stimulate employment as well as productivity which would provide increased income and purchasing power to the masses which in turn would stimulate and sustain growth with distributive justice. The recent trade (including exchange rate), industrial and budgetary policies of the Government of India make it clear that their preference is for the Fund-Bank inspired strategy. Let us examine the nature of the strategy and its possible consequences. The language of the Fund-Bank strategy has extensively percolated into most of the Indian documents, whether it is the President's speech inaugurating the budget session of the parliament, or the Finance Minister's speech or the *Economic Survey, 1990-91*. The discourse is in terms of "credible structural reforms designed to improve the *efficiency* and *productivity* of resource use (which) are inescapable necessity. If the unavoidable fiscal adjustment is not to lead to stagflation but become an occasion to import a new element of dynamism to the growth process". The centre-pieces of the strategy is to reduce the fiscal deficit from 8.4 per cent of GDP to 6.5 per cent to begin with and to stabilise prices t 4 to 5 per cent rate of inflation. So far so good. But how to achieve this? Here comes the Fun-Bank package, the most important elements of which are: (i) Correct overvalued exchange rate — *devalue*, if one still prefers to call it that way, (ii) reduce, if not outright *abolish, all subsidies*, (iii) remove all controls to eliminate directly unproductive profit seeking (DUPS) — *liberalise*, (iv) imbibe efficiency by inducting competition and disinvestment in the public sector — *privatise*, and (v) eliminate non-tariff barriers (QR) on capital and intermediate goods and reduce average tariffs on them at least in phases to not more than 20 per cent — *globalise*.

Before drawing inferences about the overall consequences of the 'package' it is necessary to examine each one of these elements. First, let us examine the reasons given for the commendation of devaluation. It is suggested that the crisis in the balance of payments of India is due to *overvaluation* of the Indian rupee in terms of hard currencies like the British Pound, the Us dollar etc. This artificially high value of rupee in terms of other currencies was not only making Indian goods more expensive thereby reducing the rate of growth of exports but also was causing capital flight. Therefore it was argued that Indian rupee should be devalued. Then follows the text book argument that it will make Indian goods cheaper making way for faster growth of exports, and imports dearer so that the imports would experience declining trend. This would result in the reduction of the deficit in balance of payments and with some more doses of liberalisation would also attract more foreign investment. Together these changes would solve the crisis.

How far are these arguments credible? Let us examine some of these propositions. First, has the Indian currency been 'overvalued'? In fact during 1980-1990 Indian currency suffered worst phase of exchange depreciation. The depreciation of the Indian rupee against the SDR was as high as 70 per cent. According to another estimate the index of real effective exchange rate (REER) of the Indian rupee declined from 100 in 1981 to 70 in 1989. Even in terms of the currencies of ASEAN countries like Singapore, Malaysia etc. the value of Indian currency has been declining after the peak of 1987. During 1980-87 the cumulative depreciation of the Indian rupee against the U.S. dollar was 47.8 per cent, against D Mark 14.9 per cent Pound (UK) 12.3 per cent and Japanese yen 58.1 per cent. (Uma Rani, 1991) Between 1987 and 1990 the depreciation was at much faster rate. These facts show that Indian currency had been experiencing *de facto* devaluation all through the 1980s and especially since 1987. Therefore there is *not* much truth in the argument that Indian rupee was *overvalued*.

Second, the argument that devaluation of the rupee would led to increase in exports also smacks of a deliberate attempt to ignore the nature of demand for the Indian exports and the nature of the world markets these exports face. Traditional exports like cotton yarn, textiles, tea etc. are not only facing stiff competition but also serious quantitative restrictions like quotas. Further, the efforts to boost exports by devaluation may lead to very severe adverse consequences in the case of primary commodities ultimately turning the terms of trade against Third World countries like India (V. Bhaskar, 1991). The markets of the developed countries are not longer the open markets as the advocates of liberalisation for the Third World would like us to believe. There are severe quota restrictions on items like cotton yarn, textiles etc. As for engineering exports, these are not likely to experience any spurt in demand because of the recessionary conditions prevailing in some of markets for the Indian goods. The new entrants in the export list like diamonds come with a heavy import content and there is not much of hope the rise in import price of raw materials as a result of devaluation would be substantially surpassed through expanded demand for finished diamond exports.

Further, there is growing evidence that the exchange rates are determined to a considerable extent by the debt service burden (Uma

Rani, 1991). The very set of policies advocated by the Fund and accepted by India are likely to push up the debt service burden and weaken the rupee exchange rate much further without any special need to resort to devaluation. That devaluation would make Indian goods cheaper is an other myth considering the way Indian prices are marked up. There is growing anarchy in the so called 'free' markets. Substantial proportion of the rise in prices of inflation in India has nothing to do with any rise in cost of production of spurt in demand or shortfall in production but just marked up through manipulation. There doesn't seen to be much that the present government could do about it. The most disturbing and recent example is the rise in the hole-sale prices of cereals by 25.35 per cent in 1990-91. There was actually an increase in production, no increase in the procurement prices and no reason to expect any sudden spurt in the demand either. What is sought to be achieved through devaluation, viz cheapening of the Indian goods in terms of foreign currencies is undone by the engineered inflation. To make the long story short, devaluation may *not* bring about any substantial *increase* in India's *exports*, certainly not as much as to fill the growing trade gap.

Third, let us see the validity of the argument that devaluation would make the imports expensive and thereby reduce the quantity of imports and the import bill. This is yet an other myth, given the essential nature of most of the imports and also some inessential but high-tech oriented recent additions as a result of liberalisation. The major items of imports include petroleum and petroleum products, fertilizers, edible oils, capital and intermediary goods. It is obvious none of these items could be reduced and therefore all the *increase in the prices due to devaluation* would only become an additional burden on balance of payments.

Contrary to the IMF propagated view that devaluation would help solve the balance of payments crisis, it would actually not only aggravate the payments crisis, but also worsen the economic situation in the country. Let us have a quick look at the devastation. The immediate result of devaluation of the Indian rupee meant that with one stroke the rupee value of foreign debt which was estimated at Rs. 1,32,000 crores or 38 per cent of GDP in June 1991 increased to Rs. 1,61,000 crores or 47 per cent of GDP. The debt-service ratio (DSR the value of debt service as a proportion to goods and services exported) would increase to 58 per cent in 1991-92 compared to 26.3 per cent in 1989. In fact, there was a continuous rise in the debt-service ratio since 1985 at an annual rate of 7 per cent. Devaluation *would make matters worse* beyond imagination.

Devaluation meant that India needs to raise the quantity of exports by 23 per cent just to keep the earnings in dollar terms at the same value as before. It can bring about any benefit only after taking care of this compensatory volume of increase in the goods exported and it is doubtful whether the quantity rise would go beyond 23 per cent.

Let us look at the oil bill which will increase by Rs. 1000 crores. If we import the same quantity of oil as last year we end up paying Rs. 1000 crores more with all its cascading effect on transport costs, costs of inputs in industries like fertilizers, energy etc.

The direct (Rs. 27,000 crores) and indirect (Rs. 3000 crores) effects of devaluation on power projects during the eighth plan is estimated to be an *additional* expenditure of Rs. 30,000. Whatever happens to the cost of power generation is anybody's guess. Most of these power projects are to be financed by borrowing from abroad and the foreign loan requirement for power projects alone would increase by Rs. 25,000 crores and would amount to Rs. 1,30,000 crores! The per mega-watt cost of thermal plants would increase from Rs. 2.5 to Rs. 3 crores to Rs. 3.5 crores, thanks to devaluation.

All this, not to bother about minor owes like what happens to the paper prices which have gone up by Rs. 2000 to Rs. 3000 per tonne, the import of books and journals which were already under strain because of jacked up prices and subscription rates. Devaluation is certain to spell disaster to most of the institutions of higher learning with the cost of their laboratory equipment, books and journals becoming prohibitively expensive.

With all the evidence to the contrary, why is devaluation thrust through the throats of the economies like India? Are there no alternatives to devaluation?

Second the question of reduction, if not abolition, of subsidies bristles with problems which have to be necessarily understood in the light of the nature of the State, its class interests, and legitimisation compulsions. While food subsidies which buy legitimisation certainly helps the poor, there are myriad other implicit and explicit subsidies which keep all the classes in the coalition — the rich farmer, the bourgeoisie including the comprador, and the bureaucracy — appeased at heavy cost to the state. The central government budgetary or explicit subsidies which began with Rs. 40 crores in 1950-51 shot up to Rs. 11035 crores by 1989-90, more than one-tenth (11.5 per cent of the

Central government expenditure. This, not to speak of several implicit subsidies like low power tariff, irrigation charges etc. According to one study the implicit state and central subsidies on agricultural inputs as a whole amounted to Rs 11,793 crores or about 18, per cent of the GDP in 1986-87. (Ashok Gulati, 1989).

An other important study shows that the overall implicit and explicit subsidies of the state and the Union governments are heavily in favour of economic services while subsidies to social services like education, health, etc. assume only secondary importance. (Sudipto Mundle and M. Govinda Rao 1991). It is fairly well known that most of the benefits of subsidies on economic services would directly benefit the 'haves' much more than 'have nots', while social services are biased in favour of the poorer classes. The kind of class interests in which the question of subsidies are enmeshed, makes any 'rational' or 'simplistic' suggestions to appear very naive. Not that subsidies should not be abolished, atleast most of them should be. But given the conflicting interests of the coalition of ruling class interests and their survival urge to appease the masses in their legitimation (Bardhan 1988), in the name of abolition of subsidies, many implicit or explicit subsidies that benefit the poor, like the ones on school education, health or food may suffer a set back while subsidies on fertilizers, exports and the like may only undergo a change in the form and may get concealed. A classic case is that of fertilisers which captures all the dimensions of an inequitous and corrupt system.

While the move to reduce fertilizer subsidies which admittedly benefits more the profit making farmers who account for about 70 per cent of the consumption and to a lesser extent the large majority of small and marginal farmers who account for only 30 per cent of fertilizer consumption raised lot of controversy with much dilution of the measure in the guise of helping the small and marginal farmers. What did not receive much attention is that substantial proportion of fertilizer subsidies accrue to the fertilizer industry. The administering of fertilizer prices are done by the government of India by what is known as Retention Price System (RPS). According to RPs the ex-factory price for each plant is on the basis of "normative cost of production" plus equated freight. The government guarantees a minimum of 12 per cent return on the investment subject to meeting certain capacity utilisation. Subsidy on domestic fertilizer is defined as the difference between the normative cost of production and the price charged to the farmer. The difference is paid to the manufacturer. The "normative cost of production" has been the cause of not only a chaotic cost structure which varies from plant to plant but also has been the source of deliberate manipulation of the cost of plant and equipment. It is for this reason that a question is raised whether "fertilizer subsidy is a subsidy to the farmers, to the fertilizer industry or even to the feedstock supplying industries?" (Ashok Gulati, 1989). There is a very wise variation in the cost-structure, the retention price and the feed stock. For example the retention price of urea in 1985 varied from Rs. 1705 per tonne to Rs. 4506. What more? Most of the fertilizer subsidies at the farmers' end reach only a few agriculturally developed states. For instance in 1984-85 and 1985-86 four states, U.P., Punjab, A.P. and Tamil Nadu together accounted for 54 per cent of fertilizer subsidies of the country (Ashok Gulati, 1989).

Thirdly, let us turn to the 'liberalisation' and 'privatisation' measures together. To appreciate the implications of this policy suggestions, it is essential to link it to the World Bank's ideological prescriptions for the Third World as it has been unfolding during the last few years. We may call this the Bank-Fund ideology. A few years ago, the World Bank, as a part of its annual *World Developmental Report 1987*, dished out a theoretical attack on State regulation and control. For quite some time there has been some orchestration of academic analysis against trade regulation regimes in the Third World countries (Bhagwati and Krishnan, 1975) State regulation of trade was theorised as leading to rent seeking activities of such rents sought as a share of the GDP were prepared (Kreuger, 1974). Recently there has been revival of these 'theoretical' efforts in the name of 'new political economy' (Srinivasan, 1985). These are generalised and popularised as the 'DUPS' (Directly Unproductive Profit Seeking) of public regulation. The essence of this proposition is that public regulation and control, like licencing, will act as a disincentive to the private productive activity and promote unproductive profit seeking through corruption and red tape. Therefore its recommendation has been, that third world countries can improve their efficiency only through removing all regulations like licencing. Further, about two or three years ago the World Bank encouraged the publication of works eulogising the *private provision of public goods* like even education, health and urban transport facilities, not to speak of other public sector enterprises which were described as highly inefficient and a heavy drain on the State's resources. The recommendation has been that the third world governments should disinvest by privatising public sector units. Thus 'privatisation' becomes the policy prescription. India, perhaps, wanted to prove that it did not large behind, when the succession of the recent governments proposed to 'disinvest' by selling the shares of profit making public sector undertakings to the private parties. The new industrial policy is the culmination of these 'privatisation' and 'liberalisation' urges. Often attention is drawn to Taiwan, South Korea, Singapore and Hong Kong which until recently were known as the 'gang of four, in the literature but now suddenly described as 'Asian Tigers'. Indian itself is referred to as 'caged tiger' (*The Economist, 1991*). What indeed is relevant to India could be the Latin American experience and not the Tiger story.

Fourthly, the recent unfolding of the 'globalisation' 'restructuring' or 'structural adjustment' in all its dimensions as revealed by the much debated World Bank document on India in circulation viz. *Strategy for Trade Reform, India* needs to be looked closely. The kind of suggested 'restructuring' of India is baffling. In simplest terms the recommendation of this document is that Indian economy should restructure itself to accommodate itself in the world market structure — to become a market for the capital goods of the developed countries, that is. The package recommended to India is as follows: (i) remove all non-tariff restrictions or quantitative restrictions (QR) on capital and intermediate goods, (ii) reduce the average tariff on all capital and intermediate goods to 20 per cent and (iii) make the exchange rate more realistic, a euphamism for devaluation. In other words, make India a market for the capital and intermediate goods of the world. What happens to the production of capital and intermediate goods production in India? By the World Bank's own estimate they will decline rapidly. What happens to the 85 per cent self-reliance of India in these goods achieved by 1980? Even the small doses of liberalisation during 1980-81 to 1989-90, increased import share of capital and intermediate goods from 15 per cent to 25 per cent. The tragic irony is that much of the trade deficit — as much as 87 per cent of it — is caused by none other than the rise in the imports of capital and intermediate goods!

III

The present economic crisis, as observed earlier, is a product of the compulsions of a dominant coalition of classes with conflicting interests. Ignoring the source of the crisis, the problem is sought be presented as one of economic management. The liet-motive of the policy, therefore, is that the Indian economy, in particular its external sector, must respond and adapt to structural changes in the world economy promptly rather than slowly and with flexibility rather than rigidity." It is the promptness and the flexibility with which the Fund-Bank package is ushered in causes concern especially when one considers the experience of the Latin American countries and the known on the ineffectiveness of these measures.

Based on a number of studies, some by the IMF staff themselves, adequate evidence has been compiled (T.K. Arun, 1991) to show that the impact of the IMF package on growth, inflation, income distribution and stabilisation are of doubtful success but often of very adverse consequences. In as many as in 88 per cent of the cases "the Fund sponsored stabilisation either actively aggravates or fails to control inflation", with half of the cases without any positive impact on balance of payments and with only 25 per cent finding favourable effects on growth. An empirical study of the "quantitative effects of IMF sponsored adjustment programme on income distribution found that in 18 Latin American countries, the labour share of income fell subsequent to stabilisation exercise prescribed by the IMF". The fund's own internal evaluation of the stabilisation programmes of nine countries which accounted for high-conditionality commitments in 1980s found that "not a single country could achieve the initial objectives of stabilisation".

The experience of ABC (Argentina, Brazil and Chile) should at least be an eye opener. These countries which went in for 'liberalisation' and 'globalisation' packages have ended accumulating debt which is almost unpayable. Resort is made to 'sell' the debt at a discount on world market and bought again by west, which is swapped for equity in various companies of Latin America. (Gilbert Lobo, 1991). Debt for equity swaps have become common. "Loans are converted into equity much like the money lenders who bought the land from the insolvent peasants. To cite only a few instances, Argentina sold the state airline, television and radio stations, petrochemicals etc., Brazil sold two largest steel plants and Mexico began with the selling of telephone company followed by state-run banks. Such sordid details abound in liberature on the experience of Latin America with liberalisation (D. Padmavathi, 1987). All those who are celebrating the ushering in of a new era in the Indian economy with the globalisation would do well to reflect on the kind of shambles into which resource rich Latin America is reduced. Latin America was hauld on a path similar to the one that is unfolding before India. Alternatives do exist if one recognises that development should be understood from the perspective of the masses who are looking for better education, employment, health facilities, and power to decide issues which affect their livelihood.

REFERENCES

"A Survey of India" ("India Caged Tiger") *The Economist* May 4, 1991.

A. Uma Rani 'Exchange Rate Modelling of Rupee-Dollar' Unpublished M.Phil. Dissertation, Department of Economics, University of Hyderabad, Hyderabad, 1991.

A.O. Kreuger "Political Economy of Rent-Seeking Society" *American Economic Review*, June 1974.

Arun Ghosh, "Trade Reform for Restructuring the Economy" *Economic and Political Weekly*, June 15, 1991.

Arun Ghosh, India : Big World's View of 'Small world'", *Economic and Political Weekly*, June 1-8, 1991.

Ashok Gulati "Input Subsidies in Indian Agriculture: A State-wise Analysis". *Economic and Political Weekly*. June 24, 1989.

Aspects of India's Economy, 2 (Oct-Dec 1990) & 3 (Jan-March 1991), Research Unit for Political Economy, Bombay.

D. Padmavathi Liberalisation : An Evaluation of the Indian Experience Unpublished M. Phil. Dissertation, Department of Economics, University of Hyderabad, Hyderabad, 1987.

Deepak Lal, *The Poverty of Development Economic's*, Institute of Economic Affairs, London, 1983.

Gilbert Lobo, "Collapse of rouble", *Financial Express*, April 3, 1991.

GOI, *Economic Survey, 1988-89, 1989-90*, and *1990-91*, Ministry of Finance, New Delhi.

J. Bhagwati and T.N. Srinivasan, *Foreign Trade Regimes and Economic Development : India*, Columbia University Press, NBER, 1975.

John Toye, *Dilemmas of Development*, Basil Blackwell, Geford, 1987.

K.S. Gill "Budget Deficit of the Central Government", *Economic and Political Weekly*, January 5-12, 1991.

P. Patnaik "On Political Economy of Economic Liberalisation" *Social Scientist*, Vol 13 No. 7-8, 1985.

Pranab Bhadran, *Political Economy of Development in India*, OUP, 1985.

S. Gangadharan "Fiscal Disequilibrium: Glaring Mismatch Between Receipts and Expenditure", *The Economic Times*, 18 July 1991.

S.D. Tendulkar "Abject Surrender, but not to the IMF", *The Economic Times*, 16 and 17 September, 1991.

Sanjay Baru "Foreign Debt : From a Lender's Log Book", *The Economic Times*, 16 Sept. 1991.

Sudipto Mundle and M. Govinda Rao "Volume and Composition of Government Subsidies in India, 1987-88", *Economic and Political Weekly* May 4, 1991.

T.K. Arun "Structural Reform : A Short in the Dark", *The Economic Times* 13 August 1991.

T.N. Srinivasan "Neoclassical Political Economy of State and Economic Development" *Asian Development Review*, Oct 1985.

V. Bhaskar "Export Promotion, Exchange Rates and Commodity Prices", *Economic and Political Weekly*, May 18, 1991.

11

EXTERNAL CRISIS, SWEEPING CHANGES IN MACROECONOMIC POLICIES AND THE UNION BUDGET: An Impeachment

S. KRISHAN RAO

Prelude

WITHIN WEEKS of assuming power, the non-majority Narasimha Rao government effected sweeping changes in Exchange Rates, Trade, Industrial and other policies. All the same, for some reasons the much vaunted 8th Plan has been shelved or continuously postponed and even if it commences from 1992, the role of "invisible hand"will be placed at the centre stage, marginalising the status of the state and bidding goodbye to the cherished goals of poverty abolition, self-reliance and reduction in concentration of economic power. A cursory review of the 1991-92 Budget Proposals read with the industrial and other policies gives credence to the apprehension. The opening and closing weeks of July 1991 are turning point in the restructuring of the Indian economy on the lines suggested by the Fund-Bank authorities. The restructuring in fact commenced from the early 80s. The public at large is in dark and at disadvantage, for contradictory views are being expressed by different segments of the media, economists and the authorities. While one section holds that the changes are in the right direction, others dub them as mortgage of India, total disrespect for democracy and steps directed towards further ruination of the Indian economy. What is the truth? Where are we going to land?

In this context, this paper aims at raising the following issues and attempts to shed light on them. Is the balance of payments (BOP) position of India so bad as to compel us to prostrate before the Fund and other international lenders under humiliating conditions? Is there no alternative? Does the Fund-Bank assistance conditioned by market-orientation, liberalisation and privatisation serve as cure of do they make the disease worse. Does, the BOP crisis alone need our concern? Does not the vast unemployment-poverty problem deserve more or equal attention? Has the BOP crisis emerged suddenly? Granted that India is under serious crisis and therefore permit the authorities to take all steps, howsoever nausiating, will the authorities ensure that the history will not repeat? Is this assurance technically feasible with the cruel medicine being prescribed? Whether devaluation will reduce imports and boost up exports? if yes, under what conditions and what was our experience with the 1966 devaluation? What should be the role of international trade in the development of India characterised by widespread poverty unemployment, vast domestic market and supply rigidities? Should India blindly emulate the Asian Tigers as to outward-orientation or should the accent be on inward-orientation? Should we go back to the Nehruvian strategy, underlining growth with equity and self-reliance? Or should be adapt Gandhian policies consistent with the 1990s situation? Does the 1991-92 Budget, Trade and Industrial Policies reflect obedience to the Fund's stipulations and what will be their impact on real growth, social justice and inflation?

Before we discuss the aforementioned issues, it should be noted that the Budget, Devaluation, changes in Trade and Industrial policies should all be considered in unison. However, for orderly analytical discussion, it becomes necessary to arbitrarily divide them under some convenient rubrics. With this caution, the paper is organised under seven sections. Section II analyses the trends in current account balances as a first step to appreciate the swelling external financial gap. Magnitude, structure and causes of the external debt are taken up in Section III. Section IV examines the relevance and impact of devaluation. Section V, we present a critique of the trade and industrial policies. In Section VI the focus is on the 1991 Budget and its impact. In the final Section a way out of the present crisis is suggested, followed by a brief summing up.

II

Trends in Current Account Balances

On the eve of First Five Year Plan, our exports and imports were about

Rs. 650 crores (crores) each, leaving a negligible trade deficit (Rs. 4 crores) but Rs. 39 crores current account surplus (Table 11.1). To cope up with the needs of planned development, there has been almost a continuous rise in our merchandise. Today our exports are over Rs. 32500 crores and imports peaked to an alarming level of over Rs. 43000 crores. While the trade deficit is about Rs. 11000 crores, the current account deficit (which is net of invisibles surplus) is much higher — nearly Rs. 20000 crores. It may be noted here that trade deficit after approaching 4 digit level, (Rs. 977 crores) in 1974-75, rose to Rs. 1843 crores in 1978-79. Two years later current account deficit too reached to 4 digit level. We now take a snap shot of trends in annual average changes in the current account.

TABLE 11.1: External Current Account and Foreign Exchange Reserves

(Rs. in crores)

Year	Imports	Exports	Trade Balance	Current Account Balance	Foreign Exchange Reserves
1	2	3	4	5	6
1950-51	650	647	–4	+39	911
1951-52	963	730	–233	–163	947
1960-61	1106	631	–475	–392	186
1970-71	1720	1403	–318	–331	438
1980-81	12544	6576	–5967	–1657	4822
1981-82	13887	7767	–6121	–2317	3355
1982-83	14913	9137	–5776	–2296	4265
1983-84	16039	10169	–5871	–2262	5498
1984-85	18680	11959	–6721	–2852	6817
1985-86	21164	11578	–9586	–5927	7384
1986-87	22669	11315	–9354	–5830	7645
1987-88	25963	16396	–9226	–6293	7287
1988-89	34202	20647	–13556	–10410	4802
1989-90	35412	27681	–8330	–13883	3692
1990-91	43170	32527	–10643	–19858(e)	2400(e)

Source: Currency and Finance, R.B.I. and Economic Surveys, Ministry of Finance, Govt of India.

Note: (e) estimated

In the first decade of planning average annual growth of imports was about 7 per cent to 9 per cent and that of exports less than 10 per cent (Table 11.2). During the early sixties, the average growth of imports and exports was almost equal. Between 1966-67 and 1970-71, growth of imports was twice the imports. But in the next 5 years, both grew almost at the same rate. In the past 15 years. imports and exports moved up by about 13 per cent to 14 per cent. Thus the record of merchandise does not permit to discern any clear trend.

TABLE 11.2: Average Annual Per Cent Change

Period	Imports	Exports	As proportion of National Income				Exports as per cent of Imports	Foreign Exchange Reserves as % of Imports
			Imports	Exports	Trade Deficit	Current A/c Deficit		
1	2	3	4	5	6	7	8	9
1950-51 to 1955-56	7.1	0.6	8.5	6.7	1.0	0.02	88.5	114.0
1956-57 to 1960-61	9.4	0.02	8.4	5.3	3.9	2.8	58.5	28.8
1961-62 to 1965-66	4.8	4.7	7.2	4.4	2.7	2.3	61.3	14.1
1966-67 to 1970-71	6.6	13.1	6.4	4.5	1.9	1.9	72.9	22.9
1971-72 to 1975-76	23.5	24.7	6.2	5.2	1.0	⊕0.1	83.3	22.8
1976-77 to 1980-81	22.4	9.7	8.5	6.6	2.0	⊕0.9	80.9	61.9
1981-82 to 1985-86	11.1	10.3	8.2	4.9	3.3	2.5	60.0	29.7
1986-87 to 1990-91	15.7	23.1	8.1	5.5	2.7	2.7	67.2	18.5

Source: Economic Survey and Currency and Finance, Reserve Bank of India.

As proportion of national income, in the first decade of planning and in the recent 15 years, imports were about 8 per cent to 8.5 per cent and in the 60s and early 70s they were a little more than 6 per cent to 7 per cent. As against the imports, the proportion of exports is relatively lower — 4 per cent to 6.5 per cent. This is reflected in the trade deficit (col. 5). It varied between one per cent and 3.9 per cent of national income. Net credits from invisibles served to neutralise or more than neutralise the trade deficits (col. 6). However, in the recent decade, it is around 2.5 per cent of national income. Looking at exports as per cent of imports, barring the First plan period, exports financed about 60 per cent to 80 per cent of our imports (col 7). With regard to reserves of foreign exchange, they were barely sufficient to finance two months imports during early 60s and in the late 80s (col 8). To sum up, although India made attempts to raise exports, due to higher propensity to import, trade and current account deficits witnessed deterioration, especially in the recent decade. Foreign exchange reserves steeply depleted and today they can not meet even a month's needs of our imports. We defer the detailed enquiry. Suffice to note here that there must be something wrong with our development strategy and macroeconomic policies adopted. Let us now shift to the task of quantification of the debt and its burden.

III

Debt Crisis – Magnitude of Balance of Payments Gap

At the outset it should be conceded that the present BOP deficit is quite alarming and certainty the economy is on the brink of bankruptcy as to the external front only. In the recent decade (1980-91), while the trade deficit rose from about Rs. 6000 crores to over Rs. 10500 crores registering an increase of 78 per cent, current account deficit shot up aggressively to about Rs. 20000 crores from about Rs. 1600 crores which means a steep rise of 1000 per cent (Table 11.1). During the 1980s due to contraction of export markets abroad, and liberalization of import policy, trade deficit began to show progressively its ugly teeth. Trade, current and overall balances all moved upwards, giving warning about the imminent crisis. To visualise the overall gap, to the current account deficit we have to add about Rs. 6000 crores representing repayment of scheduled instalments of principal, (Table 11.3). Thus roughly the current outflow from India is around Rs. 260 billion (bn). How did the huge commitments arise? Surely, it is not momentous. To get an insight into the crisis, let us scrutinise first the structure and trends in India's external outstanding debt.

Outstanding Debt—Composition

Our external debt (long and short term) in 1983-84 was Rs. 27641 crores and including NRI deposits it was Rs. 30510 crores, (vide Table 11.4). But due to reckless borrowing and spending, the debt excluding NRI liability mounted to the level of about Rs. 1100 bn. or about $73

TABLE 11.3: Repayment of Scheduled Instalments

(Rs. in crores)

Year	Repayment of Principal	Payment of Interest	Debt Service
1	2	3	4
1984-85	1195	1328	2523
1985-86	1594	1700	3294
1986-87	2644	2087	4731
1987-88	3715	2375	6090
1988-89	4249	2788	7037
1989-90	4808	3559	8367
1990-91	5259(e)	4556(e)	10085

Source: CMIE, August, 1990.
Note: (e) estimated.

TABLE 11.4: Composition of Outstanding External Debt of India

(Rs. in crores)

Year	Govt. a/c Incl. from IMF	Non-Govt. a/c & Commercial Borrowings	Total Debt	N.R.I. Deposits	Grand Total (5=3+4)
1	2	3	4	5	6
1983-84	24440	3201	27641	2869	30510
	(88)	(12)	(100)		
1984-85	28554	7171	35725	3819	39544
	(80)	(20)	(100)		
1985-86	31303	8388	39691	5650	45341
	(79)	(21)	(100)		
1986-87	37138	11210	48348	7847	56195
	(77)	(23)	(100)		
1987-88	40926	13483	54409	10014	64463
	(75)	(25)	(100)		
1988-89	50185	18646	68831	14154	82895
	(70)	(30)	(100)		
1989-90	56417	23675	80132	17831	97963
	(70)	(30)	(100)		
1990-91	N.A.	N.A.	110000*	20000*	13000*

Source: CMIE, August, 1990 and Economic Survey 1990-91.
Note: 1. * Provisional
2. Figures in parentheses are percentages.

billion[2] by 1990-91, registering a growth of 4 times during 1983-91. If we include NRI deposits the debt is around Rs. 1300 bn. Ignoring the NRI deposits, in the total debt of India, today the share of government is about 70 per cent as against 88 per cent in 1983-84 (col. 1). It signifies that in the recent 8 years, non-Government, and commercial borrowing have been on the rise. When we consider only long term outstanding debt, in 1980 the relative share of loans of commercial banks was just 11 per cent and the balance of 9/10ths we owed to official creditors and other institutions, (vide Appendix A). Due to certain reasons, continuously India stepped up commercial borrowings and by 1990 its share was about two/fifths.

The annual inflows from the overseas commercial banks were within prudent limits during 1980-87–around Rs. 15 bn.[3] Due to severe debt problem in the Latin American Countries, business of the commercial banks dwindled. Coupled with this, as India had a high credit rating, from the mid-80s they diverted attention to India. Further, as India could not obtain adequate aid from the multilateral institutions, she was compelled to borrow from the commercial banks. Consequently in 1989-90 alone, India borrowed from them record amount of about Rs. 55 bn.

The real magnitude of the debt and its burden can better be appreciated in terms of certain ratios — debt to exports of goods and services, debt to G.N.P. and, amortisation and interest to export revenue (debt-service ratio). In 1980 our external debt was 37 per cent higher than export earnings and today it is 200 per cent higher than our export revenue. As proportion to GNP, debt was 12 per cent in 1980 and today the proportion is twice that of 1980. The debt service ratio was less than 10 per cent in 1980 and today it is around 30 per cent.[4] It is held that 20 per cent debt-service ratio is to be targeted for comfortable management of international transactions. In sum apart form the monstrous absolute size of the debt, relatively too it is very high and almost appears as unmanageable under the present international milieu. This is a reflection of India living beyond her means. It is unfortunate that the symptom of huge international financial gap (excess of outflows over inflows both on current and capital accounts) over the years was over-looked in identifying the deep rooted chronic malady.

Having sketched the trends in the trade and current account deficit as also the absolute and relative size of the outstanding debt and debt service obligations, let us now further probe into the causes which led to the ongoing unprecedented turmoil.

Causes for the Crisis

In the foregoing section it was mentioned that one of the reasons for the debt hang-over was the rising share of commercial borrowings. However, this is only an aggravating cause and not the main cause. These loans by their very nature entail short period maturity, higher interest rate and therefore the debt servicing liability will be unbearable. Higher burden of interest payments is also due to falling share of welfare-growth oriented concessional aid from IDA and somewhat costly higher credits from the World Bank. Along with this, bilateral grants have also declined. These changes in the structure of the debt reduced the average maturity, enhanced the interest burden and amortisation and hence, rise in the debt service ratio. Drastic fall in NRI funds also calls our attention. To partly overcome strains on Foreign Exchange reserves India made attempts, by providing special concessions including higher interest to attract funds from NRI in terms of both deposits (Rupee and Foreign currency) and investments. For some time (early 80s), indeed there was boom of NRI inflow but it was short-lived. These inflows dwindled due to lack of confidence in us as reflected in the swelling trade and current account deficits as well as debt service ratio. IMF's hesitation to lend India is also treated as our low credit worthiness. Closely connected with the alarming size of the current account deficit is our excessive dependence on the invisibles net revenue. Reliance on this to meet trade deficit is deceptive.

Dependable solution lies in raising exports at least equal to imports with a view to achieve equilibrium in the medium long term. During 1950-91, barring a couple of years, always we had surplus in the invisible account and therefore we could partly offset the trade gap. This apart, in 10 years net credits in the invisible (Table 11.2) head not only could meet the trade gap but also served to reduce capital account deficit. Per contra, from the mid-80s current account balance has been deteriorating pointing towards grave position and in the recent 2 years, the deficit in current account exceeded trade gap implying net deficits in the invisible account (Table 11.1).

Da Costa in his recent study[5] identified proximate and ultimate determinants of trade balance. The former are volume of exports and imports, net barter terms of trade which incorporate relative prices of imports and exports. These proximate determinants are ultimately influenced by external and internal developments viz. changes in real incomes and inflation in the IACs, trends in our real income, changes in real effective exchange rates of India and the import liberalization policy. He holds that the 1980s import liberalization policy pushed up imports and our import dependence enhanced. It is reported that the average import-GNP ratio was only 4.9 per cent in the 70s which shot up to 6.6 per cent during the 80s. The concludes that in the 80s dominant forces at work on our terms of trade were external in origin — real growth and inflation in the IACs. Sunil Mani[6] too concludes that import dependence of the Indian economy increased during the post-liberalisation period (i.e. after 1985-86). All the 3 measures employed by him (Net Foreign Exchange Inflow Rate, Import intensity Rate and Direct Costs of Technology Imports Rate) unmistakably pointed the same conclusion.

The precarious present BOP is partly due to the 1990 Aug Gulf War. The rise in the trade gap by Rs. 2313 crores (from Rs. 8330 crores to Rs. 10643 crores in 1990-91, (Table 11.1) was mainly due to increase in the oil bill by Rs. 4546 crores (to Rs. 10820 crores in 1990-91), a consequence of spurt in World oil prices, caused by Iraq's invasion on Kuwait. Due to the Gulf crisis, India suffered a total loss of Rs. 5180 crores, of which Rs. 3625 crores was on account of additional oil import bill, Rs. 500 crores due to export loss to West Asia and Rs. 490 crores being the loss in remittances of NRIs (staying in Iran and Kuwait).[7]

A proximate cause for the swelling debt may be traced to the linkage between budget and trade deficits. It is well documented that there exists monetary linkage between a fiscal deficit financed with domestic credit and its impact on BOP.[8] Unabated steep rise in Non-Development[9] and Non-Plan expenditures[10] tied to ad hocism in policies and populist-cum-socialist gimmicks were responsible for the widening deficits both in the Revenue and Capital accounts. For e.g. the Loan Waiver scheme of the NF Government burdened the exchequer to the extent of Rs. 5500 crores (and including the State Governments Rs. 7434 crores). It is worth to note here that up to 1978-79, revenue account of the Government of India showed surplus, and hence it could meet a part of capital expenditure. Since 1979-80 not only revenue account started exhibiting negative balance but the revenue gap has been widening. This deficit, along with the compulsions to undertake huge planned investment, necessitated ever increasing reliance on market borrowings and credit from the R.B.I. Due to laxity in raising revenues and lavishness in unproductive spending, domestic avenues dried up. Consequently, successive Congress Governments preferred the sort option of borrowing from abroad including short term higher interest bearing commercial loans.

Today while the revenue deficit is about Rs. 130 bn., the overall deficit is about Rs. 110 bn., or about 3 per cent of G.D.P. The concept of fiscal deficit which includes all types of borrowings including from the Central Bank has become popular under the aegis of IMF. Our fiscal deficit stood at[11] 8.3 per cent of GDP in 1990-91 or in absolute terms about Rs. 434 bn (vide 1990-91 RE). In the world of IMF, prudent level of budget deficit is to be 1 per cent to 1.5 per cent of GDP and that of fiscal deficit 3.5 per cent. As a digression, here it is worth to note a popular misconception. Empirically, one may find positive close association between budget and current account deficits. However, as long as the current account deficit is around 1.5 per cent of GDP, there should not be embargo on budgetary deficit, subject to the proviso that the funds raised are used for planned development. Viewed in this perspective the magic fiscal deficit figure of 6.5 per cent of GDP prescribed by the IMF has little relevance. For fiscal health, the relevant one is revenue deficit and not fiscal deficit which is wrongly emphasized by the IMF. Let us revert to the more fundamental causes so that medicine prescription will not be problematic.

Deeper Cause

Manifestation of the present "Debt-Aid-Trade" crisis is the result of interaction of diverse forces operating over years. Often, in analysing a country's BOP difficulties, the incidence of powerful international factors, including covert and overt dynamics of international capitalism, are glossed over and domestic factors including fiscal deficit are over played. An important exogenous factor for the grave BOP is intensified protectionist policies pursued by the IACs. But unfortunately, this is given lukewarm treatment in analysing BOP problems of third world countries. The contribution of Fund-Bank mechanism and their (pseudo) advice are not seriously diagnosed. We hold that the present grave BOP is not an aberration but an integral part of the functioning of global capitalism. Ghosh neatly sums up how the aggressive industrialisation policies adopted by the OECD nations (or the developed capitalist societies) led to increased dependence, and how human nature and national considerations resist it.[12] Aggressive industrialisation demands higher levels of accumulation, finer global division of labour, more materials and transnational assured markets. These necessitate direct and indirect control over other nations and on financial-trade channels. In the changed post-II World War conditions, international capitalism for its survival and growth evolved new forms and methods of exploitation. They are : Neo-Imperialism. Neo-Colonialism, aid as bait, tied assistance and ill-suited obsolete technology transfers, flotation of pseudo democratic multilateral institutions, like the Fund-Bank and their affiliates (such as IDA, IFC, Mechanism of Paris Club and Aid-India Consortium controlled by the Fund-Bank) to subserve the interest of overseas commercial banks and capitalist nations. Today, the twins of Bretton Woods instead of easing-out liquidity problem and promoting economic development, assumed the role of cruel policeman, to discipline the debt-trapped nations and leaving the IACs scot free. Under the grab of structural adjustment or macroeconomic reforms, the two global institutions adopting allopathy therapeutics prescribe strong antibiotics to cure only the outward manifestations. Needless to say that they are highly poisonous but euphemistically called "Side effects".[13] They dictate stringent and time-bound specific policies to any aid seeker including to the trouble torn USSR. Their so-called austerity-cum-structural adjustments may be summed up under 4 Ds— Devaluation, Deflation, Delicencing/Deregulation and Denationalisation. The same, Arun Ghosh[14] calls "standard IMF package" comprising fiscal discipline (mainly drastic cuts in subsidies and finances given to public sector units) currency depreciation, trade reforms and liberalization. We are told that the aforesaid are spelt out in the World Bank's "Trade Reforms Report on India" of November, 1990 which was kept as a guarded secret by the bureaucracy and not even shown to the then Prime Minister. Their policy prescriptions no doubt rectify the short term fiscal and trade imbalances but severely inhibit growth and distribution. In other words their strategy, based on demand management through market mechanism, warrants sacrifice of long term socio-economic goals. Their package do not even mention about home market development and socio-economic institutional reforms. The impact of austerity measures will be heavier on the poor and character of growth will be more inequitous.

Experience of Other Countries

The perversions can easily be verified from the experience of Latin American and African countries which were subjected to the draconian discipline of the IMF. They were made to do everything to increase exports and follow deflationary austerity programme and open their economies to the global nations. The whole burden of adjustment fell on them and the IACs refused to restructure their economies, reduce their revenue deficits or relax protectionist policies. It is to be noted here that the main problem in raising exports continues to be quota barriers and declining demand from the US, UK and Western Europe. Adjustment is easier when the IACs experience high growth. But this is not so at present. Average unemployment rate in the OECD countries during 1980-90 was around 7 per cent[15] and GDP growth about 3 per cent.[16] The message from the history of industrialisation of the OECD countries is that the development was substantially the result of extreme protection at home and collective effort of targetting abroad[17]. England, the so called champion of free trade, resorted to protectionism centuries ago (recall here the Corn Laws controversy during Ricardo's time). Faced with competition from the Indian cotton textiles, England adopted restrictive policies even in the 19th century.

In Japan, free market is an anomaly. They protect indigenous efforts, import only the basic plant and adapt it to suit local needs. They open up gradually only those sectors which can readily face international competition. We are often glamoured by Japanese model of industrial development by without knowing their modus operandi in trade and industry. Although the stage of our development is far behind Japan and other IACs, it is unfortunate to find from the Indian economists loud talk about the market economy and liberalized trade and industrial policies. The benevolence of invisible hand to provide public welfare has been long back contested and disproved. But the 1991-92 budget and the recent radical changes in Industrial and Trade policies downgrade the role of public enterprises and planning process. We ignore with all our wisdom the traumatic experience of the Latin American countries in the 80s. Liberalization and foreign direct investment may permit access to global technology. But they will have stifling effect on the development of indigenous technology and unemployment. Already Indian economy is import-biased and with the sweeping changes announced on 24th July, 1991, import-intensity will further rise and dumping of goods from foreign countries is sure to kill Indian industries. We are on the verge of facing a second dose of de-industrialisation (the first one was in the early 19th century).

A country plagued with domestic and external deficits must restructure its economy and follow austerity but adjustment and austerity demand sacrifices. The laudable principle is that the costs of adjustment should be borne by all sections in proportion to their abilities. But experience of India and other nations does not give assurance to the adoption of the principle. Always the poor are made to swallow a major part of the bitter pills.

IV

Let us now examine in some detail the relevance and impact of devaluation affected in the first week of July 1991. We should note that this is another pet remedy of the IMF, and the most stringent of the conditionalities. Also it is part of Trade Reforms Package suggested by the IBRD for India recently.

Relevance and Impact of Devaluation

We start with the question, whether the recent two-stage devaluation wa unavoidable? Will it have salutory effect on trade balance in the medium and the long terms? Devaluation of currency is regarded as the last resort to achieve favourable balance of trade. Economists hold that it is a delicate weapon and a major operation on the economy. Therefore, it should be used cautiously when all other attempts fail. Its success depends on a host of domestic and international conditions including higher elasticities of demand for the country's exports and imports. The domestic economy should have capacity to raise production, generate surplus and the rest of the world should have ability and willingness to absorb the imports.

If devaluation is undertaken without regarded to these conditions, the cure is worse than the disease. The recent devaluation is a pointer in this regard. So far in India *de jure* devaluation was effected first in September, 1949 by 30.5 per cent and second in June, 1966 by 36.5 per cent. Since the mid-seventies, we have only depreciation and technically not devaluation, It may be noted here that up to 1971, the Bretton Woods system could ensure reasonable stable exchange rates. Consequent to the mid-seventies Us dollar crisis, the system came to an end and was replaced by floating exchange mechanism. From 1975 India too left Rupee to float. Since then the RBI has been fixing Rupees external value almost on daily basis in terms of a basket of currencies, comprising our major trading partners.

Faced with meagre reserves of foreign exchange, widening external financial gap and pressure exerted by the IMF, government of India devalued Rupee by 17 per cent to 19 per cent in two instalments as detailed in Table 11.5 The government argued that it was routine adjustment and not devaluation. Notice here the odium attached to the world devaluation. It is now a dirty word and hence the sugar quoted modern terminology "Realistic Exchange Rates". Whether or not the government concedes the de jure devaluation, what is important to note is that without any provocation from the rest of the world in the recent months, Rupee's external value substantially declined. After the second devaluation in 1966, in the history of the Indian currency, it has no parallel. As noted above, there is nothing wrong with devaluation, if the currency is relatively over valued. We are joining issue with the government about the relevance of the devaluation and its magnitude, not on the basis of its link with IMF's advice. We are aware that a policy can not become good or bad simply because it is suggested by an external agency. Nonetheless we can easily establish IMF link with the devaluation and covert motives.

As mentioned earlier, since 1975 external purchasing power or Rupee has been determined by the RBI on daily basis in relation to a basket of currencies with some degree of discretion. Rupee has been almost continuously losing its value in terms of major currencies and SDRs, as vouched by Table 11.5. Between 1970 and 1990, is value eroded to the extent of 57 per cent, 81 per cent, 41 per cent, 83 per cent and 67 per cent against the US Dollar, DM, Pound Sterling, Yen and SDRs. in that order. In the recent 5 years (1985-86 to 1990-91), Rupee's depreciation ranged between 7 per cent and 15 per cent in terms of four major currencies. Even if we consider only the recent one year, loss of value was about 20 per cent. The previous government of Chandra Shekhar refused to devalue on the ground that on a routine basis anyhow Rupee's external value declined by about 20 per cent during 1990 and hence there was no need to devalue.[18]

Not only the nominal value of Rupee fell but also NEER and REER (Table 11.6). Between 1980 and 1990 while NEER went down by 57 per cent, REER declined by 31 per cent. Between June 28 and 3rd July 1991, Rupee lost value by about 19 per cent in terms of NEER. The foregoing clearly supports the hypothesis that the government of India was rather compelled to devalue Rupee by about 20 per cent, which is generally a precondition of the IMF to sanction loan.

TABLE 11.5: Indices of Exchange Rates of Indian Rupees

(1950 = 100)

Year	Per US$	Per DM	Per UK £	Per 10 Yen	Per SDRs
1	2	3	4	5	6
1950	100	100	100	100	100
	(4.76)	(1.14)	(13.34)	(1.32)	(4.76)
1960	100	99	100	100	100
1970	158	180	135	158	158
	(7.50)	(2.05)	(18.0)	(2.08)	(7.50)
1980	165	380	137	263	215
	(7.86)	(4.33)	(18.29)	(3.47)	(10.23)
1990	365	923	228	908	481
	(17.37)	(10.52)	(30.37)	(11.98)	(22.89)
1991					
Jan	382	1041	259	1017	—
	(18.20)	(11.87)	(34.57)	(13.43)	—
Feb	390	1075	267	1057	—
	(18.55)	(12.25)	(35.55)	(13.95)	—
June	421	999	250	1061	—
	(20.3)	(11.39)	(33.33)	(14.10)	—
June 28	446	1025	258	1158	—
	(21.22)	(11.69)	(34.35)	(15.29)	—
July 1	486	1119	281	1271	—
	(23.130	(12.76)	(37.48)	(16.77)	—
July 3	547	1246	313	1415	—
	(26.02)	(14.20)	(41.72)	(18.68)	

Average Annual Loss of Rupee in Terms of (per cent)

Period	US $	DM	£ Sterling	Yen	SDRs
1950-65	0.0	0.3	0.0	0.0	0.0
1965-80	3.2	8.3	1.0	6.2	4.8
1980-88	9.1	7.8	2.8	14.1	3.7
Per cent decrease between June 28, and July 3, 1991	18.7	17.2	17.4	18.3	N.A.

Source: CMIE, 1990 August and *Economic Times*, July 10, 1990

Notes: Figures in parentheses are Rupees.

TABLE 11.6: Nominal and Real Effective Exchange Rates of Rupee

(1980 = 100)

Year	Nominal Effective Exchange Rate	Effective Relative Price	Relative Effective Exchange Rate
1	2	3	4
1980	100.0	100.0	100.0
1981	96.1	105.1	101.0
1982	94.9	103.9	98.5
1983	87.2	110.8	96.6
1984	84.6	117.3	99.2
1985	78.2	122.9	96.0
1986	64.8	133.7	86.7
1987	57.3	141.6	81.1
1988	50.7	149.7	75.8
1989	45.6	154.0	70.3
1990	43.2	160.5	69.3
1991			
January	41.9	—	—
June	37.6	—	—
June 28	36.0	—	—
July 1	32.9	—	—
July 2	32.9	—	—
July 3	29.2	—	—

Source: *Economic Times*, July 7, 1991.

Note: 1. NEER, (Col. 1), is the export-weighted (average for 1980-90) geometric average of bilateral NEER of Rupee with 18 principal countries.

2. ERP (Col. 2) is relative price change in India and abroad.

3. REER (Col. 3), is calculated by adjusting NEER (Col. 1) with the ERP (Col. 2).

To judge the impact of the devaluation on trade account, let us once again look at Table 11.2 and take note of our experience as to the 1966 devaluation. In the first year of post-devaluation (1966-67) imports moved up faster than exports (45.5%, 38.5%). In the second year also, imports increased but exports grew at a higher rate (3.3%, 15.7%). It is only in the next two years, imports actually witnessed decline and exports maintained up movement. On the whole during the five-year period of post-devaluation, imports and exports rose at an annual average rate of 6.6 per cent and 13.1 per cent respectively. The beneficial impact of devaluation seemed to have exhausted after

1970-71. In brief, India's experience with devaluation was mixed and that too shortlived. Devaluation alone can not reduce imports and encourage exports. Other conditions referred to earlier are to be satisfied. Domestic production capacity and foreign countries' ability and willingness to absorb our exports are the principal factors. To a large extent, the present domestic and international milieu is not conductive to gain from devaluation. Initially India suffers on account of increase in the value of outstanding external debt, interest burden and oil imports, leave alone the controversial benefits of rise in exports and fall in imports. A large part of our imports are non-commercial on government account. Devaluation cannot benefit these imports. It means that the devaluation forces us to export more to import less. Out outstanding external debt which is about Rs. 1300 bn will be up valued (by about Rs. 260 bn) and its consequential higher level of interest payments to the extent of about Rs. 9 bn. Today our oil bill in the total imports accounts for about 23 per cent (Rs. 100 bn) and due to the devaluation we have to shell down Rs. 20 bn more. It is true devaluation of Rupee makes Indian goods cheaper to the foreigners. But making goods cheaper by itself does not constitute sufficient condition to actually enhance exports. Our major importers should be ready to absorb them. Some of the Newly Industrialised countries (NICs) like Brazil made every effort to produce more and sell at abroad. But the IACs followed intensive protectionist policies and thereby prevented NICs efforts. This is why the World is moving towards 'Customs Unions' which permit controlled competition and protection among the members.

Chandra Mohan[19] commenting on the momentous devaluation of 1991 says that support of devaluation is often based on the experience of the Asian Tigers (South Korea, Taiwan, Hong Kong and Singapore) which followed aggressive export strategies* with undervalued exchange rates. However, it is wrong to compare a subcontinent like India, possessing wide market potential and socio-economic milieu of its own, with small countries. Furthermore, the Finance Minister contended that it was not proper to compare Rupee value with major currencies of the World. We should compare with the exchange rates of our competitors like Thailand, Pakistan, China and S. Korea. It

* This is the outcome of Exim Bank International Trade Research Award of 1990 viz. "The Post-War Terms of Trade Controversy— A reexamination", cf. *Economic Times* July 12, 1991.

means that the relative positioning of Rupee *vis-a-vis* the currencics of the LDCs is more important than the major currencies. The question now is whether really our Rupee was over-valued compared with the LDCs as to warrant massive devaluation? Chandra Mohan's preliminary investigation suggests that till 1990 Rupee was not over-valued. On the other hand, it was rather competitive since the 1980s. Real bilateral exchange rate of Rupee depreciated significantly relative to the values of the currencies of S. Korea, Thailand, Singapore, Hong Kong, Malaysia, Pakistan, Bangladesh and Sri Lanka. In sum, the recent devaluation was based neither on relative position of Rupee in terms of nominal exchange rate, real bilateral exchange rates with LDCs nor with IACs. None can neglect the urgency of improving competitiveness but devaluation is not the proper tool to achieve the goal.

In the foregoing we identified the causes for the debt pile up and examined the relevance of devaluation. Let us now move to assess the impact of changes in the other macroeconomic policies and the Budget proposals.

V

Changes in Trade and Industrial Policies

A feature of the successive Government in India is that the government in power highlights a special target for its policy and uses it as a magic wand. The target for the present government is liberalisation or deregulation and it blames the previous government for the BOP mess. Recall here that economic liberalisation in internal and external economic affairs is a part of the Fund-Bank: ready made package of reforms. Government of India having fired the first shot on exchange rate downward adjustment, took up the so called complementary measure of trade reforms on 4th July, 1991, followed by new industrial policy in the 4th week of July along with the annual budget. While announcing changes in trade policy, the Minister for commerce said that the aim was to free trade from the shackles and bureaucratic controls,. make the Indian industry competitive and thereby energize the Indian exporters. It underlines liberalisation of import regime for exporters with a view to correct imbalance in India's trade. The 13 — point trade reform package contains abolition of Cash Compensatory Support and supplementary licences, introduction of uniform 30 per cent replenishment rate for exporters, issue of freely tradeable Exim Scrips, etc. In 3 years almost all import licences for capital goods and raw materials will be abolished and Rupee will be made fully convertible in the trade account. The policy insists on that public enterprises too should meet their import requirements through REP licences. One of the immediate effects of the policy is that the government will save Rs. 2400 crores export subsidy. Low import intensity industries and agricultural export will benefits the maximum.

We appreciate very much abolition of the existing too many administrative controls, lists, appendices, licences, and notorious delays, waste, inefficiency, and corruption in exim trade. However, the liberalisation is at a cost. As exim scrips are freely tradable, the premium on Rep licences is likely to zoom and may command 30 per cent to 40 per cent premium, pushing up the cost of expenditure. Any consumer or capital good whether essential or inessential will be freely imported. The Indian economy will be flooded with imported goods and technology. Need for innovations in indigenous technology will be neglected and the small industry will be adversely affected.

Having noted the features and the impact of liberalised trade policy, we now look at the new industrial policy. It encompasses industrial licencing, foreign investments and technology agreements, public sector and MRTP Act. Except for 18 industries, compulsory licencing is abolished. Licence is also not needed for substantial expansion of the existing units. New broadbanding facility for existing units to produce any good without additional investment is introduced. Public sector operations are narrowed down to only 8 industries. Even the 8 industries will be opened up selectively to the private sector. Larger industrial houses covered by the MRTP act are now free to expand, diversify and accumulate any amount of wealth for, the threshold limit of Rs. 100 crores is removed. All shackles on the big industries are taken away. In the sphere of the so called high priority areas, covering 34 industries, foreign equity up to 51 per cent is permitted and automatic approval for technology agreements will be accorded. In the case of other than these 34 industries, the government is not averse to 51 per cent foreign equity participation, but the approvals are not automatic. Even in the case of small scale industries for which some 800 items are reserved, other industrial units including foreign companies can participate in equity up to 24 per cent. Any person including a big house can establish virtually any industry of its choice anywhere in India, excepting in cities with more than 1 million population. Even in these cities also, units can be established outside 25 kms of the periphery. For all new projects, PMP (Phased Manufacturing Programme which insists upon indigenisation of production in course of time) is abolished. Privatisation of select public enterprises up to 20 per cent of government share-holding is proposed.

As to the banking and financial sector reforms, already the RBI enhanced interest rates across the board including the bank rate by one per cent point. Keeping in view the stipulated minimum lending rates, banks are given free hand to charge any higher interest rate by discriminating different customers. The same is proposed to be extended to the term lending development financial institutions with 15 per cent minimum interest rate. Already the government appointed Narasimham Committee which covers structure, organisation, functions and procedures of financial system and will suggest measures to enhance viability and improve competitive efficiency.

What will be the impact of the radical changes in the trade, industrial and financial policies on employment, social justice, nature of product-mix, disparities in income and wealth, self-reliance and balanced regional development? The government in the opening para of the document on new industrial policy notes carefully the long term objectives set out by Nehru such as rapid expansion of opportunities for gainful employment, progressive reduction of social and economic disparities, removal of poverty and attainment of self-reliance. Speeding up of industrialisation is to be viewed as an instrument to attain socialist pattern of society. Need for development and utilisation of indigenous technology has been endorsed. The goal of balanced regional development set out in the early 70s is well recognised.

The present government acknowledge these goals but only for cosmetic show. It says that any change in macro-economic policies including industrial policy must contribute to the realisation of these goals. It is strange to note and difficult to digest the assertion of the government that the new industrial policy is inspired by the aforesaid concerns. Neither the changes in the trade, industrial and financial policies nor the budget proposals accord any explicit importance to regulate the product-mix, techniques of production and conscious allocation of investment among sectors and sub-sectors. The macroeconomic policies and the budget blatantly forget the intricate relation between the type of goods produced, techniques used and the attendant distribution of income, impact on employment generation, price stability and sustainability of growth prospects. It is unfortunate to record here that our authorities ignore elementary principles of development economics such as the close nexus between production, accumulation, technical progress, employment, stability and distribution. Repeatedly, under the grab of competitiveness, survival, integration with world economy and the euphemistic efficiency unrelated to the well-being of bottom 40 per cent of the people, the present government is blindly implementing more vigorously various reforms. Which entail serious side-effects. Notwithstanding the National Renewal Fund and other measures, the interest of existing workers is at danger, let alone the fate of neo-labour force entry into the industry. Removal of bottlenecks and inefficiencies affecting growth are welcome but they undermine the desired product-mix, income distribution and employment opportunities.

We have sympathy with Yaswant Sinha who rightly described the industrial policy as a retreat and a total drift from socialist pattern charted out by Nehru in the fifties. India can not remain in isolation and the economy should be integrated with the global economies. However, we should not forget that integration has to be a two way process. The IACs shut their gates and insists on India's to be open. Unilateral integration tantamounts to object surrender in the hands of the mighty MNCs. A little knowledge of the 1990 "Trade Reforms Report on India" prepared by the IBRD clearly tells that the new industrial policy is nothing but a recipe of the world bank. We have merely put Indian label on foreign solution. We and the third world have ample experience with the MNCs who bring only second hand technology. Therefore, the 51 per cent foreign equity participation and automatic approvals for technology agreements will permit the foreigners to dump mainly their obsolete technology on the Indian soil. While privatising the public enterprises, we forget the tremendous contribution of the public sector to industrial development and infrastructure facilities. If they are inefficient and undergoing losses, the causes should be identified and remedial steps are to be taken. Nobody likes excessive bureaucratization in public sector, but privatisation is not a panacea for the ills.

As to the industries reserved for the public sector, compulsory licencing, automatic approval of foreign technology agreements and 51 per cent foreign equity participation, a few anomalies stand out. Barring rail transport, which is reserved for the public sector, other modes of transport as also electricity do not figure explicitly in any of the three annexures. From the general tone and tenor, we may infer that they are also left to the private sector. It is surprising to find sugar, paper and newsprint under compulsory licencing. We do not know why should these industries need licence. They do not fall under security-strategic fields. Finally, no convincing reason is given for the abolition of PMP. The vague reasoning is that the new policy and devaluation have built-in disincentive to use imported components (cf. TCA Srinivas Raghavan, *Economic Times*,[21] July 29, 1991). Although we welcome simplified procedures and debureaucratisation envisaged in the industrial and trade policies, we are afraid that they lead to increased concentration, retrenchment and asset concentration. Balanced regional development, self-reliance and the goals of poverty and unemployment elimination will remain only in the document of plans.

VI

Budget Proposals

Compared with the earlier budgets, the 1991-92 budget has certain constraints. Notwithstanding his ample education, training and experience, as Singh was under heavy compulsions, he could not do much justice to present a true development-oriented budget giving direction to the long term tasks. Under the given internal and external milieu, the tried to satisfy the Fund-Bank without courting much displeasure from the domestic interest groups. In fact, Singh's budget represents the tail and of the happenings and hence, it echoes the spirit of various so called reforms already effected. Within the constraints, he exhibited skill and talent to distribute the carrots and use the sticks at his command. It is more in the nature of a holding operation rather than a tool to consciously direct scarce resources. To use Singh's words, the main objective of the budget is to bring about a credible fiscal correction.

To be fair, he seems to have succeeded in reducing the deficit from 8.4 per cent to 6.5 per cent of GDP and those of revenue and the narrowly defined budget deficit by about 1 per cent point each. But the whole approach to fiscal deficit reduction is wrong. The focus is to be on pruning the revenue deficit rather than not even the traditional overall budget deficit.

Another more important issue is how the reduction in the deficit is achieved. While implementing the austerity measures, from common man's welfare point of view, the axe should fall on the people who can bear, Contrary to this principle; virtually there is no change in the relative contributions of direct and indirect taxes to the total tax revenue. It is worth to note here that in 1950 the relative share of indirect taxes was 67 per cent and today it is around 85 per cent. As proportion to GDP, it was 4.1 per cent in 1950 and today around 15 per cent. Thus the government has been relying heavily on indirect tax revenue instead of direct taxes. Remember also here that in the total revenue receipts, tax revenue accounts for a share of 85 per cent. We are afraid that the Budget proposals will entail indirect tax-GDP ratio to rise rather than decrease, and thereby contribute to inflationary pressures. One of the reasons for not raising direct tax revenue perceptibly is that the IMF is against hikes in direct taxes, for it believes that they discourage efficiency, savings and investment. The Fund is not bothered about equity or capacity to pay.

Let us consider increase in the gross tax revenue between 1990-91 (RE) and 1991-92 (BE). While the increase in the direct tax revenue is about Rs. 1770 crores, the corresponding figure for direct taxes is much higher — around Rs. 2200 crores. Notwithstanding this stark truth, the rich industrialists are making big hue and cry focusing attention only on the hike in corporation tax. Further, the increment in total tax revenue is about Rs. 3900 crores and not Rs. 2600 crores as mentioned in the budget document. To this we have to add Rs. 1600 crores due to the increase in the prices of petroleum products, Rs. 2000 crores due to hikes in fertilizer, prices, Rs. 10000 crores being the revenue from enhancement of fares and freight of the Railways and probably another Rs. 2000 crores due to the proposed increase in the prices of coal and other mineral products. All these add up to over Rs. 10000 crores. Can the economy bear these imports? What is their impact on inflationary pressures and distribution of income? It is our common knowledge that when taxes are raised or administered prices are enhanced, the traders and industrialists utilise the opportunity to add their own share and therefore pressures will be severe on cost inflation. Contrary to the view of the government which places the impact of the budget on prices at just one per cent, the rise in prices will be much higher.

Growth prospects and inflationary pressures, inter alia, depend not only on how the government operations including development outlays are financed but also on how the pooled funds are spent. Notice here that the governments are the biggest spender in the economy and their expenditure constitutes about a third of the GDP. Any significant change in its expenditure pattern is sure to affect prices and growth process. Of the total expenditure of about Rs. 1134 bn, plan expenditure is 29.7 per cent and the remainder is non-plan expenditure, (Table 11.7). In absolute terms, there is increase in the plan outlay at Rs. 430 bn but in real terms (adjusted for the present CPI of 13.6 per cent) central plan outlay records diminution. Also there is a decline in the budgetary support (from 46% to 44% between 1990-91 and 1991-92) to the plan outlay. The implication is that the public enterprises should contribute more by way of internal and extra budgetary resources. The three options for the public enterprise are improving their efficiency, increasing their administered prices and borrowing from the market. Under the present conditions, the former is only a pious hope and based on the past experience, they are sure to resort to the soft option of raising their product prices. With the present philosophy of the government, the enterprises will be forced to obtain finances from the market through the issue of bonds and debentures. It is reported that in the 8 months of the current fiscal year, central public sector units alone will float bonds worth about Rs. 6000 crores.[21] Ignoring for a moment the capability of the Indian capital market to absorb the bonds, let us enquire into its impact on costs and returns. It is feared that the increasing dependence on market finance will further blur the profitability image of the public enterprises. In cases the market fails to fully finance their needs, either the plan outlay will be compressed or the overall budget deficit will increase to maintain the targeted plan outlay. In all probability, the government will reduce capital expenditure rather than revenue expenditure. One expects from the budget an idea about the magnitudes of monetary and fiscal adjustments necessitated by the devaluation and railway budget. Unfortunately, these are not reflected in the budget. In the 1991-92 annual plan, capital expenditure in absolute terms is placed at lower level — Rs. 8395 crores as against Rs. 8857 crores in 1990-91, vide Table 10.7. As against this, there is 21.5 per cent increase in the revenue expenditure. The reason given by the government for the enhancement is that it provides safety net to minimise costs of adjustments on the poor. The higher revenue expenditure will enable enhanced outlays in social services providing work opportunities and poverty amelioration in rural area. Government professes to accord high priority to unemployment and poverty reduction of the rural masses. But a look at the allocation pattern of the plan outlay given in Table 11.7 does not vouch the concern of the government. We do not

TABLE 11.7: Plan Outlay of Government of India

(Rs. in crores)

Head of Expenditure		1990-91 (RE)	1991-92 (BE)
		1	2
I. Total Revenue—Plan Expenditure		14020	17960
of which	Central Plan	8737	10620
	Central Assistance to States & UTs	5283	6448
II. Total Capital—Plan Expenditure		15936	16657
of which	Central plan	8857	8395
	Central Assistance to States & UTs	7079	8262
III. Total Plan Outlay(I+II)		29956	33725
IV. Row III as % of Total Expenditure		28.1	29.7

Pattern of Central Plan Outlay

(per cent)

	Sector	1990-91 (RE)	1990-92 (BE)
1.	Agriculture & Rural Development	10.4	10.6
2.	Irrigation & Flood Control	0.5	0.6
3.	Energy	31.9	31.5
4.	Industry & Minerals	18.7	16.6
5.	Transport & Communications	26.7	25.4
6.	Social Services	9.5	11.5
7.	Others	3.0	3.8
	Total	100.0 (38053)	100.0 (42969)

Source: 1991-92 Budget, Government of India.
Note: Figs in parentheses are total plan outlay in Rs. crores.

find any perceptible change in the allocation pattern of the annual plan for 1991-92 compared with the 7th plan period or the interim budget of the last year. Consider allocation to agriculture and rural development. In 1991-92 and 1990-91 the allocations are almost the same — about

10.5 per cent. Similar pattern is easily observable from the Table with regard to other sectors barring social service. The latter's relative share is enhanced from 9.5 per cent to 11.5 per cent points. Also its share of 11.5 per cent is fairly higher than the 7th plan average of 9.9 per cent. In brief, both in the patterns of revenue raising and spending, we do not find any significant departure. The budget was tailored to reflect and accommodate macro economic reforms dictated by the Fund-Bank, hence, the impact of the budget on growth, social justice and price stability will be similar to the earlier budgets. But surely, the reduce capital expenditure and budgetary support to the central plan will inhibit growth prospects and impose higher burdens on the weak financial health of public enterprises.

VII

Slashing Imports and Rescheduling the Debt — the Best Solution

Importance of foreign trade in industrialisation and economic development is widely acknowledged. But to what extent and for what type of goods, a vast country like India should depend is the real issue. In the long run, we can not think of importing unless we have capacity to pay, which is conditioned by the value of our exports. Self-reliance with respect of basic goods and technology should be the long term goal. Countries such as India which began their industrialisation efforts lately are at disadvantage. Hence, to start with a country should import select crucial inputs and equipment. Gradually the basket of imports may be expanded as the country acquires capacity to export remunerative and less-import intensive goods.

LDCs have to depend for some time mainly on primary products exports to finance imports. All the same dependence on primary products exports works to their disadvantage. Compared with the earlier decades, now the empirical base of Prebisch-Singer hypothesis of secular deterioration of terms of trade of the LDCs is stronger.* It is also revealed that the LDCs relying on primary products exports

* Often the success story of South Korea is quoted to highlight the benefits of outward-orientation. Apart from her unique culture and socio-economic background, her success was due to the US Funds and assured exports. Further, the Korean government extended artificial encouragement and insured export profits. According to one estimate[20] subsidies and tax concessions accounted for 30 per cent of the total value of exports.

should not place confidence in free market. Let us scrutinize the composition of our exports to assess our disadvantage. Even now bulk of the exports are agro and extractive industries products and the 3-star sectors (Jewellery, Leather and Leather Products, etc.), Jems and Jewellery, Readymade Garments including Cotton Fabrics, Leather, and Leather manufactures together claim about 45 per cent share. The modern sectors of Engineering and Chemicals contribute only a fourth to our exports. Unless major sudden changes occur, with the existing structure of our exports it is futile to expect that India will gain from expansion of international trade. Under the scented words of competitiveness and efficiency, trade liberalisation policies are vigorously supported, notwithstanding bitter historical experience.

It is worth to record here that on the domestic front, growth profile or physical performance of the Indian economy has been fairly satisfactory, although pattern of distribution of income is awkward. Since 5th plan, average annual GDP growth rate has been around 5 per cent composed of about 3 per cent growth of agriculture and 8 per cent growth of industries. We are lucky that in a row of 3 years, agriculture recorded excellent results. Our foodgrain production peaked to the all time record of 176 mt, with 21 mt, of buffer stocks. Only with regard to external front, we are in serious troubles. To overcome the difficulty, we should concentrate on the culprit of ever growing imports. As exports can not be pushed up aggressively, the focus should be on be drastically scaling down the imports. Prabhat Patnaik informs that China adopted this route to cure her BOP problem. (cf. *Economic Times*, July 21, 1991). Let us identify the imports which need sizing. All the goods which directly or indirectly serve the elitist consumption should be the first target. Some of the major projects, requiring huge imports and needed for long term development, are to be deferred. Even in the defence imports, there is room for reduction, By restricting the production of 2-Wheelers and passenger cars, and simultaneously expanding public transport, perceptible economies in the POL bill can be realised. It is worth to recall here that this bill claims a share of nearly a fourth in the total imports. To improve terms of trade and diversify trade, SAARC cooperation is to be intensified.* As to then solution of immediate payments obligations, India should negotiate with the creditors for rescheduling the debt. A number of

* Notice here that nearly two-thirds of our exports are directed towards six IACs — USA, USSR, Japan, Germany, UK and Belgium.

Latin American countries faced with the debt hang-over adopted the method in the eighties. We may also think of sale or mortgage of the gold weighing about 300 tonnes under the custody of RBI. By doing so we get $ 4 bn. Ignoring sentiments, there is no other use to gold except its sale in times of emergency. The aforesaid are a few alternatives to the solution of high conditionality loan of the IMF and the alternatives do not endanger any "side effects".

Epilogue

In the foregoing we endeavoured to map and analyse the recent significant changes in macroeconomic policies as well as the budget for 1991-92. The external financial gap is indeed very alarming. The debt was allowed to become unmanageable by the successive governments. Since the mid 80s gaps in trade, current and overall external accounts started widening. Although both exogenous and endogenous factors worked against India's BOP, endogenous factors such as the import liberalization policy of the mid 80s and reckless spending of the government stand out singularly. Behind the liberalization policy lies the dynamics of international capitalism, functioning under the godfather of pseudodemocratic multilateral institutions viz., the Fund-Bank. Most of the present day maladies including the BOP constraints can be traced to an important policy shift in the 80s namely dilution of the role of government in industrial planning. It is this policy shift which led to boom in imports and elitist consumption without any beneficial impact on employment. The government is doing precisely the same now but more vigorously under the grab of economic reforms.

The first radical act of the new government namely devaluation was unwarranted. Relative gains are little compared to the heavy sacrifice involved. We appreciate most of the trade reforms with a few reservations. The most disquieting step of the government is with regard to the so called reforms in the industrial field. The new industrial policy in the name of competition, efficiency and integration committed crime and constitutes a big blow to the whole gamut of planned development which India carefully nursed over four decades. The goals of self-reliance, reduction in concentration of economic power, balanced regional development and abolition of poverty and unemployment are left to the winds. As the industrial policy does not even mention the required nature of the product-mix and techniques of production, under the given structure of skewed distribution of income, production will be as per the dictates of the middle and upper classes, Consequently, none will care to look into the needs of the poor and utilization of their vast un-and under-utilised manpower. The Budget presented by Manmohan Singh is merely a tail-end operation and lends support to the IMF's prescriptions. It is no more a tool to consciously direct the resources, regulate the product-mix or techniques of production.

Our debt crisis is used as an opportunity by the big powers to influence their domestic choice and impose on us their alien values, policies and pattern of development. Debureaucratisation, exchange rate adjustment, competitive efficiency, liberalization and integration with global economies are all laudable principles and form the standard IMF package. But they cannot be practised by every economy irrespective of stage of development and basic domestic problems. Blind emulation will cause further ruination.

Social and political costs of the policies are heavy. Even if the suggested policies succeed in improving the BOP position in the short run, they have a recessionary and destabilizing influence on the economy. To correct them, again we will be compelled to approach the Fund Bank under much worse economic scenario. The whole burden of adjustment under the present impaired world is thrown on the weak, without any complementary adjustments in the LACs.

The policy changes instead of strengthening our industrial structure is likely to impair and deindustrialise the economy. Unless the poisonous medicines are antedated, the economy will face low growth, high inflationary pressures, social and political tensions, rising disparities in income and asset distribution and widening dualism. The structural adjustment programmes implemented in the Latin American countries. Turkey and Sri Lanka provide ample evidence to the aforementioned evils. The unemployed and the assetless are always the victims of austerity measures dictated by the IMF. We are told that Kirit Parikh while recommending a trial to the Fund-Bank reforms, suggested an All India Employment Guarantee Scheme which may cost some Rs. 16000 crores. Pooling this amount is not difficult if the government slashes all covert subsidies and facilities enjoyed by the rich and make them to contribute their due share. It is unfortunate that the government, chose to implement the reforms without a comprehensive supporting scheme for the poor and unemployed. We are helpless to conclude that the recent changes in the macroeconomic policies and the Budget proposals will cause much damage to the Indian economy in general and the bottom 40 per cent of the people in particular, let alone the severe below to our democracy and sovereignty.

NOTES

1. I owe to Prof A. Nagraj for the continuum of invisible blessings and to Dr AK Vasudeva chary and Mr. G. Ramalingam for technical help. This is the thoroughly revised version of the author's earlier paper presented to the SEMINAR on "India's Economic Crisis & Policy Options", organized by the Deptt. of Economics, OU, Hyderabad on July 31, 1991.
2. Government of India : *Economic Survey, 1990-91*, Ministry of Finance, Delhi, 1991 and *The Economic Times*, July 21 '91.
3. CMIE: *Basic Statistics Relating to the Indian Economy*, Vol.I, Bombay, Aug, 1991, Table 21.6.
4. According to the Economic Survey, 1990-91, it is 21 per cent. However, this excludes obligations of NRI and other short term deposits.
5. GC da Costa : *India's Balance of Payments*, Himalaya, Bombay, 1990. [See review of the Book by M Anagol, *EPW*, 26(27&28), 1991].
6. Sunil Mani : "External Liberalisation and Import Dependence", *EPW* 26(27&28), 1991.
7. PA Seshan : "Severity of Gulf Crisis:, *The Hindu, July 25, 1991*.
8. E Weisner : "Domestic and External Causes of the Latin American Debt Crisis", *Finance and Development*, 22(1) 1985.
9. While Non-development expenditure : (such as interest, defence and public administration) may be treated as necessary evil, Non-plan expenditure confers real benefits. The latter is incurred for running and maintaining already completed projects, as also improvements in Non-plan services. With regard to Development expenditure financed from Capital and Revenue accounts, it is incurred to provide social, community and general services. It is interesting to point out here that while interest, defence and subsidies are all shown under Non-Plan, subsidies are classified under Development (Revenue) expenditure and those of interest and defence are treated Non-Development, for details see,
   S Krishan Rao : "India's Rising Internal Debt: Is it Bane or Boon?", *Indian Economic Association*, Conference No., 1989.
10. During 1980-91, while plan expenditure rose at 12.8 per cent p.a., Non-Plan expenditure increased at 19.4 per cent p.a. With regard to the relative share of plan expenditure in the total government expenditure (which was around Rs. 107000 crores in 1990-91 RE), the proportion has been declining and today it is 28 per cent. For details see, budget proposals of Government of India, presented to the Parliament on 24.7.1991.
11. Government of India, *Economic Survey*, op.cit.
12. D. Ghosh : "Global Resources and International Conflict", Review of AH Westing's Book, *Economic and Political Weekly*, 22(27), 1987.
13. We discussed at length similar agenda elsewhere. For details see,
    S Kishan Rao : "International Debt-Aid-Liquidity Crisis", *Indian Economic*

Association, Conference No. 1987.

14. A Ghosh : "IMF Loan" Some Implications" *The Hindu*, July 7, 1991.
15. *Financial Times*, London, July 21, 1991.
16. IBRD : *World Development Report 1990*, Washington, DC, 1990, p. 230.
17. R Ramachandran : "Liberalisation, Japanese Style", *Economic Times*, July 7, 1991.
18. *Economic Times*, July 2, 1991.
19. N Chandhra Mohan : "Devaluation — Unwarranted on Merits", *Economic Times*, July 7, 1991.
20. EE Hagen, *The Economics of Development*, RD Irwin, Illinois, 1975, p. 475.
21. *Economic Times*, July 29, 1991.

APPENDIX

OUTSTANDING EXTERNAL DEBT OF INDIA

(US $ mn)

Year	Public/Publicly guaranteed		Private Non guaranteed	Total long term Credit (4=1+2+3)	Short term Debt	Use of I.M.F. Credit	Total External Debt
	Official Creditors	Private Creditors					
1	2	3	4	5	6	7	8
1980	16315	2007	336	18658 (2130)	926	977	20561
1981	17313	811	873	18997	1204	659	20860
1982	18462	1289	1239	20990	1827	2279	25096
1983	19627	1783	1767	23177	1573	3899	28449
1984	19065	6139	1341	26545 (5962)	2856	4456	33857
1985	22483	8944	1497	32924 (8295)	3129	4832	40885
1986	26064	12872	1350	40286 (11108)	3297	4768	48351
1987	30052	16079	1652	47783 (14364)	3519	4023	55325
1988	31056	18639	1473	51168 (16518)	3772	2573	67513
1989	33075	23732	1520	58387 (21602)	4022	1701	64050
1990	35529	28373	1598	65500 (25509)	4283	—	—

Source: CMIE, August, 1990

Note: Figures in parentheses are total debt to commercial banks.

12

X-CRISIS*

J.S. NARAYAN RAO and Y. PUSHPALATHA

THIS IS a small note on export-crisis, X-crisis, of the Indian Economy, which is made out to be "the Mother of all Crises" facing the economy, resulting, among other things, in the unprecedented "devaluation", officially described as exchange rate adjustment, of the rupee twice to the extent of 18 per cent in the first week of July 1991,[1] and of the X-policy of "do-or-die",[2] to meet the BoP crisis of some Rs. 10,000 crores, for 1991-92,[3] which has sent the nation scurrying of the IMF for a loan of some $ 7 billion.[4]

The crisis seems to be a quite long-standing[5] which it seems, is getting aggravated with the passage of time.[6] In what follows, we make a note of the "Crisis", and see how it can be met.

The importance of Xs, as one of the sources of National Income (x-M), for the economy, needs no argumentation.[7] India, for long, was associated with Xs and a leading X-er.[8] After Independence, it should have gone back to this position. Contrary, however, to this, India's position in the world-x-trade is nose-diving, Table 11.1, which is a folk table.

The falling share of India in the world X-trade is the crisis of India's Xs. The trend needs to be reversed, and it seems a bit already in the 80s (Table 12.1 col. and row 5). It means that Indian goods, relatively, are selling less and less in the world markets. There in other words, they are not rated much. This is a big loss of external economic face. That means, in Xs, we are not living up to our Joanses. The

* Dedicated to the halpless Indians, we included, groaning under the increasing obligation to X-port at any cost.

nation, in sum, is counted as an inferior X-nation, meaning the economy has either no goods to export or that they are not much in demand. The results of this crisis of X-trade are terrible, or can be envisaged to be so. It means, at some two per cent share of world X-trade, loss of some Rs. 80,000 crores Xs in 1989-90. Now, the question is whether the economy has so much X-capacity? Certainly not. Accordingly, Xs needs to be helped through massive productions, at competitive rates, of exportable commodities. Poor nations, in short, cannot be great X-ting nations. They may be great M-ing ones, which India appears to be notwithstanding its poor FOREX reserves. The declining share is at the back of the X-crisis.

TABLE 12.1: India's share in world Xs

(Rs. in crores)

Sl. No.	Year	World Exports	India's Exports	Exports as % of World Exports
(1)	(2)	(3)	(4)	(5)
1.	1950-51	27318.19	601.00	2.2
2.	1960-61	55018.34	606.22	1.2
3.	1970-71	243676.20	1535.16	0.63
4.	1980-81	1560697.70	6711.00	0.43
5.	1989-90	4943035.75	27681.00	0.56

Source: Economic Intelligence Service, *Basic Statistics*, Vol. I, August, 1990. Bombay, 1990.

Note: Xs given in Uncle Sam's $ for Indian Public consumption are given in rupees though the rupee is made out to be a worthless commodity.

Did 1949, 1966 Devaluation Help?

Are we helped by the 1949 and 1966 devaluations?[9] Have they, in other words, helped restore the nation's position in the world export-trade and bridge the M-X gap, if not turn it into X-M? Definitely not, according to the facts. India's J-Curve appears to yet take-off or turn upward. In the 80s, it started looking up a bit, from 0.43 per cent to 0.56 per cent (see Table 12.1). But, it is due to the exchange rate adjustment said to be in vogue since 1983, resulting in some 70 per cent devaluation of the rupee *vis-a-vis* U.S. $ or the Hindu rate of growth of some 3.5 per cent becoming > 5 per cent Indian Xs, in devaluation, are said to flicket only a bit.[10] The approach is monetarist". The fault is not too much money, but money failing to deliver the goods.

Notwithstanding Manmohan Singh,[11] India appears to have not come out form X-Fatalism. When things are looking up a bit, blow appears to have been struck to X-confidence of the nation, through a third devaluation, seeing that the first and second devaluations had not much salvaged the situation. The rupee was not overvalued. It could not have been with so much of deficit financing, inflation in evidence in the economy.[12] We anyhow were self-deprecating through the so-called exchange-rate adjustment, calling for no further devaluation. One wonders whether any nation with so much lack of self-assurance can make a mark in X-trade. We Indians are trying to exchange the old East India Company for new East India Companies, like old lamps for new in the Aladdin story, and others to fight our X-battles. We seem to feel good for nothing.

The reason for the fall of India in world X-trade is that the pattern of world Xs might have changed greatly and we are not moving with the times. The recent move appears to have only elongated the Indian J-curve, or further pulled it down. Devaluations appear to give us only T, not J-Curves, viz. further depreciate our Xs.

That Xs are failing us in a number of ways can be discerned from a number of ways. First, the X-sector is shrinking *vis-a-vis* the domestic economy (Table 12.2).

TABLE 12.2: Share of Xs in national income.

(Rs. in crores)

Sl.No.	Year	Y	X	X/Y
1.	1950-51	9136	601.00	6.57
2.	1960-61	13999	660.22	4.72
3.	1970-71	42879	1535.16	3.58
4.	1980-81	136125	6711.00	4.93
5.	1989-90	433192	27681.00	6.39
6.	1990-91	493243.25	36500.50	7.40

Source: Economic Intelligence Service, *Basic, Statistics,* Vol. I, August, 1990, CMIE, Bombay, 1990.

Apparently, the 50s and the 60s were specially bad for Xs. They started looking up or brightening from the 70s and picked up to the 80s, and may look forward with confidence for the 90s. Thus, Xs not only lost in foreign ground but domestic ground also. That is, Indian trade looked more and more inside or became introvert rather then extrovert. The trade, export, seemed more and more inward looking. That means, as could be very well understood, so much loss of national income, FOREX, employment and modernisation. Now, happily, Indian X-ers appears to have become more and more assertive and outward looking.

Yet, the situation of (M-X) is worsening, in spite of Xs picking up both in terms of Xl/Xw and X/Y, viz. as share in world Xs and share in National Incomes, both in terms of trade, BOT, and trade and services, BOP, which can be discerned from Tables 12.3 and 12.4.

TABLE 12.3: **Balance of trade**

(Rs. in crores)

Sl.No.	Year	M	X	BOT
1.	1950-51	650	601	-49
2.	1960-61	1106	630	-476
3.	1970-71	1826	1404	-422
4.	1980-81	12544	6576	-5967
5.	1990-91	44000	3650	-7500

Source: Economic Intelligence Service, *Basic Statistics*, Vol. I, August, 1990, CMIE, Bombay, 1990.

TABLE 12.4: **Balance of payment**

(Rs. in crores)

Sl. No.	Year	BOT	Net invisible earnings	BOP
1.	1950-51	-49		-49
2.	1960-61	-476	+83	-393
3.	1970-71	-422	-28	-450
4.	1980-81	-5967	+4311	-1656
5.	1988-89	-14002	+3573	-10428

Source: economic Intelligence Service, *Basic Statistics*, Vol. 1, August, 1990, CMIE, Bombay, 1990.

Obviously, LDCs, of which India is an excellent case in the sense of a well-underdeveloped nation,[13] imports goods, raw-materials and machinery, which must be met by Xs. In this, Indian Xs, seem to be greatly failing. Both BOT and BOP are negative due to a crisis in Xs, or the failure of Xs to keep up with Ms.

Why Prod a Dry Cow?

BoT and BoP are increasingly in the red, meaning rising M-X. Xs are not keeping up with Ms. But, as there are limits to X-capacity, there should also be M-capacity of a nation. We, however, appear to be oblivious of that import capacity, and for an undeveloped nation we appear to like to enjoy the best "fruits", and "wines"of all nations. That is, unless Ms are reined in, Xs may not run beyond their capacity, however hard we may flog them. What is the use of, say, prodding a dry cow? For, afterall, we should not be "one-eyed Jacks", oblivious to M-performance. That Xs are rallying and are trying to come out of the woods of stagnation can be seen in Table 12.5, but are falling behind Ms.

TABLE 12.5: X and M growth (Compound) (%)[14]

(p.a.)

Sl.No.	Year	M	X
1.	1948-49 to 1965-66	6.0	3.0
2.	1966-67 to 1972-73	-1.8	9.3
3.	1973-79 to 1989-90	16.8	16.2

Source: Economic Intelligence Service, *Basic Statistics*, Vol. 1, August, 1990, CMIE, Bombay, 1990.

That Xs are picking up and trying to even up with Ms is to be seen in Table 12.5. There growth rate during 1948-49 has gone up, from a bare 3 per cent, well behind M's 6 per cent, to 9.3 per cent in 1966-67 to 1972-73 to further 16.2 per cent during 1973-74 to 1989-90. Where from here? What is more, they are trying to even up with Ms which stand at 16.8 per cent.

Now have we gone back on our earlier assertion of a grave X-Crisis facing the nation? No. Then, what are we trying to drive home? That the scenario is improving bit-by-bit. Quite Herculean tasks are needed to take the share of India's Xs to 2.2 per cent level of world X-trade. We are, indeed, in deep X-crisis. The crisis, truly, must be related to this. All other symptoms of the crisis flow from this. The crisis is deep and it is related to the general economic crisis.

In Tables 12.6–12.12, we present further profiles of Xs, regarding the direction, composition, determinants, etc.

First, direction X-destinations are six: 1. Africa, 2. USA, 3. Central and South America, 4. Asia, 5. West Europe, and 6. East Europe.

Of these the USA and Europe may be regarded as the X-Meccas. BOT with these were shown in 12.6.

Thus, barring the USA, a chance surplus of Rs. 319 crores, and with Eastern Europe a substantial Rs. 1,408 crores due to rupee trade which, with the disappearance of the Eastern Block, may not be now forthcoming, the nation is running deficits of trade with every trading destination (see Table 12.7). And of the 10 major trading partners, viz. USA, USSR, Japan, U.K., Germany, UAE, Belgium, Italy, Saudi Arabia and France, the nation, strangely, has X-M with only the USA and USSR to the extent of some Rs. 1,000 crores (see Table 12.8).

In other words, X-crisis is multi-dimensional. Vide Table 12.9, X-commodities fall into the following five categories: 1. Agricultural and Allied Products, 2. Ore and Minerals, 3. Manufactured Goods, 4. Mineral Fuels and Lubricants, and 5. Others.

Of these, the third, manufactured goods, happily are the bed-rock of Xs to the extent of 62.7 per cent. Given, however, industrial inelasticities of the nation, such as infrastructural, how far Xs of these goods can be pushed up is a question.

Again, giving India's share (see Table 12.10) in world tea, spices, tobacco, iron ore, leather goods, textiles and cotton Xs, in which the nation has an X-name, much to our discomfiture, even during the X-dynamic 80s, the nation's share is falling except in iron and spices meaning that the nation is becoming less and less competitive X-wise. Thus, the crisis appears to encompass major goods with which the nation's name is greatly associated in world X-trade. As such, wherever we turn there seem to be dark clouds on X-horizon. They appear to be up against the hills and fighting a losing battle. Still, devaluation appears not to be the sole remedy. It appears to devalue Xs.

TABLE 12.6: **Regional imbalances:**

Sl.No.	Country	1970-71	1980-81	1988-89
1.	Africa	(-)	(+)	(-)
2.	USA	(-)	(-)	(+)
3.	C. and S. America	(-)	(-)	(-)
4.	Asia	(+)	(+)	(-)
5.	W. Europe	(-)	(-)	(-)
6.	E. Europe	(+)	(-)	(+)

Source: Worked out.

TABLE 12.7: Region-wise foreign trade

(Rs. in crores)

Sl.No.	Region	1970-71			1980-81			1988-89		
		X	M	BOT	X	M	BOT	X	M	BOT
1.	Africa	139	170	-31	435	265	170	497	1016	-519
2.	North America	235	583	-348	806	1851	-1045	3934	3623	+311
3.	Central and South America	10	16	-6	36	380	-344	119	606	-487
4.	Asia	481	300	+181	2267	5741	3474	6417	10872	-4461
5.	West Europe	299	349	-50	1653	3017	-1364	5474	104114	-4640
6.	Eastern European	362	226	+136	1486	2390	-904	3356	1948	+1408
7.	Countries									.1408
	Total	1535	1634	-99	6711	12549	-5838	20295	28194	-7899

Source: Economic Intelligence Service, *Basic Statistics*, Vol. 1, August, 1990.

TABLE 12.8: India's trade with top ten trading partners

(Rs. in crores)

S.No.	Year	USA	USSR	JAPAN	UK	West Germany	UAE	Belgium	Italy	Saudi Arabia	France	Total Include all
1	2	3	4	5	6	7	8	9	10	11	12	13
1.	1980-81	-778	+212	-241	-338	-309	-198	-151	-91	-375	-133	-5838
2.	1981-82	-485	+524	-181	-397	-547	-260	-335	-79	-650	-106	-5802
3.	1982-83	-499	+257	-254	-491	-491	-161	-418	-106	-1269	-280	-5490
4.	1983-84	-378	-417	-618	-661	-716	-58	-434	-119	-855	-129	-6060
5.	1984-85	+65	+92	-211	-321	-801	-90	-601	-84	-991	-166	-5390
6.	1985-86	-90	+328	-610	-326	-1031	-379	-726	-113	-573	-380	-8763
7.	1986-87	+445	+862	-1257	-961	-1185	-81	-753	-151	-649	-414	-7644
8.	1987-88	+918	+355	-513	-813	-1110	-453	-886	-14	-488	-418	-6503
9.	1988-89	+540	+1351	-471	-1236	-1235	-455	-1152	+37	-1568	-390	-7899
10.	1989-90	+244	+702	-129	-874	-451	-294	-696	+32	-396	-139	-3131

Source: Economic Intelligence Service, *Basic Statistics*, Vol. 1, August, 1990.

TABLE 12.9: Exports by major commodity groups : value and percentage

(Rs. in crores)

Sl.No.	Commodity Group	1960-61	1970-71	1980-81	1986-87
1.	Agricultural and Allied Products	258.70 (40.70)	487.01 (31.7)	2056.66 (30.7)	3422 (27.5)
2.	Ore and Minerals	77.00 (11.9)	164.02 (10.7)	413.56 (6.2)	717 (5.7)
3.	Manufacture Goods	277.72 (43.1)	771.97 (50.3)	3741.81 (55.8)	7808 (62.7)
4.	Mineral Fuels and Lubricants	7.4% (1.1)	12.60 (0.8)	27.85 (0.4)	418 (3.4)
5.	Others	21.49 (3.2)	99.56 (6.5)	465.82 (6.9)	87 (0.7)
6.	Total	642.32 (100)	1535.16 (100)	6710.70 (100)	12452 (100)

Source: A.N. Agrawal and others, *Indian, Economic Information Year Book*, 1990, p.185.

Note: Figures in brackets indicate percentage to the total.

TABLE 12.10: India's share in world exports of principal commodities

Sl.No	Commodity	percentage	
		1980	1986
1	2	3	4
1.	Tea and Mate	27.7	16.3
2.	Species	14.5	15.5
3.	Tobacco and Tobacco manufactures	2.4	0.6
4.	Iron ore and Concentrates	6.3	8.5
5.	Leather Manufactures and Dressed for Skin	6.8	5.4
6.	Textile Yarn, Fabrics, etc.,	2.3	1.7
7.	Coffee and Coffee Substitutes	2.1	1.4
8.	Pearls, Precious and Semi-precious Stones	3.1	10.00
9.	Feeding Stuff for Animal	1.6	1.1
10.	Others	40.00	39.5
11.	Total	100	100

Source: A.N. Agrawal and others, *Indian Economic Information Year Book, 1990.*

TABLE 12.11: Imports of principal commodities

(Rs. in crores)

Sl.No.	Items	1950-51	1960-61	1970-71	1980-81	1987-88
1	2	3	4	5	6	7
1.	Cereals and Cereal Preparations	99	181	213	100	33
2.	Cashewnuts	3	10	29	9	63
3.	Cotton (raw)	101	82	99	—	N.A.
4.	Wool (raw)	6	10	15	43	79
5.	Crude Rubber	3	11	4	32	108
6.	Mineral Fuels, lubricates and related materials	56	70	137	5266	4083
7.	Animal and Vegetable Boils and Fats	4	5	38	709	N.A.
8.	Organic and Inorganic Chemicals	9	39	68	358	1050
9.	Medical and Pharma-ceutical Products	10	16	24	85	137
10.	Iron and Steel	14	122	147	852	1273
11.	Non-ferrous Metals	28	47	119	477	576
12.	Metal Manufactures	14	23	9	89	177
13.	Machinery and Traces, Port Equipment	124	333	395	1821	4749
14.	Miscellaneous	—	17	33	212	N.A.
15.	Total: Including others	650	1122	1634	12549	22399

Source: Economic Intelligence Service, *Basic Statistics*, Vol. 1, August, 1990.

Meanwhile, giving the imports of some 14 principal commodities in value terms for 1960-61, 1970-71, 1980-81 and 1987-88 (see Table 12.11), fuels, metals and machinery appear to impose heavy M-burden. So, one likes it or not, import suostitution in these matters seems an imperative. The superstructure of Xs, it seems, cannot be built without a sound economic structure.

Yes, Indian Xs are lagging. They are in a crisis. How is the situation to be met? For this, we make a passing foray into the field of X-determinants at rather superficial and layman's level.

X-Determinants: Table 12.12 gives Index numbers of the following variables for the 70s and 80s: 1. Exports (Xs), 2. Imports (Ms), 3. Prices (P), 4. Cash Compensatory Scheme (CCS), 5. Rupees per dollar (S:Rs.) and 6. Gross National Product at Sector Cost (FNP).

TABLE 12.12: Index 1970-71 = 100

Sl.No.	Exports (Y)	Imports X1	Prices X2	CCS X3	Rupees for Dollar value X4	GNP X5
1.	100	100	100	100	100	100
2.	104.75	111.69	102.22	137.25	101.2	107.28
3.	128.40	114.26	113.33	156.24	99.06	118.34
4.	164.36	180.84	137.77	158.00	108.00	143.96
5.	216.87	276.60	173.33	191.35	111.74	170.25
6.	263.32	322.82	186.66	389.70	119.46	183.24
7.	335.05	310.53	197.8	935.33	116.53	197.60
8.	350.09	368.80	222.22	891.55	109.2	223.68
9.	373.00	416.83	222.22	1027.83	108.4	242.82
10.	417.80	559.55	233.33	985.56	104.80	267.27
11.	437.19	768.00	242.22	1078.00	115.46	317.80
12.	508.60	232.8	275.55	1295.39	126.13	372.18
13.	580.33	878.6	293.33	1287.57	134.66	413.09
14.	642.80	964.68	335.60	1244.56	151.46	480.61
15.	772.31	1051.00	377.8	1396.36	164.94	535.99
16.	679.03	1112.2	380.00	1622.94	168.13	609.59
17.	825.21	1229.2	397.80	2093.95	173.06	608.50
18.	1024.30	1367.4	407.90	2582.50	185.60	770.08
19.	1322.14	1725.5	420.60	3420.42	216.26	906.86
20.	183.32	2166.0	425.70	5083.00	230.94	1011.81

Source: Economic Intelligence Service, *Basic Statistics*, Vol. 1, August, 1990.

Xs be Growth-based

In Table 12.12, Ms over-running Xs may be seen. XMs appear to have the closest possible affinity, nearly 1:1. Then the so-called inflation factor, not much, appears to be not much dampening to Xs. Cash Compensation appears to be bloating without fattening Xs. The so-called devaluation appears to be not of much relevance too. Even if it is, its contribution to X-drive is to be put at around 10 per cent. Then the D-School (Devaluationist School) may argue that the rupee is not sufficiently humbled. It is still keeping its head high where it has to keep low. The affinity between X and Y appears to be > 1, establishing the hypothesis of this piece, viz. that Xs be growth-based.

Conclusion

In sum, there is no denying the fact that the Indian economy is in a deep X-crisis. For instance, in 1988-89, where, at 2 per cent share in world Xs, it should have been X-ing worth some Rs. 1,00,000 crores, it is found exporting about Rs. 28,000 crores.[15] The nation has lost ground very steeply in X-trade in the last so many years, from which it is looking up a bit only now.

But, still, there are dark clouds all over the X-horizon, whether in terms of regional trade balances, or falling share in important goods and others.

So, the nation, it seems, needs to branch off into new avenues of Xs. Simultaneously, even though blasphemous to some structuring the base of the economy has also to take place. Because of the bulgeoning BOP, X-crisis may look a national tragedy and of epic dimensions. But the more villainous oil Ms seem to be making Xs look villainous.

However, for X-growth, X-sector need to be treated on more solid and scientific lines than the present *ad-hoc* and perfunctory lines. Indeed, the challenges of X-crisis are formidable. In meeting them, *ipso facto*, we shall meet the other challenges and crises also, significantly.

NOTES

1. *Economic and Political Weekly*, Vol. XXVI, Nos. 27, July 28, 6-13, 1991, pp.1636-37.
2. *The Economic Times*, July 21, 1991, p.1.
3. "IMF Loan to meet Rs. 1,000 Crores Soon", *The Economic Times*, March 25, 1991, New Delhi, p.9.
4. Ravikanth, D., "$ 7 Billion bridge loan sought", *The Economic Times*, May 14, 1991, p.1.
5. Jha, L.K., *India's Foreign Trade*, Eastern Economist Pamphlets, 9, New Delhi, 1950.
6. See the BOP Crisis of India even in the X-dynamic 80s.

(Rs. in crores)

Sl.No.	Year	BOP
1.	1980-81	-1657
2.	1985-86	-5927
3.	1988-89	-10429

Source: Basic Statistics, *op. cit.*

7. Prashad, P., *Some Aspects of Indian Foreign Trade: 1757-1839*, S. King and Sons Ltd., London, 1932, Venkatasubbaiah H., *The Foreign Trade of India*, OUP,

Bombay, 1946.

8. Varshney Roshan Lal, *India's Foreign Trade*, Kitab Mahal, Allahabad, 1954.
9. Sidney S. Alexander, "Efforts of a devaluation on a trade balance", *IMF Staff Papers*, Vol. II, April, 1952, pp.263-78, Bhagawathi, J.N. and Srinivasan, T.N., *Foreign Trade Regimes and Economic Development*, The Macmillan and Company of India Ltd., New Delhi, 1966.
10. Jha, L.K., *India's Foreign Trade*, *op. cit*.
11. Manmohan Singh, *India's Export Trends*, Oxford University Press, New York, 1964.
12. "Present rate of inflation is 12.1 per cent, Economic Survey 1990-91". *The Economic Times*, July 21, 1991, p.11.
13. Varma, S.C., *Millions in Poverty*, Kunj Publishing House, New Delhi, 1984.
14. Our Decade to Decade "Compounds" are:

(p.a.)

Sl. No.	Year	C.G.
1.	1950-60	-0.0669
2.	1961-70	10.3
3.	1971-80	19.35
4.	1981-90	15.02
5.	1950-90	10.79

Source: Estimated.

15. Even for 1991-92, X-targets are only Rs. 41.00 crores, which are quite punny compared to our historical share, *The Economic Times*, July 21, 1991, p.6.

SELECTED BIBLIOGRAPHY

Abhijit Sen, "Payments Crisis : A Different Solution", *The Economic Times*, July 12, 1991, p.8

Alexander S.S., "Effects of a Devaluation on a trade Balance", IMF Staff Papers, Vol. 2 (April, 1952), pp.263-78.

Allen, W.R., "A Note on the Money Income Effect of Devaluation", *Kyklos*, Vol. 9, 1956, pp.372-80.

Brems, H. "Devaluation of Marriage of Elasticity and Absorption Approaches", *Economic Journal*, Vol. 67, March, 1957, pp.49-64.

Brown, A.J., "Trade Balances and Exchange Stability", *Oxford Economic Papers*, No. 6, (April, 1942), pp.57-75.

Chandra Mohan, N., "Devaluation: The rupee takes a pounding", *The Economic Times*, 4-7, 1991, p.6.

Chandra Mohan, N., "Devaluation: Unwarranted on Merits", *The Economic Times*, July 17, 1991, p.10.

Jagdish, N. Bhagwali and Padma Desai, *India Planning for Industrialization*, London, Oxford University Press, 1970.

Kanoria, R.V., "Foreign Investment: Need for Policy Change", *The Economic Times*, July 23, 1991, p.8.

Kasbekar, S.R., "Coping with the Economic Crisis: A debate", *The Economic Times*, July 18, 1991, p.13.

Mohan Sule, "Three Days that Shook the ex-World", *The Economic Times*, July 14, 1991, p.6.

Pahariya, N.C., *Indian Exports Structure and Determinants*, RBSA Publishers, Jaipur, 1988.

Shonfield A., *International Economic Relations*, Sage Policy Papers, Georgetown University, Washington, 1945.

Special Report, "What the Economists Say", *The Economic Times*, July 7, 1991, p.7.

Tandon, R., *Some Perspectives on India's Trade Policy*, Chugh Publications, New Delhi, 1983.

The American Economic Association, *Readings in International Economics*, published for the Association by Richard D. Irwin, Inc House Wool, Illinois.

Thomas, T., "Devaluation only the first step", *The Economic Times*, July 9, 1991, p.8.

Varma, M.L., *Export Effort of India*, IIFT, New Delhi, 1986.

13

IMPORT POLICY, INDUSTRIAL GROWTH AND BALANCE OF PAYMENTS

RAJEEVA SINHA

Abstract

OVER THE past decade the import policy developments in India point to its greater market orientation. The changes reflect the debate that has taken place in development literature. The discussion in the literature poses a restrictive import regime (policy oriented) or a liberal import regime (market oriented) as the two choices. What is underemphasised is that given the basic constraint of foreign exchange gap, both the choices have to have a design of an import regime. There is an objective necessity to control the volume of imports. The relative efficiency of policy or market as an input in deciding the composition of imports is not the central issue. The focus of the discussion should be on the design of an import regime.

Import policy has been the subject of an old and continuing debate in development literature. Broadly, import policies have been classified as restrictive or liberal. The terms 'liberal' or 'restrictive' do not impart any exactitude to the character of the import regime. There is no controversy regarding the necessity of control over the volume of imports in developing countries. The pressure to import for production/consumption is many times more than the foreign exchange availability. The appropriate mechanism for determining the composition of imports has been the point of departure between a restrictive and liberal import regime. A restrictive import regime has emphasised the role of development policy in determining the composition of imports. A liberal import regime has, on the other hand, laid emphasis on the market for determining the composition of a country's imports.

The liberal import policy protagonists base their case on three points :

(1) An overriding faith on the functional efficiency of the market mechanism.
(2) A weak empirical evidence based on the success stories of four East Asian countries (one country and three city states).
(3) The general poor performance of the countries with restrictive import policy.

The restrictive import regime derives its justification from the historically given realities of the economic environment. What it fails to comprehend is that these very contradictions undermine the success of the import regime it professes.

> "In actual practice, however, protectionist policies have rarely been adopted out of a reasoned consideration of how protectionism might improve the terms of trade, raise the savings ratio, take account of external economies, or overcome distortions in labour market. On the contrary it has been the persistent shortage of foreign exchange that has dominated considerations of trade policy and protectionist policies have been much more in the nature of *ad hoc* responses to recurrent balance of payment crisis". (Meier, 1984, p. 486).

The controversy in the literature between a liberal or a restrictive import regime is misleading. It fails to capture the significance of the design of an import regime in the success or failure of an import policy. The design of the import regime is given a serious consideration neither in the policy perspective nor in the market perspective. In the former, it becomes a victim of adhocism induced by the angularities of the environment, the very genesis of the policy perspective. In the latter, the design of the import regime is overlooked as it is presumed that the market knows best. The need to properly incorporate the market signals in the design of an import policy is underemphasised (See Datta, 1987).

The following are the important considerations in designing an import regime. First, the import policy has to be properly integrated with the strategy of industrial and economic development. As the major concern of import policy is industrial growth it is crucial that the industrial strategy should have a basic validity. Then only the success of an import policy can be ensured.

The second crucial component of a properly designed import policy, particularly market oriented import regime involves the perceptions of the parties to whom it is addressed, viz., the domestic and foreign capital. This area has been left unexplored in the evaluation of the success stories of the East Asian countries.

> "One issue that we were not able to consider in this study is, why the Korean government was able to interfere in the manner it evidently did. It could well have courted disaster, not so much because of misconceived intervention as such but because of an inability to implement them in the face of opposition, or the business determination to circumvent them. (Luedde Neurath, 1986, p. 188)

Finally, the viability of an import regime will depend upon its implications for the balance of payments (bop). It should be able to ensure a fundamental equilibrium in the bop in the medium and long term.

II

In India also, the question of import policy is a longstanding controversy. The explicit acceptance of a liberal import policy was the outcome of the Memorandum of Understanding signed by the Indian Government for the SDR 5bn., loan from the IMF in November, 1981. However this was not a turnaround in policy. It was definitely within the ongoing changes that were taking place in the perceptions of the policy makers in India. There was an increasingly articulate viewpoint even prior to the IMF loan that India's import policy was too restrictive and in the specific context of industrialisation, was breeding inefficiency. The answer lay in allowing for a greater role for the market forces. Import liberalisation was seen as a crucial component of the new policy emphasis on a more liberal economic regime. However, a comparative study of the Sixth Plan document finalised in February 1981 and the IMF's Memorandum signed in November 1981, clearly provides evidence that the case for import liberalisation was clinched subsequent to the IMF loan (See Sau, 1983).

The current phase in our import policy has been undertaken with a view to carry out technological upgradation of Indian industry. This policy has led to a more open attitude towards import of technology, capital equipment, and direct foreign investment. This is visualised as the path to greater efficiency in Indian industry. Greater efficiency it is asserted will mean not only a greater capability to compete in the international market but would also lead to a higher growth rate for industry. Import liberalisation is thus the major policy thrust to bring about an improvement in the character and pace of industrialisation.

An efficient and growing industry is also seen in the present policy perspective as the path to a viable balance of payments, India's dismal performance in non-traditional exports even during the period 1960-73 when the world economy was in an expansionary phase, is attributed to the high cost industrial structure arising out of the protected domestic market for Indian industry.

It is crucial to examine the validity of these policy perceptions. A failure of this policy will not only have severe disruptive effects for industry but will also have the effect of foreclosing the future policy options for the Government and domestic capital. Foreign capital and the oligarchic institutions like the IMF will have a greater say in India's economic policy. The scenario of the debt trap could as well became a reality.

An evaluation of the prospects for the success of this strategy entails a closer look at the following questions :

1. How far is the present emphasis on technological upgradation a valid strategy for industrial growth?
2. Even if it is accepted that Indian industry is inefficient is it right to see a solution to it in mere technological upgradation?
3. Does the policy perception on import liberalisation mesh in with the industry's perception?
4. As has been noted earlier a major objective of import liberalisation is to ensure a viable bop in the medium and long term. The possibility of this could be examined at two levels. First, will the developments in the domestic industry as a consequence of import liberalisation lead to a greater supply of exportables? Secondly, is it realistic to expect that an enhanced capability to export would be translated into an actual increase in exports? Or is it that the understanding of the Abid Hussein Committee that export promotion and efficient import substitution are two sides of the same coin, a gross

simplification?

III

There is a large volume of literature which seeks to explain the stagnation in Indian industry (See Ahluwalia, 1985). Among the constraints that have been found to have empirical validity are the demand constraint (agriculture drag, slowdown in public investment) and the supply bottlenecks (structural as well as policy induced).

The present emphasis on technological upgradation for industrial growth is more in line with a clearer recognition of the demand constraint on Indian industry. The attempts to widen the demand base for Indian industry by institutional reforms in the rural sector in the 70's have failed. The impact of import liberalisation on demand is visualised at two levels. First increased factor productivity is seen as the source of greater income generation and thus a greater demand for industrial goods. Second, higher level of exports is expected to ease the demand constraint.

It needs to be reasserted, however, that the ignoring of institutional issues in agriculture has and will prove inimical to industrialisation. A more egalitarian agriculture provides deeper and wider home market for labour intensive mass consumption products which in turn allows the industrial structure to absorb more labour in the primary import substituting phase and to maintain a high level of employment even beyond that. The width and depth of the home market for mass consumption products have more importance in densely populated countries like India. Their absence in India has rendered the import substituting industrialisation quite ineffective.

The developments in agriculture are disquieting in the context of our concern for industrialisation. It has been pointed out that the small farms (less than 2 hectares) the area under fertiliser over total irrigated area is less that unity while the ratio is greater than one and keeps on increasing for larger farms (Sau 1983). As prices of fertilisers rise this discrepancy is bound to increase. The overall productivity per unit of fertiliser can be expected to decline. With the growing reliance on intensive agriculture for increase in agriculture output, agriculture can be expected to stagnate for small farms. As 4/5 of workers depend on agriculture for their livelihood, this will have far reaching consequences for demand from domestic industry.

The developments in public sector are equally ominous. The prices of commodities and services going into fixed capital formation are rising faster that the general price index. The public sectors output is mostly in this category of investment goods. Further upward revisions of their prices as is proposed in the present policy emphasis would only aggravate this trend. As a result the relative prices of capital goods would rise and hence the rate of profit would decline. Savings would transform itself into unproductive assets like construction or high profit areas of industry where the intensity to import is high. The public sector being the largest producer of capital goods would therefore face demand recession.

All this goes to prove that the issues pertaining to demand constraint remain. Choice of new avenues will not solve the problem but in a limited sense might postpone it.

Besides the factor intensity of the technology and capital equipment imported will be more in line with the factor endowments of the developed countries. Such technology imports would lead to an increase in income of capital. Here it must be pointed out that restrictive import regimes have also not been able to check this tendency (Streeton, 1973). However, the ramifications of this under a liberal import regime will be more serious. This tendency reflected in demand will lead to a rise in demand for technology and import intensive, sophisticated items. This will lead to a stratification of the production structure. The dynamic area of industry as reflected by demand characteristics will get further delinked from the industrial structure. Given the level of technology available domestically it will lead to a greater reliance of the enclave industries on imports. Similar developments can be expected because of the present emphasis on exports.

The evaluation of the efficiency question in Indian industry needs to be undertaken at two levels. First we need to examine the evidence on inefficiency in Indian industry and secondly, it is important to examine how far the framework under which efficiency has been discussed is appropriate.

The empirical evidence on inefficiency of Indian industry has been computed in terms of macro aggregates like Effective Rate of Protection, Domestic Resource Cost and Total Factor Productivity. The first two being the evidence and the third being the empirical source of declining efficiency. As is the problem with macro aggregates the computation procedure has been accused of errors. Further, multidisciplinary studies by World Bank also provide evidence to the contrary of the commonly held belief regarding inefficiency in Indian industry (See Chandra, 1986).

The empirical basis for declining productivity is in terms of trends in Total Factor Productivity. The evidence on this is very hazy and it is surprising how argument of a general decline in productivity in Indian industry since the 50s came to be accepted. All possible evidence seem to indicate a positive rate of growth of productivity. Though it is a different question whether the positive rate increase could have been higher or not (See Ahluwalia, 1985).

What is of more serious concern is the framework under which productivity increase is sought to be discussed. The overriding role in productivity increase is seen to be of technology. This follows form the production function frame of discussion on productivity (Ahluwalia, 1985). This implies that the discussion takes place in the context of a set of ethereal assumptions (perfect competition, perfect mobility) and what is more important, in the comparative statics framework. The impact of technological improvement in the production function is to shift the production function and this is how industrial growth and efficiency is sought to be brought about by the present policy emphasis.

This approach is unrealistic at the policy level because of the following reasons (See Nelson, 1984):

1. The time series of observed inputs outputs and prices are presumed to have been generated by a moving competitive equilibrium.
2. The effects of various variables on output growth are treated separately. There is nothing in the theory that provides for strong interactions, or packages of elements.
3. Institutional complexity is ignored. The theoretical economic universe consists of perfectly competitive firms, workers and resource owners and consumers. There is not much room here for a serious analysis of the effects of institutional complexities.
4. Short run fluctuations in the degree of capacity utilisation and unemployment are treated as phenomena calling for adjustment of the data so that cycle and trend need not be compounded. The particular productivity growth models do not have anything in them suggesting that the short run and long run interact in complicated and perhaps durable ways.

The drawbacks of the present production function approach become clear when we examine the considerations behind efficiency with the help of another neoclassical tool, the production possibility frontier (ppf). An efficient production structure will be one where actual production takes place at the frontier. However, setting up such a structure implies the establishment of price ratios as would be relevant in light of full flexibility, full mobility and availability of information on the endowment of factors and comparative advantages of the economy (Brahmananda, 1982). Such issues imply that attainment of efficiency cannot be merely linked up with technological upgradation. The objective of efficiency becomes all the more complicated when we keep in mind that in the context of development, the ppf is itself shifting outwards and what is more important distributive questions cannot be ignored. Distributive questions, as has been the experience of most of the developing countries, are not merely a normative necessity but an objective necessity for growth and developments.

In the light of the evaluation of the issues undertaken above it is difficult to accept the argument that the industrialisation process in India could be speeded up by a mere emphasis on technological imperatives and by a implicit sidelining of the institutional issues.

As noted above even if an import liberalisation policy is properly conceived its success depends upon the perception of the policy by the parties to whom it is addressed to, that is the domestic and foreign capital. It is important to ascertain the common ground between the policy perception and the capitalists' perception regarding import liberalisation.

Within domestic capital it is important to make a distinction between individual capitalist and the capitalist as a group. Investment decisions are taken by the capitalist acting individually and not functioning as a group. For an individual capitalist, technology imports are a softer option given the time, risk and investment required to develop indigenous technology. This inclination coupled with the demand characteristics of industrial products (discussed earlier) can make technology imports repetitive.

At the input stage a liberal import regime may be used to enhance the competitive position by one firm over other firms in the industry. This may not necessarily imply a lower price as competitiveness does not mean price competitiveness alone. Improved competitiveness may also result because of demand preference for foreign goods assembled under various collaboration agreements. The experience of BHEL is revealing in this regard. BHEL had come to acquire a position where it was in a position to bag overseas orders and also domestic orders floated under global tenders. Today it has gone in for foreign collaboration to reach even the domestic market. When there are global bidding for projects or when the companies also provide credit or bilateral aid, BHEL has found itself non-competitive under the present import regime. Its strategy has changed from independent functioning to collaborating with foreign firms in domestic markets. All this when none of the developed countries allow import of power equipment. (TOI, March 21, 1987).

The age structure of the technology and capital equipment imported gives indication that the motivation behind technological upgradation is competitiveness in the domestic market and not the firms competitiveness in the international market (Table 13.1). It is not uncommon to come across import of 'junk' technology or capital equipment by the firms.

TABLE 13.1: Age Structure of Imported Designs

(per cent)

Age (in yr)	Tech. collaboration	Joint venture	Foreign controlled firm
1-5	12.5	-	20
6-8	33.3	33.3	40.0
9-	54.2	66.7	40.0

Source: UNCTAD. 1983 from Niramal Chandra (1986).

Secondly, import liberalisation has also been induced by the pattern of demand on the product side. The past decade or so has been marked by an increase in the intensity of the international demonstration effect. There is distinct demand preference for internationally traded consumer goods. The domestic consumers have sought to satisfy this either through visits abroad, a sizeable workforce in foreign countries or through informal methods like smuggling. One is not sure about the exact magnitude, but the full page advertisements in national dailies for products not marketed in India, indicate that this market should be sizeable. Given the demand constraint in the Indian economy this phenomenon has had the effect of further constricting the demand for domestic products. One finds an increasing tendency of domestic capital to act as the middlemen in this transaction between international producers of these consumers goods and domestic consumers. The import of these goods in completely knocked down (CKD) or semi-knocked down (SKD) conditions are a growing phenomenon in industrial imports. Thus instead of a dynamic and efficient industrial structure, a tendency towards assembly in production or what has been termed as the dominance of screw driver technology, is taking place.

The attitude of foreign capital will also run contrary to the objectives of the import liberalisation strategy. Technological upgradation of Indian industry via import liberalisation is to be achieved on the basis of harmonious interaction between domestic and international capital. It will be more logical to expect the relationship to be antagonistic. The perennial interest of the international capital, varying in intensity, depending upon cyclical conditions in the industrial countries, has been to gain access to the Indian market. At the same time they would not like to encourage greater competition in the low growth areas of industrial countries, the likely thrust areas of Indian exports, All this has been brought out in a number of studies of collaboration agreements in India industry. On the other hand the domestic capital in spite of its emergent middleman role in a number of industries will not like to share the narrow domestic market and would be theoretically interested in expanding its operations in the international market. Thus the perceptions of domestic capital and foreign capital differ from the policy perception regarding their relationship subsequent to import liberalisation.

The implication of import liberalisation on the BoP front has to be assessed in the context of the new export pessimism (See Cline, 1982; Streeton, 1982). Sustainable import liberalisation will require a concommitant growth in exports for a viable balance of payments position. The Abid Hussain Committee does not examine the question of export prospects deeply except that it goes by the perception that it should not be very difficult to expand India's share in the total world's exports from its present low of 0.4 per cent. It emphasises the importance of marketing strategies for exports in this context.

Prospects of exports for developing countries like India is primarily based on the multistage comparative advantage and the gradual moving up of the ladder view point. This understanding is beset with a number of problems. The conventional trade theory places very little emphasis on the demand question. The relative sectoral growth rate in the two group of economies, developed and less developed are different. The less developed economies like India have very little potential to meet the import requirements of the high growth areas of the industrialised countries. When we talk of technological upgradation to make the domestic industry internationally competitive, we approach the problem of modernisation in the present context of industrial development in India i.e., in the area of traditional industries. There are precisely the low growth areas of industrialised economies. Any increased ability on the part of less developed countries to export these products has met with resistance in commercial policy of developed countries as these are also the employment sensitive areas in the developed countries and a sector of the economy where the trade unions are strong. There is considerable evidence of the tariff and non tariff barriers to less developed countries exports (See Anjaria *et al.* 1985). The developed countries have indicated reluctance to structurally adjust their economies in light of their changing comparative advantage. Evidence of this is provided in the developments relating to the Multi Fibres Agreement (MFA). Under the MFA the US has attempted to reverse its comparative disadvantage in the textile sector by carrying out the necessary structural adjustment. Instead of graduating out of this industry the US has attempted to structurally adjust this industry. By introducing greater capital intensity in production the effort has been to make US textile competitive with third world's textile exports.

South-South trade has been suggested as an alternative. However, expansion of South-South trade is difficult. First, the manufacturing activities of the various group of less developed countries tend to be overlapping. Their non-traditional exports often tend to be competitive. This makes their export markets a crowded one, an update of the terms of trade argument. On the import front the major requirements of less developed countries are not the exports of developing countries. Further the import requirements of LDCs are coupled with the question of foreign exchange availability. Even when a LDC is in a position to meet the import requirements of another LDC they are unable to do so because of inability to provide resources to finance the purchases.

IV

From the above discussion the following conclusions can be drawn:

1. The present policy emphasis displays an over reliance on

technological upgradation for a dynamic and efficient industrial structure and underemphasises the institutional questions affecting industrialisation in India.

2. The policy of import liberalisation assumes a complete unanimity of interests between the policy makers and industrial capital ; and further between the domestic and foreign capital.
3. On the export front the policy does not account for the fact that the thrust areas of countries like India lie in low growth rate sectors of advanced countries.

The present import liberalisation strategy takes a very simplistic view of the problems of industrialisation and balance of payments. It might as well evolve into a situation of the tail wagging the dog, where considerations in the foreign trade sector condition the responses in the domestic economy. Besides having a disruptive effect on industrialisation it will lead to a further deterioration in the balance of payments. This development should be taken in conjunction with India's growing foreign debt servicing obligation. Given the non-discretionary character of two-thirds of our imports, in face of a foreign exchange crunch, the first area which will experience a cutback in imports would be the capital and other industrial imports. This would have a further disconcerting impact on the pace and character of industrialisation.

The viability of balance of payments could as well have been ensured by reducing imports through appropriate measures thus reducing the desperateness on the export front. Considerable scope for reducing imports have been suggested (See Bhaduri, 1980). The present policy is unwilling to take the difficult option of rationalising our imports and tackling the structural contradictions in the domestic economy. This is typical of Myrdal's 'soft states' aided and abetted in its responses by international institutions like the IMF.

REFERENCES

Ahluwalia, I. J. : Industrial Growth in India, Stagnation since the Mid-Sixties, Oxford University press, Delhi. 1985.

Anjaria, S. J., Kirmani, N. and Potersen, A. B. : Trade policy issues and Development, Occasional paper 38, International Monetary Fund, Washington, D. C., July 1985.

Bagchi, A., Ghosh, A. and Dasgupta, S. : Industrial policy and the Economy, *Social Scientist*, September, 1985.

Bhaduri, A. : in the Committee on Export Strategy for the 1980s : Final report, Ministry of Commerce, New Delhi, 1980.

Brahmananda, P. R. : Productivity in the Indian Economy, Rising Inputs For Falling Outputs, Himalaya Publishing House, Bombay, 1982.

Chandra. N. : Modernisation for Export Oriented Growth. A critique of Recent Indian Policy, *Economic and Political Weekly*, July 19, 1986.

Cline, W. R. : Can the East Asian Model of Development be Generalised? *World Development*, February, 1982.

Datta, A. : Understanding East Asian Economic Development, *Economic & Political Weekly*, April 4, 1987.

Linder, S. B. : Trade and Technical Efficiency, in Bhagwati, J. N. and others, (Ed), Trade, Balance of Payments and Growth, Papers in International Economics in Honour of C. P. Kindleberger, North-Holland publishing Company, 1971.

Luedde - Neurath, R. : Import controls and Export Oriented Development, A Reassessment of the South Korean Case Westview Press, 1986.

Meier, G. M. : Leading issues in Economic Development, Oxford University, 1984.

Meier, G. M. : The old and New Export Pessimism : A critical survey, paper read at the VIIIth World Economic Congress of the International Economic Association New Delhi, 1986.

Raj, K. N. : New Economic policy, V. J. Krishnamachari Memorial Lecture, Institute of Economic Growth, November 20, 1985.

Sau, R. : Structural Adjustment in the Indian Economy, IMF Model of Import Pushed Growth, *Economic and Political Weekly*, Annual Number, May 1983.

Streeton, P. : Trade Strategies for Development : Some Themes for the Seventies, World Development, July, 1987.

Streeton, P. P. : A cool look at 'Outward Looking Strategies for Development, The World Economy, September, 1982.

Times of India, : Capital Goods Sector Hit Hard, March 21, 1987.

UNCTAD, : Technology Issues in the Capital Goods Sector : A case study of Leading Machinery Producers in India, UNCTAD/TT/55 of September 6, 1983 Reproduced by the Centre for Monitoring Indian Economy, January 1984.

14

ECONOMIC CRISIS IN INDIA AND EXTERNAL FINANCE

SUMITRA CHISHTI

THE INDIAN economy is facing a grave crisis in the beginning of the nineties. The Finance Minister, Dr. Manmohan Singh, said in his budget speech of 1991-92 : "we have not experienced anything similar in the history of India". He also went a step further by stating that this crisis was the result of economic management by the government after November 1989 thus implying that the entire crisis grew within a short period of twenty odd months. As he put it, "The new government, which assumed office barely a month ago, inherited an economy in deep crisis".[1] This interpretation of the Indian economic crisis of the government made by one of the outstanding economists of India, who definitely knows better than what he has said, shows an extremely incorrect understanding of the Indian economic crisis a statement about which has been made for purely political reasons.

Economic crisis in varying magnitudes has been with India since it launched developmental efforts. The criteria to judge an economic crisis vary. The discussion of economic crisis very often overlooks certain basic elements of the crisis. Be as it may, the present crisis as is being seen now dates back to the early eighties. It is important, therefore, to analyse the nature and components of this crisis.

First, an assessment of the Indian economy in the eighties, especially during the period 1985-90 applying the following criteria does not give rise to the conclusion of about its being deep in an unprecedented crisis: (i) Growth of national income; (ii) growth of agricultural production (this is very important for India for the share of agriculture in national income and employment is substantial; (iii) growth of industrial production; and (iv) savings of the Indian economy.

The *Economic Survey, 1990-91*, states that it is a measure of the inherent strength of the economy that it withstood the effects of shocks of various types like the shocks of the Gulf crisis and political uncertainties. Table 14.1 gives the performance of Indian economy during 1985-86 – 1990-91.

TABLE 14.1: Indian Economic Performance During the Period 1985-91

	1985-86	1986-87	1987-88	1988-89	1989-90	1990-91
Gross National Product	4.1	3.6	4.2	10.6	5.2	5.0
Agricultural Production	2.5	-3.7	-0.8	21.0	1.7	4.5
Foodgrains Production	3.4	-4.7	-2.7	21.0	0.4	3.9
Industrial Production	8.7	9.1	7.3	8.7	8.6	8.4
Gross Domestic Savings at current price	19.7	18.4	20.3	21.1	21.7	N.A.
Imports at current price	14.7	2.2	10.7	26.9	25.4	21.9
Exports at current price	-7.2	14.3	25.9	29.1	36.8	17.5

Source: Economic Survey, 1990-91.

Again, to quote *The Economic Survey:* "The underlying strength of Indian economy is revealed by the fact that many of the targets set for Seventh Plan were exceeded, which was partly attributable to the performance of Indian economy in 1989-90. Thus, the average annual growth rate of GDP worked out to 5.6 per cent as compared with plan target of 5 per cent. In agriculture the average annual growth rate at 4.1 per cent exceeded the target of 4 per cent despite the run of the poor monsoon in the first three years of the plan. The overall industrial production increased at an average rate of 8.5 per cent narrowly missing the plan target of 8.7 per cent per annum. . . . There has been an encouraging trend in the rate of overall domestic savings which showed an improvement during Seventh Plan. The ratio of gross domestic savings to GDP, at current market prices, which declined continuously from 21.6 per cent in 1979-80 to 18.2 per cent in 1984-85 improved to 21.1 per cent in 1988-89 and further to 21.7 per cent in 1989-90. With this, the average gross domestic savings during the Seventh Plan works out to be 20.2 per cent compared with 19.6 per cent achieved during the Sixth Plan".[2]

It is unnecessary in the light of this statement to elaborate that the Indian economy judged from these criteria is not in the crisis at all. In fact, if has performed much better than in the previous years. It is important to recognise this before we work into other aspects of Indian economy which have resulted in the suggestion of Indian economy having in deep crisis.

In some respects Indian economic growth has not percolated down to provide benefit to the larger section of the population. The first criterion normally used in the context of India is to what extent the number of people below the poverty line has been reduced. In other words has there been any reduction in the incidence of poverty? The Government of India claims a larger decline in the incidence of poverty than the estimates made by experts. It suggests that in the Seventh Plan the part of the population below poverty line has been 29 per cent. However, this estimate has been questioned. According to Minhas *et al* the incidence of poverty declined in rural India from 58.8 per cent in 1970-71 to 50.8 per cent in 1983 and 48.7 per cent in 1987-88. In the urban sector the corresponding decline in poverty incidence was from 46.2 per cent in 1970-71 to 39.7 per cent in 1983 and 37.8 per cent in 1987-88. For rural and urban India taken together, the incidence of poverty declined from 56.3 per cent in 1970-71 to 48.1 per cent in 1983 and further to 45.9 per cent in 1987-88. What is important for the present discussion is the decline in poverty incidence in the Seventh Plan period as compared to the previous plan periods. The evidence in this respect has been disquieting. As they say, "To put it differently, the annualized rate of decline in rural poverty incidence as a whole was steeper between 1970-71 and 1983 (1.2%) than in the later period from 1983 to 1987-88 (0.9 per cent). In urban sector, the corresponding decline was about 1.1 to 1.2 per cent per annum during both the periods. "The absolute numbers of the rural poor (in million) on the other hand, rose from 257.9 (1970-71) to 276.8 in 1983 and further to 283.7 (1987-88)".[3]

Yet another indicator that should be used is to see as to what extent this growth has generated employment opportunities. In other words, how it has reduced unemployment in India? In fact the Economic Advisory Council under the chairmanship of Sukhmoy Chakravarty has emphasized the importance of employment generation. For the widespread unemployment and the resulting acute mass poverty are the gravest problems confronting the Indian economy.

As the report puts it, "The trend rate of growth of GDP for the decade of the 1980s would be around 5.3 per cent per annum, while the aggregate growth performance of the economy would appear to be an improvement over the preceding decades . . . there are reasons for serious concern on the employment side. Growth of output has not been matched by a corresponding growth in employment".[4]

In aggregate terms the growth rate of employment has actually declined during the period 1983 to 1987-88. During 1972-73 to 1977-78, the growth rate of employment was 2.82 per cent which declined to 2.22 per cent during 1977-78 to 1983 and 1.55 per cent during the period 1983 to 1987-88. The decline is marked in manufacturing industries. During the period 1972-73 to 1977-78 the growth of employment was as high as 5.10 per cent which declined to 3.75 per cent during 1977-78 and further to 2.10 per cent during 1983 to 1987-88. In agriculture also a similar decline has taken place. During 1972-73 to 1977-78, the rate of growth was 2.32 per cent which steadily declined to a very low figure of 0.65 per cent during 1983 to 1987-88. It is estimated by 1995 India will have to generate 65 million jobs during the Eighth Plan including for increased educated unemployed.[5] This and other indicators like illiteracy, lack of basic needs, etc., do indicate the existence of a deep of crisis.

The crisis that is being discussed presently, however, does not refer to the above elements of the situation. The focus is entirely different. It refers to three elements: (i) growth of fiscal deficit; (ii) deteriorating balance of payments; and (iii) mounting international debt of India. The panicky behaviour of the Government of India is with regard to the management of the latter two elements of this crisis. This needs elaboration.

Fiscal Deficit

Fiscal deficit is defined as the difference between the total deficit of government expenditure and government revenue while budget deficit is conventionally defined as the difference between all receipts and expenditure. To quote Dr. Manmohan Singh, "The fiscal deficit of the Central Government, which measures the revenue receipts and total expenditure, is estimated at more than eight per cent of GDP in 1990-91 as compared with 6 per cent at the beginning of the eighties and 4 per cent at mid-1970s. The fiscal deficit has to be met by borrowing. As a result, internal public debt of the Central Government has accumulated to about 55 per cent of gross domestic production,

GDP".[6]

The *Economic Survey, 1990-91*, clearly spells out the steady and significant growth of that deficit in the Sixth and Seventh Plans which the statement of Finance Minister attempts to conceal. While the budget deficit as a proportion of GDP increased from 0.9 per cent in 1981-82 to 2.4 per cent in 1989-90, the gross fiscal deficit as a proportion of GDP increased from 5.4 per cent to 8.0 per cent over the same period. Thus the fiscal imbalances worsened during the eighties, as the fiscal deficit, on an average, rose from 6.3 per cent of GDP in the Sixth Plan period to 8.2 per cent of GDP in the Seventh Plan period. It is significant to see (Table 14.2) that the gross fiscal deficit was 7.8 per cent of GDP in 1988-89 which went up to 8.0 per cent in 1989-90 and to 8.4 per cent in 1990-91. In the year 1986-87, it was as high as 9.0 per cent.

TABLE 14.2: Budget Deficit and Fiscal Deficit of India as percentages of Gross Domestic Product at current market prices in the Eighties.

Year	Budget deficit	Gross fiscal deficit
1975-76	0.5	4.1
1980-81	1.8	6.2
1981-82	0.9	5.4
1982-83	0.9	6.0
1983-84	0.7	6.3
1984-85	1.6	6.3
1985-86	2.0	8.3
1986-87	2.8	9.0
1987-88	1.7	8.1
1988-89	1.4	7.8
1989-90	2.4	8.0
1990-91	2.1	8.4

Source: Economic Survey, 1990-91, p.100.

Another disturbing feature of fiscal imbalances is that deficits on revenue account, that is, the difference between current revenue and current expenditure is growing. The revenue deficit as percentage of GDP had steadily gone up from 0.6 per cent in 1980-81 to 2.1 per cent in 1985-86 which shot up to 3.4 per cent in 1990-91.

It is important here to mention the price situation in the country.

The inflation in India was steadily growing. The wholesale price index registered a rise, especially in essential products, during the last two years. Indian people are highly sensitive to inflation because of their low income. The annual inflation rate in the Seventh Plan is less than the inflation rate in the Sixth Plan. But during the last two years inflation has grown. The annual inflation rate increased on a point-to-point basis from 9.1 per cent in 1989-90 to 12.1 per cent in 1990-91.

While this crisis was growing, the real alarm came from the external sector of the economy. The panic response of the government of India is caused by a number of developments in the country's international payments.

External Payments Crisis

The external payments situation of India has never been viable. Over the Plan periods very often India had to cut down its investment and consumption in order to meet the payments crisis. India had experienced a similar crisis during the Second and Third Plans. All other plans had also been subject to constraints on this front. However, the present external payments situation has a number of features and it deserves a detailed and understanding. The eighties witnessed a fast deterioration in the external payments position of India as seen in Table 14.3.

TABLE 14.3: External Payments Situation of India in the 1980s

(Rs. in crores and figures in brackets as percentage of GDP)

	1980-81	1984-85	1985-86	1986-87	1987-88	1988-89
Balance of trade	-5967.2	-6721.1	-9586.0	-9353.9	-9296.1	-13555.6
	(-4.4)	(-2.9)	(-3.7)	(-3.2)	(-2.8)	(-3.5)
Net invisibles	4310.6	3848.5	3630.2	3523.9	3003.5	3145.6
	(3.2)	(1.7)	(1.4)	(1.2)	(0.9)	(0.8)
Balance of payments	-1656.6	-2094.9	-5927.3	-5830.0	-6292.6	-10410.0
current account	(-1.2)	(-1.2)	(-2.3)	(-2.0)	(-1.9)	(-2.7)
Foreign exchange reserves at the end of financial year	5544	7243	7820	8151	7687	7040
Total debt service			3162.0	4552.0	5861.0	6919.0

Source: Economic Survey, 1990-91.

The above table does not provide figures for the year 1989-90 and 1990-91. There are figures available, although not comprehensively, as given in Table 14.4.

India has been depending on external finance to supplement its domestic savings. This has primarily come in the form of official development assistance till 1980. After 1980, that is, from the beginning of the Sixth Plan, commercial borrowings and large borrowings from the International Monetary Fund to finance increased deficit in balance of payments contributed substantially to the flow of external finance into India.

TABLE 14.4: External Sector

	1989-90	1990-91
Balance of trade	7735 (-2.3)	10644
Foreign exchange reserves	6251	5092.0 (11416.0)
Debt services	8402	9630

Note: It is necessary to state here that the foreign exchange reserves stood at the end of 1990-91 at Rs. 11416 crores because the gold holdings of the Reserve Bank of India were revalued closer to international price in October 1990.

Source: Economic Survey, 1990-91, p.153.

TABLE 14.5: External Capital inflows during the period 1985-86 to 1990-91

(Rs. in Crores)

	External Assistance	Commercial Borrowings (authorization)	IMF Borrowings		Non-Resident Deposits
1985-86	5650	1700	4665	1985	3819
1986-87	6160	1395	4826	1986	5650
1987-88	9265	2654	4348	1987	7847
1988-89	13070	4314	3347	1988	10054
1989-90	10826	5479	2362	1989	14154
1990-91	6252	3414	4389	1990	17831
				1991	20542

Source: Economic Survey, 1990-91.

While domestic savings were high compared to many countries, which in fact increased during the period 1984-85 to 1989-90, the gross domestic investment also increased. The gross domestic savings increased from 18.2 per cent of GDP in 1984-85 to 21.7 per cent in 1989-90; the gross domestic investment increased to 19.6 per cent of GDP to 24.1 per cent of GDP during this period. The gap between domestic investment and domestic savings had to be financed by an inflow of foreign capital to the tune of 2.4 per cent of GDP during the Seventh Plan. This was far less than the difference financed by external capital in the Sixth Plan which was 1.4 per cent of the GDP.

The total international debt of India in 1989-90 (including NRI deposits) is estimated by the Government of India to be Rs. 97,966 crores, which amounted to 22 per cent of the GDP. The preliminary estimate for the year 1990-91 (March 31) is Rs. 120,000 crores. The World Bank, however, gives a figure of 24 per cent of the GDP as accounted for by the external debt of India.[7]

The terms have also changed as debt magnitude has changed. The average interest rate was only 2.4 per cent in 1970 but it went up to 6.4 per cent in 1989. Similarly the average maturity in years has also gone down. It was 34 years in 1970 which declined to 20 years.[8]

The debt stock of India also changed its character. At the beginning of the Sixth Five-Year Plan external debt stock consisted mainly of external assistance which constituted almost 90 per cent of debt stock. Since then the share of external commercial borrowings has registered the fastest growth accounting for 27 per cent of the debt stock.

The Collapse of Confidence

In the preceding pages a detailed picture of the deteriorating external payments position of India and the changing nature of external capital flow has been made. It is very important now to analyse what factors contributed to this deterioration leading to the collapse of confidence of the Government of India.

It is appropriate to highlight here some of the dramatic elements of this crisis.

(a) India's credit rating in the international banking system went down drastically.

One of the major reasons which sent perhaps premature alarm bells was the credit rating of India. Moody's, the New York-based credit rating agency took the initiative in placing India on credit watch with an intention to downgrading it, on August 1, 1990, which was followed up by other credit rating agencies placing India on watch, such as Standard and Poor and Japan-based Research Institute. This indeed is mysterious for in July 1990, there was no special factor which warranted such an assessment. Judged from any criteria, foreign exchange, debt servicing, trade balance, orderly change in the government, there was no major development during the first half of 1990 which necessitated changes in India's credit rating.[9]

Nobody is in a position to give a clear answer why India's credit rating went down in August 1990. Some argue that Moody's took a dim view of India's political uncertainties. International bankers too believe that Moody's assessment was based on political rather than economic factors. Even conceding, as Moody's explained, the factors such as long-term debt accumulation, ability to repay, foreign trade difficulties, etc., there was no immediate cause for India to be downgraded in credit rating. But all the factors that Moody's mentioned were well-known in 1989 itself. Why, then, July 1990? It is likely that Moody's precipitated a crisis by an excessively negative assessment of India. Some commentators raise questions as "Did they induce complacency earlier on, through 1988 and 1989, by offering excessively upbeat assessments of India's credit worthiness? Was India first enticed into borrowing more than it should have, and then deprived of further assistance and, thereby wittingly or unwittingly, forced into undertaking painful structural adjustment policies? Was this the result of a poor rating ability or part of a conspiracy? Available evidence does not answer that question conclusively".[10]

(b) The normal roll over facility granted by the international banks did not come by consequent to this credit rating. In fact, it is this that precipitated the crisis leading to the possibility of default in repayment on the part of the Government of India which had a record of a worthy borrower hitherto.

(c) The delay in commitments coming forward from foreign governments such as the UK, the USA, Japan as well as international financial institutions such as the IMF and the World Bank, caused further difficulty.

(d) India's eagerness not to default payments as a sovereign borrower resulting into pledging a part of official gold reserves with the Bank of England and pledging of gold by the State Bank of India to make debt repayments aggravated the crisis further.

It must be stated here that this crisis in external payments could be anticipated. It was built-in in the strategy of financing investments and imports. Prudent external borrowing was an important feature governing India's policy till 1980. This prudent policy was given up in the early eighties when India went in for controversial borrowing from the International Monetary Fund in 1981, which it did not utilize completely for various reasons. Since 1985, very good credit rating prompted many to suggest that India should avail of this opportunity and borrow external funds to finance consumption and investment. Some of the sceptics who feared that India would be in the company of heavily indebted countries like Poland, Mexico, Argentina and others, if it pursued this reckless dependence on borrowings, were outvoted with an accusation that they did not know how best to draw the benefits of international capital to India and were too narrow in their national sentiments. Well, as things have moved it appears that these sceptics knew India better in terms of its capacity to generate funds to repay the international debts especially in the short-and medium-terms.

It is considered that import growth caused reliance on external borrowings. Import growth has been attributed to this crisis by a number of experts. Imports did grow in the second half of the decade of eighties barring 1986-87. In the entire period it grew by 16.0 per cent in rupee terms and 8.2 per cent in dollar terms. However, the share of imports in GDP was 8.3 per cent, similar to the share experienced in the period 1980-85 in value terms.

Imports in volume terms grew more than was targeted for. The target growth rate was 5.8 per cent for the period 1985-90 while actually imports grew by 9.8 per cent in volume terms. This is contrary to the experience of the Sixth Plan when in volume terms imports were less than the target.

It is significant to observe that the composition of imports has changed during the above period. Normally, there is a tendency to attribute the growth of imports to petroleum and petroleum products. But the share of imports of these products in the Sixth Plan period was 35.8 per cent of the total imports while in the period 1985-90 (Seventh Plan period) it fell down to 17.9 per cent. Capital goods, chemicals, etc., increased their share correspondingly. Petroleum price hike during 1990 caused increase in imports, but the general import growth cannot be attributed to this price rise. Therefore, it is not far fetched to say that the liberalised import policy did have its role in the growth of imports.

This is particularly reinforced by the fact that exports during this period performed much better. While the share of exports in GDP remained almost constant in the entire decade of 80s, the value as well as volume of exports grew. In value terms, be it in dollar terms or rupee terms, exports registered higher growth rate in the Seventh Plan period than in the Sixth Plan period. It also reached the expected targets of growth in volume terms in the Seventh Plan.

The remittances which were an important means of financing merchandise deficit did not increase substantially during these years. There was a marginal increase in 1987-88 and 1988-89. Figures are not available for the latter two years. The year 1990-91 had perhaps experienced a decline in the inflow of private remittances. But in the entire period there has been no dramatic decline in remittances.

It is relevant in this context to examine why the Government of India became a liberal borrower from the international banks and thus exposed itself to the expected risk of not being able to repay. The reasons for this lie in a number of factors.

The official development assistance, the mainstay of India, continued to be forthcoming. According to the *Economic Survey, 1990-91*, the disbursement of external assistance actually accelerated during the Seventh Plan. Of course, the grant component of external assistance fell. Except in the year 1990-91 when the authorization of external assistance declined markedly, the period did not witness any marked deceleration of official development assistance.

The Government of India might have considered that reliance mainly on external assistance was not enough to finance its growing needs. There were questions about India's inability to utilize the aid from bilateral sources as well as aid from multilateral institutions. Donors, particularly in the Aid India Consortium, had begun questioning increased authorization of aid in the face of tardy utilization. In fact the Seventh Plan period experienced a decline in the utilization of aid. Table 14.6 gives authorization and aid utilization in the last five years.

TABLE 14.6: External Assistance: Authorization and Utilization

(Rs. in crores)

Year	Authorization	Utilization
1985-86	5650.4	2936.0
1986-87	6159.5	3605.0
1987-88	9265.3	5051.9
1988-89	13069.8	5304.4
1989-90	10826.0	5802.5
1990-91	6251.9	6660.1

Source: Economic Survey, 1990-91, p.S95.

With the exception of the year 1990-91, utilization has fallen short by nearly 50 per cent. The total authorized aid in the pipeline is estimated to be around Rs. 30,000 crores.[11] The massive underutilisation has not only adversely affected the pace of growth in the country but also India had to pay a charge on unutilized aid. This also reflects the poor economic management that had set in for reasons of non-utilization of aid primarily arose from the failure of recipient authorities of the State and Central Governments to make use of the aid because of cumbersome procedures and non-availability of local finance.

The utilization of commercial borrowings has been substantial. Table 14.7 gives authorization and disbursement in the same period.

TABLE 14.7: Utilization of External Commercial Borrowings

(Rs. in crores)

Year	Authorization	Disbursement per cent
1985-86	1700	1799
1986-87	1396	2474
1987-88	2654	2252
1988-89	4314	4069
1989-90	5479	4196
1990-91	3414	3050

Source : *Economic Survey, 1990-91*, p 166.

From the above, it can be seen that the commercial borrowings lent themselves to easy utilization through quick disbursement without being linked to any specific projects. Hence this preference to this source of funds.

It is important here that while the Government of India took recourse to easy financing facility mainly for its current expenditure no adequate strategy and plan was made in the economy to provide for debt servicing. In this case one can cite the example of South Korea. While South Korea depended on external commercial borrowings in the 70s and early 80s and its international debt mounted, it planned and built in increased export capability in the system thus insuring itself against any debt crisis. Regrettably, when borrowings were effected by the Government of India a corresponding effective strategy was not built into the economy to develop the necessary repayment ability.

Flight of Capital

In the entire discussion of India's balance of payments crisis, it is important to recognize that India during the decade of eighties suffered a massive capital flight. This capital flight in the regime of strict control of export of capital can take place in the following manners : (i) Trade misinvoicing, that is, exports under-invoicing and import over-invoicing, provides conduits for capital flight. In India there has been evidence that there has been misinvoicing of trade. (ii) Cash transfers of hard currency can take place by smuggling hard currency from India purchased from the black market through persons. It is well known that India has developed flourishing black market in foreign exchange. (iii) Kickback or commission which are similar to over-invoicing. The foreign supplier pays the recipient a portion of the proceeds of goods and services which will be directly deposited abroad in the name of the recipient. (India has such payments going on as mentioned in the government study of aspects of black money in India.) In the purchase of major civil or defence equipment from abroad the sending company makes payments usually into accounts held overseas to key participants or their agents in the decision to award the contract. This will become cost of imports. (iv) Inter-bank transfer by the foreign banks could be a conduit for despatching the money aborad.

The estimates of capital flight reveal that during the eighties it grew substantially. Table 14.8 gives the annual flow of capital flight.[12]

TABLE 14.8: Estimated Capital Flight from in India in the Period 1980-1986 in Constant 1986 US Dollar

(in millions)

1980	3119	1984	–1659
1981	884	1985	2840
1982	3158	1986	3058
1983	3087	Total	21103

Source: "The Hidden Balance of Payments, 1971-1986," *Economic and Political Weekly*, July 28, 1990, p. 16.

The total stock of capital flight for the period 1971-1986 is estimated to be $ 21 billion. If the imputed interest is included it goes up to $28.6 billion. The stock of $ 28.6 billion in 1986 capital flight as a proportion of total international debt of India, $ 70.0 billion in 1990, would be 43 per cent.

Let us examine what options India has to recover from this strangulation of crisis caused by external finance. The Government of India has indicated two options in its policy response: (i) IMF loan, and (ii) increasing foreign direct investment. We shall first deal with the latter and then discuss borrowings from the IMF.

Foreign Direct Investment and Transnational Corporations

It has been argued that a country can finance the needs of its external finance by liberally permitting foreign direct investment including transnational corporations.

The decade of the nineties had inherited during the eighties an altered appreciation of the role of transnational corporations (TNCs) in the developing countries. The decade of the seventies had witnessed deep concern of the academics, policy formulators, governments and international institutions with regard to the threats that the TNCs posed to the economic development and political stability of the developing countries.

There was almost a consensus that the TNCs, if allowed to function unregulated by the governments, would disturb seriously the priorities of developing countries in their developmental effort by diversion of resources to undesirable sectors as well as siphoning off of substantial amount of resources from them. Hence, a whole set of policies aimed at regulating the TNCs came into force in addition to a series of guidelines in respect of their functions agreed to by international institutions such as the Organisation of Economic Cooperation and Development (OECD).

The United Nations also took an active part in this endeavour by establishing a Centre on Transnational Corporations (CTC) in New York to study and formulate policies on TNCs with a view to primarily assisting the developing countries. It also undertook to develop a code of conduct, yet to be finalised, to direct the functioning of TNCs with a special emphasis on their functioning in developing countries. However, in the eighties, this apparent consensus was broken down because of a number of factors.

First, a large number of developing countries emerged as debtors. The financial flows to these countries got reduced substantially. The official development assistance to these countries did not rise to the expected level of 0.70 per cent of GDP of the advanced countries: it never exceeded 0.38 per cent on an average. In some years even this level could not be achieved. The boom in funding by the international banks also came to a standstill as the huge borrowers from the developing countries were unable to repay their debts. Hence, they were unwilling to lend substantially any new finance to developing countries. In the mid-eighties, the developing countries began to experience net transfer of resources to developed countries amounting to 3 per cent of their GDP. The developing countries as a group increased their net transfers to the rest of the world in 1989 to $ 47.9 billion from a figure of $ 37.6 billion in 1988. Consequently, it is felt that the primary mechanism of transfer of resources to developing countries can only be the foreign direct investment, especially by the TNCs.

Second, there has been substantial change in the ideological environment in the world economy. The early eighties witnessed the establishment of governments in the UK and the USA which believed in the primacy of the market accompanied by the reduction of the state's role in economic life: this gave rise to a proposition that the economies must strive for efficiency regardless of their impact on various sectors/population of the nation/world. The TNCs, it is argued, were eminently suited to achieve the objective of efficiency. Hence they must be allowed to function efficiently, nationally and globally and all factors which impede the growth of TNCs must be eliminated.

Third, it is argued that aid and commercial bank loans bring along with them only financial resources. What the developing countries need now is not only financial resources but also technology, marketing and management resources. The TNCs, being the leading organizations, are the right institutions to provide these necessary resources, according to this argument. Hence, they must be nurtured not only by eliminating the obstacles to their functioning but also by providing positive incentives to them.

Fourth, the international economic institutions such as the International Monetary Fund and the World Bank which have been active in helping developing countries not only through their resources but also through their advice, such as policy dialogue, have emphasized the importance of the TNCs. In fact, inviting foreign direct investment (FDI), especially from TNCs, has been a part of the conditionality package. Obviously, the developing countries could hardly maintain any different approach to the virtues of TNCs other than what these institutions proposed.

Finally, the developments in Eastern Europe and the Soviet Union contributed to the breakdown of consensus on TNCs that prevailed in the seventies. These countries which were highly critical of the TNCs' role in the developing countries subsequently abandoned their historical position. In keeping with the trends of the time, they are now inviting TNCs to their own countries by offering a large number of incentives. They believe now that without their assistance they cannot succeed in their reconstruction programmes.

Even under the Uruguay Round of multilateral trade negotiations, developing countries are under pressure to give up their selective foreign investment policy requiring the TNCs and foreign investors to perform. The bilateral pressure from the US government under Super 301 to liberalised performance requirements are well known.

The Government of India in 1991 declared a policy of foreign direct investment which is expected to remove the constraints that the foreign investor was facing in the country in a bid to get FDI. *First*, a large number of industries are open to foreign investors including TNCs. *Second*, one of the most important elements of India's foreign investment policy since independence (linking foreign direct investment to technology) has been removed. *Third*, the embargo on 51 per cent equity on a number of industries is also removed. *Fourth*, automatic licence is issued if the foreign investor finances from his capital all the import requirements of capital goods. *Fifth*, the foreign investor can invest 25 per cent of the equity in small scale industries. A number of other facilities with regard to royalty payments and divided remittances have been made.

The expectations are that with this liberalization India will emerge as the recipient of foreign direct investment in a large measure thus reducing the need to depend on external assistance and external commercial borrowing.

It is not within the purpose of this article to debate the effects of the foreign direct investment policy. The only concern here is: can it be an alternative source of the external capital for India? The chances of foreign direct investment becoming an alternative source of capital are rather limited. The reasons for this pessimistic assessment have been the following.

Since the mid-eighties, barring a few developing countries in South East Asia, foreign direct investment has not gone into developing countries. It could, however, be argued that India can become an attractive centre for foreign investors including TNCs. It is not disputed that the foreign investor does consider growing domestie market of India as attractive. It can be seen that when foreign investment policy was liberalized in the eighties the number of collaboration agreements increased rapidly. During the six calendar years (1985-91) more than 5000 collaborations were approved. Of these, 1390 collaborations were financial involving foreign investment amounting to Rs. 1,520 crores, i.e., an annual inflow of Rs. 200 crores. Therefore, this liberalization was not followed up by any dramatic increase in foreign direct investment.

What could encourage a foreign investor to bring more money into India than what he is doing? For a TNC or any other foreign investor can achieve the corporate objective in India, i.e., taking an increasing share of the growing domestic market without recourse to his substantial investment. This is so because by selling his technology occasionally the second generation foreign investor can acquire necessary clout in the company with minority participation. He can also use his marketing assets, such as brand names and trade marks to the Indian collaborator for which there is a premium in the domestic market, and earn enough. Further, he can use the domestic savings of India to finance the required investment. In fact, he is precisely doing this. Thus, with limited exposure of his capital to risks he can enjoy the benefits of Indian market which he is actually doing.

Too much emphasis has been laid on the importance of equity holding of 51 per cent by the foreign investor. Very often, it is argued that this gives the parent company of the investor necessary control over the Indian company. There has been substantial evidence to show that the TNC does not need 51 per cent of equity to control the company. It can control the associated company with far less holding of he equity. It can do it eminently with 40 per cent and less as has been the case of India where all others are small investors.

Another specious argument offered for 51 per cent equity is that it would enable the TNC to use its subsidiary in all its financial and accounting aspects as an integrated part. But TNCs all over the world have developed adequate techniques and procedures to deal with their associated companies. In fact, this associated status sometimes facilitates their exemption from certain legal requirements imposed by the host countries.

Given this understanding, can India hope to get substantial foreign investment in the immediate future resulting from liberalization? The answer is a categorical 'no' because of a number of factors.

Indian political uncertainty which was never there has become a factor to be considered in the risk perception of TNCs.

The demand for foreign investment has grown substantially all over the world. In fact, the developed countries have become major recipients. The USA took nearly 40 per cent of all direct investment in 1988. The 'Europe-1992' whose main objective is to facilitate intra-community investment will make European investment Euro-centric.

Added to this, the emergence of the East European countries and the Soviet Union with liberalized foreign direct investment policies there will be additional competion for this form of investment.

The Japanese investment has an increasing tendency to go into south-east Asia in addition to the USA and Europe. Hence it may not be a major investor in India.

Above all, there are inadequate savings in the world which is bothering many including international financial institutions. In the face of increased investment demand this factor will also put a constraint on the increased flow of resources to developing countries.[13] How much India can attract in this situation is anybody's guess. All the evidence is that India will not become a more attractive country to invest in than the present competitors and emerging nations which may become more favourable hosts.

It is useful to highlight other implications of this liberalized foreign investment policy. The trade off that is expected to be made to get increased investment by suffering certain disadvantages may actually lead India with the worsts of both the worlds.

The increased role of TNCs in India means that these companies would increasingly enter into high profit consumer goods sector. Even under so called restricted foreign invesunent policies, the TNCs dominated the high profit sector.[14]

Technology may not be actually flowing especially in view of the fact that the TNCs are increasingly apprehensive of technology diffusion leading to reduction in their monopolistic advantages.

Contribution to improvements in balance of payments from the operation of TNCs could not be as expected, i.e., export will grow and would not only pay for the remittances and imports but will also lead to a surplus. The past history of companies with 51 per cent equity shows that their activities in India have resulted in net outflow thus deteriorating the balance of payments of India.

The apprehension that the foreign investor will thwart domestic/national entrepreneurs, especially the small and medium ones, is brushed aside saying that Indian entrepreneur has come of age to survive the competition offered by the TNCs. National entrepreneur in India has indeed grown in a number of industries. One should not overlook the role of government policies in promoting this enterprise. Once they are removed it may be that the Indian entrepreneur will face a blizzard of competition for he has not yet arrived completely. Development of entrepreneurial capability is a long-term task.

Assistance from the International Monetary Fund and the World Bank

In order to solve this crisis of international payments of India, the government of India has sought assistance from the IMF and the World Bank under various facilities. Some of the proposed borrowings come under stiff conditionalities linked with structural adjustment programmes. It is believed that India is expecting to get 4 billion dollars from the IMF in the next two to three months. It is also negotiating for a loan of $600 million from the World Bank under Sectoral Adjustment Lending.

India has been dealing with the IMF since its inception especially after Independence not only as a member, but also an active one, endeavouring to represent developing countries. By accident of history, India was also a permanent member on the Board of Governors till the mid-seventies.

India has borrowed from the IMF under arrangements which have not demanded high conditionality. However, there were two occasions when India's relations with the IMF had come under severe criticism at home. In 1966, India appeared to have devalued its currency by 57.5 percent on the basis of the advice of the IMF with rather unfavourable effects on India's balance of payments and Indian economy.

The second important borrowing was in 1981 when India went in for a massive borrowing of 5.1 billion SDR, under Extended Fund Facility with conditionality. There was tremendous criticism of this borrowing. But India took only two tranches without taking the third one. It was argued that India's balance of payments position had improved hence it was unnecessary to draw the third tranche. This was in any case the official position. Unofficially, it is argued by some that India was not in a position to meet the stiff condition of reducing budget subsidies. Hence India avoided it by refusing to draw the third tranche to avoid the embarrassment that would have been created by the refusal of the IMF to release the third tranche because of the failure of the Government of India to meet the specified conditionality of reducing budget deficit through reducing subsidies. Table 14.9 gives the debt that the Government of India has incurred and repayments to IMF since 1985-86.

TABLE 14.9: IMF Loans and Repayments

Years	Debt outstanding	Authorization	Interest payment	Total debt
1985-86	4665	245	375	620
1986-87	4826	624	334	958
1987-88	4348	1163	338	1501
1988-89	3347	1472	277	1749
1989-90	2362	1402	273	1675
1990-91	4389	1056	218	1274

Source: Economic Survey, 1990-91.

The issue now is to seek 7 billion SDR loan from the IMF as Structural Adjustment Funds which is to be a loan under concessional finance with stiff conditions. It is argued that in a bid to get the loan the Government of India has introduced policy measures stipulated by the IMF. These include pursuing a 'realistic exchange rate policy' which is equivalent to devaluation, reduction in budget deficit., liberalized imports, liberal foreign investment policies and privatisation. The government has brought about the policy changes which include devaluation of the rupee by 22 per cent, liberalization of the foreign trade regime, liberalization of foreign investment policies, reduction of fiscal deficit to reach 6.0 per cent of GDP, liberal foreign investment policies, removal of licencing to a large number of industries, almost scrapping the conditions for MRTP companies in a bid to get lower conditionality by the IMF at the time of borrowing to satisfy the domestic criticism of being guided by the IMF.

Assuming the IMF grants to India 7 billion SDRs to meet its emergency requirement and India fulfills the conditionality, is it possible for India to find a solution to its economic crisis, especially of the crisis in external payments? No doubt, if India borrows from the IMF, there are three things which would happen immediately. *First,* India's creditworthiness will go up in the international banking sector. *Second,* India can meet her import requirements and thus perhaps maintain the industrial production. *Third,* other donors may come forward to lend. Thus in the immediate period, the external financial crisis will be temporarily solved.

There are two important questions which have not been sufficiently raised in the debate. Will the policy mix adopted result in the improvement of the Indian economy?

To answer this question it is vital to see how the adjustment programmes have influenced the developing countries. "The World Bank in its latest World Development Report has to say: "Have they succeeded? Answering this question is not straightforward".[15] A number of studies find improvement in the balance of payments, but the evidence on growth and inflation is inconclusive.

Table 14.10 gives the findings of 13 cross-country studies examining the adjustment programmes and their impact on those countries which accepted the programme. They differed from one another in terms of methodology, statistical techniques employed and coverage as regard the number of countries and the period of study.

TABLE 14.10: Number of Findings on the Impact of Stabilization

	Overall balance of payments	Current Account	Inflation	Growth
Improvement	6	5	2	4
Deterioration	3	2	10	7
No Change	4	5	4	5

It is clear from the above table that as many as ten countries experienced deterioration in inflation and in growth, while inflation and growth remained unchanged in five. Only in the case of current account balance there is an improvement in some cases, that too in a period when international banks were competing with each other to lend them. Even the immediate stabilization objectives have not been achieved. The study of 105 programmes during 1969-78 found that targets for government revenues could not be achieved in 40 per cent of the cases while expenditure exceeded stipulated limits in 60 per cent of the cases. Further, the effects on income distribution have been negative. Mamel Pashor in an empirical study on the impact of adjustment programme on income distribution found that in 18 Latin American countries, the labour share of income fell subsequent to a stabilization exercise prescribed by the IMF.[16]

The IMF itself conceded that the success of its programme depends on political commitment to the programme and high external finance. The political commitment, as the IMF sees it, is that the government should abandon all its welfare measures, become insensitive to the sufferings of large masses for basic needs. This is not the time for India to receive high finances as has already been discussed.

These measures are draconian and have naturally affected adversely the poorer sections of the population. They normally are expected to bear the burden of adjustment. The adjustment "with a human face" will not yet come about. Reduction in subsidies benefiting the poor, decline in employment and high inflation can hardly create a situation for adjustment "with a human face."

The additional debt burden which this temporary relief grants would make India borrow more to finance its imports. This will lead to increased debt burden with inadequate repayment capacity thus leading India into a vicious circle of debt burden. What India needs now is not to integrate totally with the world economy by pursuing policies over which it has little control. The need of the hour is to rethink about creative national development. The kingpin of this creative national development is to retain its complete sovereignty to take all decisions affecting its economic and political destiny. This creative national development should keep the priority of objectives of improving the lot of the masses as well as building in the system adequate impulses to achieve efficiency. This can be achieved by a close cooperation between government, industry and labour. The political consensus for this effort is a prerequisite for India to seek such a developmental path. This creative national development is not autarkic as some critics allege. It aims at developing a strategy which will incorporate a choice for the country, whereas the total integration in the world economy negates it.

NOTES

1. Budget speech of the Finance Minister 1990-91, *Economic Times*, July 25, 1991.
2. Government of India, *Economic Survey, 1990-91*, p. 4.
3. See for detailed discussion, B. S. Minhas, L. R. Jain, S. D. Tendulkar, "Declining Incidence of Poverty in the 1980s, Evidence versus Artefacts," *Economic and Political Weekly*, July 6-13, 1991, pp. 1673-82.
4. *Towards Evolving an Employment Oriented Strategy for Development in the 1990s*. See for discussion of this report, "Search for Employment Oriented Growth Strategy — A Discussion," *Economic and Political Weekly*, May 26, 1990.
5. Arun Ghosh, Eighth Plan : Challenges and Possibilities-III, 'Employment, Core of the Plan' *Economic and Political Weekly*, Feb-2, 1991. p 197.
6. Budget Speech of the Finance Minister 1990-91, *Economic Times*, 25 July, 1991.

7. *World Development Report*, 1990, p. 250.
8. *Ibid.*
9. See for an excellent analysis, G. Balachandran, "Mystery of the Sliding Rate", *Economic Times*, 12 August, 1991.
10. "A study in uncertainty, The Economy: Indian Credit Rating", *Economic Times*, Aug 12, 1991.
11. Statements made by former Finance Ministers Mr. S. B. Chavan and Mr. Madhu Dandavate to the Press.
12. See for detailed discussion Meenakshi Rishi and James K. Boyce, "The Hidden Balance of Payments, Capital Flight and Trade Misinvoicing in India, 1971-1986", *Economic and Political* Weekly, July 28, 1990.
13. See the speech of IMF Managing Director in Economic Social Council, 1991.
14. See for detailed discussion, IIFT, *Foreign Investment and Technology Transfer in India, Singapore and Malaysia* (mimeographed).
15. World Development Report 1991; p. 115. The columns do not add up to 13, the number of studies, because either some studies employ more than one method to assess the same target or a study does not evaluate one of the targets listed. Summarized by T. K. Arun, in "Structural Reform: A Shot in the Dark", *Economic Times*, 13 August, 1991 from Mohsin S. Khan, "The Macro Economic Effects of Fund Supported Adjustment Programme", *IMF Staff Papers*, vol. 37, no. 2, June 1990.
16. *Ibid.*

15

RURAL ENERGY CRISIS: Process and Prospects

S. GIRIAPPA

Introduction

THE PRESENT global energy crises are more due to factors of political economy through concentric effects of natural endowments and superfluous consumption patterns. While the current estimates of exhaustible energy recovery are optimistic for another 80 to 120 years, the development of renewable sources both highly sophisticated (technologies like photovoltaics, wind farms and wood gasification with long term perspectives) and less sophisticated (biogas, cookstoves and energy plantations with short term amendments) along with electricity (hydro, thermal and nuclear) and coupled with energy conservation and sustainable consumption (no more, no less) could ameliorate the crisis situation in the long run. Of course, the chances of negentropy will have its surprise entry any time during the crisis regimes.[1]

Biased resource endowment, inequitable consumption amongst different systems, regions, sectors, programmes and delivery groups have made the energy scenario at least in some years or sectors or regions or groups look crucial and problematic. When compared to urban areas, energy sources in rural areas because of their low sophistication and multiple uses have become characterized by lower levels of intensity and efficiency.

Types of Energy

Energy sources can be classified into exhaustible, commercial, non-commercial, conventional, non-conventional, renewable or a different combination of one or more of these. Thus, thermal, nuclear energy and natural gas are exhaustible, commercial and non-conventional. Coal and oil products are exhaustible, commercial and conventional energy sources. Amongst the renewables, hydro-electricity is commercial and conventional. Fuelwood is partly commercial and conventional and renewable with a time lag. Crop residues, cattledung, etc. are non-commercial and conventional sources. Biogas, forms of biomass energy, solar energy, wind energy, etc, are both non-commercial and non-conventional.[2]

Problem of Renewable Development

The problems with most of the renewables are that they are not primarily intended for use as fuel, and they require conversion for transformation and exploitation according to the given urgency of the priority of enduse. Renewables unlike exhaustibles are less intense and recovery cost would increase with the scale of operation. Though interest in renewables was refurbished especially after the oil shocks, the development has not become significant and competitive with the fossils. Relative short-term stability of fossils and fear of the oil cartels that if oil price is kept very high it will affect their longrun prospects via cheaper renewables (development of which would be quicker as a result of very high oil price) have made the development of both sophisticated and less sophisticated renewables tardy and time consuming.[3]

Commercialization and increasing efficiencies of different energy sources depend upon the nature of (sophisticated) technology that is available to convert the particular source (direct or indirect) into competitive use. Even among the fossils, a more sophisticated technology will emerge when the existing less sophisticated levels become uncompetitive and inefficient. Though the block of recoverable oil is not that encouraging when compared to that of say coal, yet in terms of exploration and distribution, oil is still the cheapest fuel in spite of recent price increases. At a time when oil price quadrupled, interest in renewable development and oil conservation methods were initiated. It took over 6 to 8 years to introduce fuel efficient cars and other conservation measures such that dependency on oil was reduced to a great extent in the heavily oil importing developed countries like the United States and Japan. Solar and wind energy development, sophisticated processing of coal, nuclear energy, bioenergy, etc., received importance. In the oil importing developing countries, the process of sophisticated technology in conserving, recycling and adopting to new sources has been slower. Energy has not been the prime factor of development in such counties but its importance is being felt in recent times. It could be that the developing countries are in the second or third stages of energy development and their achieving the most sophisticated conversion technology would result from high economic growth rather than any other factors.[4]

Since biomass is the principal primary energy resource in the oil importing developing countries and owing to the scarcity of fossils, it is but natural to expect these countries to stimulate renewable resources. Failure or slow progress in this regard leads to problems not only in the renewables but also in the case of fossils which may not be able to cope with the rising expectations of growth. And the intensity of the problem may or may not be uniform throughout the economy or regions or sectors or individual consumers. In the interfuel economy, exhaustible and commercial sources would be normally appropriated by the urban industrial and service sectors. Agriculture and rural domestic sectors have long been associated with non-commercial and biomass sources or energy for different enduses. The generation, distribution and efficiency of different energy sources differ according to the given endowment and use patterns. For example, the landed households by virtue of possessing fuel biomass base, may not experience the problem of energy crisis in normal times. Whereas in the landless and poor households, the crisis may be reflected either in the form of very low energy consumption or effecting transfers between different energy sources including labour. Thus, human labour may be expended in fuel gathering to ameliorate the woodfuel crisis resulting from low bargaining power.[5]

Since different energy sources are used simultaneously, (the co-existence pattern being at both macro and micro levels), different levels of integration among these sources are warranted. The management of exhaustible resources is centralized, whereas biomass energy management may be local-based and operated on a small scale in the absence of high sophistication. Since endowments of fossils are centralized, integration in them may be easily tackled, whereas in the different biomass sources, integration may be difficult and time consuming. Further, integration between less and high sophisticated levels becomes problematic and may lead to less sustainability.

Energy use in Rural Areas

This paper attempts to view the nature of energy crisis at the micro levels of households and also at the village level taking into consideration use and shortages over years.[6]

Udupi taluk of Dakshina Kannada district in Karnataka is one of the integrated rural energy programme (IREP) blocks since 1981-82. With 60 per cent subsidy biogas development in the block has been quite remarkable. Of the 3,000 plants in the 8 taluks of the district, Udupi shares about 25 per cent. Even in the case of improved cookstoves, the block shares over 20 per cent. Besides these, solar cookers, solar water heaters, solar street lights, solar stills, wind mills, etc., have been introduced on experimental basis. The proportion of forest to total geographical area is about 5 per cent, but the area under miscellaneous trees and groves and private forestry accounts for over 20 per cent of the land area. In this respect, the block is not wood deficit in relative terms when compared to many other interior blocks of the state. The proportion of net area sown is 40 per cent with a cropping intensity of 1.5. The percentage of net irrigated area is 25, with an average annual rainfall of about 400 cm. However, the irrigation intensity is only 1.1. Of the total crop area, rice shares about 55 per cent, other important crops being pulses, coconut and cashewnut.

The uncultivable waste and fallow lands produce biomass sources for fuel and other purposes; besides, plantation crops like coconut arecanut and cashewnut also yield a certain proportion of biomass energy. Marginal and small holdings account for about 88 per cent of the total number of operational holdings and 49 per cent of the operated area. Semi-medium holdings account for 8 per cent of the holding and 24 per cent of the area. Medium holdings share 3 per cent of the holdings and 19 per cent of the area. Large holdings share less than 0.5 per cent of the holdings and 8 per cent of the area. Area per holdings is one of the lowest in the block at 0.97 ha.

The results are based on a survey on IREP covering about 12 per cent of the villages of rural Udupi undertaken with reference to 1988-89. About 1200 households belonging to big farmers, medium farmers, small farmers, marginal farmers, rural industries and artisans, fisherman, service and business people, agricultural labourers and non-agricultural labourers were covered. Considering energy endowment and other particulars, these were grouped into: (i) big and medium farmers, (ii) small and marginal farmers, (iii) artisans, rural industries and fishermen, (iv) services and business and (v) agricultural and non-agricultural labourers. Energy consumption pattern according to these 5 groups and also between 5 income ranges (less than Rs. 7,500 to above Rs. 22,500 with a class interval of Rs. 5,000) according to different enduses like domestic, agriculture, industry and transport was analyzed. Based on energy equivalence, integration into joules was attempted. Further, energy demand and supply estimates have been for 5 years for the entire rural block.

For a particular group of households, energy shortage may be in some sources during some years or in some seasons. Energy shortage may become a problem factor and in some problem groups, the crisis may be endemic. Since energy intensity is part and parcel of the general economic growth process, any addition to energy should invariably result in improved lifestyle but in some cases superfluous and conspicuous consumption may result which would intensify the crisis stage for other groups.

Per Capita Energy Consumption

Table 15.1 describes per capita annual energy consumption in the five groups as regards domestic sector. The average quantity of fuelwood consumption was 350 kg, being higher than the average in groups I and II and lower in others. Fuelwood was used for cooking (83.4%) and heating (16.6%) only. Per capita consumption in fuelstick and crop residues was 554 kg, higher in the I, II and last groups and lower in the middle groups. Fuelstick was used for heating (78%) rather than for cooking. Cattle dung consumption was very low at 2 kg, groups II and V reporting a slightly higher level of consumption.

Kerosene was used mainly or lighting (97.1%); cooking (2.3%) and heating (0.6%) were minor end-uses. The average kerosene consumption was 9 litres, lower for the I group, average for the middle groups and higher for the lower groups. The proportion used for cooking was higher in the upper groups. Electricity consumption was 11.8 kWh, the labour groups reporting a very low average. Electricity was used mainly for lighting purpose (91.6%); cooking, heating and other uses shared more or less equally the remainder. LPG (0.7 kg) and biogas (11.8 cubic metre) were consumed at a higher level by the upper groups and very little or nil by the last group.

TABLE 15.1: Per Capita Annual Fuel Consumption Groupwise (domestic)

Source	Big & Medium farmers	Small & marginal farmers	Artisans @	Services & business	Labourers*	All
Fuelwood(kg)	553.0	353.7	299.6	266.1	241.8	350.0
Fuelstick + crop residues (kg)	610.6	561.0	435.8	471.6	579.5	544.0
Cattle dung (kg)	0.8	3.8	0.8	0.6	2.7	2.1
Kerosene (l)	6.5	9.0	8.9	11.2	9.9	9.0
Electricity (kWh)	14.6	11.6	11.2	16.7	6.5	11.8
L.P.G. (kg)	1.2	0.6	0.2	1.7	0.01	0.7
Biogas (m^3)	21.2	19.2	2.5	5.3	-	11.8
Total cons (Giga.J)	20.6	16.0	12.71	12.80	13.65	15.50
Average income (Rs)	16,022	9,108	9,415	16,903	7,197	11,108

@ including rural industries and fishermen.
* both agricultural and non-agricultural+rural.

The average per capita annual domestic energy consumption as 15.5 Giga. J (10^9 joules). The consumption level in group I was the highest (20.6 GJ) and slightly above the average group II (16 GJ). The consumption level in groups III and IV was the lowest but similar and it was slightly higher in the last group. It is interesting to note that the labour groups had a higher consumption level than the artisans and service groups. The higher level of consumption of fuelstick and crop residues was the factor behind this.

Energy Purchases

When compared to income levels, the service and business units fared better with an energy intensity of 0.76 mega (10^6) J/Rs (for a income of Rs. 16,903), followed by big and medium farmers (1.28 MJ/Rs), artisans (1.35 MJ/Rs), small and marginal farmers, (1.76 MJ/Rs) and labourers (1.89 MJ/Rs) as against the average intensity of 1.40 MJ/Rs.

The proportion of owned and gathered fuelwood, fuelstick and crop residues was lower for the farmer and labour groups but higher for others. According to Table 15.2, the proportion of purchased fuelwood for all groups was 21.1 per cent, higher for rural industries, fishermen, services and business, moderates for medium farmers and the labour groups, very low for small and marginal farmers and nil for the big farmers. Big and small farmers had no purchases of fuelstick and crop residues; medium and marginal farmers had very low purchases. Rural industries, services, business and non-agricultural labourers had a higher proportion of purchase than the average purchase ratio (5.8%). In crop residues also, these classes reported a higher proportion of purchase (over 10 per cent as against 6.4 per cent average. Fishermen in fuelwood (70.3%) and crop residues (19.4%) and rural industries in fuelstick (20.7%) had the higher proportion of purchases. It is evident that non-agricultural labourers, rural industries, fishermen, services and business had to depend upon external sources of fuel biomass when compared to the four farmer groups and agricultural labourers.

TABLE 15.2: Proportion of Purchased Fuelwood, Fuelstick and Crop Residues

Group	Fuelwood	Fuelsticks	Crop residues	Domestic energy as % to income	All energy as % to income
Big farmers	—	—	—	1.7	12.7
Medium farmers	13.7	3.6	1.3	3.9	14.6
Small farmers	6.3	—	—	2.7	7.1
Marginal farmers	6.3	5.2	3.1	4.2	11.6
Rural Industries	66.3	20.7	16.6	12.7	19.4
Fishermen	70.3	2.8	19.4	6.5	9.2
Services	56.5	17.1	12.0	4.3	15.8
Business	59.7	20.4	13.8	5.6	15.9
Agril labour	15.2	5.3	3.2	3.8	3.9
Non-agrl labour	23.0	15.5	8.2	6.6	7.4
All	21.1	5.8	6.4	4.6	12.1

The nature of the problem could also be seen by considering the proportion of household income spent on different energy sources across the different groups. On an average, 4.6 per cent of household income was spent on purchased energy in the domestic sector. The proportion was lowest for the big (1.7%), small (2.7%), medium (3.9%) and marginal farmers (4.2%), services (4.3%), and agricultural labourers (3.8%); rural industries had the highest proportion (12.7%) followed by non-agricultural labourers (6.6%), fishermen (6.5%) and business units (5.6%). When energy use for domestic, agriculture, industry and personal transport was considered, the proportion of household income spent on purchased energy increased to 12.1 per cent for all the groups. Big and medium farmers, rural industries, services and business units had a higher proportion while agricultural labourers, non-agricultural labourers, small farmers and fishermen had lower averages.

Income-rangewise Energy Consumption

The problem can also be considered according to different income levels (Table 15.3). The proportion of households in the lowest income range (less than Rs 7500) was 28.5 per cent; it was 38.3 per cent in group II (Rs. 7,501-12,500), 28.2 per cent in group III Rs. 12,501-17,500), 8 per cent in group IV (Rs. 17,501-22,500) and 5 per cent in the last group (above Rs. 22,501). The average household income for the sample as a whole Rs. 11,108, being very high for the big farmers, medium for services, business and medium farmers, around average for fishermen and small farmers and lower for artisans and labourers. In terms of energy intensity, groups IV and V were efficient (0.83 and 0.64 MJ/Rs respectively) when compared to others. In fuelwood consumption, income group I had a lower level and other groups either average or higher level of consumption. In the case of fuelstick and crop residues, the first and last income groups had higher averages than others. The lower income group had a higher cattle dung consumption. In kerosene consumption, the upper income group had a slightly lower consumption. Electricity, LPG and biogas consumption increased with increasing income levels.

TABLE 15.3: Per Capita Fuel Consumption, Income Rangewise (domestic)

Source	Less than Rs. 7,500	Rs. 7,501-12,500	Rs. 12,501-17,500	Rs. 17,501-22,500	Above Rs. 22,500
Fuelwood (kg)	295.4	352.8	362.6	397.2	394.4
Fuelstick + crop residues (kg)	600.6	528.0	461.8	514.2	663.7
Cattle dung (kg)	3.0	2.3	1.3	0.2	—
Kerosene (l)	9.1	8.8	9.7	8.3	8.9
Electricity (kWh)	8.8	10.6	16.2	12.9	18.9
L.P.G. (kg)	0.3	0.5	1.1	1.0	1.9
Biogas (m^3)	6.8	8.4	21.2	21.5	13.2
Total cons (Giga. J)	15.15	15.25	14.79	16.17	18.25
Average income (Rs.)	5,803	9,473	14,151	19,298	28,555

While the difference between lowest and highest consumption levels in the 5 social groups was about 8 GJ, it was only 4 GJ in the different income groups. High consumption of owned and gathered fuelstick and crop residues in the lower income groups had presented a slightly lower but nonetheless satisfactory consumption level for them. However, in consumption of all other energy sources, the lower income groups lagged behind others. High energy consumption seemed to be influenced least by income differences.

Supply-demand Gap

Extrapolating the different social classes existing in the sample villages to the entire rural block, an analysis has been attempted to view the supply-demand gap for different energy sources for five years up to 1993-94 keeping 1988-89 as the base. The analysis shows the nature of deficit energy across different consuming groups (Table 15.4). The attempt has been made only in respect of fuelwood, fuelstick and crop residues, kerosene and electricity. As regards LPG, petrol, diesel and biogas, there is a vast scope for improvement and higher future growth rate. Moreover, the deficit situation would arise especially when the normal supply is restricted at times of macro crises. Being more or less non-conventional in the rural areas, their supply-demand gap will have little meaning unless adopted in large scale. Hence these have been left out of estimation.

TABLE 15.4: Extent of Deficit Energy Across Different Consumer Groups (%)

Group	Fuelwood		F.S. & C.R.@		Kerosene	Electricity	
	1988-89	1993-94	1988-89	1993-94	1988-89	1988-89	1993-94
Big farmers	—	3.0	—	—	1.5	18.5	6.0
Medium farmers	1.5	5.0	—	—	3.0	12.0	5.0
Small farmers	4.5	10.5	1.0	1.5	4.5	11.0	5.0
Marginal farmers	7.0	13.0	—	—	8.0	10.0	3.0
Rural industries	5.0	18.0	3.0	3.0	15.0	14.0	7.0
Fishermen	10.0	16.5	5.0	5.0	10.0	10.0	2.0
Services	5.0	12.5	—	—	12.5	14.5	3.0
Business	5.0	10.0	—	—	10.0	20.0	5.0
Agrl. labour	3.0	6.0	5.0	8.0	10.0	12.5	1.5
Non-agrl. labour	4.0	8.0	5.0	11.0	10.0	7.5	1.5
All	4.6	10.4	1.7	2.6	8.5	11.9	3.7
Deficit villages	8.7	21.6	2.7	5.4	12.8	14.3	5.3

@ = fuelsticks and crop residues.

In respect of fuelwood, the supply-demand gap was 4.6 per cent of demand for all the groups in 1988-89 and the gap would increase to 10.4 per cent in 1993-94. Big farmers had no deficit in the base year but the gap will increase to 3 per cent in the terminal year. For the medium farmers, the gap will increase from 1.5 to 5 per cent and for the small farmers from 4.5 to 10.5 per cent. The deficit rate for the marginal farmers was high at 7 per cent in the base year and would increase to 13 per cent in the terminal year. The deficit rate for fishermen was the highest at 10 per cent and would increase to 16.5 per cent in the terminal year; for the labour groups the deficit rate (3 to 4%) would double in the course of five years. For rural industries, services and business, the 5 per cent deficit would increase to 18, 12.5 and 10 per cent respectively. Rural industries, fishermen, marginal farmers and services would have a larger deficit in the terminal year. Not only the proportion of deficit will increase over the years, new social groups may be added to the high deficit range.

Of the 12 sample villages, 5 villages had no deficit of fuelwood or fuelstick, though some groups in them had. For the deficit villages, the overall proportion of fuelwood deficit was 8.7 per cent which would increase to 21.6 per cent in the terminal year. When compared to the general average, the deficit villages had almost 90 per cent more deficit but in the terminal year the difference would increase to 108 per cent. The worst effected groups would be fishermen, rural industries, marginal farmers, services and small farmers.

In the case of fuelstick and crop residues, big, medium, and marginal farmers, services and business had no deficit. The average deficit rate was 1.7 per cent in the base year, increasing into 2.6 per cent in the terminal year. Rural industries, fishermen, agricultural labourers and non-agricultural labourers would be having a larger deficit in both the base and terminal years. The labour groups, owing to their higher dependency on these resources would be worst effected. The deficit villages will have an additional deficit of 60 per cent in the base year and 108 per cent in the terminal year. For all the biomass fuels, deficit in the terminal year would be substantial from 6.3 to 13 per cent for all the villages and from 11.4 to 27 per cent for the deficit villages.

As regards kerosene, the overall deficit was 8.5 per cent in the base year. In the terminal year, the estimated deficit would be very little owing to fuel substitution. The deficit would be larger in the case of rural industries, services, fishermen, business and labourers. For the deficit villages, the proportion of deficit was higher at 12.8 per cent.

It is in respect of electricity, the proportion of deficit was the highest at 11.9 per cent for all the villages and 14.3 per cent for the deficit villages. Almost all the social groups experienced inadequate electricity supply. In the terminal year however, a lower proportion of deficit had been envisaged owing to new projects in the region and the larger incidence of gaseous fuels, in the absence of which the deficit rate is bound to increase. At the household levels, deficit may not be experienced by some groups like big and medium farmers but at the village level there may be overall deficit. Conversely, households belonging to labourers, artisans, etc., may experience deficit but the particular village may experience little deficit.

For a particular social group, energy use may be in commensurate with the given lifestyle though not average annual income. But when compared to high consuming groups, the lower groups might face a seasonal or annual shortage and cumulatively a crisis may follow thereon. If basic minimum need of energy is considered, it may vary between different groups. Without considering basic minimum needs for the entire households, it may be under or over estimating the energy needs. As such, a large proportion of the lower groups may said to be experiencing shortage of basic energy if shortages of most of the basic needs are experienced. High energy use without fulfilment of basic needs has little meaning. Also, the high energy intensity households would sooner or later face energy crisis unless conservation and more efficient measures are adopted.

Share of Energy Sources

Table 15.5 presents the effective share of deficit energy sources in different sectors of rural Udupi, based on extrapolation in the sample villages during 1988-89. The thermal efficiency ranges from 7 per cent in fuelstick and crop residues to 70 per cent in LPG and electricity. In absolute terms, total energy use across different sectors was 6.13 PJ (10^{15} joules). The share of fuelwood was 42.9 per cent and that of fuelstick and crop residues 50.3 per cent. When effective energy use is considered, total energy use was only 11.8 per cent of the gross value (i.e. 722.7 Tera J- 10^{12} joules). The effective share of fuelwood at 10 per cent efficiency would be only 36.5 per cent and that of fuelstick and crop residues (at 7 per cent efficiency) 29.8 per cent. The effective share of these two biomass resources would be around two thirds of total energy use as against 93 per cent in absolute terms. Electricity (8.1%), kerosene (12.9%) and petrol (6.7%) would have a larger share after the biomas energy sources. The share of diesel was 2.6 per cent, that of LPG 0.9 per cent and biogas 1.6 per cent in effective terms.

TABLE 15.5: Effective Share of Different Energy Sources in Rural Udupi

Source	Fuel cons 10^9 MJ	Effective		Effective Share %	Domestic	Agrl.	Industry	Transport	EKJ/Rs*
		%	10^6 MJ						
Cattle dung	0.01	12	0.6	0.08	100.0	—	—	—	2738
Fuelstick@	3.08	7	215.5	29.82	100.0	—	—	—	2663
Fuelwood	2.63	10	263.4	36.45	99.9	—	0.01	—	3864
Charcoal	0.02	25	5.8	0.80	—	—	100.0	—	3905
Biogas	0.02	60	11.8	1.63	100.0	—	—	—	5925
Kerosene+	0.16	60	93.5	12.94	78.2	16.5	5.3	—	9091
Petrol	0.08	60	48. 7	6.74	—	—	—	100.0	2789
Diesel	0.03	60	18.5	2.56	—	34.5	35.0	30.5	6606
Electricity	0.08	70	58.5	8.10	35.1	64.2	0.7	—	3602
L.P.G.	0.01	70	6.4	0.88	100.0	—	—	—	6792
All	6.13	11.8	722.7	100.0	591.09	59.37	17.90	54.34	—
				%	81.79	8.22	2.78	7.51	

* Effective kilo joules per rupee.
@ Includes crop residues.
\+ Including lighting and heating.

The entire quantum of cattle dung, fuelstick and crop residues, biogas and LPG were used in the domestic sector. About 99.9 per cent of fuelwood, 78.2 per cent of kerosene and 35.1 per cent of electricity were also used in that sector.

In agriculture (irrigation pumps), 16.5 per cent of kerosene, 34.5 per cent of diesel and 64.2 per cent of electricity were used. The entire quantum of charcoal, 35 per cent of diesel, 5.3 per cent of kerosene, 0.7 per cent of electricity and 0.1 per cent of fuelwood were used in rural industries. The entire quantum of petrol and 30.5 per cent diesel were used in the personal transport sector.

The effective energy used in domestic sector was 81.79 per cent followed by agriculture (8.22%), transport (7.51%) and rural industries (2.48%). The relative efficiency of different sources shows that kerosene, LPG, diesel and biogas have a better productivity (above 6 MJ/Rs) while cattledung, fuelstick and petrol have lower productivity levels.

Conclusion

It has been estimated for the sample block that an investment of Rs. 103 mil in biogas plants (44%), improved cookstoves (32%), wood gasifier and solar energy (15%) and farm forestry (9%) over a five year period would yield an additional energy besides saving fuel biomass to the tune of Rs. 119 mil, thus favouring the strengthening up of the renewable strategy. Of course, effective energy management (local as well as bureaucratic) and making the alternative technology economic and competitive are essential ingredients of the conservation process.

It may be pointed out that due to the above constraints, the existing system of improved cookstoves has had limited impact on rural households in the region, biogas programme is yet to take off and solar and wind energy still in demonstration stages. Except fuel biomass, other forms of renewable energy sources are still economically unviable, though they have been proved socially advantageous. In the absence of any incentives like cash subsidy, the adoption of these unconventional energy sources would be practically insignificant.

From the study of energy use pattern in a micro-region, the following types of consumption may be established. Owing to high energy intensity (when considered to income levels), inefficient energy consumption results in certain groups like labourers and marginal and small farmers. Second, high level of consumption (sometimes superfluous) especially in the high income groups with high energy intensity results in inequality in consumption levels. Lastly, insufficient consumption in the lower income groups with or without high energy intensity aggravates the process of energy crisis. This has to be considered especially when the fuel biomass deficits are estimated to increase in future, more so in the case of lower income groups and villages having inadequate woodlot. Adequate supply of electricity, LPG, kerosene, petrol conservation of fuel biomass through farm forestry, integrated methanization, improved cookstoves and better conversion processes like wood gasifiers and photovoltaics would enable to contain the shortages in the shortrun (through small scale and less sophisticated renewable technology) as well as in the long-run (through largescale and sophisticated renewable technology).

There is a lot of scope to reduce fuel biomass. Since it has multiple uses including that of environment subsidy, its choice as energy has to be very selective and recycling-oriented. Because this will depend on the capacity of other alternatives (including efficient use), redevelopment of the same would become a basic need. Improper use of renewables may aggravate the environmental crisis, besides the negative impact of fossils. For an oil importing energy deficit country like India, the crisis has been there in some form or other, sometimes turning to be catastrophic. The crisis may be embodied in periodical shortages, low consumption levels, high prices, inefficient use or superfluous consumption. Underutilization of renewables and over-dependence on scarce fossils should not in no way discriminate against rural areas which also require high energy intensity for improved productivity and sustainability. The question is at what cost or transfer or time, sustainable energy could be managed to be achieved within the overall development perspective of the economy.

NOTES

R.L. Pirog and S.C. Stamos Jr. *Energy Economic Theory and Policy*, Prentice-Hall Inc., New Jersy, 1987, p.4.

See also D.W. Pearce and R.K. Turner. *Economics of Natural and the Environment*, Harvester Wheatsheaf, New York, 1990, Chaps. 16 and 18.

L.G. Hines. *The Market, Energy and the Environment*, Allyn and Bacon Inc., Boston, 1988, Ch. 6.

W.S. Chern. "An Assessment of future energy demand in Developing Countries", *Natural Resources Forum*, Vol. 9, No. 4, 1985, pp.303-309.

For a description of the exchange process between fuel energy and human labour, see M.R. Bhagavan and S. Giriappa. "Class character of rural energy crisis : Case of Karnataka", *Economic and Political Weekly*, Vol. XXII (26), 1987, pp.57-69.

S. Giriappa, Integrated Rural Energy Programme Udupi block, Dakshina Kannada, *Survey Report*, Mangalore University, Mangalagangotri, 1990 (mimeo).

16

FOOD SUBSIDY IN THE CONTEXT OF REVENUE DEFICIT: Diagnosis and Treatment

K.N. REDDY and V. SELVARAJU

Introduction

WHILE PRESENTING the Budget for 1991-92, on July 24th, 1991, the Finance Minister, Dr. Manmohan Singh observed that the Indian economy is in deep economic crisis, with ever growing revenue deficit/budgetary deficit/and fiscal deficit, and balance of payments deficit on the one hand and spiraling price level on the other. He tried to reduce the deficit through raising of resources and halting/reducing the growth of certain items of expenditure — defence and subsidies — hitherto considered impossible. The urging of arresting the growth of defence expenditure, interest payments and subsidies was recognised long ago — i.e., at the time of presenting the Long Term Fiscal Policy (LTFP) in 1985 itself. But the Finance Ministers since then were not bold enough to make efforts to reduce them. For the first time, Dr. Manmohan Singh made efforts to keep defence expenditure at the previous year's level (or reduce it in real terms) and reduce expenditure on subsidies by 15 per cent from Rs. 12,121 crore (RE) in 1990-91 to Rs. 10,395 crore (BE) in 1991-92. But the interesting part of it is that while expenditure on export subsidies was brought down considerably by adopting suitable changes in trade policies, similar efforts were not made in expenditure on food subsidies. Contrary to expectations, expenditure on food subsidies went up from Rs. 2,450 crore in 1990-91 (RE) to Rs. 2,600 in 1991-92 (RE). Whatever little efforts made in reducing expenditure on fertilizer subsidies were knocked out by diluting it at the time of passing the budget in Parliament.

What is interesting and intriguing is the hike in expenditure on food subsidy and the reason associated with it. The reason mentioned was the likely increase in procurement prices of wheat and rice to farmers to compensate for the inevitable increase in the prices of fertilizers consequent upon the reduction in fertilizer subsidy to indigenous manufacturers. This is understandable since the attempt is to provide incentive to farmers. What is not understandable is the hike in procurement prices (and hence increase in food subsidy) without increasing the issue prices of commodities sold under Public Distribution System (PDS). Even the much talked to targeting of foodgrains was not attempted. In our opinion, there is scope to reduce growth of food subsidies buy looking at the whole issue afresh, particularly at the functioning of Food Corporation of India (FCI) and targeting the food subsidies to the deserving classes only. In what follows attempt is made towards that end.

Section II discusses the description of events that led to the governmental intervention in the distribution of foodgrains at subsidised rates and the entry of FCI in the sale and purchase of foodgrains to serve as a background for the study. Section III discusses the factors responsible for the growth of food subsidy and identifies the areas for action. Section IV suggests steps for reducing/arresting the growth of food subsidy in the years to come.

II

Background of Food Subsidy

Until 1943, foodgrains economy of India was virtually a free market economy, wherein foodgrains prices were determined by market forces. The World War II disrupted the imports and internal transport system and consequently free foodgrains market collapsed during mid 1940s. In economic terms market failed to be "Pareto efficient" due to externalities. Market failure resulted in deprivation among the poor and compelled the Government to intervene and improve the functioning of foodgrains market. The correction of externalities formed the rationale for Government intervention (Burgess R and N Stern, (1989), Social Security in Developing Countries: What, Why, Who and How? Working Paper No: DEP 23, ST-ICERD, University of London).

The Government intervened by setting up a Foodgrains Policy Committee in 1943 to review the foodgrains situation in the country. The Committee after a detailed review, suggested a system in which a Central Government agency would participate in the procurement and distribution of foodgrains parallel to private trade and creation of Central reserve of foodgrains. In the initial years, the Government mainly confined to importing of foodgrains and distributing them through ration shops rather than procuring them from domestic supplies. The policies related to foodgrains underwent drastic changes and there was no stable policy. There were controls and regulations which were ad hoc in nature for temporary problems. The need for a long term foodgrains policy was realised in 1964 when the prices of foodgrains increased by 27 per cent. It was also recognised that to implement the controls successfully, adequate preparations before enforcement were necessary, and the State must build up sizeable stocks of grains (R. Radhakrishna and S. Indrakant., (1988), Effects of Rice Market Intervention policies in India: The Case of Andhra Pradesh, in Evaluating Rice Market Intervention Policies: Some Asian Experiences, ADB, Manila).

In this context, FCI came into existence in 1965 to deal with foodgrains trade and was expected to act as a countervailing force to the speculative activities of the private traders. The functions of procurement, storage and distribution were handed over to FCI which were hitherto handled by Department of Food in several States. In addition, FCI was asked to handle all imported grains and their distribution and implement the food policy objectives namely, (i) self sufficiency, (ii) assuring the supply of adequate foodgrains in all parts of the country with special emphasis on safeguarding the interests of low income consumers along with price stability and (iii) assuring reasonable and incentive prices to the producers.

Gradually the task of food management got extended from the disaster and drought management to enlarged distribution function directed towards vulnerable sections of the population. In fact, FCI grew manifold and emerged as an effective instrument of the Government in implementing food policy objectives. But along with its expansion, its losses also went up – from Rs. 865 crore in 1980-81 to Rs. 2,061 crore in 1988-89 and thus recorded 14.62 per cent growth (Table 16.1). Consequently food subsidy which was Rs. 650 crore in 1980-81, rose to Rs. 2,200 crore in 1988-89 – a stupendous increase of 19.68 per cent.

TABLE 16.1: Trends in the Losses of Food Corporation of India : 1980-81 to 1988-89

(*Rs. Crores*)

Year	Sale Receipts	Value of Sales	Other # Expenses	Total Losses	Food Subsidy	Actual * Consumer Subsidy
1980-81	2759	2971	653	865	650	212
1981-82	2814	2955	784	925	700	141
1982-83	3173	3355	893	1075	710	182
1983-84	3530	3854	1036	1360	835	324
1984-85	3169	3476	1235	1542	1100	307
1985-86	5106	5430	1704	2028	1650	324
1986-87	5202	5656	1818	2272	2000	454
1987-88	5975	6627	1715	2367	2000	652
1988-89	4752	5307	1506	2061	2200	555
	10.13	10.76	13.52	14.62	19.68	18.67

Source: 1. FCI Annual Reports.
2. Economic and Functional Classification of Central Government Budget, Ministry of Finance.

Note: # Other expanses include freight, handling, salaries and wages etc., rent, depreciation, interest and miscellaneous expanses.
* Value of sales minus receipts.

III

Factors Associated with the Growth of Food Subsidy

It is not difficult to visualise the factors responsible for the rapid growth of food subsidy. At least two factors can be mentioned immediately – one is the very policy of government in reimbursing the losses of FCI and the other is the operational efficiency of FCI. Since the objectives for which FCI was set up are such that losses are bound to occur, and will occur in the future also. Only political decision could change the losses of FCI. To be more clear, look at what food subsidy is meant and the components constituting it.

Food subsidy refers to the amount paid by Government to FCI towards reimbursement of (i) the difference between the "economic cost" of foodgrains and their issue prices, (called as consumer subsidy), and (ii) the carrying cost of buffer stocks. "Economic cost" comprises of (a) procurement prices and (b) procurement incidentals for indigenously procured as well as imported foodgrains and (c) distribution incidentals of foodgrains comprising of their movement, storage, handling, interest charges etc. Issue prices refer to the average price of sales realised under various schemes such as Integrated Tribal Development Programme (I.T.D.P.), Rural Landless

Employment Guarantee Programme (R.L.E.G.P.), National Rural Employment Programme (N.R.E.P.), Jawahar Rojgar Yojana (J.R.Y.), P.D.S. and open sales (i.e., sale of damaged foodgrains). By and large, food subsidy is influenced by (a) socio-economic policy of the government, and (b) by the operational efficiency of FCI. Therefore, if savings have to be effected in food subsidy or growth of subsidies has to be contained, steps are needed on both the fronts. Since, improvement in operational efficiency of FCI lies in the hands of government administration and amenable for pressures, it will be discussed first. The changes needed in socio-economic policy shall be taken up later.

Operational Efficiency of FCI

It needs no mention that higher the operational efficiency of FCI, lower shall be the subsidies. It is therefore necessary to examine inefficiencies, if any, in its operation and see whether they can be removed. There are three constituents in operational efficiency of FCI. First is the way the procurement incidentals were incurred. Second, the way the distribution incidentals were incurred and the third the way the carrying costs of buffer stocks were incurred. Any neglect in the management of either of them or all of them would escalate inefficiency of FCI and consequently its looses. In what follows operational efficiency of is looked into in respect of two major commodities — wheat and rice — leaving the rest for the present. In fact, wheat and rice constitute more than 80 per cent of the total value of foodgrains brought under the fold of FCI.

Procurement Incidentals refer to the costs incurred by the FCI in procuring the foodgrains, i.e., the costs incurred to move the foodgrains, from the places of purchase to the godowns which incidentally include mandi charges costs of gunny, purchase/sales tax, interest charges storage charges, mandi labour charges, forwarding charges, internal movements, establishment charges, others. Tables 16.2 and 16.3 show the procurement incidentals incurred on wheat and rice respectively. It can be seen (Table 16.2) that procurement incidentals of wheat grew at the rate of 7.61 per cent per annum during 1980-81 to 1988-89. In absolute terms, they increased from Rs. 21.31 in 1980-81 to Rs. 36.36 per quintal in 1988-89. It appears that much of the increase was on account of rapid increase in the costs of gunny, interest charges, storage charges and internal movements. In absolute terms, cost of gunny, purchase/sales tax and mandi charges account nearly 70 to 80 per cent of total procurement incidentals of wheat.

Procurement incidentals of rice grew at the rate of 6.70 per cent per annum – registering a smaller increase than that of wheat. In absolute terms they increased from Rs. 10.05 in 1980-81 to Rs. 16.91 in 1988-89 per quintal (Table 16.3). Here again cost of gunny and purchase/sales tax contributed maximum (i.e., 70 to 80 per cent) of total procurement incidentals on rice; But unlike in the case of wheat, forwarding charges, are increasing at a faster rate.

In fact, procurement incidentals of wheat are almost one hundred per cent more than that of rice. One important reason seems to be that mandi charges, which grew relatively fast, account for 15 to 20 per cent of total procurement incidentals of wheat. But in the case of rice no mandi charges are involved and consequently no mandi labour charges too. Another important reason seems to be the purchase/sales tax, which also grew relatively fast, accounts for 20 per cent of the total procurement cost of wheat whereas it accounts for 10-15 per cent only in the case of rice. Other charges such as interest charges, storage charges, internal movements, etc., also were relatively higher in the case of wheat.

Distribution Incidentals refer to the costs incurred by FCI for distributing the foodgrains from godowns to distribution centres. They are pooled incidentals for wheat and rice and no separate incidentals are available for each commodity as the foodgrains meant for sale are generally distributed together or jointly. It can be seen from Table 16.4 that distribution incidentals increased at the rate of 10.38 per cent per annum during 1980-81 to 1988-89 – from Rs. 29.05 to Rs. 72.38 per quintal. Much of this increase was on account of storage charges, handling charges, administrative overheads and freight charges which increased at the rate of 14.92 per cent, 13.56 per cent, 13.34 per cent and 12.17 per cent respectively during 1980-81 to 1988-89.

Carrying Cost of Buffer Stocks is yet another important component of operational efficiency of FCI. Its incidentals went up from Rs. 34.00 in 1980-81 to Rs. 61.84 in 1988-89 per quintal – registering an annual increase of 4.12 per cent. And much of this was on account of sharp increase in storage charges, administrative charges, and handling charges (Table 16.5). In absolute terms storage charges went up from Rs. 8.30 per quintal in 1980-81 to Rs. 40.83 per quintal in 1988-89, whereas administrative charges, and handling charges went up from Rs. 1.60 per quintal to Rs. 7.16 per quintal and Rs. 1.58 per quintal to Rs. 5.09 per quintal respectively.

TABLE 16.2: Procurement Incidentals — Wheat : 1980-81 — 1988-89

(*Rs. per quintal*)

	Items	1980-81	1981-82	1982-83	1983-84	1984-85	1985-86	1986-87	1987-88	1988-89	Gr Rate(%)
1.	Mandi Charges	3.96	3.82	4.30	4.44	3.92	4.22	5.17	6.23	6.40	6.37
2.	Cost of Gunny	6.04	5.88	6.18	6.71	8.25	11.30	11.32	9.54	9.95	9.02
3.	Purchase/Sales Tax	4.54	4.70	5.38	4.51	5.09	6.53	6.28	5.72	7.75	5.84
4.	Interest Charges	1.99	2.42	2.64	2.52	2.71	2.73	3.89	4.57	3.72	9.17
5.	Storage Charges	0.59	0.59	0.50	0.50	0.52	0.57	1.37	1.51	1.30	14.50
6.	Mandi Labour Charges	0.99	1.06	1.11	1.12	1.17	1.32	1.83	1.75	1.65	8.17
7.	Forwarding Charges	0.78	0.89	0.63	0.54	0.50	0.48	0.62	0.46	0.88	−2.71
8.	Internal Movements	1.47	1.89	2.25	2.45	2.76	2.99	2.96	2.93	3.38	9.41
9.	Establishment Charges	0.95	1.07	1.29	1.36	1.33	1.41	1.37	1.42	1.33	4.00
10.	Others	—	—	—	0.02	0.06	0.06	—	—	—	—
	Total	21.31	22.32	24.28	24.17	26.31	31.61	34.81	34.13	36.36	7.61

Source: Annual Reports of FCI : 1980-81 to 1988-89.

TABLE 16.3: Procurement Incidentals — Rice : 1980-81 — 1988-89

(*Rs. per quintal*)

	Items	1980-81	1981-82	1982-83	1983-84	1984-85	1985-86	1986-87	1987-88	1988-89	Gr Rate(%)
1.	Mandi Charges	—	—	—	—	—	—	—	—	—	—
2.	Cost of Gunny	6.21	6.05	6.26	7.18	12.37	9.80	8.25	8.54	10.68	7.02
3.	Purchase/Sales Tax	1.46	1.27	1.05	1.10	1.64	2.00	1.79	1.30	2.16	5.66
4.	Interest Charges	0.22	—	0.18	0.52	0.14	0.34	0.36	0.27	0.45	−0.17
5.	Storage Charges	—	0.02	0.08	0.45	0.29	0.08	0.07	0.05	0.07	−15.19
6.	Mandi Labour Charges	—	—	—	—	—	—	—	—	—	—
7.	Forwarding Charges	—	0.73	0.85	0.84	1.14	1.28	1.26	1.71	1.60	9.86
8.	Internal Movements	0.80	0.43	0.46	0.66	0.74	0.66	0.38	0.38	0.62	−2.89
9.	Establishment Charges	0.96	1.04	1.01	0.97	1.01	0.97	0.87	0.91	1.33	1.01
10.	Others	0.40	—	0.05	0.27	—	0.05	—	—	—	—
	Total	10.05	9.54	9.94	11.99	17.32	15.18	12.98	13.16	16.91	6.70

Source: Annual Reports of FCI : 1980-81 to 1988-89.

TABLE 16.4: Pooled Distribution Cost : 1980-81 — 1988-89

(*Rs. per quintal*)

	Items	1980-81	1981-82	1982-83	1983-84	1984-85	1985-86	1986-87	1987-88	1988-89	Gr Rate(%)
1.	Handling Charges	2.11	3.33	3.62	3.71	3.51	3.87	7.18	5.57	6.79	13.56
2.	Storage Charges	2.77	3.28	3.08	3.06	2.97	3.35	3.61	5.54	13.60	14.92
3.	Interest Charges	7.16	7.96	9.08	12.95	18.20	17.39	15.34	15.09	10.74	8.48
4.	Freight Charges	9.64	13.92	17.08	16.83	17.17	20.45	26.08	25.92	26.09	12.17
5.	Admins. Overheads	2.13	2.49	2.89	2.80	3.16	2.84	3.13	3.90	9.54	13.34
6.	Transit Shortages	3.91	5.17	6.58	6.20	6.11	4.42	4.91	4.84	4.16	−1.45
7.	Storage Shortages	1.33	1.72	1.58	1.32	0.77	0.87	0.98	1.19	1.46	−3.47
	Total	29.05	37.87	43.91	46.87	51.89	53.19	61.23	62.05	72.38	10.38

Source: Annual Reports of FCI : 1980-81 to 1988-89.

TABLE 16.5: Carrying Cost of Buffer-Stock : 1980-81 — 1988-89

(*Rs. per quintal*)

	Items	1980-81	1981-82	1982-83	1983-84	1984-85	1985-86	1986-87	1987-88	1988-89	Gr Rate(%)
1.	Storage Shortages	4.28	5.34	4.94	3.73	2.19	2.72	3.06	3.77	4.24	−3.85
2.	Handling Charges	1.58	2.50	2.87	2.78	2.64	2.91	3.72	4.20	5.09	12.00
3.	Storage Charges	8.30	9.83	9.61	9.19	8.94	10.21	11.28	17.04	40.83	15.12
4.	Interest Charges	18.24	22.24	22.83	22.91	25.84	28.52	28.00	8.88	4.52	−12.05
5.	Admins. Charges	1.60	1.87	1.98	2.10	2.38	2.14	2.37	2.94	7.16	13.75
	Total	34.00	41.78	42.23	40.71	41.99#	46.50	48.43	36.83	61.84	4.12

Source: Annual Reports of FCI : 1980-81 — 1988-89.
Note:# Includes transit loss and freight charges of Rs. 2.88.

Briefly speaking, operational efficiency of FCI has been going down; for, the cost per quintal with respect to either procurement incidentals, or with respect to pooled distribution incidentals or with respect to buffer stock incidentals has been going up. It is contrary to the theoretical reasoning and common belief that cost of operation per unit comes down as the scale of operation increases. During the past one decade the scale of operation has been considerably increasing and the costs per unit were also going up. It is suspected that prime reason is the underutilisation of storage capacity. In fact, the increase in handling charges, storage charges and administrative charges as well as decline in the storage losses and interest charges indirectly confirm the underutilisation of storage capacity — i.e., when lesser quantity of grains are stored in huge godowns, handling charges, storage charges and administrative costs per unit of stock would go up and storage losses and interest charges per unit of stock would decline.

As mentioned earlier, decline in operational efficiency of FCI is only one part of the story in ever increasing food subsidies. The other part of the story, the most important one, relates to the movement of procurement prices and issue prices which are not under the control of FCI, but are directly under policy making of the government from time to time. Apart from these, the very policy as to whom PDS should serve and in what quantity (targeting of foodgrains subsidy) are in the hands of government.

Trends in Procurement and Issue Prices

It can be seen from Table 16.6 that procurement prices of both wheat and rice increased, but the prices of rice increased slightly faster than that of wheat. Similarly issue prices of both wheat and rice increased, but here again, the price of the latter increased faster than the former. What is important from the point of savings in food subsidy is the level of difference the government wants to maintain between wholesale prices and procurement prices on the one hand and issue prices and consumer prices on the other. The experience of 1980s was that while procurement prices of wheat and rice increased by 4.43 per cent and 4.98 per cent respectively, the wholesale price index of wheat and rice increased by 6.31 per cent and 5.44 per cent respectively. It logically follows that procurement prices of foodgrains were kept much below the market prices, and this might not be possible now and in the years to come. Any attempt to fix procurement prices much below the wholesale prices might prove counter-productive and may endanger the very objective of providing incentive prices to the farmers under food policy.

TABLE 16.6: Pattern of Changes in Procurement, Issue, Wholesale and Consumer Prices : 1980-81 to 1988-89

Year	Procurement Price (Rs. per quintal)		Issue Price (Rs. per quintal)		Whole Sale Price Index 1970-71=100		Consumer Price Index Food Average 1960-100
	Wheat	Rice	Wheat	Rice	Wheat	Rice	
1980-81	117	105	145	150	206	176	419
1981-82	130	115	160	165	226	192	476
1982-83	142	122	172	175	257	214	508
1983-84	151	132	172	188	292	218	581
1984-85	152	137	172	208	273	210	607
1985-86	157	142	190	217	284	226	638
1986-87	162	146	195	231	302	239	700
1987-88	166	150	204	239	326	259	759
1988-89	173	160	204	244	364	292	839
Growth Rate	4.43	4.98	4.71	7.15	6.31	5.44	8.53

Source: 1. *Economic Survey.*
2. *Bulletin on Food Statistics.*

In regard to issue prices, of wheat and rice, it needs to mention that they have been kept much below the consumer prices of industrial workers. In can be seen that from Table 16.6 that issue prices of wheat and rice rose by 4.71 per cent and 7.15 per cent respectively. But, consumer price index of foodgrains rose by 8.53 per cent. In other words, the rate of increase in issue prices was lower than that of consumer price index.

Now having toed a particular policy line for so long a time and made certain commitments to supply foodgrains at reasonable prices to people there may be very little scope to reduce subsidy on this count. The only possibility open to government is to rationalise the PDS and supply foodgrains only to those who are in need, and ask the rest to purchase in open market. Perhaps such a policy, (viz., targeting of PDS) might help contain food subsidy as well as meet the fundamental objectives of food policy.

Targeting of Foodgrains

But targeting of foodgrains to specified income classes is a complex matter. It is complex in the sense that given the diverse nature of population with high degree of inequality in the distribution of income and wealth it is difficult to identify what and who actually constitute the target group. Any study in this direction is possible only when a detailed analysis on the pattern of distribution of supplies of PDS among different strata of consumers is known. In this connection, results of the 42nd Round of National Sample Survey Organisation on Social Consumption conducted for the year 1986-87 are useful.

Distribution Pattern of PDS Users and Supplies

The distribution pattern of wheat under PDS across different classes of consumer (see Table 16.7) reveals, that in rural India, 38.12 per cent of the supplies of wheat is purchased by 46.87 per cent of users belonging to bottom 40 per cent of the consumer expenditure class. The middle 20 per cent class accounts for 21.09 per cent of users and 14.72 per cent of purchases. The top 40 per cent of expenditure class account for 47.16 per cent of purchases with only 32.04 per cent of users. Almost similar trend is seen in the case of urban India also.

TABLE 16.7: Percentage Distribution of PDS Users and Quantity

	Wheat				Rice			
	Rural		Urban		Rural		Urban	
	Persons	Quantity	Persons	Quantity	Persons	Quantity	Persons	Quantity
0-10	12.71	10.85	10.78	9.33	14.97	14.44	12.97	16.53
10-20	10.50	11.17	11.64	12.55	11.49	13.01	10.51	16.16
20-40	23.66	16.10	25.57	13.70	24.23	14.98	25.34	14.17
40-60	21.09	14.72	21.80	17.83	19.64	13.25	23.99	15.05
60-80	17.14	16.18	17.12	15.12	18.36	15.27	16.35	14.01
80-90	9.03	15.38	7.81	16.72	6.82	15.16	6.75	12.83
90-100	5.87	15.60	5.28	14.75	4.49	13.89	4.09	11.25
Total	100.00	100.00	100.00	100.00	100.00	100.00	100.00	100.00

Source: National Sample Survey, 42nd Round.

Of the total users of rice (under PDS) in the rural India, bottom 40 per cent of expenditure class account for 50.69 per cent, while the quantity purchased by them is only 42.43 per cent of the supplies. The middle 20 per cent class account for 19.64 per cent of users and 13.25 per cent of supplies. On the other hand, 29.67 per cent belonging to top 40 per cent of the expenditure class account for 44.32 per cent of purchases. The picture is almost same for urban India also.

The distribution pattern of PDS and thereby food subsidies aggravated the level of inequality in income distribution in the country. This emerges from the fact that the bottom 40 per cent of consumer class, though account for about 50 per cent of PDS users, get less than 40 per cent of the quantities supplied by PDS. This implies that the per capita subsidy accruing to the bottom 40 per cent of the consumer class is less when compared to their counterparts, (i.e., top 40 per cent of the consumer class). This is true for both the commodities (wheat and rice) and for rural and urban sectors.

IV

Steps for Reducing or Arresting the Growth of Food Subsidies

Then what steps should be taken to achieve the real intent of government and reduce the growth of subsidies? If the foregoing analysis is of any guidance:

(1) Operational efficiency of FCI should be improved considerably, particularly in regard to (a) procurement incidentals, (b) distribution incidentals, and (c) costs of buffer stock operations. Attention must be paid to costs on gunny bags, purchase/sales tax, interest and storage losses as these contributed largely to the increase in operational costs. Measures like, substitution of durable synthetic or nylon bags, instead of jute bags should be tried out. The purchase/sales tax on the foodgrains purchased under PDS, can be urged for reduction; efforts should be made to explore the possibilities of abolishing it altogether, as it is more or less inter-departmental/or inter-governmental transfer. Unutilised storage capacity should be fully utilised or some of the godowns, not being in use, or being underutilised, should be given up for some other purpose to make it more economical.

(2) The personnel policy of FCI should undergo drastic change as the increase in administrative expenses contributed to operational costs. In fact, the number of staff of the category level I increased from 744 in 1980-81 to 820 in 1988-89, whereas the staff of the category level of IV declined from 32,067 in 1980-81 to 25,498 in 1988-89. While the reduction in staff of category IV is on the right direction, the increase in staff of category I is unwarranted. Moreover, the practice of dumping the surplus staff of different Ministries of Government on FCI or FCI being used as a transit place for State officials looking for green pastures should be given up. FCI should assert itself and function as an autonomous organisation and not as a wing of the Ministry of Food and Agriculture as it is giving impression to people at present. FCI should change its recruitment policy at all the levels and build up its own cadre by appropriate training to them periodically.

(3) Government policy, regarding the fixation of procurement prices and issue prices, should be realistic and should not unduly raise the subsidy. Such a policy would be in line with the objective of providing incentive to the farmer and reasonable subsidy to the consumer. It is easy to be populistic and generous at the expense of somebody, but difficult to take hard decisions that impinge on the popularity of government. The issue prices should be revised frequently, based on the movement of consumer price index (food index).

(4) The practice of subsidised distribution of foodgrains to all citizens, irrespective of the level of income, should be changed. There is no strong reason as to why the people of middle income and upper income group should receive subsidized foodgrains. Proper targeting in the distribution of foodgrains would help reduce the growth of food subsidy and at the same time provide opportunity to distribute to more people in remote and tribal areas. Among different income groups, discrimination could be made between the most vulnerable and the needy by introducing different types of ration cards — say, green cards for bottom 40 per cent of consumer expenditure class, yellow cards for middle 20 per cent of the consumer expenditure class and completely leave the rest 40 per cent of the consumer expenditure class to open market. In fact, this is being done in some States in one form or the other. Other States may emulate them or devise their own models.

(5) It is possible to argue that once the quantum of foodgrains distributed gets reduced, due to targeting, the PDS procurement would also be reduced, otherwise stocks with FCI would pile up and operational losses would go up and hence subsidies. If, on the other hand, FCI reduces the quantum of procurement, foodgrain prices will be affected seriously, and farmers' incentive to produce foodgrains will be reduced, and even negate the very objective of food policy. To overcome such a dichotomy, diversification of operations of FCI should be attempted. In our view, FCI should distribute subsidised foodgrains only to the target group and the remaining foodgrains can be sold at prices comparable with open market prices. Such a policy would result in not only in the efficient utilisation of the existing PDS net work but also earn some profit out of open market sales. It might reduced hoardings and also minimise exploitation of consumers and farmers by unscrupulous traders and middlemen. More importantly, it might help stabilise price level, which, indeed, is the most urgent one at present.

(6) The growth rates of sale receipts and value of sales reveal that the actual subsidy passed on to consumers is very meagre (see Table 16.1). To pass on even this much subsidy, an amount almost equal to three folds of the same (actual consumer subsidy) is being incurred on account of maintaining the net work of public distribution system. Do we need to maintain such a costly distributive system?

17

COPING WITH THE ECONOMIC CRISIS

R. CAUVERY and U.K. SUDHA NAYAK

STANDING ON the threshold of the 21st century and after 45 years of Independence it is disheartening to digest the fact that there is a crisis — a crisis in ideology, a crisis in values, a crisis in policy prescriptions culminating in a crisis on several economic fronts. If we do not solve the cluster of economic problems that confront us now, an economic Chernobyl may destroy all that has been built during the last four and a half decades. We are like a business that has become insolvent.

A stock taking of our achievements should not make us blind to the remarkable progress on many fronts. The balance sheet of development reveals positive achievements on several accounts. The basic objectives were "development along socialists lines to secure rapid economic growth and expansion of employment, reduction of disparities in income and wealth, prevention of concentration of economic power and creation of values and attitudes of a free and equal society.

The Indian economy recorded an average growth rate of gross domestic product, to the order of 5.23 per cent during 1980-81 to 1988-89 which is no mean achievements. As a consequence the per capita income went up to Rs. 2,082 in 1988-89, rise of nearly 85 per cent during the 38 year period. If this trend is sustained for another two decades a big dent would be made on poverty.

The planning process has resulted in the reduction of poverty. As against 46 per cent of the total population living below the poverty line in 1977-78, the recent evidence indicates a reduction in poverty to 30 per cent poverty in 1987-88. The various other indicators of a better quality of life also show improvement. For instance the average life expectancy has gone up to 58 years in 1988-89 from 32 years in 1950-51. The death rate too has fallen down sharply to 10.9 per thousand in 1988-89 from 32 years per thousand in 1950-51. The birth rate too revealed a declining trend of 31 per thousand in 1988-89 when compared with 1950-51 where it stood at 40 per cent thousand. There is now a better survival rate of our population in spite of the fact that 50 per cent of our population suffers from under-nourishment or mal-nutrition.

The remarkable progress that the Indian economy has made in the last four and a half decades is evident from Table 17.1.

TABLE 17.1: Per Capita Consumption of Selected Commodities 1951 and 1987

Sl. No.	Commodities (Consumption of)	1951	1987
1.	Cereals	334 gm	487 gm
2.	Edible oil	3.1 kg	6.2 kg
3.	Vegetables	10.3 kg	24.7 kg
4.	Fish	1.5 kg	3.7 kg
5.	Milk	46.8 kg	56.2 kg
6.	Electricity	2.4 kWh	27.4 kWh

Source : Ruddar Dutt, *Financial Express*, 10-2-1991.

The per capita consumption of man made fabrics went up from 1.2 metres in 1960-61. But it should certainly be at the expense of cotton cloth whose per capita consumption obviously came down from 13 metres in 1960-61 to 10.1 metres in 1987-88.

Industrial development has been significant in basic and heavy industries. There has been a remarkable diversification of our industrial base with our public sector playing the leading role. Self-reliance in consumer goods and certain essential basic commodities like steel, cement and certain fertiliser has been achieved.

During the planning era the country witnessed a very rapid and vast expansion in the educational system. A five fold increase in the enrolment from 239 lakhs in 1950-51 to 1275 lakhs in 1984-85 bears testimony to the development of human resources. Again the significant development in the growth of scientific and technical man power is crystal clear from the enrlargement of the scientific pool from 0.19 million persons in 1950-to 1.8 million persons in 1980.

An important value to be pursued in the process of development is self-reliance. It is heartening to note that we have achieved self-reliance in food-grains with our production reaching 172 million tonnes in 1989-90 as against 50 million tonnes in 1950-51.

Another achievement that merits consideration is the boost in the gross domestic saving from 10.4 per cent in 1950-51 to 23.2 per cent in 1978-79 and there upon it got established at 20 per cent of GDP.

Nevertheless, the development process has left a majority of the population untouched. The three basic values of development are ensuring balanced development, avoiding concentration of wealth and means of production and self reliance. It is these values which are now at stake. With the growing concentration of wealth and therefore of economic power and the increased disparity of income distribution these values have largely been already eroded. A dual society has been created with about 100 millions at a level of affluence and 300 millions at or below poverty line resulting in an unprecedented economic crisis.

The multiple malaise that afflicts the Indian economy to-day for several years has kept development under siege. But when it comes to the all important question of how to break this siege and infuse new life into development, it speaks in discordant and contradictory voices and falls back upon platitudinous generality.

The current economic crisis has four separate but related facts viz., balance of payments, the budget deficit, inflation and the slow down of the economy.

A major cause of concern dominating all our policies has been the balance of payments situation. The ratio of current account deficit to GDP averaged 2.2 per cent during 1985-90, far above the 1.6 per cent projected for this period in the 7th plan document. In absolute terms the current account deficit averaged 55.5 billion dollars during the sixth plan. The already difficult balance of payment situation was worsened in 1990-91 with imports of petroleum and oil products rising by 2.2 billion dollars. The growth of exports which averaged around 10 per cent per annum during 1986-87 to 1989-90, also came down substantially. Though the current account deficit is expected to come down in the wake of the devaluation of the rupee, there is still the problem of how we are going to finance this deficit. There has been a drastic change in the pattern of external assistance received during the last decade. External finance which constituted 50 per cent of total assistance during the sixth plan dwindled to 29 per cent in the seventh plan. Non-resident (NRI) deposits increased from 14 per cent in the sixth plan to 23 per cent in the seventh. IMF credit constituted 28 per cent in the sixth plan. While other commercial borrowing to the tune of 24 per cent was the major source in the seventh plan period. As a result our external reserves got corroded to the extent of 15 per cent in the beginning of '90s.

The persisting current account deficits year after year have raised the external debt liabilities. During 1990-91 the level of foreign currency assets declined from 3.4 billion dollars in March 1990, to 2.2 billion dollars by the end of March 1991, in spite of the withdrawal of 1.8 billion dollars from the IMF. In fact, by April, it had declined to 1.2 billion dollars. Political and economic circumstances have dried up some of the usual sources of financing, chiefly commercial borrowing, As a result, India had to resort to severe policy measures — internal and external to comply with IMF's specification to get qualified for its assistance. Thus the crisis on the balance of payments from is two fold: one is that the current account deficit must be brought down to manageable levels, to be sustained by normal capital flows; second, we must maintain our good record of meeting external obligations for which there must be reduction in imports.

The structure of capital account deficit has undergone changes. The sixties and the seventies saw official loans on concessional terms as the main source of financing the current account deficit. In 1980 nearly 90 per cent of India's outstanding debt was from official creditors with 85 per cent of this on concessional terms. By 1989, official loans accounted for 61 per cent of the total outstanding debt and the proportion of concessional loans had fallen to 47 per cent. The decline in concessional assistance from World Bank group has been the major cause of worry.

TABLE 17.2: Structure of India's Long Term Debt (1970-89)

(*in million U.S. Dollars*)

		1970	1980	1989
1.	Total outstanding debt	7837	18322	54776
2.	Total official debt of which concessional	7507	16315	33371
3.	Total private debt	330	2007	21405

Source : World Bank, World Debt Tables, 1990-91.

Table 17.2 shows the decline in the proportion of concessional assistance in the total outstanding debt of India which causes increasing burden of repayment.

Another related issue for balance of payments crisis is concerning foreign investment and commercial borrowing. The volume of foreign direct investment in India averaged only about 100 million dollars during the past three years ending 1989 compared to 3.4 billion dollars in China during the same period. With a view to promote indigenous capital India had to fallow a very conservative policy by restricting the percentage of equity participation. Notwithstanding the debate on pros and cons of encouraging foreign investment, empirical evidence is strongly in favour of making conditions easy for foreign investments, thanks to the example set by Asian countries like Thailand, Malaysia and Singapore which have achieved quick transformation through "foreign investments". Fears expressed by writers like Uzava and other Japanese economists as well as Fall and Streeten, that this 'tariff jumping' variant of foreign investment might taken advantage of the protected markets in the host countries and reduce their incomes.

India should think in terms of simplifying her laws relating to foreign equity investment. The volumes are so small that even a manifold increase in equity investment can do no harm. For one thing the equity investment has a gestation period in production thus shifting the burden of repayment to a later date. For another it provides immediate solution to increase our investments in fields requiring an urgent increase in production. Care should be taken to ensure that such investment is positive in terms of foreign exchange and is internationally competitive. In the case of competitive investment entry should be automative and transparent. However to the extent the foreign equity investment is going to increase productive capacity, in the long run, it is not going to help immediately to relieve the present crisis of maintenance imports and debt service obligations.

The average nominal interest rate on loans from official creditors has increased from 2.4 per cent in 1980 to 5.6 per cent in 1989. However because of the decline in interest rates, in the private capital market, the average interest rates on all loans from all creditors has not increased much (from about 5.4% in 1980 to 6.4% in 1989). But total interest payments in dollar terms have nevertheless been increasing at a much faster rate than exports. Interest in dollar terms increased at a compound rate of 21. 7 per cent per annum in 1980s as compared to 7.8 per cent growth per annum in exports.

The debt/exports ratio in India crossed 300 per cent in 1990s. Since a large part of the debt is in the public sector, the rising debt servicing burden and rising fiscal deficits have led to the emergence of a vicious circle of deficit and debt. Unless we reduce this debt/exports ratio to manageable levels, there is very little hope for inward looking investment.

By international standards, the size of the balance of payments correction required in India is relatively modest between 1 to 1.5 per cent of GDP under normal circumstances. A programme of shifting the structure of production in favour of exports as against the domestic market along with allied administrative and policy reforms should be able to accomplish this task within two or three years without causing much social cost.

India has some of the highest rates of customs duties in the world compared to even China and Eastern Europe. Whilst most countries have duties below 30 per cent, we have duties ranging from, 100 per cent to over 250 per cent. We should bring down the maximum duties to the level of 50 per cent and as a part of long term policy make an announcement of further reduction to 30 per cent in the next five years. It would also enable Indian manufacturers to import more competitively the components and machinery required to upgrade quality. There is a direct correlation between country's imports as a percentage of GNP and its exports as a percentage of GNP.

International experience has shown that exchange controls lead to distortion and corruption and actually act as a hindrance to economic development. Most countries have moved towards abolishing exchange controls. It is recommended that India, should abolish exchange controls immediately on all current payments for import of goods, machinery, travel, education etc. Controls may be retained for the next five years on capital transfer i.e., transferring the proceeds of sale of assets. Once exchange control is abolished foreign investors and NRIs will have much greater confidence in investing in existing or new enterprises in India as they do not have to be subject to controls and delays in remiting their earnings from the investment. With hike in price of travel and spending abroad the kind of ostentation by a few thousand Indians spend abroad cannot add up to more than 20 or 30 million dollars a year. Saving that amount is not worth sacrificing all the advantages of abolishing exchange controls. Several of them do it even now through illegal means. So the additional burden of legitimising it could be even smaller.

Indian manufacturers will be able to import machinery, intermediates, new materials and know how which will enable them to achieve competitive international standards of quality. This will lead to a more domestic competitive market based on quality and costs, which will benefit the Indian consumer. As domestic manufacturers do not have to obtain import licences for capital goods, it will cut down delays in the implementation of projects and consequent cost escalations. International customers will gain confidence in Indian manufacturers who will be able to respond faster and more flexibly as they will have greater freedom to do so.

In any scheme of macro economic stabilisation a major factor will be the containment of the fiscal deficit. It is now fairly well established that widening fiscal deficits in recent years have been the primary cause of balance of payments disequilibrium. It was announced in December 1990, that India's fiscal deficit would be reduced to 6.5 per cent in 1991-92 from the level of 8.3 per cent of G.D.P in 1990-91 to be ultimately reduced to 3 to 4 per cent over 3 years. The fiscal deficit measures the difference between the revenue receipts and total expenditure including capital expenditure. Fiscal deficit therefore is wider than the budget deficit. In order to evaluate the impact of reduction of fiscal deficit by 1.8 per cent on various macro-economic variables in India, a simulation exercise was adopted which has estimated that it ought to reduce the rate of growth of output by 0.6 to 1 per cent, the growth of industrial output by 1 to 1.5 per cent, and the rate of inflation was likely to be lower by 2 to 3 per cent. The effect of reduction in fiscal deficit will be only partially favourable, i.e, the improvement in the current account would be about 1/3 of the reduction in fiscal deficit in rupee terms.

In order to contain public expenditure substantial cuts will have to be made in subsidies. The overall budgetory deficit has increased from Rs. 5315 crores in 1985-86 to Rs. 10592 crores in 1989-90. Drastic steps like a reduction in Government and non-development expenditure, strict enforcement of tax laws to check evasion, widening the tax base and selective approach to subsidies would be needed to bring down the deficit. There is need to rationalise the stabilise tax structure to restore confidence of the tax payers in long term fiscal policy.

Regarding subsidies which involve social obligations steps should be taken to limit them to the vulnerable and needy sections only. Expenses on subsidies have gone up from Rs. 4796 crores in 1985-86 to Rs. 10,677 crores in 1989-90 and further to Rs. 12121 crores in 1990-91. The gravity of the burden is obviously seem from the fact that expenses on subsidies in 1990-91. Stood higher than the budgetary deficit in the previous year.

Of the major subsidies, only food and fertilizer subsidies are amenable to cut. Inadequate contribution of the public sector to finance development is one of the causes for mounting deficits. Therefore steps to improve the performance of the sector seem to be very much on the card. A fundamental reason for lack of viability of development financing of large projects in the public sector is the low productivity of these investments. An estimate of delays in the case of 63 projects in the public sector fixes the cost of delay to be Rs. 100 crores or more. Most long-term commercial loans have to be repaid in 5 to 8 years and if the public sector projects delay their production the entire repayments problems becomes burdens one for the Government. These public sector projects contribute very little to exports even after commencing commercial production causing further debt servicing problems. Therefor, priority should be given only to quick-gestation, export-oriented projects for financing through external commercial loans, which means satisfying the criteria, of low capital-output ratio and high exports.

The Government sector which now generates 30 per cent of the GDP incurs an expenditure of nearly 45 per cent of the GDP. This is a major source of crisis as this expenditure is financed only by borrowings and created money against taxes. There are two other issues. The first is related to the size of the business sector enterprises in ratio to those in the private sector and the second is related to the issue of Government controls and regulations versus the market. There is yet no settled consensus over the confusing issues of the debate. The optimism with which the public sector was launched has given way now to intense rage against it because it has let down the economy in respect of the objectives set forth inspite of huge investments. Public sector along with public bureaucracy constitutes an internal empire setting a siege against the nation. About one lakh crores of Rupee has been invested in the public sector in about less than 300 enterprises. Barring half a dozen enterprises, all of them have run in losses for years so much so some of them have eaten up the whole of their capital. The cost and time over runs have been as high as 100 to 200 per cent.

The number of profit-making public sector enterprises has increased from 94 in 1980-81 to 118 in 1988-89. On the other hand the loss incurring enterprises have gone up from 74 to 101 during the same period. In fact it is said that 55 per cent of the total profit of all the profit-making enterprises was accounted for by Petroleum group of enterprises. This reflects the poor performance of non petroleum enterprises. Apart from what it might have done to itself, the public sector has strangled itself instead of promoting growth in so far as it failed to generate its own projected surplus, plan after plan. In real terms, the gross surplus ended up at less than half the projections, thus forcing the Government to draw its budgetary resources for this sector instead of putting the sector on vanguard.

The worst role of the public sector has been its growing inefficiency and parasitism. Not only their returns on capital have declined, and in some cases capital has been consumed, this sector has been given the privilege of maintaining its share of capital formation around 42 to 45 per cent. Its share of gross domestic savings have continued to decline from about 23 per cent in the mid seventies to less than 15 per cent in the mid-eighties. A comparison with China may not be out of place because both India and China relied on the growth potential and savings on the modern sector. In China, the modern sector belonged to public sector. However, whereas in China the public sector contributed about 25 per cent of the GNP in the form of savings, these were transmitted to the fiscal budget. In India the modern sector contributed less than 4 per cent of the savings and heavily depended not only on the savings of the households which was consistent with property relations but also on the budgetary deficits, an arrangement which is now in a very deep crisis. The so called modern sector has failed India as it were.

A large part of the public sector has run out of its utility. It is draining and wasting national resources. It is caught in a vicious circle which is one of the various circles on which the economy is moving. It has been put in straight jacket by vested interests. But quite tragically there is little possibility of reform, what to say of dismantling of this sector, without this the economy will remain under siege.

The long term fiscal policy has projected that public sector savings will finance a greater proportion of the plan outlay. Indeed the share of the public sector savings in the total central sector plan outlay was expected to go up from 25 per cent in 1985-86 to as much as 43 per cent in 1989-90. There are to ways of raising the surplus of public sector undertakings (1) improving their operational efficiency (2) raising their administrative prices and output. Since the first one needs a long time, the government has resorted to the second namely it passed the cost of its inefficiency to consumers through increase in the price of its output. Steel and coal for instance are intermediate goods with high forward linkages and arise in their administered prices will feed inflation. The goods with such inflation potential should be identified. For example it is estimated that a 15 per cent average increase in the price of coal will mobilise substantial additional resources without generating much inflation. Only a judiciously selected administered price increase would contribute to bridge the resource gap for VIII plan without generating high rates of inflation.

Wherever the Government is helpless in the policy of administered prices, it should resort to privatisation of these enterprises. Privatisation need not mean a complete reversal of policy. It could mean, privatisation of management of public sector units or partial privatisation involving share holding by public. Already the government has mooted suggestions in this line for power generation, transport etc.

Thus we have paid heavily for this performance ideology over economic consideration. Public sector enterprises were mooted to remove imperfections in market or market failures. On the other hand, besides creating, massive losses in its enterprises causing tremendous fiscal damages, reducing money and capital for private sector, creating monopolies along with corruption, it looks it would have been better to let market imperfections to be a part of developmental strategies rather than that of regulations, public sector monopolies and price discrimination. The vested interests created by the government does not want free market forces again. An inefficient financially losing and corrupt public sector is the biggest enemy.

Nothing has given a serious jolt to the economic cohesion of India as inflation. The problem of inflation assumes an entirely different complexion in India; even without the agony of rising prices, our people are face to face with endless misery. Inflation has emerged as an economic and social evil because, in the last few years, it has redistributed income and wealth in various unjust, haphazard, and socially undesirable ways and also because it has caused a major disturbance in the lives of the vast majority of our people poor and defenceless.

The problem of greatest concern to the people is inflation. India's inflationary problem, in the context of abject poverty of the masses, been more grievous than in some other countries. The official index of wholesale prices which rose 32 per cent during 1956-61 have touched its peak having lodged itself at 192.7 at in end of April 1991. For the period March 1990 to March 1991, the index of wholesale prices registered a 11.3 per cent rate of expansion, compared to 8.4 per cent for the previous year and a 6.0 per cent average annual rate during the seventh plan period. The consumer price index has increased at an even higher rate of above 15 per cent, which compares even poorly with the seventh plan annual average rate of 8.0 per cent. This year's rates are clearly much above the normal and "acceptable" rates of inflation for India. The annual rates of inflation in terms of wholesale price index was 11.7 per cent in 1990-91 compared to 9.1 per cent during 1989-90.

Inflation is one form of taxation which is levied by the Government without any parliamentary sanctions. With prices rising, taxation is patched up in more ways than one. Considering the social and economic conditions in India the inflationary tax tends to be grossly inequitous. For millions of people whose budgets are gingerly balanced, this concealed tax means denial of the normal pattern and volume of consumption and a slide down in the social scale. What is even more disturbing is that the impact of inflationary taxation is both direct and indirect. Inflation is in the nature of an indirect tax on money. The rate of the rise in price is in rate of the hidden tax. The public who have stock or reserve money finds the purchasing power of rupee eroded by rising prices. To remain in the same level the public should expand the nominal amount of means of payment. This obviously refers to the fact that the public has to acquire and hold more money to have the same purchasing power as it had before inflation set in. Clearly therefore the public has to use an additional amount of money receipts, not for spending on extra good and services, but merely to keep the purchasing power of its stock of money unchanged. In effect ultimately, there is hardly any difference between this burden and the one where an explicit tax is levied. The concealed burden is disturbed according to the consumption of the "taxed" goods, the price of which keeps rising.

The basic mechanism of inflation in India are different and domestic. The current rate of price increase forebodes, ill for the future development of the Indian economy and social advancement of the people. When inflation and distortions in the present scale are stopped, as they have to be eventually, the process is bound to become much more painful the longer it is delayed. It is therefore essential that the Government should have a general strategy towards inflation. Short-term manipulations are apt to be counter productive. Normally people associate Indian inflation with enormous growth in money supply reflecting deficit financing by the Government. But this correlation between changes in money supply and fluctuations in the value of money is very much controversial. Inflation in India is a wide ranging complex phenomenon. Even if the growth of money and government deficit were intended to signify excess demand, there is no conclusive evidence of a stable relationship between the two. Particularly in the Indian conditions fluctuations in the stock of money are also not only factor that influence the general level of prices.

The reasons for the rate of inflation in 1990-91 are essentially three. First being the increase in administered prices, mainly of petroleum products and food grains; second, the monetary impact of the persisting fiscal deficits, the "liquidity over hang" in the system, third the role of speculative factors and market imperfections in a period of consistent and continuous political instability.

The role of administered price increases has been particularly important this year in explaining the increase in the price of petroleum, petro products and foodgrains. While the average rate of inflation in the case of primary products was 12.0 per cent for the period March 1990 to February 1991, in the case of primary articles this was 17.9 per cent and specifically for wheat it was 47.9 per cent. This is the "cost-push" component of the inflationary process in the fiscal year 1990-91. The experience in the last few months has belied the operation of Phillips curve hypothesis viz., it is not the wage cost as much as the raw material cost which has exerted greater pressure on the overall price level. While using foodprices have pushed up the rate of inflation, they have not been fully absorbed by the organised sector so that these have not impacted on production costs as yet. In contrast the cost rise in the industries using steel and coal is already being felt. It is the cost increase which has been passed down by these vital industries in the form of higher prices of their output that has set in motion a cost-price spiral.

The injection of excess liquidity into the system and its residual impact i.e., the liquidity overhang of the liberal credit and monetary policy of the past few years had maintained the demand pull pressure on prices. While 19.9 per cent increase in the overall liquidity (M3) during 1989-90 is ascribed as one of the factors operating on the price front, a purely monetarist solution cannot suffice in tackling the inflationary process. The growth of a parallel credit network and the vastly expanded scope of the black economy have narrowed down the margin and degree of the central bank over the money market.

Thirdly the role of speculative factors and market imperfections in a period of continued political uncertainty and administrative stasis taxes as in the case of cement price where neither demand nor cost factors can suffice to explain steep increase in prices. Such speculative pressures have been particularly active since the beginning of 1991. Owing to persisting political uncertainty and the inability of the government to exert disciplinary pressure on traders.

It should be clear that Government's counter inflationary strategy would have to include a multipronged strategy because on individual policy can be decisive on its own. The starting point of any attempt to tackle inflation is to recognise that it is a serious economic and social problem, not just a temporary economic imbalance. Even an inflation which does not escalate into a galloping hyper inflation poses a threat to society and economy. It is futile to dream of rolling back of prices to a given base period. A prudent and supple strategy to reduce the damage and the rate of inflation without nursing any illusions without chalking up quick and great victories should be evolved. The Government hopes to conquer inflation by cutting on money supply. This can have alarming results in Indian conditions. It can for example slow down the rate of growth of essential supplies if the projects are postponed and development expenditure cut in the process. Such cuts can spark off a major recession and the last decade of the century will be spent in fighting the man made calamity. In the prevailing conditions, cuts in investments or postponement of projects may mean reduced orders, increases in unutilised capacities in basic and capital goods industries and possibly retrenchment hitting to start with casual labour besides impairing growth potential of the economy in essential sectors.

The major policy to contain inflation should aim to increase production. In the first four decades of planning there was failure to utilise the full capacity on the production front. "The lost output" during this period, that is to say, the difference between potential maximum and the realised output might have the vital link in solving this puzzle. It is worth while to reconsider the basis of some of the fiscal concessions and link development rebate with production increase. Further intensive utilisation of capacity in terms of rate of growth of output should be rewarded through accelerated depreciation allowance.

The cumulative effects of the aforesaid three problems has slowed down the pace of the economic machinery. The fact that four decades after the initiation of the development planning in the county, we are still talking of a strategy of poverty alleviation. It is not just that socialism has failed and with it the concept of a dominant public sector. We have to question the wisdom of all that went in the name of anti-poverty effort – the 20-point programme, the IRDPs, the employment-oriented schemes and the populist lending of commercial and other banks. Nothing has really helped in poverty alleviation because we are still talking of policies not focusing on the 700 million poor. Things are not going to get any worse with deregulation, delicencing and free play of market forces.

The price policy of industrial products also proved inimical to the growth of capital goods industries. There has been very stringent and often economically unjustifiable controls on the prices of basic industrial products like steel, cement, aluminium, coal, chemicals, fertilizers and drugs leading to their uneconomic prices as well as black-marketing. On the other hand there was practically no price control on consumer durables or when controlled the result was black-market and black money. This has changed the priorities, morals, value system, desire to have high standard of life, work ethics and culture in the economic scenario.

There has emerged a target mentality in what we do. There is no motivation either to improve upon the performance to achieve the target or set a higher target. This is an obsession that investment is the panacea for every economic problem. Investment without people's motivation and participation will not result in any achievement and we can never come out of the crisis however much we invest. All out investments have produced sub optimal results. We have failed to provide employment opportunities to all able bodied persons and eradication of poverty still appears to be a distant dream.

There is a need now not only to reassess our theories of development but also to reconsider the data itself on which they are based. We need an innovative approach, not a mere icing on the cake of accepted fundamentals as we have been doing till now. There is not much time on hand. There is only so much gold that can be pawned.

The ongoing crisis requires a series of measures adopted as a package that make a clean break with past policies. In order to stimulate production, competition and export, it is necessary to completely abolish industrial licencing which is not only unnecessary but extremely wasteful.

India needs to attract 50 billion dollars of foreign investment over the next five years. It is far better for us to attract equity investment from foreign investors then borrow abroad from banks or even international institutions. Foreign investment need not be allowed in defence products. In agriculture foreign investors can have only minority interests. In all other sectors, foreign investment should be allowed up to 75 per cent provided the remaining 25 per cent is issued to Indian public through share offer. It there is an Indian partner the joint holding of the foreign investor and Indian partner should not exceed 75 per cent. Ninety per cent of the management staff and majority of the executive board should be Indian nationals.

In the interest of reducing the budgetary deficit, subsidies should be rationalised. Reduction in fertilizer subsidy, rationalisation of procurement prices in upward direction, income limit for recipients of subsidised food and removal of export subsidies in the wake of devaluation are other measures suggested.

If privatisation of public sector were to be resorted to in the interest of setting the public sector units in the proper gear, the shares of the loss making units should be sold through the stock exchanges. Private negotiations for share holding may favour the vested interests. Share holding by employees on a compulsory basis will results in better labour involvement in better production. All infrastructure projects like rods, bridges, rail, travels, electric power generation, water supply schemes can be handed over for future development to private sector which can recover the cost through tolls as in USA and other developed countries.

Double digit inflation requires not only stringent monetary and fiscal measures but it is high time India considers in terms of incomes policy. The system of linking wages to cost of living index through Dearness Allowance has caused a wage-price spiral. No doubt wages need to be protected against inflation through such schemes, but when labour does not act in a responsible manner to increase productivity, the system of dearness allowance linked to cost of living index sustains a wage-price spiral which feeds upon itself. Two pronged strategy is required in this connection. Permanency of jobs irrespective of motivation and productivity consciousness should be replaced by time bound contractual system as is practiced in U.S.A. Wage hikes and incentives should be linked to increase in productivity. When this policy is tried on a universal scale, prices and incomes be subjected to a freeze for stipulated periods.

The steps examined above are interlinked and have to be implemented as a total package in order to obtain maximum effectiveness. What we have to look for is not only a remedy for meeting the current crisis but also a more stable structure for higher and sustained rate of growth of the Indian economy in the future as a part of the global economy.

That the country is facing an unprecedented crisis at this juncture is not larger a point of dispute though there are divergent views about the remedial measures both short term and long term. The question is not of ideology or state but one of economic discipline. Today the ideology or a way of thinking has taken a turn for more and more acquisitiveness or consumerism.

India is faced with an economic crisis. But a crisis is also an opportunity to consider the economic strategies to be adopted and to reconsider the values.

REFERENCES

Abhijit Sen, "Payments crisis, A different solutions", *The Economic Times*, 12th July 1991.

Bimal Jalan, "India's economic crisis. They way ahead", Oxford University Press, New Delhi.

N. Chandra Mohan, "Devaluation, unwarranted as merits", *The Economic Times*, 17 July, 1991.

Deepak Lal, "The poverty of developed economics", Institute of Economic Affairs, London 1983.

R.C. Dutt- "A crisis of values", *The Economic Times*, 22nd July 1991.

Kirit, S. Parikh, "Economic policy; Need to look outwards", *The Economic Times*, 13 June 1991.

Praful Bidwai, "Dubious economics, Bad Policies", *The Economic Times*, 13th July 1991.

A.V. Rajwade, "Devaluation" was it really necessary, *The Economic Times*, 20th July 1991.

C. Rangarajan, "Devaluation: Causes and consequences", *The Economic Times*, 5th Aug 1991.

C. Rangarajan, "Payments crises and Monetary Policy", *The Economic Times*, 17th June 1991.

D.K. Rangnekar, "Vicious circle of prices and taxes", *The Economic Times*, 4th August 1991.

Ruddar Dutt, "More we develop more we go down poverty line", *Financial express*, 10th Feb, 1991.

Sanjaya Baru, "Inflation and Macro Economic Adjustments", *The Economic Times*, 15th May 1991.

J.D. Sethi, "Economy under siege", *Financial Express*, 29th Aug. 1991.

T. Jhomas, "Devaluation : was it really necessary", *The Economic Times*, 19th July 1991.

18

THE CRISIS OF ECONOMIC DEPRIVATION IN INDIA AND THE REMEDY

K.K. DAS GUPTA

Introduction

THE PURPOSE of this paper is to examine some facets of a critical dimension of the Indian economy, namely, poverty and unemployment. Of late, hundreds of pages have come in print on how to combat the present crisis of balance of payment without which the prognosis of the malady of the Indian economy appears to be grave. Solutions are being sought and implemented, however controversial they might be, to overcome the present critical situation. But a lingering malady which have prevailed throughout our exercise of planned development during the last four decades, save some piece-meal attempts of amelioration and which has strengthened the underdevelopment-development cleavage according to many, is undoubtedly poverty and unemployment in the midst of favourable results of important indicators of economic development like growth, industrial productivity and so on. To put it in different terms, our planned development has neglected the requirements of human elements of the economy, if by this we do not mean only a segment but the overwhelming majority of our population. There cannot be any doubt that crisis in our economy is all pervading in spite of advancement in some spheres. The attempt here will be to isolate one malignant symptom and suggest a remedy so that at least the critical phase could be by-passed.

Lessons of Economic Planning in India

The diagnosis of a malady requires the study of its history. An examination of the emphases at different phases of our planning can provide us with this basis. As is well-known, from the very beginning of our planning, a large section of our intellectuals articulated the necessity of increasing the normative content of planning in the presence of certain age-old economic problems including poverty and unemployment which appear irremediable within the given constraints of planning. Strictly speaking, this normative content belongs to politico-economic arena of planning and it can be strengthened only by crossing the realm of arithmomorphic validity of plan exercises. If we took the Mahalanobis model, it would be evident that the solution of the two problems was envisaged through a mere gradualist path although the task of industrialisation was taken as a rigorous plan exercise with conscious determination of investments, resource allocation, division into sectors, capital intensity (its nature) and so on. But there was no specific emphasis on planned redistribution of income nor there was any conceptual input on imperative need of social security of the population. As one recalls, it was assumed in the model that the economy was closed, stock of capital could be shifted from capital goods industries to consumption goods industries and increase of investment and consumption would be a constant proportion of investment in the two sectors so that the growth of national income would follow certain predetermined path like any social model. The model did not envisage the nature of emergence of inequality of income and the resulting deprivation of the population. Rather, the model was incapable of undertaking this task because it was assumed that if the economic planning had done the magic in the Soviet Union there was no reason why, if properly formulated and implemented, Indian planning would not do the same. In this consideration, the difference in the Institutional structures was overlooked in spite of our massive planning of public sector aimed at occupying the 'commanding height'. It was true that there was a strong centralised framework of planning but at the same time the market forces were destined to play the dominant role.

It is sometimes argued that Feld'man's pathbreaking contribution on the theory of accumulation in the famous industrialisation debate in the Soviet Union was the precursor to some of the important features of the Mahalanobis model. It is true that both emphasised on the criteria of capital intensity and 'delayed effect'. The difficulty in this similarity analysis lies in the fact that the assumption of the two models were different. In the case of India the satisfaction of the above criteria was regarded as possible within the heterogeneity of a society consisting of different economic classes and strate with a mode of production whose heritage was of colonial capitalism. Excepting fiscal instruments there was no other means by which the 'relative deprivation' or even 'destitution' could be remedied. In Feld'man's model the size of the consumption basket was assumed to the same however meagre the quantum of the consumption goods could be in the given situation. Also, 'affordable' social security was a fundamental right of the Soviet citizens in Feld'man's time, that is, the very late twenties.

Was it because the planning up to the third plan which followed the model under discussion was not sufficiently centralised in content to incorporate strong 'command' elements to eradicate glaring economic injustices? Unfortunately, it was not the absence of centralism but rather the lack of vision. Centralism in any case could not have been very deep in a market dominated economy. It would be interesting to comment on a characterisation of the model by a critic. According to this author, "All the planning models, starting from the aggregative models of Mahalanobis and ending with official model used in connection with the Fifth Five Year Plan are built in such a way as to stimulate decisions taken by a *single decision-maker*. . . . The Indian plan models have implicitly vested the planner with full authority of decision-making power of all the decision variables included in the models".[1]

This comment deserves some comment. Firstly, to make economic planning effective, there has to be a planner, India being no exception. Also, the history of planning in socialist countries up to the time when India launched its Fifth Five Year Plan was mainly centralised in character although the degree of centralisation had diminished over time. As a legacy, there was a centralised element in the plan framework in India. The question is whether such a planning is appropriate for an economy where the government can enforce decisions by command only in a small part of the economy. "There are in this country, not one decision maker but some millions of them".[2] One author has correctly commented, "What is termed in India as its socialist economy is a *market economy* where planning controls the market process of production and distribution in both the public and private sectors, gearing the two to its pre-determined goals".[3]

The issue in contention is not that much whether Indian planning model had a command or indicative type of centralism but whether solution of the problem of 'absolute poverty' through employment generation and/or welfare schemes were rigorously planned. The planners always had the mistaken notion that in a gradualist framework the creation of employment *ceteris paribus* by market forces through plan and piecemeal ameliorative programmes would solve the vexed problem of destitution and unemployment.

Assuming that the economy is basically or dominantly capitalistic in character is it theoretically possible to envisage a full employment situation in India within the foreseeable future? Without engaging oneself to unnecessary extrapolation with generous addition of side-conditions it would be wise to learn from the conclusions of a great economist of the past. We came to know that after the phenomenal success of Keynes' 'General Theory' one of his admirers asked him whether he had found the solution to the problem of unemployment in capitalism, to which great economist replied with characteristic aplomb: "Nonsense, then it would be the end of capitalism". To strengthen our contention we need not bring in Marx's famous 'absolute General Law of Capitalist Accumulation' and the imperative need for the existence of 'relative surplus population' for the very survival of capitalism.

Unemployment and Poverty

If we accept the proposition that the complete solution of the unemployment problem is not possible in a market economy through creation of employment opportunities alone, then we have to look for a planned solution within the framework of the Indian planning which will be the resultant of a number of given employment opportunities and the volume of assistance given to the economically handicapped people in India. This assistance will be needed for those who could not be immediately absorbed into the working population in any gradualist framework of employment generation. This is the fundamental building block of social security. Of course, there are number of other elements as well, as is known. This approach, if taken, would go a long way towards eradication of the most pernicious malady of our economy, namely, 'extreme poverty'. For the purpose of this paper, a distinction has been made between 'poverty' and 'extreme poverty' as constituents of 'absolute poverty'.

The usual argument about unemployment and poverty boils down to the simple proposition which entails a causal connection between the two with former being the antecedent. If one however wants to avoid viewing the world through causal nexus but through tangible associations, then one is likely to confront situations everywhere with one-to-one correspondence between unemployment and poverty. This is more or less the general understanding of the phenomenon known as poverty in poor third world countries like India.

But Raj Krishna's analysis of the situation is extremely interesting and needs some thought. He has argued, quite correctly that those suffering from nutritional deficiency due to poverty may not unemployed, rather a considerable proportion of them may be working poor.[4] If it is accepted that an employed person may remain poor or even 'extremely poor' depending on size of the household, number of employed within the household and finally, the degree of employment, not in terms of man-hours alone but in terms of income per period then it is necessary to derive a measurement of rates and degrees of unemployment. No serious attempt has been done in this regard with a view to planned solution of the problem. A few remarks on Raj Krishna's criteria for defining 'state of unemployment' would indeed be useful. As is well-known, he has envisaged four criteria: (a) time criterion (working time less than some normal standard), (b) income criterion (income or consumption less than some normal standard), (c) willingness criterion (willingness to do more work), and (d) productivity criterion (productivity less than some normal standard).[5]

As is evident, criteria (a) and (b), that is, time criterion and consumption or income criterion (the latter could also be designated 'minimum subsistence' criterion) are not mutually exclusive. Raj Krishna is correct in pointing out that there is inadequacy in the classification made by Dandekar and Rath (1971) in which deficiency of consumption and deficiency in income-yielding work have been made separate. By the same token it can be said against Raj Krishna's classification that time criterion and consumption or income criterion may overlap in a large number of cases because deficiency of minimum need for many may be due to under-employment in time terms at a given wage. The 'willingness' criterion may not be a criterion of unemployment at all, as far as we are concerned.

Also, what Raj Krishna calls 'misemployed' cannot be seriously associated with specificities of poverty. Sen's recognition aspect of employment also falls within the same consideration.[6] As Sen has pointed out, "the question of recognition can influence one's choice of jobs, if such choice should arise. For example, a marked preference for working for oneself rather than for others partly relate to this problem of recognition in terms of both status and of one's reaction to being ordered around".[7]

In the absence of recognition, from the subjects' point of view, it is argued that the status could be termed 'misemployed'. Sen also holds the view that Marxian discussion of alienation relates closely to the situation. This contention is not fully correct. For example, a person may be self-employed and not 'ordered around'. So, his labour is not alienated labour. But he may find recognition hard to come by. Also, he may not be in an economic position such that he can transcend the condition of absolute poverty. So, he is not alienated in his individual work but is alienated from the economic world at large and also from the purpose of his work. On the other hand, a person occupying a good position in an undertaking with good income, although being 'ordered around', may feel satisfied with recognition in his place of work and by the fact of his occupying a good position has a good chance of being recognised in the society as well. In this case his labour is not alienated and he is not 'misemployed' although he is working for others and being 'ordered around'.

The important question – recognition where, at the place of work or outside it. Add to this the subjective craving or desire. A typical example may be a person with a certain qualification structure engaged in occupation A with salary X and recognised both within and outside his occupation. He may feel that he will not be estranged if he were in occupation B with a salary Y (Y less than X) although he may feel doubtful about his recognition outside his place of work. In a particular institutional framework with specific values associated with it, recognition of capacity in society is reflected in the earning capacity of the individual in general. In the case cited above, if the person accepts the generally held values of the society, he may consider himself 'misemployed' whereas if he chooses the alternative, others would consider him 'misemployed' and the person concerned has to weigh these considerations. It is clear that 'misemployment' may not be at a lower level of income or even be 'alienated labour'. But there may be cases of convergence of 'misemployment', 'alienated labour' and 'under-employment' simply because of our economic backwardness in a condition of total absence of a central plan of security.

The Nature of Poverty

There is no doubt that during the past twenty years a number of efforts have been made to understand the depth and nature of absolute poverty in our country and some programmes of alleviation seriously attempted but, as has been emphasised, did not constitute a comprehensive framework. Without entering into the controversy on whether the percentage of population below the poverty line is 40 per cent or 50 per cent or even smaller than that it could be concluded that the lower middle and the poorer sections of the population constituting almost the bottom half of the earners did not benefit much or at all from the planned development. Out of these, the lowest 20 to 25 per cent are in need of assistance from the society for survival. According to a 1971 study on poverty, in spite of planning, the condition of the bottom 20 per cent of the rural population had remained as miserable as before. On the other hand, the bottom 20 per cent of the urban poor had deteriorated further and another 20 per cent of the lower middle did not experience any improvement of the standard. According to the authors, "Thus while the character of rural poverty has remained the same as before, the character of urban poverty has deepened further".[8]

In a 1984 study, it has been claimed that up to 1979-80 an estimated 51 per cent of the population was below the poverty line. The Government expected it to fall to 37 per cent by the middle of the eighties. It expected the rate to fall further to 23 per cent by the end of the Seventh Plan, thus making the poverty rate half within a span of 10 years.[9] In pursuance of these objectives programmes like IRDP were launched and vigorously implemented. More on this later.

One of the important reasons for aggravation of the nature of the poverty during the entire plan period has been the incapacity of the theoreticians of planning to understand that the poorest decile or 10 per cent consisting mainly of destitudes, invalids, old and others were not actively in the economic stream and hence were incapable of receiving any economic benefit from planned development. From the very condition of existence of these persons they needed social assistance, if there are no other avenues of financial support.

A suitable indicator if not essential could be the 'critical line' of poverty below which the population will be entitled to social assistance. In the present condition of our economy at least 20 per cent of our population, both urban and rural could be assumed to be under the 'critical poverty line'. This is the most important segment of the population for the determination of policy measures for combating poverty.

In analyses of poverty, reference to percentages of households below poverty line alone creates some conceptual ambiguity for policy measures. When we talk of households below the poverty line or 'critical' poverty line, if this distinction is accepted, the specific economic position of households has to be brought under consideration. It depends on the number of members in the household and the number in the employable age-group. Also, let us take the case of invalids and old age pensioners and non-pensioners in households. Although we are inclined to agree that these persons are outside the stream of benefits generated by planning, their status, by itself, should not give entitlement to them for assistance. With the structure of family and households in our country, many invalids and old members of the household are looked after by the relatives who are better off but may not be residing in the same household. So, given the conditions of the economy, one has to determine who are economically deserving and who are not. The best approach for determining the distinction should be: to ascertain (a) the number of families below the 'critical line' with surplus hands in the employable age-group, (b) the number of families in the same category with no additional work hand, and (c) families with no actual or potential work hands for the present but are getting some income enough to survive somehow by all conceivable means. It has to be mentioned that condition (b) will be deemed to have been satisfied only if the engaged work hands of the family are in the employable age-group. If child labour constitutes a part of the labour offered by the family for regular family incomes, then for the purpose of social security assistance, the family would be considered to have satisfied condition (c). This change of condition does not entail a shift in public policy directed to such groups of families. The policy should be aimed at providing employment guarantee to families in category (a) and assistance to (b) and (c) as the benefit of employment has no meaning for the last two categories. If the above classification is accepted as useful, some work has to be done for determining employment status according to the rules mentioned above of households below the 'critical poverty' line. It may be remembered that United Kingdom, before and during enactment of various poor laws made it a point to have a complete census of the poor.

Determination of the poverty status on the basis of consumption standard through sample surveys is adequate for limited purposes, but a complete picture of the degree of 'immiseration' of a section of our population has to be obtained at the quickest possible time if tangible *demarche* has to be made for amelioration. In the meantime policy framework, norms of implementation must be formulated and also actual implementation must start and continue. The proposed 'census of the poor' will make the whole attempt comprehensive and complete.

TABLE 18.1: Population Below Poverty Line

Sector	1977-78	1979-80	1984-85	1989-90
		Poverty Ratios (%)		
Rural	51.2	53.6	39.9	28.2
Urban	38.2	42.9	27.7	19.3
Total	48.3	51.1	36.9	25.8
		Number of Poor (Million)		
Rural	253.1	273.0	222.2	168.6
Urban	53.7	66.0	50.5	42.2
Total	306.8	339.0	272.7	210.8

Source: A.N. Agarwal (ed.), *India: Basic Economic Information*, New Delhi, 1986, p. 34

As is evident from Table 18.1 both the poverty ratios and the number of poor have declined in India within a span of slightly over a decade. As regards improvement in the poverty ratios and the number of poor in the rural sector, the contribution of IRDP and employment and income guarantee schemes in a number of States with Maharashtra taking a leading role has been enormous. On the other hand, the improvement of the two indicators in the urban sector may have been due to an encouraging growth among other things, of durable and semi-durable consumption goods industries after liberalisation of industrial policy in the early eighties, which also has been responsible to many including the present author for the present crisis in balance of payment. It has been argued quite convincingly in recent past by a number of economists that the improvement of poverty ratios could have been brought about by a healthier approach to economic and industrial development.

Nature and Magnitude of Unemployment

Whereas there is no definite correlation between employment and absence of poverty if all the cases are considered, there is definitely a one-to-one relationship between unemployment (involuntary) and poverty especially in families within lower income groups. Recent trends of both magnitude and nature of unemployment as has been shown and analysed by Arun Ghosh are extremely revealing. Firstly, as he has indicated, overall growth rates of employment are going down steadily over time and more so in the recent period. Secondly, with the acceleration in the rate of growth of GDP, the employment growth did not show an increase, rather it was significantly lower than the growth rate of population.[10]

Another disturbing feature has been the absence of growth in the rate of employment in the organised manufacturing sector. These and other factors have led, according to Ghosh, to a structural change, "an increase in open unemployment, as compared to the long, historical tradition of underemployment (as well as low productivity employment) in the country".[11] The shift from underemployment and low-productivity employment to open unemployment has a clear politico-economic explanation. It also signals the consolidation of scales of production in both rural and urban sectors which calls for a lower labour-capital intensity. As is known from economic history of developing countries, shift in the scale and level of technology also creates a shift in the nature of unemployment.

In the recent past, especially during the past five years, the issue of 'right to work' has become quite prominent among economists, policy makers, planners and so on. During the short tenure of the National Front Government, a serious endeavour was made to understand the implication, nationwide of the 'right to work'. It has to bee emphasised at the very outset that 'right to work' does not mean the right to obtain a work according to one's qualification structure or desire. It is a right granted to a citizen who is in need of it and the guaranteed remuneration is a statutory minimum wage. Along with the right to work, the 'right to minimum income' becomes operative. This is rather a combined social security package. The right to minimum income is exercised by those, who cannot exercise the right to work inspite of the best efforts by the government. The remuneration in this case is lower than that obtained according to minimum wage.

It was estimated by the Planning Commission in 1990 that the labour force was to increase by about 37 million during 1990-95 and by another 41 million during 1995-2000. In other words, new employment to the order of 65 million have to be generated if unemployment has to be tackled completely by 1995. New jobs have to be created for 106 million if the problem has to be tackled by the end of the century.[12] For this to be effective, the planners must consider this as a cause and then must make a comprehensive plan for it. The present five-year plan, if the pronouncements are any pointer, does not seem to have taken up the issue at all with that amount of seriousness that it deserves.

The Two Important Programmes of Poverty Alleviation

The Integrated Rural Development Programme (IRDP) for the country as a whole and the Employment Guarantee Scheme (EGS) for Maharashtra are two examples of serious poverty alleviation programmes, the former by creating conditions for increase of production and productivity in the agricultural sector and allied sectors by better utilisation of resources like land and water and at the same time endeavouring resource and income development of vulnerable segments of the population in the entire rural India.[13] The main objective of the latter was to offer a guarantee of employment to all able-bodied persons which was regarded as constitutional right to every citizen.

After a decade of its implementation and experimentation by widening its areas of operation and greater financial commitment over the years, IRDP has really been the subject of wide discussion. It has been hailed by many as the key programme of poverty alleviation in rural India. As has been mentioned before, the decrease in the poverty ratios and the number of persons below poverty level, especially in the rural sector could considerably be attributed to the success of this programme. But there are important critics as well of the programme. The main points in the criticism have been whether the objective of equity envisaged in the programme could be achieved, or even with proper implementation the programme would reach or has reached the poor.

According to Dantwala, "Equity oriented policies and programmes pursued within the cast iron inequitious structure of. ownership of assets will not only be self-defeating, but may prove counter-productive through a 'tickle-up'. Here simply a direct attack on poverty without an equally direct attack on structure, which has bred poverty and continues to do so, is an illusion at best, fraud at worst".[14] No one will contest the truth of this argument because the programme of asset creation among the poor or the very poor is likely to be an exercise in futility because of the state of poverty of the recipients. At the same time it has to be emphasised that the task of changing the structure which breeds poverty is not at all easy if possible at all. To start a programme of poverty alleviation we have to start with the given and has to come with programmes of relief, temporary and long term as far as possible without arguing for a change which will only delay whatever alleviation is possible at present. It is one of the lessons of the history of economic development of developed countries that in spite of enormous wealth and extreme inequality of incomes, the government has stepped forward to ensure conditions of existence of the poor. The objective of IRDP basically has been this.

According to Kurien, "It is argued that even if the programme is implemented and planned, without any malpractices or leakages, the benefits to the poor (through IRDP) may not be significant or sustainable. A good part of what is given to the poor through IRDP will be taken away, through the social process and market operations dominated by the rich and powerful". This problem can only be tackled by economic vigilance. In any case it is better to have a comprehensive programme in spite of some defects which are pronounced.

In reply Dantwala's comment would be useful. In spite of his reservation, he has said that one need not wait, in the wings, for a total revolution to occur which would transform the structure at one stroke. Instead, the attempt should be to progressively erode the structure through constructive programmes. One such programme has to be *to compensate the loss due to leakage or corruption by social assistance to the poor (emphasis added).*

All said and done, it cannot be denied that 26 million households have benefited up to July 1988 through the programme since its inception in 1978. According to the mid-term appraisal of the Seventh Plan, sectoral shifts in allocation have been increasing over time. The primary sector coverage has gone down drastically from 94 per cent in 1981 to 55 per cent in 1985 and to 41 per cent in 1988. Consequently, the coverage in the secondary and tertiary sectors has been increasing.[15]

Coming to Maharashtra, where the EGS is a state effort for poverty alleviation, it was stipulated in the scheme that if a group of 50 persons approached the government for employment that would be provided work by starting a new project within an area of 5 miles radius from the place of residence of the job-seekers. There was a provision for daily wage of Rs. 3 per day initially in 1972 and what is equally important was that those who were unable to obtain work were entitled to employment assistance of Re. 1 per day. With the passage of time the wage rate and the employment assistance have changed, and the scheme has become an example to those states where the social assistance is under consideration.

The scheme had to face certain initial problems. The idea of offering work to all able-bodied persons is commendable. But the purpose of the scheme, namely, putting a check on the deteriorating economic condition of the rural poor, may be defeated unless there is provision for discrimination before offering work on ground of poverty status. Otherwise, it has been heard that persons who are not that needy take advantage of the scheme in some cases while the demand of the genuinely deserving people is ignored. Secondly, the minimum number of 50 to form a group to be eligible to seek work was found to be unpractical in many cases. There were two reasons: (a) so many persons may have not been known to one another and even if contacts were established, the proximity clause may not have been satisfied thus providing impetus to bureaucratic inaction; and (b) the size of the number of itself may create a new type of employment guarantee contractors. Originally, it was not very clear whether entitlement to employment assistance was for a group of fifty or a single individual irrespective of the total number. Right of assistance of a single individual willing to work is obviously the best alternative. At present an individual has entitlement irrespective of the number of job-seekers.

In spite of the significance of EGS, it should be supplemented by an Assistance Guarantee Scheme (henceforth called AGS), as, according to the provisions of the former, a household without a person of working age is doomed to destitution. Under such circumstances wanton exploitation of child labour takes place. Only desperate economic circumstances force families to take recourse to such inhuman steps for survival. Standard economic literature does not say whether such employment is unemployment, underemployment, misemployment or employment proper. From a social standpoint the only suitable description would be 'expoitative employment'. There is imperative need for AGS to prevent this state of affairs.

After about a decade since its inception, it was found out that although there was definite improvements in the conditions of recipients of benefit in the EGS scheme, 79 per cent of them however did not obtain enough, due to family size, so as to maintain minimum nutritional standard.[16] Hence the need for a combination of EGS and AGS. The present author's contention, as opposed to a number of official spokesmen, that there is a sizable chunk of population who are capable of being in the stream of economic activities but are not, is thus demonstrated to be not so incorrect. If not, EGS would not have been necessary. Secondly, this contention is borne out by the fact that the programme of economic development for almost four decades (if we included the plan holidays) has not contributed considerably towards solving one of the main tasks of planning.

In spite of some of the inadequacies of the EGS in Maharashtra, mentioned already, full credit should be given to its sponsors for bringing the issue of minimum welfare and the right of minimum subsistence to the highest plans of consideration. But what about such measures for the urban poor? Hunger and destitution do not discriminate between rural and urban populations. There is a partly mistaken notion, fostered by many researchers on poverty that the intensity of urban poverty and destitution are mostly due to migration from rural areas.[17] Whereas this conclusion may be true for new urban agglomerations, the old parts of India, in spite of expansion, have been breeding not only wealth but also poverty. So, any State which has introduced schemes like EGS of Maharashtra must be prepared to bring the urban poor also into its fold and in this regard Maharashtra should take leadership.

The Hypothesis of 'Trickling down' of Benefits of the Poor

In Indian economic literature, an interesting argument has been put forth in recent past on which a debate lingered on for some time and perhaps the ideas on two sides are still stuck with many. In a much discussed paper Ahluwalia contended that empirical evidence points out the beneficial effects of 'trickling down' of plan benefits for reducing the extent of rural poverty in the sixties and the seventies.[18] By the same logic of development and trickling down it must have happened in the eighties as well. As is well known, several explanations have been offered for this improvement on the basis of statistical analysis. On the other hand, Bardhan, on empirical evidences alone has contested the hypothesis of 'trickle down'.[19] The contents of the debate is known to many. The issue to the present author is not which of the two authors is more correct, the question is whether the notion of 'trickling down' could at all be semantically and epistemologically associated with the philosophy of economic planning if it is a planning at all. The theory of 'big cake' and trickling down' are rather prejudices rather than theories, because historical experiences point out, as far as present day advanced market economies are concerned, that to tackle absolute poverty within a framework of welfare state, the ideas of 'big cake' and 'trickle down' are not necessary. What is necessary is a conscious policy towards eradication of certain injustices in the society.

There is some doubt about this possibility by a section of Marxists in India. In the opinion of Sau, "What is specially noteworthy is that when the Indian economy is in the grip of big capitalists to such a great extent, when the pursuit of the capitalist path of development in the last three decades has resulted in so much poverty, unemployment and deprivation and when capitalism in India is in a crisis, it is idle to talk of need-oriented, endogenous, self-reliant, and ecologically sound development, unless due attention is paid to structural transformations".[20] This transformation is only possible according to the author by establishment of socialism but not the Indian variety already in existence.[21]

There cannot be any disagreement to what Sau is emphasising especially the complete conceptual hollowness and non-existence of socialism in practice, in spite of tall claims in our country. But many may not agree with the contention that until and unless the ideal is reached nothing should be done to take away the reality from the ideal. In fact, it has to be ascertained whether what we are aspiring for is ideal or utopian especially after recent traumatic experience of socialism in USSR (erstwhile) and Eastern Europe.

Bardhan has also made the comment that "for those who find radical institutional changes politically disturbing or infeasible, the so-called 'trickle-down' hypothesis is comforting".[22] But Bardhan perhaps was not aware of other solutions apart from 'trickle-down' effect, which can be employed in an economy like that of India and which has withstood the test of usefulness in economic history. It could again be argued that radical institutional changes are best answers to some lingering problems like unemployment, poverty, etc., in economies like India but such conclusions also smack of escapism because in these the possibility of looking for any planned action in the given circumstances is ignored.

The General Objective and Outcome of Indian Planning

Let it be recalled that Indian Planning was never aimed at bringing in a radical structural transformation. The mixed economy was a compromise to halt the march of unbridled development of capitalism in a backward economy. The philosophy of such a development was unaccepted as that would have reduced the Indian economy to *so-called* 'periphery' of developed 'metropolitan capitalism' as a logical extension of a condition of 'colonial capitalism' existing over one and a half centuries. The issue of equity, social justice, satisfaction of minimum needs of the population would have been submerged under the effects of 'underdevelopment' of the periphery.

In spite of the attempt of defeat this possibility, Indian planning has been instrumental in making capitalism stronger for which a framework of mixed economy was necessary. Even if we admitted this fact, it could not be denied that the present level of development would have been impossible with private capital alone, which for reasons best known to them, the supporters of 'privatisation' tend to conveniently forget. Whatever may have been the defects of central planning as a methodology, it at least succeeded as a paradigm for 'directed' industrial, agricultural and other developments including that of strong market relations.

Along with this positive achievement of planning, there was however no comprehensive planned task for ensuring maximum welfare to the maximum number of Indians. The result was increasing immiseration over time as has been evidenced by census data and other indirect criteria. The cause of this immiseration has to be sought mainly in the ever widening inequality of incomes during the period of planned development because there was no effort for redistribution of income. One reason of this that the planners believed that market forces would ultimately produce the solution, although economic theory points out otherwise.

It would be interesting to quote Manmohan Singh in this connection. He says, "As regards inequality in the size distribution of income, there is the famous Kuznets' inverse – U hypothesis in terms of which the overall inequality first increases and then decreases but may still be higher at the end of the process than at the beginning.

Thus, at least in the initial stages, the free play of market forces cannot be relied upon to bring about a reduction in the inequality of income and wealth. It is necessary to evolve a deliberate policy of State intervention to achieve this objective".[23] The question is : did our plans pursue this policy, especially to reduce the staggering inequality of income and wealth? The theoretical justification of the failure could be discerned in the inherent contradiction in Singh's next argument, that is, "in devising policy instrument, an important consideration must be to ensure that redistributive policies do not hurt the basic process of growth and capital accumulation".[24]

While commenting on the failure of Indian planning, an author has contended, "The failure over 30 years of planning is so consistent that one should not look for explanation. To explain away this failure on the basis of external factors and unexpected events over such a long period is no explanation at all. Unfortunately, however, the planning models assume in idealistic world in which the government is assumed to be all-powerful to pursue any policy that is necessary to fulfil the plans.[25] The author seems to have overlooked the main cause of the number of failures in various areas of Indian planning. If there were any idealism in the planning, the deviation of the attainments from the ideal was not due only to the failures of government policies in fulfilling the plan tasks but also ignorance about the right policy frame for coming closer to the ideal chosen within the institutional framework. Let us take again the issue of poverty in India. Not a single plan from the First to the Seventh and now the Eighth identified the correct means by which absolute poverty could be eliminated. Our economic plans, like similar plans of a number of developing countries, led to an excess capacity of heavy industries and an exaggerated emphasis on production of luxury and semi-luxury goods for the affluent. On the other side, there was an apathy towards solving crucial problems that affect the vulnerable segment of the population. Nicholas Georgescu-Roegen was correct when he remarked, "In some countries, such as Egypt or India, for example, where the food problem cries for immediate action, an impressive proportion of resources has been nonetheless invested in the production of consumer goods inaccessible to the rural masses (and) to urban masses as well. There is a foolish extravagance, if one pauses to think about the fact, in pushing persistently industries of automobiles, refrigerators, television sets and to other similar consumer goods, in countries whose annual income per capita is a couple of hundred dollars."[26]

One may argue that in India, even in remote villages, one can see households possessing television and similar utility goods. This does not mean that if television and some other goods are seen in every corner of India, the problem of absolute deprivation has been solved. Schumpter had once observed that during the reign of Elizabeth I, only she could wear silk stockings, but in his own time, any factory girl in Britain could afford to have a pair of silk stockings. "Before the British factory girl could afford silk stockings, the working class of that country was able to satisfy progressively some of the other more basis wants." Georgescu-Roegen then adds, "Actually economic history bears out fully the contention that the broadening of the industry or the trade of wage goods is not purely an ethical requisite of economic development, but an organic condition of it."[27] The *fait accompli* in India over time has been due to conjunction of planning and market forces and the process cannot be reversed. In the march of history, this is not an unfamiliar situation. The developed capitalist countries in the past and many developing countries at present are in such a stage of economic development, the only difference being that in the case of the former, the oppressive doctrine of *laissez faire, laissex passer* was the key to the overwhelming advantage cf elites, whereas, in case of the latter, ironically, planning has been the *deus ex machina*.

Concluding Remarks

In the situation that confronts us today in matters of poverty and unemployment, the solution has to be the same as has been indicated by the course of economic history, namely 'transfer of income' as an essential component of an 'affordable' social security. This has to be achieved through a 'voluntarist' rather than a 'gradualist' planned approach. Strictly speaking, a 'gradualist' approach to planned eradication of absolute poverty is a contradiction of terms. It reminds one of the famous 'Zeno's paradox' in mathematics. However, this suggestion of a 'voluntarist approach' does not entail a sweeping change in property relations. What is imperative need in today's crisis situation is a rigorous sub-plan for its solution with dominance of directive element in this sub-sphere of the plan. The rest of the plan could proceed as before. Even if we recalled some features of French planning of the years immediately after the war, the slogan at first was *'Modernisation ou Decadence'* (modernisation or destruction) and Jean Monnet had to introduce *dirigisme* (directivism) in full swing to combat a crisis of unforeseen dimension.[28] And France was a full-fledged capitalist economy. Could we not take genuine lessons from these and come out with the slogan 'poverty alleviation or economic decadence'? Finally, it has to be emphasized that in the vigorous campaign in favour of market relations and privatisation and against government intervention in India, it is argued that the problem of poverty and unemployment has to be solved through the market forces. Tragically, the perfect solution of the two through market can only be achieved *by destitution and starvation*. Free market enthusiasts should remember this.

NOTES

1. A. Rudra, "Planning in India: An Evaluation in Terms of Its Models," Economic and Political Weekly (EPW), April 27, 1985, p. 762.
2. *Ibid.*, p. 763.
3. B. Singh. "A Planned Market Economy," in B.P.S. Bhadouria (ed.) *Reflections on the Indian Economy*, Delhi, 1987, p. 1.
4. Raj Krishna, *Rural Unemployment — A Survey of Concepts and Estimates for India*, Delhi, 1976, p. 18.
5. *Ibid.*, p. 14.
6. Amartya Sen, *Employment, Technology and Development*, OUP, 1976, pp. 5-6.
7. *Ibid.*
8. V.M. Dandekar and N. Rath, *Poverty in India*. 1971, p. 32.
9. Bharat Dogra, *Poverty Development and Poverty*. New Delhi, 1984, p. 38.
10. Arun Ghosh. "Eighth Plan : Challenges and Possibilities III, Employment : Core of he Plan," *EPW*, February 2, 1991, p. 197.
11. *Ibid.*, p. 198.
12. *Ibid.*
13. J.S. Sodhi, *Poverty Alleviation and Rural Development*. New Delhi, 1990, p. 14.
14. Quoted by Sodhi, *op. cit.*, p. 14.
15. *Ibid.*
16. K.K. Das Gupta. "Case for Public Assistance in India," *Mainstream*, February 21, 1981, p. 25.
17. See for example, Dandekar and Rath, *op. cit.*, p. 32.
18. See M.S. Ahluwalia. "Rural Poverty and Agricultural Performance in India," *Journal of Development Studies*, April 1978 and by the same author, "Rural Poverty, Agricultural Production and Prices," in J.W. Mellor and G.M. Desai (eds.). *Agricultural Change and Rural Poverty*. Johns Hopkins University Press, 1986.
19. Pranab K. Bardhan. "Poverty and 'Trickle-down' in Rural India: An Quantitative Analysis," in Mellor and Desai (eds.), *op. cit.*, p. 84.
20. Ranjit Sau, *India's Economic Development*. New Delhi, 1981, pp. 81-82.
21. *Ibid.*, p. 82.
22. Bardhan, *op. cit.*, p. 76.

23. Manmohan Singh. The Quest for Equity in Development. R.R. Kale Memorial Lecture, 1986 — Gokhale Institute Publication, Pune, p. 5.
24. *Ibid.*
25. Kirit S. Parikh. "Planning Without Policy," in S. Guhan and M. Shroff (eds.). Essays on Economic Progress and Welfare — In Honour of I.G. Patel. OUP, India, 1986, p. 24.
26. N. Georgescu-Roegen. Entropy Law and the Economic Process. Harvard University Press, 1971, p. 314.
27. *Ibid.*, p. 315.
28. Claude Seibel. "Planning in France," in Morris Bornstein (ed.). *Economic Planning: East and West.* Mass., U.S.A., 1975, p. 155.

19

FOREIGN EXCHANGE, ECONOMIC REFORMS AND POLICY FREEDOM

RAJAT DEB and M.J. FERRANTINO

AROUND THE middle of June, 1991, India was losing foreign exchange from its NRI (Non-resident Indian) accounts at the rate of Rs. 100 crores a week. A "gold swap" of 20 tons of gold failed to stem the tide. The rupee was devalued on 1 July and again on 3 July by about 20 per cent in all. Reserves had been drawn down to levels so low that they were only enough for a few weeks of imports. A major foreign exchange crisis was at hand. India flew 25 additional tons of gold to London on collateral for future loans and waited on IMF approval of a short term loan of over $ 1.75 billion. At the same time, Dr. Manmohan Singh, who had been sworn in as Finance Minister less than three weeks earlier, announced a major economic policy initiative. The devaluation was to be followed by a policy of fiscal restraint, trade reforms, delicencing and decontrol of industry, elimination of subsidies, and special incentives for foreign investment. Even privatisation of the public sector was to be looked at. These, however, were measures which had for a long time been recommended by the IMF and rejected by the Indian government! Are these policies good for India? Or are they being dictated by foreign interests with the finance minister "sacrificing national interest at the altar of the IMF"? (*Economic Times*, 25 July 1991). To understand the recent changes in Indian economic policy it is best to look at the relationship among economic development, exchange rate policies and policy freedom. By policy freedom we mean the ability to set domestic economic policy without foreign interference.

Growth, Foreign Exchange and Policy Freedom

Any overpopulated developing country like India, attempting to achieve rapid industrialisation and growth, inevitably comes up against two major resource constraints: (a) savings and (b) foreign exchange. With a large portion of the population living at the subsistence level, domestic savings to fund development can either be obtained from the wealthy few through financial markets, through direct taxation (which at least partially crowds out private savings and investment) or through indirect taxation. Failure of taxes to fund government projects results in budget deficits and implicit regressive indirect taxes in the form of inflation.

Foreign investment can fill the gap caused by inadequate domestic savings. However, even the ability to mobilise adequate savings domestically is usually not enough because critical inputs (like oil) and sophisticated technology may have to be imported from abroad and paid for in foreign exchange. The cost of foreign exchange in terms of domestic resources depends on the rate of exchange. In India's case *other things being the same*, the stronger the rupee, the fewer the number of rupees that have to be paid per unit of foreign exchange and consequently smaller the cost in real domestic resources of a given amount of foreign exchange. Indeed, if the rupee can be kept strong in the face of an increase in domestic (relative to world) prices, the real cost of foreign exchange would decline. This method of keeping foreign exchange costs low and stimulating growth by overvaluing the exchange rate is a great temptation to developing countries.

What determines the value of the rupee? One may distinguish among four different values: the free market value, the market value, the official value and the black market value of the rupee. The free market value is one that would prevail for a freely convertibly rupee by the supply and demand for foreign exchange in the absence of any tariffs and quotas. To make the rupee stronger than its free market value, the government has used export and other incentives to artificially increase the supply of foreign exchange and a set of tariffs and quotas restricting imports to reduce the demand for foreign exchange. The value of a convertible rupee that would prevail with the supply and demand curves for foreign exchange as modified by these policies will be called me market value or foreign exchange. The rate at which the rupee is actually traded, the official value of the rupee, is set by the government through the RBI. This may be higher than, lower than, or equal to the market value. Even at this rate, the rupee is not convertible. The sale of foreign exchange is controlled by the RBI using quotas. To avoid these quotas, the rupee trades illegally for foreign exchange at its black market value, usually considerably lower (in, i.e. dollars/rupee) than the official value.

A policy of using a free market for foreign exchange would have the possible disadvantage of making imports unacceptably expensive (from a political standpoint) because of a weak rupee. It would, however, have the advantage of rewarding exporters, penalising importers and removing all profits from black marketers of foreign exchange.

A policy of having a convertible rupee traded at a market value (after the trade policies have had their impact on the supply and demand for foreign exchange) would possibly make foreign exchange less expensive than under a free market and would reduce somewhat the profits in the black market; nevertheless trade controls would invariably have adverse incentive effects. Excessive trade controls could conceivably lead to incentive effects sufficiently perverse to make the market value of the rupee lower than the free market value.

The impact of using (as is currently done) the official rate would depend on whether this rate is above, below, or equal to the market value of the rupee. A policy of overvaluing the rupee – setting a rate such that fewer rupees are traded for a unit of foreign exchange than that which would be determined by the market value – would lead to an outflow of reserves. The difference between the demand and the supply of foreign exchange would have to be covered by depleting foreign exchange, gold, or other reserves held by the RBI. If such a policy leads to drastic reserve losses, a foreign exchange crisis would be precipitated whereby India would either have to default on its foreign obligations or its government would have to borrow abroad to meet in obligation. Such borrowing would be costly as lenders may insist on preconditions for making loans. These would normally include, but not be restricted to, devaluation. Since the government would have little choice but to comply with these preconditions the cost would be high not only in terms of real resources (a weaker rupee means more Indian goods must be given up for any bundle of foreign goods, given the same domestic prices) but also in terms of policy freedom. Thus such a policy of overvaluation trades off policy freedom for lower foreign exchange costs in the short run. A policy of undervaluation of the rupee would have exactly the opposite effect.

Foreign exchange costs would be higher in the short run leading to slower growth; reserves, however, would continue to accumulate allowing for the possibility of not only safeguarding policy freedom but also of lending to others, gaining leverage over other countries' policies, and being able to sustain temporary outflows of foreign exchange if necessary. A policy of setting the exchange rate equal to the free market rate leads neither to loss of policy freedom not does it provide leverage to control the policy of others.

The Market Value of the Rupee

The evidence on the appropriate market value of the exchange rate is somewhat mixed. Most Indian goods are low priced by would standards even when valued at the official exchange rate. Theoretically, in the long run, an exchange rate should be based on the concept of purchasing power parity (PPP), equating prices of Indian and foreign goods valued in any currency. Thus, in the long run, the rupee could be substantially stronger than it is today. However, it is also the case that India has run chronic trade deficits since Independence and has lost foreign exchange reserves steadily since early 1987. These facts could be taken as *prima facie* evidence that the rupee is overvalued and should be set at a level sufficiently low to improve india's international competitiveness and achieve balanced trade. Conversely, to establish an exchange rate based on purchasing power parity at the present time would have disastrous consequences for India's foreign exchange position.

Figure 19.1 presents the actual exchange rate (in dollars per rupee) and two alternate concepts of the exchange rate. For convenience the ratio of exports to imports is also presented as measure of the trade balance. The first concept of the exchange rate which we have calculated reflects the rate at which merchandise trade would be likely to balance. Under the well-known Marshall-Lerner theorem, a devaluation will improve the balance of trade so long as exports and imports are sufficiently responsive to price. Specifically, it is required that η, defined as the sum of the price elasticity of export demand and the price elasticity of import demand, be greater than 1 in absolute value. The more elastic are export and import demands, the smaller is the devaluation required to bring about balanced trade. Estimates of the demand for Indian exports reveal a fairly high degree of price elasticity. Khan (1974)[1] estimates a price elasticity of aggregate demand for exports at 1.7 and for imports at 0.7, while Lucas (1988),[2] working with disaggregated data for 18 categories of goods, reports export demand elasticities ranging from 0.7 for basic chemicals and metal products to 6.2 for railway equipment with the midpoint at around 1.3. Import demands are likely to be relatively inelastic as these have been determined largely by government fiat. Accordingly, we consider a value of $\eta = 2.0$ as being representative; the values obtained would be not too different for other reasonable values of η. Large values of η would give estimates more closely approximating the actual exchange rate, and *vice versa*.

Second, we consider the value of the rupee which would be necessary to equate the price of Indian and foreign goods, relying on the results of the International Comparisons Project.[3] The difficulties here are first, obtaining appropriate definitions of internationally comparable goods; second, that many goods (e.g. housing, personal services, local transport) are not internationally traded and are not suitable for making judgments about the exchange rate; and third, in the presence of tariffs, quotas and exchange control even traded-goods PPP is unlikely to hold in the long run. We make two choices; first, to use the relative India/rest of world prices for investment goods rather than the prices for all of gross domestic product or for consumption goods; and second, to assume that short-run PPP held in 1975. The PPP exchange rate for investment goods may be a better guide since investment goods are more likely to be tradeable internationally than consumption or government goods. Among recent years, 1975 as the year most approaching balanced trade as measured by the export/import ratio. This implies that the actual rupee rate at this time was appropriate to achieve trade balance. Assuming that the exchange rate in 1975 (the year most closely approaching trade balance) was "correct", we calculate the rupee rates needed to adjust for changes in relative Indian and world prices before and after 1975.

By either measure, the rupee has been chronically overvalued since the mid-1970s, but not drastically overvalued. The appropriate rate for 1990 seems to lie around Rs. 20-21/dollar while the actual exchange rate averaged Rs. 17.5/dollar for the year. The above figures suggest that the July 1991 devaluation may have been roughly of the right order of magnitude. However, it is unrealistic to except a sudden improvement in India's trade performance. If there is delay between the devaluation and the time that Indian exporters adjust their rupee prices (and foreign exporters to India adjust their domestic currency

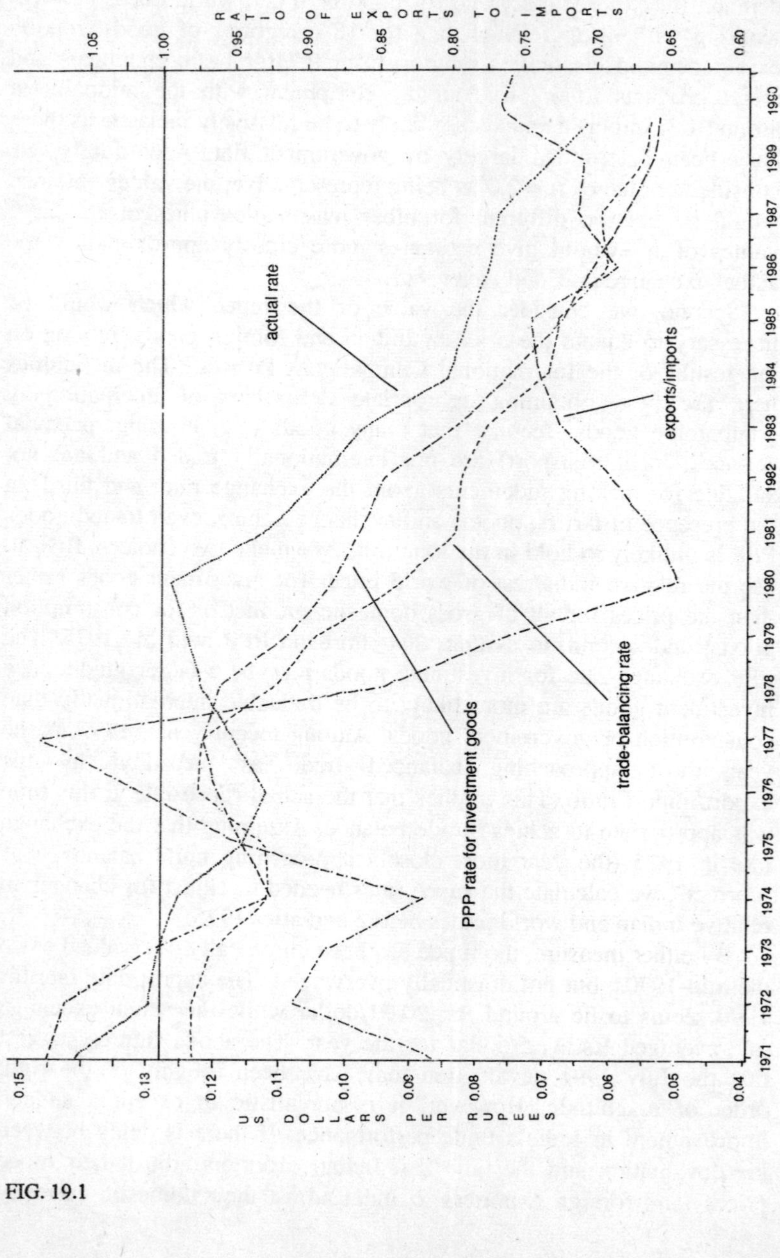
actual rate
exports/imports
trade-balancing rate
PPP rate for investment goods
RATIO OF EXPORTS TO IMPORTS
US DOLLARS PER RUPEE
1971
1972
1973
1974
1975
1976
1977
1978
1979
1980
1981
1982
1983
1984
1985
1986
1987
1989
1990

FIG. 19.1

prices) to reflect the devaluation, that the short-run trade balance will deteriorate due to the well-known J-curve effect, but will eventually get better. Additionally, a long period of rupee overvaluation will have induced a number of behavioral effects in Indian exporters who have become accustomed to poor results, and it may take longer for a devaluation to correct these effects. This source of sluggishness in the trade balance has been widely analyzed lately under the name of hysteresis.[4]

The Reserve Position

It is, of course, possible to have chronic trade deficits without an unsustainable loss in foreign exchange reserves, as long as foreign exchange inflows from other sources are available to compensate. These sources may include borrowing, foreign investment, remittances, foreign aid, services, or returns on India's investments overseas. Until recent years these sources have prevented any unsustainable loss in reserves.

India's foreign currency reserves peaked in the first quarter of 1987 at US $5.924 billion. These reserves had fallen to $3.754 billion by the third quarter of 1988, remained at $3.103 billion as late as August 1990 (by which time India had spent an additional $645 million represented by its reserve position in the IMF , which it relinquished) and collapsed to $1.205 billion by December 1990. The IMF loan agreed to in January 1991 by the Chandra Shekhar administration was responsible for temporarily doubling this amount, but by the June election foreign exchange reserves had dwindled back to $1.124 billion, with the devaluation and second IMF loan following immediately in July.

India's additional reserves include "paper gold" in the form of SDRs, which have also largely been spent, and actual gold. In October 1990 India took the unusual step of re-valuing its gold from the official price of around $15 an ounce to the world market price of around $350 an ounce signaling to world markets the possible necessity of financing international transactions with gold. If the entire gold stock could be liquidated at the world price, it would fetch around $3.6 billion dollars, enough to finance the trade deficit for seven months if there were no other source. Against this possibility must be reckoned the downward pressure on gold prices induced by expectations that the Soviets (as well as India and some others) may be gold sellers in the near future. Accordingly, it is necessary to turn to the other items in the international accounts for potential sources of funding while the trade deficit persists, as well as potential origins of the problem.

Table 19.1 depicts the recent balance of payments position of India insofar as it was available at the time of writing. We have not adopted the usual arrangement of the items but rather have organised them according to their usefulness in financing of imports, with the largest items first. (By this convention, an outflow of reserves has a positive sign.) It can be readily seen that the gap between imports and exports was steadily increasing, requiring the need for more finance. An additional drain on foreign exchange reserves was generated by India's gradual repayments of loans granted under the IMF's Extended Financing Facility during 1982-84 in the wake of the second oil crisis. This balance as largely paid off by 1990.

TABLE 19.1: Trade Deficit and Methods of Financing (current $US million)

	1984	1985	1986	1987	1988	1989	1990
Items To Be Financed							
Imports	14216	15081	15686	17661	20091	22220	22110
Payments for services	3619	3878	3920	3363	3790	—	—
Income of foreigners	1188	1372	1606	1646	2319	—	—
Methods of Finance							
Exports	10192	9465	10248	11884	13510	18080	20140
Government borrowing	2064	1692	2244	4208	5284	—	—
Income from services	3232	3384	3228	3363	3790	—	—
Net remittances	2287	2456	2223	2636	2295	—	—
Private nonbank capital inflows	881	1518	1837	1570	2014	—	—
Outflow and revaluation of reserves	--1595	538	891	800	1184	—	—
Borrowing from IMF	494	–177	–512	–954	–1197	–1086	–858
Overseas income of Indians	481	487	529	518	450	—	—
Foreign aid	492	320	399	370	457	—	—
Statistical discrepancy (black money?)	368	500	197	–409	–112	—	—
Deposit money banks	100	72	–88	–44	–57	—	—
Exceptional financing	32	37	30	21	29	—	—
Memorandum Items							
Trade balance	–4025	–5616	–5438	–5777	–6581	–4160	–2050
Total IMF credit & loans outstanding*	4529	4354	3918	3175	2282	1440	804
Foreign exchange*	5034	5549	5444	5603	4148	3105	1205

* at year's end.

An important traditional source of financing for the balance of payments, remittances from NRIs, remained flat in dollar terms during the period. Since both money and real incomes of NRIs presumably increased in the general economic expansion of the 1980s, this implies that NRIs devoted a smaller proportion of their income to remittances in 1990 than in 1984. A non-traditional source of financing, "private nonbank capital inflows", increased in the mid-80s as a result of Rajiv Gandhi's more favourable attitude towards foreign investment (unfortunately the government does not report direct and portfolio investment separately .)

The two methods by which the foreign exchange deficit was financed were (a) an outflow of reserves, as discussed above (b) increased government borrowing from sources other than the IMF. These include the World Bank and its agencies, individual foreign governments and apparently some on the private capital markets. This is not just a matter of shifting lenders. Since government borrowed over $15 billion during 1985-88 while retiring only $2 billion of IMF debt! The unsustainability of this policy is evidenced first, by the increased payments of "income to foreigners" which largely represent interest on the new debt, and second, by the sharply negative turn of the statistical discrepancy (usually thought to reflect black markets) almost as soon as the policy began, reflecting a lack of confidence in the policy.

The net effects of the policy are visible in the trade balance for 1989 and 1990, which show a forcible narrowing of the gap between imports and exports. This is typical of a country in debt crisis; Brazil and Argentina went suddenly from trade deficit to trade surplus in the early 1980s. The levelling off of imports simply reflects the inability to sustain financing of import growth at the previous levels. Whether the rapid export growth reported for 1989-90 is the result of government promotion of exports, increased competitiveness, good luck, or statistical artificial is unclear.

Appropriateness or Policy for Achieving Stable Reserves

As discussed above, the magnitude of the July 1991 devaluation seems appropriate, but its effects may take some time to manifest themselves fully. In the discussion below we compare some of the policy reforms outlined in the Finance Minister's July speech with India's policies in the past, with the goal of identifying (1) to what extent the new policies reflect a loss of policy freedom as induced by India's dwindling reserve position and (2) whether the reforms as announced seem appropriate for achieving a stable external position.

One important source of financing has of course been the loan from the IMF itself. It is well known that countries which borrow from the IMf must sign a letter of intent indicating changes in future policies which will hopefully improve the country's net external position and render future IMF financing unnecessary. Although some details of the reforms are left to national discretion, too great a deviation from the general understanding can cause the IMF to refuse to dispense the latter instalments of the loan payment and certainly make the process of applying for future loans much more difficult.

The policy package of devaluation, government budget reduction (to deflate the economy and reduce import demand), liberalisation in product and financial markets and movements towards free trade and liberalised foreign investment is a familiar feature of IMF conditionality as expressed in the letter of intent. Clearly agreeing to this conditionality represents a reduction in policy freedom. The perception of externally imposed policies has aroused substantial political criticism in India. However, if external balance is to be achieve, some combination of these policies would need to be agreed to voluntarily in any event.

The argument that IMF conditionality serves to manipulate the Indian economy at the behest of Western monied interests is a flimsy one when analyzed carefully. Taken in turn and together, the policies recommended have the effect of reducing the need for further foreign exchange loans and thus, of further IMF intervention. There are numerous instances of countries managing their own affairs after an initial IMF loan. A liquor store, desiring the addiction of its customers, would hardly offer them free treatment for alcoholism as well. Yet this is effectively what IMF conditionality amounts to.

By contrast, a full exploitation of a country's lack of international reserves in order to induce compliance with foreign desires would be represented not by IMF conditionality, but by something like the U.N. sanctions against Iraq. By embargoing oil and other Iraqi exports and freezing Iraq's overseas assets, foreign exchange reserves were effectively forced to zero. This is a state which can be prolonged indefinitely. If it were really desired by the IMF to dictate terms to India, a policy of letting India completely run out of foreign exchange and then doling out small loans under Draconian terms could have been devised, or else policy of permitting easy loans and then suspending them suddenly. Neither course is being followed here.

The only other new source of import financing besides borrowing has been private foreign capital inflows. This source seems to have reached its limits to expansion by 1986. This corresponds to the nature of the policy towards foreign investors, who may only invest in certain sectors, only with approval, and (until recently) only as minority shareholders. India vets foreign direct investment more thoroughly than any other mixed economy. To the objection that foreign investors are just as bad as foreign creditors, since they will repatriate foreign exchange in the form of profits or dividends rather than interest (thus contributing to the rising "income of foreigners" item), it must be admitted that this is true. Nonetheless direct investment is preferable to debt since debtors are owed a fixed contractual obligation of interest. Foreign investors are stakeholders in the firm; they can only repatriate profits when the firms are profitable and must be content with less when the firms are less profitable; thus they can be made to bear some of the risk of India's fluctuating foreign exchange position in a way that foreign creditors cannot. It requires no particular government intervention to shift the risk in this fashion. Besides inducing risk-sharing, foreign investment involves responsibility sharing as well since foreign managers can be held accountably for the success or failure of their business plans while foreign creditors have no comparable accountability for any actions taken in India's economy which might further her welfare. Furthermore, when profits are good one can often anticipate that foreign investors will choose to reinvest, rather than repatriate, the proceeds on hopes that such profits will continue. The example of China, in which the growth of production and exports by foreign-owned firms has been rapid. indicates that the potential is great when there is significant policy alteration towards foreign investment even in an otherwise hostile political and economic system.

The policies which have been announced represent at best a modest increase in incentives for foreign investment and are unlikely to have much impact. The permitting of 51 per cent foreign equity if of minimal impact since (1) it only applies to "key industries" (2) there are many ways to get effective control with the 49 per cent the old law permits, so the advantage of majority shareholding is less than it may seem (3) there were already exceptions to the policy anyway. In addition, two requirements which have the goal of insuring that foreign ventures have positive short-run impacts on the foreign exchange position may have negative long-run impacts by scaring away good projects altogether. The necessity of paying for imported capital inputs with enough equality to cover their foreign exchange is problematic since (1) it eliminates the possibility of investing a stock of foreign exchange up front to get a slow but steady stream of foreign exchange which will eventually amount to more, consistent with traditional principles of capital budgeting and (2) under the 51 per cent rule, it is also required to find an Indian partner willing to put up the 49 per cent in rupees, thus effectively limiting the size of equipment that can be imported. The requirement that export earnings of foreign ventures balance off against dividends "over a period of time" seems designed to be misadministered.

The benefits of increased foreign investment include imports of technology, access to foreign markets and the demonstration effect of international standards of production and managerial efficiency. But these are not to be attracted easily in the current international environment. Many countries have policies towards foreign direct investment which are much more inviting than those of India and have taken further steps in recent years.

In 1982, the U.S. Department of Commerce surveyed overseas affiliates of U.S. firms to find out what types of incentives and restrictions they experienced in various countries. Comparing only other LDCs to India, in about 3 per cent of the cases were firms subjected to a restriction on the foreign exchange balance (as vs. 6 per cent for India), in about 13 per cent of the cases were they subjected to ceilings on the percentage of foreign equity (vs. 54 per cent for India), in about 3 per cent of the cases were they subjected to import ceilings (vs. 8 per cent for India) and so on. these survey differences probably understate the true differences since some firms are unlikely to report negative treatment by a host government even if it exists and since the survey could not reflect the experiences of firms so deterred by the investment regime that they did not invest at all and is biased towards survivors who will be relatively well-treated.

Since 1982 a host of countries have undergone liberalisation programs, particularly in Latin America. International Business Communications Ltd. of London publishes a guide to country risk for use by multinational firms. This guide rates countries on a scale of 1 to 100 with scores above 70 reflecting low risk and below 50 reflecting very high risk. Countries are ranked on political risk (corruption, realism of policy), financial risk (threat of exchange controls, loan defaults) and economic risk (possibility of inflation, debt-service costs, etc. In August 1991, India was rated at 43 overall and 34 on political risk. This compares to other LDCs as follows; Malaysia, 77.5 and 71; South Korea, 73.5 and 63; Mexico, 70. 5 and 71; Indonesia, 68.5 and 57; Thailand, 68 and 57; Brazil, 62 and 67; China, 60 and 58; Niger, 49 and 45. Fair or not, this probably reflects accurately international opinion as to the relative riskness of India's business climate, which depends largely on domestic policies.

Thus, a substantial shifts in India's policies would be required to induce the perception that they are now internationally comparable. Let us now consider some of the other proposed policy reforms.

To attract funds from NRIs the government proposes to establish a commissioner to case procedural difficulties for investing in joint projects in selected sectors, acquiring property and investing on a non-repatriable basis. Furthermore, remittance rules for NRIs would be relaxed and special tradeable five-year bonds with exchange protection and tax privileges would be made available to NRIs. These suggested policies represent marginal changes in existing procedures and are unlikely to result in a large inflow of foreign exchange from NRIs. In particular the tradeability feature, which permits NRIs to resell bonds only to other NRIs, is not worth very much since such persons could always buy fresh bons directly from the government anyway.

In its attempt to meet the IMF stipulation that the deficit he reduced from 8.4 per cent of GDP to 6.5 per cent of GDP, the Finance Minister has announced a number of austerity measures. These include cuts in defence and removal of export subsidies as well as sugar and fertiliser subsidies. To the extent these policies can be successfully implemented (and there has already been political opposition to specific budget cuts and tax increases) there would be a favourable impact on the trade balance since a reduction in aggregate demand would lower import demand as well. Reduced deficits also imply a reduced need for Reserve Bank credits to the government, which induce inflation through money creation, and thus may be favourable for preserving the rupee's long-run value.

The simultaneous lowering of customs duties and export subsidies minimises some of the tensions inherent in the current policy position. These policies have the beneficial long-run effect of subjecting Indian firms to international competition and helping sort out the country's eventual comparative advantage. But in the short run both policies have fiscal costs (running against the objective of reducing budget deficits) and costs in terms of the trade balance (more imports from duties reduction, fewer exports due to subsidy reduction). Probably this is one area where the IMF's philosophical predilection towards free trade can be seen in the policy mix.

If anything is to be gained by opening up the country to international competition at world prices, it will be necessary for labour and capital to move freely from industry to industry in the process of identifying national comparative advantage. But this will be difficult under current policies. In many ways, the comprehensive licencing and trade restrictions imposed in the past have led to the current impasse. Although imports are heavily regulated and access to foreign exchange is tightly controlled, this has not stopped import growth from outstripping export growth. Exporters do not benefit fully from their earnings of foreign exchange. Under the scheme of export replenishment licences (REPs), the vast majority of export earnings were taken away from firms by government and assigned to other firms bureaucratically. Importers thus had no particular incentive to conserve the scarce asset of foreign exchange after having assured that they stood in the appropriate political circumstance to obtain some. Exporters, keeping only a fraction of foreign exchanged in the REP, were deprived of the full incentive to export which they would have received by keeping all of the foreign exchange, and selling openly the amounts not needed their own imports. The canalisation of foreign exchange to preferred importers, which was intended as a rational response to the trade deficit, has ended up worsening the trade deficit. Substituting resalable EXIM scrip for the REP licences of exporters, as has been proposed, is preferable. Although the retention of only 30 per cent of export earnings by firms still represents a substantial hand of government in allocating foreign exchange, at least the retained foreign exchange can be sold openly rather than illegally.

It may be objected that the falling rupee has at least caused rupee prices of imports to rise in the past, and that this would causes firms to conserve on imported inputs even if they had unlimited bureaucratic allocations of foreign exchange. This is true insofar as it goes. However, other aspects of India's industrial and labour policy have served to limit the impact of this incentive. For example, the falling rupee has increased the rupee price of oil, an important import whose price OPEC denominates in dollars. To conserve oil in the production process generally requires substituting equipment for oil or labour for oil. If equipment is added on anything other than a small scale, endless delays may be encountered in the licencing system.[5] If labour is substituted for energy, firms run up against the provisions of the Factory Act designed to prevent workers from being dismissed. Since, if the price of energy were to fall in the future, the firm could not shed labour and use more energy, it may be reluctant to hire labour to replace energy in the first instance. Again, a policy designed to preserve employment may not only have inhibited employment but cost the country foreign exchange as well.

This is at least some recognition in the proposed reforms that intersectoral mobility of resources is vital to exploiting the opportunities created by an opening to world markets. The talk of easing the licencing regime is welcome, as are the initial steps towards a fee exit policy implied by the suggested procedures for winding up failed public-sector enterprises. Again, the risk is that these will not be general reforms but will be privileges allotted to "key industries" or on an experimental basis. India as undergone several rounds of licencing reform on a "key industry" basis before. Such "reforms" amount to little more than a marginal increase in the group of industries granted privileged access to the bureaucracy. It is hoped that this trap will be avoided.

Conclusion

India has been led by a series of policies to become a net consumer of foreign goods. This has led to increasing needs for external finance culminating in a loss of reserves and the associated loss of policy freedom. New policies must be tailored to those who are in a position to provide foreign exchange (the IMF domestic exporters, NRIs, foreign multinational firms). This is a natural consequence of having lost the foreign exchange in the first place. If one wished to do with less or no IMF financing, it would be necessary to undergo even more strenuous efforts to entice one of the other foreign-exchange-providing agencies.

The Government's policies as announced represent steps in the right direction insofar as they are designed to provide natural market-based incentives to private agents to increase India's foreign-exchange position and reduce reliance on the IMF. However, in each case (foreign investment, NRIs, export policy) the proposals appear to be only marginal adjustments in the *status quo*, and in other areas where complementary policy changes are urgent (licencing and exit policy), the proposed changes seem slow and tentative. This leaves the unpleasant prospect of a fiscal austerity which will both be painful and possibly inadequate to produce the desired effect by itself. It should be well-understood that failure to generate sufficient positive incentives for attracting foreign exchange to the country only invites further returns to the IMF and more severe policy conditionality from them.

If a failure of political courage to alter domestic policy now means renewed dependence on the IMF later, this would be most unfortunate. Of the various constituencies that can be potential sources of foreign exchange, India possesses the least influenced over the IMF. Domestic exporters and foreign investors in India are always within reach of the government, and the NRIs may at least possess special good will for India in a way that the IMF cannot be expected to. Ultimately, there are some priorities in the Indian budget which can best be identified and preserved by Indians themselves, and it is the freedom to set these priorities which is ultimately at stake.

NOTES

1. Mohsin S. Khan, "Import and Export Demand in Developing Countries", *IMF Staff Papers*, November 1974 pp. 678-693.
2. Robert E. B. Lucas, "Demand for India's Manufactured Exports", *Journal of Development Economics*, Vol. 29 (1988) pp. 68-75.
3. Robert Summers and Alan Heston, "The Penn World Table (Mark 5); An Expanded Set of International Comparisons, 1950-1988", *Quarterly Journal Of Economics*, Vol. 106 No. 2 (May 1991), pp. 327-368.
4. Avinash Dixit, "Hysteresis, Import Penetration and Exchange Rate Pass-Through", *Quarterly Journal of Economics* Vol. 104 No. 2 (May 1989), pp. 205-229; Richard Baldwin and Paul Krugman, "Persistent Trade Effects Of Large Exchange Rate Shocks", *Quarterly Journal of Economics* Vol. 104 No. 4 (November 1989), pp. 635-654.
5. That this can happen in the case of energy substitution is illustrated by the case of Ponni Sugars Chemicals in Erode. Ponni is vertically integrated with a paper mill and desired to use bagasse from sugarcane as a fiber in paper-making. Since most factories burn bagasse to generate steam electricity, Ponni required a coal-burning boiler to make this feasible. Although the proposition was sensible on economic grounds, such an attempt to diverge from industry norms for energy added years of licencing delay to the start-up of the project.

REFERENCES

Baldwin, Richard and Paul Krugman, "President Trade Effects of Large Exchange Rate Shocks", *Quarterly Journal of Economics,* Vol. 104 No. 4 (November 1989), pp. 635-654.

Dixit, Avinash, "Hysteresis, Import Penetration, and Exchange Rate Pass-Through", *Quarterly Journal of Economics,* Vol. 104 No. 2 (May 1989), pp. 205-228.

Economic Times, 25 July 1991.

International Business Conditions Ltd., *International Risk Guide,* New York: August 1991.

Khan, Mohsin N., "Import and Export Demand in Developing Countries", *IMF Staff Papers* (November 1974), pp. 678-693.

Lucas, Robert, E. B., "Demand for India's Manufactured Exports", *Journal of Development Economics,* Vol. 29 (1988), pp. 68-75.

Summers, Robert and Alan Heston, "The Penn World Table (Mark 5); An Expanded Set of International Comparisons, 1950-88", pp. 327-368.

20

INDIAN ECONOMIC CRISIS: Need for a New Paradigm of Growth

JITENDRA DHOLAKIA

THE TERM economic crisis indicates the current state of the Indian economy. If one focuses on the situation with regard to inflation and balance of payment position and also on the declarating trends in the rates of agricultural and industrial growth, the prevailing situation in India can aptly be described as one of multiple crisis. The inflation is currently estimated at about 14 per cent rate which has adversely affected the living standards of the poorer and weaker sections of the Indian people. These poorer Indians do not have the protective cover of the rising dearness and the other compensatory allowances to neutralise economically bad effects of a raging inflation. The major cause of inflation is unduly high rate of growth of money supply as well as budgetary deficits. There is then the chronic imbalance between aggregate demand and aggregate supply. The current level of buffer stocks of foodgrains and other essential wage goods is not sufficient enough to cushion the inflationary pressures in the Indian economy.

Another facet of Indian's current economic crisis reveals several disconcerting features of the balance of payment position. Despite official claims that in the past three to four years exports have been increasing by leaps and bounds, the trade deficit on the current account has been widening at an alarming rate. In the foreign trade sector, imports have continuously outpaced exports and the magnitude of the trade deficit grew particularly large with the deficit hitting a peak of Rs. 13,100 crores in 1990-91. This fact was disclosed for the first time by the recently released annual reports of the Reserve Bank of India. Thus our current account deficit is U.S. dollars 7.3 billion accounting for 2.5 per cent of GDP at current market prices. A number of factors have been responsible for our deteriorating balance of payment problem. Among them are the import liberalisation, growing import-intensity of exports, declaration in the workers remittance from abroad, rising domestic demand for petroleum products and domestic macro-economic imbalance spilling on the balance of payments. The liberalisation measures have certainly aggravated the balance of payment position. A look at the import statistics reveals that capital goods imports have increased from Rs. 1910 crores in 1980-81 to Rs. 8831 crores in 1989-90. Despite increasing recourse to borrowing from abroad, the foreign exchange reserves have fallen substantially. In mid-January 1991 India had barely enough funds to finance 10 day's imports. The sources of external imbalance are partly from the trade account and partly from the deterioration on the invisible and capital accounts of the balance of payment. The net result of all these developments on the external front is a serious payments crisis.

Moreover, India's growth rate has not been accelerating at a rate which could generate sufficient economic surpluses from agricultural and industrial sectors to mitigate the adverse effects of inflation and disequilibrium in the balance of payments. Agricultural growth rate has been volatile and has not got diversified by crop and region. The industrial growth rate is expected to fall below six per cent, last year it was well over eight per cent. If one judges the value of over-all economic growth in terms of the progress in reducing poverty and unemployment, the performance of the Indian economy has been far from satisfactory. The multiple economic crisis is reflected in the deplorable standards of living of the poorest sections of the Indian population. 2.20 million persons living below the official poverty line do not have enough food to eat. And a very few of 3,80,000 fair price shops are able to supply basic essential items like wheat, rice, sugar and edible oil to the poor. The society has not been able to protect the right of poor to a minimum quantum of food. 66 per cent of Indians do not have access to safe drinking water. The economic crisis is really the crisis of the levels of living and denial of better life chances to the poorest strata of the Indian society. Poverty, unemployment and income-disparity ratios are rising along with the impressive growth rate recorded in certain islands of affluence in the Indian economy. There is a dual economy where the top 20 per cent of Indians appropriate 63 per cent of the country's total white and black income, whereas the bottom 20 per cent of the poor Indians have a meagre share of 7 per cent of this total income. Therefore those who design the policies and programmes of resolving Indian's economic crisis should not be oblivious of the needs and opportunities of improving the life styles of the abysmally poorer sections of the Indian society.

In response to the crisis situation of inflation, external imbalances and slowing down of economic growth, the government of India has taken several far reaching measures to grapple with the current crisis. These measures include reduction in the fiscal deficits, devaluation of Indian Rupee major reforms in trade policy and announcement of the new industrial policy. The main intention is to tackle inflation and external imbalance and to promote growth of the Indian economy by opening it up to forces of world trade and international competition. The general thrust of the policy measures seems to be correct. We have to get out of the rigid thought-patterns and grooves and ghettos of the economic ideologies of both socialism and free markets. In any economic situation, the real forces and factors concerning excessive money supply, export sluggishness and export pessimism, useless import and exchange controls and bureaucratisation of the decision making are far more damaging than the so-called socialist models. There is neither pure socialism nor unalloyed, free markets anywhere in the world. It should now be clear to all that we as a nation have been wasting out time in a futile debate about whether the socialist planning or free market is important or not for economic growth and welfare of the poor. If there is any lesson that we have to learn from the present economic crisis it is this: without promotional guidance of the government and broadly competitive framework of the Indian economy, neither economic growth nor well-being of the poorest can be maximised by anybody at anytime. Indian should cease to be a land of ideologies, whether of left or right economic philosophy. The Indian economists should jettison preconceived notions and the economic policy should be formulated in the contextual reality of the needs and potentials of the vast, Janus faced Indian economy. If economic welfare of the poorest strata of society, efficiency-oriented growth of the economy and equality are considered socially desirable, let us say it so in a positive way and design means and instruments to realise these desirable goals. Then competition, liberalisation, removal of controls and direct action for reduction of poverty and unemployment are of instrumental value. One might argue that the socially desirable ends acceptable to people is also a kind of ideology. But let there be a clear cut distinction between what the society considers its worthwhile goals and instruments and means to fulfil these goals. Given the rational and realistic approach ideological debates about socialist planning versus free economy can be rendered otiose. The critical insight requires that the right instruments and right measures be devised to grapple with any crisis in the light of changing economic conditions and circumstances.

It is not possible to provide against each and every likely uncertain condition or circumstance. But given the correct approach to the crisis, one may have high hopes for the success of the measures recently taken by the government of India. There can be little doubt that the demand-driven inflation can be contained by reducing the fiscal deficit. But the focus should not be exclusively on the reduction of fiscal deficit. Genuine, not spurious, efforts must be made to step up the rate of public savings. Let us recall, it consists of the revenue surplus of the government plus the retained profits of the public enterprises. A rise in the ratio of the public savings to the aggregate national savings of the economy should be one of the major components of the strategy of curbing inflationary pressures. Therefore the reduction in the fiscal deficits and revenue deficits should be the agenda for macro-economic management. The new measures do not spell out any tolerable rate of price inflation for the economy. One may ask: Why not reduce the inflation rate to zero over a period of three to five years? If the rate of inflation is reduced to zero, one can then get rid of the need to depreciate the rupee. In order to bring about the zero rate of inflation, it will be imperative to improve productivity, factor-efficiency and to create a durable environment for healthy competition between the public and private enterprises. Moreover, it will be necessary to give incentives for increasing the rates of governmental corporate and household savings. By stepping up the domestic savings, the exchange gap can be at least partly breached. More real savings mean more exports, less imports and closings of the savings investment gap. The policy of zero inflation and that of stepping up of the rate of domestic savings is one of the effective ways of tackling the disequilibrium in the balance of payments. There is a strong empirical support for the hypothesis that the excess of monetary investment over real savings widens the trade gap. Therefore the incentives of raise the over-all savings ratio and the zero rate of inflation should be the corner stone of the macro-economic management.

The diminishing foreign exchange reserves brought about a very critical payment crisis which made it imperative for the country to seek external commercial borrowings. General shortage of liquidity in the international financial markets and erosion in India's credit rating almost dried up commercial borrowings as a source of finance. Under the uncharitable and uncertain circumstances, a strong policy measure like devaluation of the Indian rupee became inevitable. As indicated by the fluctuating purchasing power parity of the rupee vis-a-vis the major hard currencies of the world, the rupee was over-valued before the latest exchange depreciation. What would have been the cost of not taking up the devaluation of the Indian Rupee? Over-valued rupee would have reduced our exports by keeping their foreign currency prices unduly high as well as by shifting domestic production pattern from exports to the non-traded goods. Devaluation alongside Exim Scripts would re-orient the Indian production pattern in favour of exports and it would also enhance India's competitive capacity in the global markets. But whether the foreign exchange receipts will increase will depend on the elasticity of demand for exports and elasticity of supply. In the immediate short-term, there would not be any sizeable increase in the foreign exchange earnings. But over a period of three years, there would be an important break-through in the foreign trade sector and devaluation would be useful as a step towards greater convertibility of the Indian rupee. During the period of transition, a number of follow-up measures will have to be taken to reap the maximum benefit of the devaluation.

The optimal measures pertain to improving Indian's competitive skills in selected global industries and hard currency markets. India will have to evolve a new paradigm of growth demonstrating its corporate cost advantage in the global markets of the dollars 2 trillion world trade of value added goods. Indian agriculture and industry will have to become innovative, productive and cost-effective. Indian can certainly develop global competitive advantage because it has many building blocks in place; its scientific, technological and managerial manpower, expanding frontiers of new technology and emerging developmental contracts with the foreign companies. India is on the threshold of momentous economic changes. The Indian governments, industrialists and the people of at large should not react to foreign private investment with a sense of fear and difference. We are a free country and like China, we must so arrange our macro-economic management that the foreigners and multinationals earn foreign exchange for us, not of all repatriations, remittance of profits, fees and other costs. The fears in some quarters that the multinationals will dominate the indigenous economy are vastly exaggerated and more ideological than anything. Foreign equity is not going to come running to our industries because we will have to do a lot to correct the negative image of bureaucratic decision making, infra-structural infirmities and irrational controls. Indian will have to market itself in a new, luminous light globally. This is going to be a very tough job and we therefore need a new paradigm of growth through innovation and globalisation.

But what is to be done in the immediate short-term period? The social costs of macro-management of the current crisis should not be disproportionately borne by the poorer strata. It is in this context that the role of the state as a promoter and provider of well-being of the poor becomes very crucial in India. There must be direct and efficient public provision of the basic human needs of the poorer sections of the society. Indian has tremendous experience of running public distribution of wage goods and also in implementing other pro-poor programmes of employment generation and asset creation for the poor. We must strengthen these programmes and improve the quality of service provided under these programmes.

The task of tackling a severe economic crisis is doubtless daunting. It is also appropriate to stress that structural imbalances in the Indian economy cannot be corrected at once. In the immediate period, we will have to tap external source of finance just to maintain our sound credit rating in the international financial market. India has therefore approached the IMF and it has approved a loan of $635 million under the Compensatory and Contingency Financing Facility. The Finance Minister is on record as saying that the government of India may go to the IMF for a fresh loan of $ 5 to 7 billion. But these loans and investments of the non-resident Indians in the India Development Boards bonds will give our country the necessary breathing time. These are not the lasting solutions. In the medium term the real solution lies in India becoming globally competitive. India must have an ambitious goal scaling the acme of excellence in capturing the world markets for some of our most promising areas of manufacturing activity. We must announce and strive to achieve a target of exports of 18 to 22 per cent of Gross National Product. This must be categorical imperative because India's external debt of around $ 70 billion places it as the third largest indebted country in the world after Brazil with the foreign debt of $ 122 billion and Mexico with that of $ 101 billion. Moreover, the recent borrowings from the IMF and other sources such as deposits and bonds of the non-resident Indians will impose additional burden of the servicing of the ever-mounting debt. Thailand,

Malaysia, Indonesia and China within a period of three to five years within very recent period have pulled themselves up by their boot straps from the gravitational pull of declining foreign trade by becoming globally competitive. A cross-country comparison with South-Korea, Singapore and Taiwan and other newly industrialising economies of Asia suggest that India can certainly become globally competitive. In order to accelerate the pace of globalisation of the Indian economy, it will be needful to design a creative paradigm of growth. But what matters most in this context is the efficiently operated domestic competition. Without greater competition in the domestic economy as a first step, opening up of the country to the forces of foreign competition would not be very productive. We must have a competition — fostering, innovative domestic environment. In order to brıng about a new economic order within our country, we will have to alter fundamentally many of the behaviourial parameters such as managerial autonomy and accountability, participatory production and work ethics, attitudes and norms of efficiency. This calls for a veritable over-haul of the prevailing system of whole of the industrial and business organisation. Looking to at the countries which have successfully built up comparative trade advantage, it is evident that India will have to gird up its loins and convert the current crisis into a conduit for moving into a more productive and innovative trajectory of growth. There are no soft options. India either becomes globally efficient or does not matter at all for the rest of the world.

21

EMERGING ISSUES IN POLICY PLANNING

A. VAIDYANATHAN

THE DECISION of the Government to postpone presentation of the annual Budget in Parliament, the delay in the finalisation of the Eighth Plan and the continued problems on the external payment front continue to focus attention on the need to come to grips with certain systemic weaknesses in the Indian economy. Many of the problem facing the economy, particularly the fiscal and current account deficits, are the culmination of policies which have been in operation for several years and cannot be solved by short-term policy adjustments. Remedial measures to tackle these deficiencies must, of necessity, be fairly drastic, far-reaching and of a long-term character.

Both inflation and the recourse to the IMF are the culmination of policies which have been in operation will before the Gulf crisis. The rate of inflation has averaged seven per cent a year through the eighties; the BoP deficit has risen steadily and strongly in the past decade, largely due to a rise in import payments and a slowdown of remittances while exports have in fact done rather well. The rise in import payments is not all due to the liberalisation policy though this has certainly contributed to some extent. The liberal spending on imported military hardware and commercial aircraft in the early eighties was as important, possibly more. That the deficits have had to be increasingly financed by loans on harder terms (interest and period of repayment) adds to the burden. It needs recalling that the debt service ratio had already reached close to 30 per cent before the Gulf crisis.

The inflation rate (in terms of the wholesale price index) has quickened in 1990-91. There has been an alarming deterioration in the budgetary situation, with governments – Central and State – having to borrow even to meet their current expenditures. And the magnitude of this dissaving in the Budget has increased rapidly through the 1980s. While public enterprise performance (in terms of their savings relative to the GDP) has not deteriorated, it has fallen way short of Plan assumptions. It would have fared worse but for the liberal and frequent recourse to administered price increases. With governments unable or unwilling to contain expenditure, pious declarations to the contrary notwithstanding dependence on borrowed funds has been much higher than projected and the cost of borrowing—as a matter of deliberate policy—has risen.

No Easy Solutions

The belief that opening the door wide for private foreign investment will take care of the BoP and resources problem is a pipe dream: the magnitude of deficit is far too large; what foreign investors find profitable or attractive may not serve the country's long-term the interests; and the large competing claims of East Europe and the USSR may, for various reasons, be more attractive to the MNGs. Nor on the NRIs likely to bring in large additional flows; they are mostly professionals seeking safe investment and are more attracted by FCNR deposits, rather than equity investment. Investments in the FCNR area are already quite sizeable.

Nor can we hope to manage the situation by import compression. A large part of our imports—like POL, fertilisers and non-ferrous metals—consist of essential inputs of which there are no ready or quick domestic substitutes. Many items of intermediate product and capital goods which are either not produced at home or are far too costly or time-consuming to produce will also have to be imported on a larger scale as the economy expands. Imports of defence items, food products and luxury consumption goods are large, but does any government have the political will to take on the constituencies which will be adversely affected by curbing them?

One can, however, hope to contain the growth of inputs through a series of well-planned measures over the medium term. Fuller use of capacities already established obviously would help contain import needs. More comfortably raising the efficiency in the use of import-intensive (inputs, especially POL) and fertilisers, for which there is a great deal of scope, would mean that the projected overall growth of the economy can be sustained with a substantially slower growth of demand for such inputs. They will also have the incidental effect of reducing costs throughout the economy. Similarly, the need to import food products can be contained if, besides achieving faster, more diffused growth of agriculture, the scope and scale of subsidised public distribution of essential commodities is restricted to the poor; and by altering investment priorities and the fiscal regime to discourage import-intensive consumption.

But with all this, import compression can only go a limited way. It is, therefore, imperative to mount a more aggressive, resilient and long-range strategy for export promotion of viability if the BoP is to be restored. A target of 15 per cent annual increase in foreign exchange earnings at constant price is the minimum necessary for this purpose. To achieve this in the face of a prospective slowdown in the developed economies and dislocations in our own economy which might result from continued confusion (and worse) in the Middle East is obviously difficult. Our advantage is that we are a small player in should make exports and work in collaboration with exporters to evolve and enforce a long-range programme for a few selected thrust areas and facilitate resilient adaptation to changing market conditions.

Recourse to Foreign Borrowing Unavoidable

With the best will and effort all this will take time to come to fruition. In the meantime continued recourse to foreign borrowing on a substantial scale seems quite unavoidable. With no prospects for a substantial increase in official aid flows, the exposure to commercial borrowing being already at an uncomfortably high level and the tightening of the issue capital markets, we really cannot avoid recourse to the IMF. Nor is this undesirable. The objections to IMF conditionalities should not really bother us. We need to take many harsh steps to restore better health to BoP and the fiscal position. What we should be doing is to work out, on our own, a package of measures which will cause minimum hurt to the really poor and underprivileged. We should take the initiative in implementing such a package before going to the Fund asserting our entitlements. To do otherwise will only make us more vulnerable.

The other important problem area is government fiscal management. Here again the problem lies more in the Government's profligacy and its uttar unconcern for effectiveness of public spending than in inadequate revenue. This is not to suggest that there is no scope for raising revenues by more effective collection of levies in force and by extending the coverage and raising the effective rates of levy of both direct and indirect taxes on the well-to-do segments. But with the tax ratio (20%) already quite high for a country at our level of development, can we really raise this ratio substantially? At any rate, it cannot be the primary means of reducing the budget deficit.

Meanwhile, it is necessary to take a hard look at expenditure. Do we need to spend as much as we are on defence? We need an institutional mechanism where the various parameters of medium- and long-term defence planning can be discussed and critically evaluated with greater openness, information and involvement of non-government experts. The scale of a operation of paramilitary forces has been rising at an alarming rate and has not really succeeded in preventing a deterioration of "law and order" reflecting deeper social turning. Do we need them and can we afford them ?

Periodic revision in pay allowances had led to a rapid increase in the salary bill of the Government. Decisions by the States to bring their salary bills on a par with the Centre has added substantially to staff costs. Altogether salaries and pensions of government employees between 1980-81 and 1986-87 have risen from Rs 8,000 crores to Rs. 20,300 crores. And there are constant pressures for increase in them. The Government's finances do not allow this to go on indefinitely without cutting into development programmes. Raising the efficiency of public employment—for which there is obviously much scope—is essential to contain the growth of salary cost without sacrificing the range, volume or quality of essential services they are supposed to render.

Undeserved Subsidies a Drain

The total quantum of subsidies, according to the national accounts estimates for 1987-88, is of the order of Rs 14,000 crores. The NAS definition of subsidies is, however, much too restrictive and does not include a great many hidden/implicit subsidies. A recent study by the NIPFP, undertaken at the instance of the Planning Commission, estimated that the Government (including departmental enterprises) spends nearly Rs 62,000 crores for the users of these services. They recover barely Rs 20,000 crores from the users of these services. The unrecovered costs are partly attributable to the inefficiency of the

Government agencies (leading to higher costs)—partly to subsidies in the strict sense of charging below what the market will bear. There are of course services (of which elementary education and basic healthy care are the most important) which the State should provide at subsidised rates to the poor in the larger social interest. Even allowing for these, there is clearly great room from improving cost recovery both by more efficient management of public services and by trimming subsidies which benefit the better-off segments of the population. Effective cutting of subsidies benefiting the better-off is equivalent to raising taxes on them and there is much more room for the former.

Strong Grounds Against Public Enterprises

Subsidies, both explicit and implicit, are also part of the reason for a low return on investment in public enterprises. The inability of public enterprises, to generate surpluses for reinvestment and to become a progressively more important source of both aggregate saving and finance for public investment has been a major failure of our planning. Excluding oil, the Central public enterprises taken as a whole, are recording losses after meeting interest charges and depreciation. The State electricity boards and transport corporations are posting large and mounting losses despite pretty hefty and sustained rises in prices of their products. This situation is unsustainable and provides strong grounds—both ideologically and in practical terms—for those opposing public enterprise.

Norms of accountability of public enterprises for economic construction of projects and their efficient operation remain ill-defined and such mechanisms as exist to enforce accountability are notoriously weak. The widespread tendency to use public enterprises as a vehicle of political patronage, excessive interference by the political executive, Parliament and State bureaucracy in the details of management rather than focusing on performance in relation to well-defined overall goals, the problem of maintaining high levels of operational efficiency and achieving the dynamism to adapt to changing market and technological environment are all well-known symptoms of the weaknesses. A major structural reform involving a trimming of the extent and scope of activities of public enterprises; limiting involvement of the Parliament, political functionaries and executive ministries in the affairs of the enterprises to clearly defined mattes of general policy; evolving a set of rules and transparent mechanisms governing matters relating to investment decisions, personnel policy, enterprise objectives and performance evaluation has been long overdue. Everyone recognises the problem but no one seems to grasp this nettle.

On the larger question of planning and development strategy we should not shy away from a ruthless appraisal of our own experience of the past four decades, and the massive retreat of the socialist countries from the planning system which had inspired us to a significant extent. There is a fundamental similarity in that both are reacting to the excesses of detailed centralised planning and State control. In our case the reaction has found expression in a strong and increasingly vocal lobby for "liberalisation" on the one hand, and a concern for dealing more effectively with persistent large-scale unemployment or underemployment and poverty on the other.

The "liberalisers" speak of leaving the private sector free to decide what investments are to be made, where and for what purpose in the light of market conditions; restructuring the foreign trade or investment policy by dismantling the system of import licencing in favour of a rationalised, low-tariff system; redressing the imbalance in the incentives for exports as against import substitution; and generally reducing the effective protection enjoyed by domestic producers and allowing free flow of private investment as a vehicle of both funds and technology. These measures are seen as the core of structural reform.

Abrupt Transition Not Advisable

While there is much to be said in favour of switching from a system of import controls and licencing to a system which relies on tariffs and exchange rates, the transition to such a regime cannot be abrupt. In any case the present BoP situation does not permit us to embark on it right away. A full-scale liberalisation will not only necessitate considerable and necessarily painful, adjustments in domestic industry, it will also give rise to a substantial increase in the demand for imports thereby increasing the already unmanageable BoP deficit.

Therefore, without finding some ways and means of financing the extra deficits, the process cannot be sustained long enough for the beneficial effects to be realised. External liberalisation must, therefore, be highly selective focusing initially on areas which will augment exports, save on scarce imported inputs and/or raise the efficiency of intermediate and capital goods production. There is no warrant for free inflow of capital and technology for finished consumer goods under foreign brand names.

One can grant that the system of direct control on investment, import of technology, scale and output has not really worked, and in several important respects has even proved counter-productive. The proposition that it is desirable to move from a detailed discretionary control to indirect, strategic intervention cannot be said to find a very wide acceptance. Strategic intervention should operate at a few selected points, such as interest rates, exchange rates and tax-subsidy policy, to promote certain broadly deconsumption and output patterns, technology choice, indigenous innovation spatial dispersal and the like. Greater freedom of entry and exist are necessary to create and sustain pressures for efficiency and improvements on the producers.

MRTP Relaxation not Disastrous

In this connection the relaxation of MRTP restriction is not necessarily disastrous when we consider that the "large business houses are far move numerous and diversified now than 20 years back and, more importantly, public financial institutions hold a large proportion of the equity of the big corporation. (The latter opens up the possibility of "strategic" guidance for the policies and programmes of the private sector without direct control, but that will require a very different mode of operation of public financial institutions.)

Internal liberalisation should, however, make sure that the emergence of monopolies in particular products is effectively contained; that sufficient time and, where necessary, assistance to manage the transition problem is given; and that the interests of small businesses and traditional industry which provide a large volume of employment are given reasonable protection.

The tendency to focus on "liberalisation" as the central issue of economic reform should be strongly resisted. Its concern for the most part is with organised industry. No one can seriously maintain that licencing and controls are holding back agricultural development small industry and several other sectors operating more or less in a free market environment. It is arguable, on the other hand, that if agriculture is to grow faster than it has, or if regional disparities in this sector are to be reduced, the State has to intervene more purposefully and strongly in terms of the scale, effectiveness of spatial distribution of public investment, and in terms of better management of common production resources like land water. And without faster, more diffused agricultural growth, we cannot expect decontrol of industry to produce any miracles in terms of further overall growth.

More generally, the growth of industry even in a "free market" regime will depend critically on the availability and cost of energy, transport, water supply, trained manpower and other similar elements of infrastructure which, even liberalisers concede, should be in the public sector. If, as is widely accepted, the bottlenecks caused by inadequate and unreliable infrastructure services are a major problem, a significant improvement in public sector performance in these spheres, and in the production of key intermediate products, should receive as much emphasis as any other reform. If anything it should be given much greater emphasis inasmuch as the reform is wholly an internal matter, and any improvement in performance will help save investment and foreign exchange besides reducing the necessity for frequent, large increases in the price of these inputs. This, as well as the various measures needed to improve the fiscal situation, involves far-reaching systemic changes in the way the Government and the public enterprises work.

This brings us to the much larger and more central question of the role the State should play in the development process. While the nature, scope and level of details of controls on private industry need substantial changes, a great many other functions must continue to be performed by the State, but performed more effectively than at present. It has to make sure that the growth of the economy is not impeded by inadequacies in quantity an/or quality of infrastructure; that the services are produced and supplied as economically as possible; that the long-term problems be it in terms of building indigenous technological capability, protecting the environment, exploring alternative sustainable life-styles for the masses are anticipated and corrective action taken.

Unemployment and Deprivation need Immediate Attention

Above all the State has to address the problems of unemployment and deprivation here and now rather than wait for them to be taken care of gradually as a byproduct of growth. The need for such intervention is hardly a matter of controversy. Over the years compulsions of competitive mass politics has led to the adoption of targeted anti-poverty programmes aimed at particular backward regions/classes; for positive discrimination to correct historical accumulation of disadvantages or particular social disadvantages for particular social groups arising from the caste system; and a variety of social security programmes for the destitude and handicapped. All of this is relevant, but they have become far too populist leading to a mindless proliferation of programmes, whose effectiveness is seriously compromised by the fragmentation concept and in implementation as well as their ubiquitous use as a vehicle of patronage.

The overall scale of these programmes has now become quite large and is close to one-fifth of the public sector Plan. A larger allocation in both absolute and relative terms may well be justified, but the potential gains of restructuring and rationalisation the programmes are very large, and should be the main focus.

The essential ingredients of such restructuring include:

- A pooling of the allocation for anti-poverty programmes (along with minor irrigation, social conservation, rural roads, rural water supply, social forestry and such essentially local development programmes) and distributing the pool through the States to the districts in proportion to the volume of unemployment and poverty.
- The content of programme in each district (and within the constituent parts of each district) to be decided and implemented by the elected representatives in the light of its felt needs and the potential.
- The role of State agencies to become supportive — helping with technical advice, professional supervision, evaluation and the like — instead of deciding on their own what programmes are to be taken up, where and on what scale.
- Periodic elections to the Panchayat Raj institutions being made mandatory.

Actual Fund Allocation the Real Test

Besides this change in the approach to rural development the State should give overriding priority — and the test of it would be in actual allocation of resources — for eradication of illiteracy, restructuring of education towards imparting skills, and improvement in basic health care. This is an area where mass mobilisation of the kind attempted in the Jana and Gyan Vigyana Jatha has a vital role to play. Without it, the State cannot hope to accomplish the task in a reasonable period.

The third element is a border social security programme to provide a safety net to the aged, the handicapped and widows, of the poor class; and for contingencies (like accident and death of the breadwinner) leading to significant loss in the means of livelihood of agricultural labourers and other poor households. Such a comprehensive scheme has, in fact, been introduced in Tamil Nadu since last year. It is quite affordable.

All this calls for radical changes in the structure of local government institutions; the relation between these institutions and the authorities (political and administrative) at the State and Central levels; far greater information on the people's entitlements under various programmes; mechanisms and acceptance by all political parties of a degree of restraint in abusing such programmes for populist purposes.

This is all tall order perhaps, but such is the agenda that any serious attempt at restructuring the State to safeguard the interests of the poor, the dispossessed and the underemployed would require even as the basis is laid for a more equitable society. And without it we are bound to pay dearly for the unbridled populism which has taken over our policy.

IMF RECIPE FOR INDIA'S BALANCE OF PAYMENT CRISIS:
A Critique

A.C. MINOCHA

THE MAIN object of this paper is to analyse the factors which have contributed to the present crisis on the balance of payment front and examine critically the relevance of IMF recipe for overcoming the crisis in the context of Indian economy. The paper also presents the outlines of an alternative strategy.

The present economic crisis which the country is facing has not come to us suddenly. Its roots can be traced to the policies that we have been following in the past, more particularly since the '80s, when the policy of liberalisation was pursued vigorously and indiscriminately. The two important manifestations of the current economic crisis are the fiscal imbalance and the external imbalance which are inextricably linked with each other.

The fiscal imbalance has been caused largely by mounting deficits on revenue account escalating to a record figure of 3.4 per cent of GDP in 1990-91. To meet these deficits on revenue account, the Government of India had to borrow repeatedly in the capital market without yielding any return, with the result that the public debt of the government has burgeoned substantially from Rs 30,864 crores in 1980-81 to Rs 1,51,352 crores in 1990-91 and interest payments swallowing more than 34 per cent of non-plan expenditure and 21.4 per cent of total expenditure of the central government in 1990-91. These mounting deficits have been caused by increasing expenditure on administration, interest payments, subsidies and defence. Apart from subsidies on three important items, viz. food, fertiliser and exports which accounted for 18 per cent of the current revenue of the central government in 1989-90, there are many explicit and implicit subsidies running into crores of rupees on social services and many commodities produced in the public sector taken together, accounting for 14 per cent of the GDP. The beneficiaries of most of these subsidies are the upper income groups and the benefits enjoyed by them are many times the combined total of subsidies on public distribution system and the amount spent on anti-poverty programmes.

At the macro-economic level, fiscal deficits inevitably spill into balance of payments problems and create inflationary pressures. The demand induced growth of the 80s characterised by rising budget deficits and the declining saving ratio could not be sustained against the worsening position on the supply side, represented by low rate of addition to capacity, shortage of power and foreign exchange bottle-necks. The over-all saving rate nose-dived from 23.2 per cent to 18.2 per cent between 1978-79 and 1984-85 and then crawled to 21.2 per cent in 1989-90. This decline in saving rate may be largely attributed to the poor performance of the government in this regard between 1977-78 and 1989-90, public sector saving registered a fall from 4.6 per cent to 1.7 per cent of GDP.

Table 22.1 presents investment-saving gap in the government sector, rate of inflation, revenue deficit, budget deficit, fiscal deficit and import-export gap.

The demand generating impact of the investment-saving gap in the public sector as well as of revenue and fiscal deficits in the budgets on price level and import-export gap, is to be seen from Table 22.1.

Increasing fiscal deficits varying from 7 to 8 per cent of the GDP have led to expansion of money supply and excess liquidity in the economy. Money supply grew at an average annual rate of about 17 per cent during the first four years of the Seventh Plan and went up by as much as 19.7 per cent during the final year of the plan. This contributed in a large measure to the double-digit inflation during 1990-91, exceeding 15 per cent currently. The infrastructure sector has started showing deceleration and the growth rate of industrial output has started declining. Despite achieving a 5.3 per cent growth rate on average per annum in the Seventh Plan period and coming out of the syndrome of the Hindu rate of growth of 3.5 per cent per annum in the earlier period, unemployment has been increasing, prices have been rising, rupee has been depreciating and our foreign exchange reserves have been depleting. The higher growth rate of the Seventh Plan may be attributed to higher growth rate of tertiary sector and of the consumer durables. The economy is drifting into stagflation with low growth, high inflation and increasing unemployment. The latest annual report on Currency and Finance of the RBI, has drawn our attention to the likely deceleration in the economy in 1991-92.

TABLE 22.1: Investment saving Gap in Government Sector

(as percentage of GDP)

Year	Public sector investment	Public sector saving	Investment saving gap in public sector	Revenue deficit	Budget deficit	Fiscal deficit	Import-export gap	Inflation rate
1980-81	8.7	3.4	5.3	0.6	1.8	6.2	4.4	16.7
1981-82	10.5	4.5	6.0	0.1	0.9	5.4	3.8	2.4
1982-83	11.3	4.4	6.9	0.7	0.9	6.0	3.2	7.2
1983-84	9.8	3.3	6.5	1.2	0.7	6.3	2.8	7.2
1984-85	10.8	2.8	8.0	1.5	1.6	7.5	2.9	6.0
1985-86	11.1	3.2	7.9	2.1	2.0	8.3	3.7	4.8
1986-87	11.7	2.7	9.0	2.7	2.8	9.0	3.2	5.1
1987-88	10.4	2.2	8.2	2.7	1.7	8.1	2.8	10.7
1988-89	9.9	2.0	7.9	2.7	1.4	7.8	3.5	5.7
1989-90	10.7	1.7	9.0	2.7	2.4	8.0	2.9	9.1
1990-91	NA	NA	NA	3.4	2.1	8.4	2.9	10.3
1991-92 (BE)	NA	NA	NA	2.4	1.3	6.5	NA	11.0

Source: Economic Survey, Govt. of India, 1990-91.

The balance of payment difficulties are mainly the outcome of growing internal imbalances, making the rupee weak internally as well as externally, causing an appreciable increase in imports to sustain mainly the investment pattern for catering to the needs of the top decile of population.

The balance of payments difficulties have been with us since the beginning of the second plan, sometimes assuming alarming proportions, forcing us to devalue the rupee, as we did in 1966 and borrow from time to time from the IMF and other sources. Since 1966, the rupee has depreciated to the extent of 300 per cent and yet exports as percentage of national income and overall global exports have declined. The second half of the 80s has witnessed the worst phase of trade and current deficit when exchange depreciation of the rupee between 1985-90 has been of the order of 68 per cent but without causing any appreciable increase in exports. Table 22.2 presents data in respect of foreign trade and exchange rate.

TABLE 22.2: Foreign Trade and Exchange Rate

(as percent of GDP)

Year	Exports	Imports	Net invisible	Trade balance	Current account balance	Rupee-dollar exchange rate
1980-81	4.8	9.2	3.2	-4.4	-1.2	7.9
1981-82	4.9	8.7	2.4	-3.8	-1.5	9.0
1982-83	5.1	8.4	2.0	-3.2	-1.3	9.7
1983-84	4.9	7.7	1.7	-2.8	-1.1	10.3
1984-85	5.2	8.1	1.7	-2.9	-1.2	11.9
1985-86	4.4	8.1	1.4	-3.7	-2.3	12.2
1986.87	4.5	7.7	1.2	-3.2	-2.0	12.8
1987-88	4.9	7.7	0.9	-2.8	-1.9	13.0
1988-89	5.3	8.9	0.8	-3.5	-2.7	14.5
1989-90	6.4	9.3	0.6	-2.9	-2.3	16.6
1990-91	6.3	8.4	NA	-2.1	NA	17.9

Note: All figures except rupee-dollar rate, are percentages of GDP.
Source: *Economic Survey, 1990-91* - Government of India

The exchange rate of rupee in terms of dollar has depreciated continuously but without any impact on either trade balance or current account deficit, as is clear from Table 22.2.

The trade deficit has more than trebled in the Seventh Plan and was of the order of 3 per cent of GDP in 1990-91, when the deficit had touched the record figure of Rs 10,643 crores. In absolute terms, the current account deficit averaged Rs 7772 crores per annum in the Seventh Plan as against Rs. 6091 crores in the Sixth Plan. Throughout the Seventh Plan period, the balance of payment was under pressure. In 1990-91, imports registered an increase of 21.9 per cent compared to the previous year, whereas exports increased by just 17.5 per cent as against 36.5 per cent in the previous year, the result was that the trade deficit was higher by 38 per cent than 1989-90. There was rapid run-down of foreign exchange reserves which plummeted to such a low level in June 1991, that we could not meet more than a weeks imports with these reserves. Table 22.3 presents India's, trade balance since 1960-61.

TABLE 22.3: India's Trade Balance

(in crores of Rs.)

	1960-61	1970-71	1980-81	1985-86	1986-87	1987-88	1988-89	1989-90	1990-91
Imports	1109	1822	12,513	19,658	20,096	22,399	28,194	35,411	43,170
Exports	630	1404	6,576	10,895	12,452	15,741	20,302	27,681	32,527
Trade balance	-479	-417	-5937	-8763	-7644	-6658	7892	-7730	-10,643

The short-term and the immediate contributory factor was the Gulf crisis which led to disruption in supplies and a sharp increase in the prices of crude oil and petroleum products. The cost of POL imports during 1990-91 escalated to Rs 10,820 crores as against the original estimate of Rs 6400 crores. The Gulf war also resulted in decline in workers remittances, additional burden of repatriating and rehabilitating NRIs from the affected zone of West Asia. The crisis hampered trade flows, having adverse effects on our exports. The direct overall adverse effect of Gulf war has been put at Rs 5180 crores in 1990-91 *(Economic Survey, 1990-91)*.

The medium term factors identified are plateauing of indigenous oil production in the face of continuously rising domestic demand for petroleum, levelling off of workers remittances from abroad, erosion of surplus on invisible account, unfavourable climate for external assistance, increasing recourse to commercial borrowings and increasing debt-servicing obligations. The problem became more serious due to decline in the role of net invisibles in financing trade deficits. Net invisibles had financed more than 60 per cent of trade deficit in the Sixth Plan but only 23 per cent in 1990-91.

Difficulties on the balance of payment front are partly of our own creation. Gradual import liberalisation set in motion since 1977-78, contributed to the emergence of trade balance gap in combination with other growing macro-imbalances. Our industrial structure, by and large, has become elitist-oriented, highly capital intensive, import intensive and environment polluting. It makes a large draft on our scarce resources, thereby denying even basic necessities to the majority of the people. Whereas per capita availability of some essential commodities life pulses, cereals in some parts of the country, edible oil, vanaspati, cotton cloth, has declined over time, the availability of luxury and semi-luxury goods has increased. Higher growth rate is no guarantee for poverty reduction and employment generation. Among the industry groups, the highest rate of growth has been manifested by the consumer durables in the 80s. Import guzzling pattern of industrial development has been exacerbated by larger inflow of foreign capital during the 80s. During 1990 alone 660 foreign collaborations were approved by the government. There is a good case for the induction of foreign capital in areas where we need technological upgradation and export promotion. But there is no case for opening up the economy to free inflow of foreign capital, with all its disastrous effects on internal and external balances. The nexus between direct foreign investment and promotion of consumerism among upper and middle class is palpable from the behaviour of multinationals already operating in India. Mostly these MNS are engaged in the production of soft drinks, cosmetics, food products, electronic toys, motor vehicles, VCRs, tape recorders, etc. The export performance of multinationals has been dismal. Their entry into Indian market, on the other hand, has led to greater imports of raw materials, components, spare parts and technical know-how.

It would be quite interesting to analyse as how the deficits on current account were financed. These deficits were mainly financed by substantial inflow of foreign capital in the form of loans from bilateral and multilateral sources, commercial borrowings and inflow of funds from the NRIs. Net availability of assistance on concessional terms has been declining. This has led to large increase in commercial borrowings and NRI deposits which are costly. This is amply reflected in the contrasting modes of financing the deficits in the sixth and the seventh plans. During the VII Plan, loans from concessional assistance provided 29 per cent of the financing need, commercial borrowings provided 25 per cent, NRI deposits 23 per cent and other capital transactions about 13 per cent. In contrast, during the VI Plan period, external assistance financed 55 per cent of the deficit, commercial borrowings 18 per cent, NRI Deposits 17 per cent and 10 per cent by making a draft on foreign exchange reserves.

Indias foreign debt has risen significantly from Rs 39,619 crores in 1985-86 to Rs 1,20,027 crores by the end of March, 1991. Table 22.4 presents the pattern of external liabilities of India.

In 1991, the total foreign debt of India was represented by external assistance to the extent of 56.9 per cent, commercial borrowings 22.7 per cent, borrowings from the IMF 3.6 per cent and NRI deposits 17 per cent. The NRI deposits and commercial borrowings taken together, accounted for 39.3 per cent of total foreign debt outstanding in March, 1991. The newly emerging pattern of external liabilities has steadily pushed up debt-servicing liability as percent of exports from 9.4 per cent in 1980-81 to 26 per cent in 1990-91. We are fast heading towards debt trap.

TABLE 22.4: Pattern of External Assistance

(in crores of Rs.)

End of March	External assistance	External commercial borrowings	Liabilities to IMF	NRI deposits	Total	Col. 3+5 as per cent of total
(1)	(2)	(3)	(4)	(5)	(6)	(7)
1985	24,004	6,908	4,888	3,819	39,619	27.1
1986	26,638	8,075	5,271	6,650	45,634	32.3
1987	32,312	11,243	5,548	7,847	56,950	33.5
1988	36,578	13,543	4,732	10,054	64,907	36.7
1989	46,838	19,147	3,696	14,154	83,835	39.7
1990	54,095	24,500	2,573	17,831	98,999	42.7
1991	68,390	26,706	4,389	20,542	1,20,027	39.3

We were on the brink of external bankruptcy in the sense of being in the danger of defaulting in our debt-servicing payment which had ballooned as a result of borrowing spree indulged in by successive governments in the 80's. We had applied for a big loan to the IMF. Given the genesis and the magnitude of the present economic crisis, the moot question in whether the IMF-WB model of growth which the IMF tries to impose on the borrowing country through its conditionalities would provide solution to the basic problems of our country. Does the model fit into the objectives of our plans? The IMF recipe to achieve balance of payment adjustment within an open trade regime is essentially through deflation via cut-backs in public expenditure. Its important conditionalities are: realistic exchange rate, reduction in fiscal deficit, liberalisation and privatization.

We would also like to see the fiscal deficit narrowed down to contain inflation but not with the same objective which underlies the conditionality of the IMF. The IMF emphasis on reducing fiscal deficit raises a strong suspicion that the purpose is not so much to control inflation as to constrain the role of the government in the economy. Such a strategy would affect demand and employment and entail cut in social services and developmental expenditure, adversely affecting both redistribution and growth. The budget for 1991-92 has reduced expenditure on employment generating programmes. Our view is that fiscal deficits should be narrowed down by abolishing such subsidies which benefit the rich and continuing only such which are targeted to the poor, exercising utmost economy in expenditure, appropriation of a part of the huge gains from public investment accruing to the private sector, making public sector enterprises autonomous and accountable, raising more resources through direct taxes by reducing exemptions, concessions and loopholes and by tightening tax collection machinery, transferring all centrally sponsored schemes to the state governments or to village panchayats and local bodies. The IMF, on the other hand, lays stress on reducing the role of the government in the economy.

The 1991-92 budget of the central government was prepared under the pressure of the IMF conditionalities, though it is a half-hearted exercise in that direction. The alibi of the Finance Minister has been short time available to design the budget. In fact, the half-heartedness is mainly due to political constraints for a government which is in minority. The fertiliser subsidy had been reduced but the proposal could not be implemented under the pressure of lobby of the big farmer, cutting across party lines. The hefty hike in procurement prices announced on 4th September, 1991, has compensated the large farmers more than what they will lose in terms of small rise in prices of fertilisers. The inflationary forces will gather further momentum due to hike in procurement prices of foodgrains and other agricultural products. The cascading effects of food prices would be felt soon on other essential goods. The common man will bear the brunt of so called structural adjustments being made in the economy at the behest of the IMF.

The share of direct taxes has virtually stagnated since 1950-51. It started out at 2.47 per cent of GDP in 1950-51 but after touching 3.26 per cent in 1963-64, it had gone down to 2.49 per cent of GDP in 1988-89 (Table 22.5)

Faced with resource crunch, when budgetary allocations have had to be trimmed, it has been invariably the capital expenditure that has had to be axed while revenue expenditure has gone on increasing. Powerful vested interests have emerged to keep the fiscal economy running in this manner. Gross capital formation out of the budgetary resources which comprised 40 per cent of total expenditure in 1980-81, has steadily gone down to 32.7 per cent in 1990-91. In the 1991-92 budget, revenue expenditure on current consumption of the government is estimated to increase by 8.5 per cent. On the other hand, capital expenditure will increase only by 0.9 per cent over the previous year. The much-vaunted reduction in fiscal deficit from 8.5 per cent to 6.5 per cent of GDP as demanded by the IMF, besides being illusory and not likely to be realised in practice, has been attempted by diluting the developmental role of the government.

TABLE 22.5: Tax/GDP Ratio Total Tax Revenue (all-India)

Year	Direct	Indirect	Total
1950-51	2.47	4.23	6.69
1960-61	2.48	5.85	8.33
1970-71	2.34	8.67	11.01
1980-81	2.41	12.21	14.61
1985-86	2.38	14.10	16.48
1988-89	2.49	14.62	17.11

Source: Indian Economic Statistics (Public Finance) Ministry of Finance, 1990.

The Indian rupee was devalued by 22 per cent, though euphemistically called "structural adjustment" in exchange rate. This has been done in the wake of a big bout of depreciation already taken place. Indian rupee is linked to the basket of important currencies of major trading partners and its value has been adjusted from time to time to promote the competitiveness of the rupee. It is doubtful whether exports will increase to the desired extent. Devaluation has raised the rupee cost of imports all along the line at the first go. Domestic costs are bound to rise and, therefore, export prospects are dim. In the post-devaluation period, the rate of inflation has escalated to more than 15 per cent per annum on point-to-point basis. Our import bill of oil and petroleum products, edible oil, fertiliser, newsprint, steel, copper and capital goods has gone up. The burden of debt-servicing has also gone up because of devaluation. The devaluation of rupee at a time when both domestic economic growth and world trade are likely to decelerate, is not likely to have favourable impact on export performance. Of course, profitability of exports has improved. But imports have become costlier, forcing us to make further downward adjustment of exchange value of the rupee. Increase in exports will depend upon elasticity of demand for our exports. Much of our exports either have structurally low price elasticity or face inelastic demand owing to protective import policies pursued by our major trading partners. Increase in exports will depend upon factors like, degree of elasticity of demand for our products in world markets, price competitiveness, quality, trade policy of other countries and world demand for our goods.

The trade and tariff reforms that have been introduced will now throw open the gate to imports which would be either totally unnecessary or be at the expense of well-established domestic industry, specially capital goods industry in regard to which we have achieved a reasonable degree of self-sufficiency. The package of new trade policy announced along with devaluation on July 4, 1991, aims at reducing control over imports, particularly import licencing, strengthening export incentives and linking practically all non-bulk imports to exports through the instrumentality of REP, now designated as EXIM scripts. All exports will have uniform REP rate of 30 per cent of the FOB value, which is a substantial hike from the earlier rates which varied between 5 per cent to 20 per cent of the FOB value. The new EXIM scripts can be freely traded. The new REP scheme aims at giving maximum incentive to exporters whose import intensity is low. Subsequently, as part of the supplementary package, certain items like value-added agricultural products, electronics, bulk drugs and formulations, marine products, certain categories of advanced engineering goods have been made eligible for an additional EXIM scripts of 10 percentage points, taking the total EXIM scripts to 40 per cent of FOB value. Special rates for gems and jewellery, certain metal-based handicrafts and books and magazines will continue. All user imports and OGL imports have been virtually directed to buy import entitlements from exporters to meet their import requirements. With the devaluation of the rupee and liberalisation of REP, the Cash Compensatory Scheme (CCS) for exporters has been abolished. Now, both exporters and rich farmers have emerged as the most important economic agents in the system, enjoying total exemption from income tax and also getting benefits of new package of reforms.

The idea of flat rate of REP is misconceived. Many exports do not need imports at all and still they are entitled to get EXIM scripts. The REP should have been graded according to the nature of the products. Under the present dispensation, importers of luxury goods by bidding higher prices of EXIM scripts, will pre-empt bulk of such scripts. This will give further fillip to imports of luxury goods and a boom in the life style of top decile of population which commands nearly 25 per cent of purchasing power in the country. The tariff structure has been revised and the maximum tariff has now been brought down from 300 per cent to 100 per cent.

Nearly 40 per cent of our imports are in the nature of bulk imports and the remaining 60 per cent non-bulk imports. The Government has decided that 60 to 70 per cent of foreign exchange would be allocated directly by it and the remaining 30 to 40 per cent can be left to the market mechanism. EXIM scripts may not be adequate for meeting the requirements of non-bulk imports. This fact may further push up the prices of imported goods.

The new industrial policy announced on the day the budget for 1991-92 was presented, has supplanted the Industrial policy Resolution of 1956. The new policy envisages measures to unshackle industry from administrative and legal controls, abolition of industrial licencing for most of the industries, exemption from licencing for all substantial expansion of existing units, abolition of convertibility clause, direct foreign investment up to 51 per cent of equity, creation of a specially empowered Board to negotiate with a number of international firms to approve direct foreign investment in selected areas, removal of threshold limit for MRTP companies and dominant undertakings, offering a part of equity of public sector undertakings to mutual funds, financial institutions, workers and the general public, adoption of open door policy to foreign capital and foreign technology. The priority areas now numbering 8 left to the public sector will be, arms and ammunition and allied defence equipment, defence aircraft and warships, atomic energy, coal and lignite, mineral oils, mining of iron ore, manganese ore and other vital minerals and railway transport. It may be recalled that the Industrial policy Resolution of 1956 had allocated 17 industries to the public sector. The nine industries now left out are: iron and steel, heavy plant and machinery, heavy electrical plant and machinery, heavy casting and forging of iron and steel, air transport, ship building, telephones and telephone cables and related products and generation and distribution of electricity. Not much remains of the edifice of the 1956 industrial policy. Instead of physical controls, the new policy relies more on fiscal and monetary policy to achieve the objectives of planned development. Since the financial system itself is being liberalised, it is doubtful whether we can achieve the objectives of industrial policy through the instruments of fiscal and monetary policy.

Liberalisation may not lead to larger inflow of foreign capital. Notwithstanding assurance of hospitality to foreign capital towards the close of 80s, there has been deceleration in inflow of foreign capital. Foreign capital prefers to flow to growing economies and flourishing markets and wants safety of investment, quick returns and repatriation of surplus that is generated. The foreign investors are not standing in a queue to enter India. To rely on foreign capital for solving the balance of payment problem, achieve development goals or subserve social priorities, is a fanciful notion. Direct foreign investment tends to emasculate impetus for economic growth which satisfies mass needs and promotes self-reliance. Multinational corporations will have to be cajoled to come to us with capital, technology, management and marketing expertise on their own terms. Hence the decision to appoint a High Powered Special Board. Joint ventures will now involve both joint trading and production ventures in which MNs are invited to come in with high technology and global marketing net-work and Indian firms will play the role of sub-contractors and provide cheap-shop floor operations and labour. The components and parts will also be supplied by foreign corporations and assembled into finished products by Indian labour. A new phase in growth process is planned to be opened through direct foreign investment primarily aimed at the satisfaction of elitist consumption demand in the domestic market and secondarily for exports. This fits very well with the investment pattern and production structure to subserve the social milieu and life style of the upper decile of population but having little relevance to the living standards of the masses. The common man is bound to be squeezed further because of lesser availability of essential commodities and rising prices. The recent hefty increase in minimum support prices of agricultural products will further accentuate inflationary tendencies already fuelled by devaluation and other policy measures initiated at the behest of the IMF.

The policy of liberalisation initiated in early 80s and implemented with greater vigour in the second half of the 80s has failed to deliver the goods, as was promised. How can acceleration of the same policy achieve growth with social justice ? When growth remains uncertain, the market forces will boost up labour saving and capital intensive and import intensive technology and accentuate further concentration of economic power. The new policy has no features which will deal with some of our major problems like poverty, unemployment, regional inequalities, etc.

We do not advocate a command economy for India but such an economy where planning becomes effectively decentralised and more powers and finances are transferred to village panchayats and local bodies, where there is genuine democratisation of the Indian polity, where private sector is regulated for channelising investment according to plan priorities, where public sector is made more efficient, where internal competition between private and public sectors in encouraged, where there is selectivity in permitting imports and foreign capital and foreign technology, where there is social transformation to change the existing power balance in the economy, where production structure is geared to the production of articles of mass consumption but at the same time catering to the needs of the growing middle class. At the macro level, the most important objective must be to stop up the over-all saving rate, more particularly the saving rate of the government sector. The focus of the fiscal policy should be to close the revenue deficit and not so much the fiscal deficit.

The IMF assistance can provide only temporary relief but cannot be a substitute for measures intended to solve the basic problems of poverty, unemployment and inequalities. In our enthusiasm for the new policies we have forgotten these problems and planning given a go-by. It is only through structural changes in the internal economy that we can tide over the present crisis on a lasting basis. The alternative to IMF assistance would be restricted imports as well as inflow of foreign capital, narrowing down of the fiscal deficit through a cut in subsidies to the rich, increase in direct taxation, economy in expenditure and change in production structure. The private sector will not adhere to the socio-economic objectives of the plans. Let public sector units compete with private sector units in certain areas so that overall operational efficiency of both the sectors improves. Monopolies in both the sectors should be curbed.

The IMF recipe for macro-economic adjustment is fraught with grave consequences for the Indian economy. The economy will experience a decline in growth of output both in the agricultural and industrial sectors, a strengthening of inflationary tendencies and a sharp rise in the incidence of poverty, inequalities and unemployment. It will also cause further distortions in the Indian economy.

REFERENCES

1. Studipto Mundle and Govind Rao — Volume and composition of Government subsidies in India — *EPW*, May, 4, 1991
2. B.B.Bhattacharya — Macro imbalances, stabilisation programmes and the Union budget — *EPW*, 24th, August, 1991
3. D.T.Lakdawala — New Policy measures, *EPW*, August, 24, 1991 p. 1992.

23

LIBERALISATION, GROWTH STRATEGY AND THE PRESENT ECONOMIC CRISIS

AJIT KUMAR SINGH

IN THE recent months a view has been aggressively proclaimed by the government and the media that the India economy was currently passing through a severe crisis. As a supposed response to overcome this crisis the government has come out with unprecedented haste with a whole package of economic policies of far reaching consequences for the future economy and polity of the country. The very first question, therefore, is to examine what is the nature of this crisis.

The most immediate facets of the economic crisis were mentioned to be the drastic depletion of the foreign exchange reserves of the country, the feared run on the NRI deposits in the country, the threat to the solvency of the country to meet its foreign debt obligations and drying up of sources of foreign capital in view of the plummetting of the credit rating of the country in the international capital market.

Though certain negativities in the economic situation are indeed there and have persisted for quite some time of which the most critical is the foreign exchange crisis, it is a moot point whether the panicky policy response of the government was called for of not. In fact, the state of the economy is basically sound as a look at the real indicators is concerned (Table 23.1). During the last decade the economy recorded a growth rate of around 5 per cent, though annual fluctuations were there. During 1990-91 the agricultural growth rate was expected to be a very satisfactory 4.5 per cent, while that of industrial production was expected to be 8.4 per cent and the overall GNP growth at 5.0 per cent. The saving rate was rising and was at a fairly high level of around 21.7 per cent during 1989-90. Country's infrastructure was also in a satisfactory state. The Indian economy has acquired over the years a high degree of diversification, dynamism and resilience to withstand short period shocks. Yet through bad economic management we find ourselves in the present sorry pass. One is left wondering whether this great hue and cry about a serious crisis was generated to push the economy in an altogether different policy direction.

TABLE 23.1: Selected Economic Indicators

(Percentage Change over Previous year)

Economic Indicators	1981-82	1982-83	1983-84	1984-85	1985-86	1986-87	1987-88	1988-89	1989-90 (P)	1990-91 (P)
Gross National Product	5.8	2.6	7.9	3.8	4.1	3.6	4.2	10.6	5.2	5.0*
Agricultural Production	5.6	-3.8	13.7	-1.2	2.5	-3.7	-0.8	21.0	1.7	4.5*
Foodgrains Production	2.9	-2.9	17.7	-4.5	3.4	-4.7	-2.1	21.0	0.4	3.9*
Industrial Production	9.3	3.2	6.7	8.6	8.7	9.1	7.3	8.7	8.6	8.4
Electricity generated	10.2	6.7	7.6	11.9	8.6	10.2	7.6	9.5	10.8	7.1
Wholesale Price Index	2.4	7.2	7.2	6.0	4.8	5.1	10.7	5.7	9.1	12.1
Monetary Resources (M3)	12.5	16.1	18.1	18.9	15.9	18.6	15.9	17.8	19.4	15.1
Imports at current prices	8.4	5.0	10.8	8.2	14.7	2.2	10.7	26.9	25.4	21.9
Export at current prices	16.3	12.8	11.0	20.2	-7.2	14.3	25.9	29.1	36.8	17.5
Foreign Exchange Reserves (Rupees Crores)	4024	4782	5972	7243	7820	8151	7687	7040	6251	11416
Foreign Currency Reserves (Rupees Crores)	3355	4265	5498	6817	7384	7645	7287	6605	5787	4388

* Anticipated (P) Provisional.

Source: Government of India, *Economic Survey 1990-91*, p.1.

The present malaise can be better described as a self-inflicted growing paralysis rather than a sudden stroke. The Indian economy was suffering during the last several years from certain imbalances, particularly in the fiscal and the trade sector, to which economists and even government's own policy makers had been drawing attention. This state of affairs could not be expected to continue for long, though the day of reckoning came sooner than expected thanks to political unstability and inertia and the strain in balance of payment caused by the Gulf War.

Roots of the 'Present Crisis'

The fiscal and the trade deficit, which are at the Centre of the present economic impasse, are the outward manifestation of the strategy of growth followed during the eighties and the pattern of financing public expenditure adopted by the government. Most of the discussion of the present 'economic crisis' which has displayed rightly a concern for the twin deficits has, however, by passed the issue of the growth strategy of the eighties and its political economy. As a result what we find is an effort to suppress the symptoms rather than to control the disease.

The growth strategy of the eighties popularly called liberalization of the economy has been more appropriately described as 'demand led industrialization (Kurien, 1989). The strategy relied on giving a boost to the purchasing power of the organized sector of the economy of which the large bureaucracy and army formed an important component by giving them hefty salary increases. The other politically important sections – the exporters, big industrialists, rich farmers – also received bounteous and ever increasing subsidies. The lowering of direct tax rates and various tax concessions also had the same impact. To beguile the poor programmes of the populist nature in the name of poverty alleviation and employment generation were undertaken. But the large sums spent on these programmes only helped lining the pockets of the bureaucrats and the middle men thanks to the large leakages in the system. These policies gave a big boost to demand for the consumer durable goods by the the rich and the upper middle classes. Thus between 1981-82 and 1989-90 the index of industrial production for consumer durables went up by as much as 167 per cent against an increase of only 39 per cent in that of consumer non-durables and 94.8 per cent increase in that of industrial production (Table 23.2).

Liberalisation of the industrial and foreign trade regime to meet the demand for consumer durables was a necessary concommitant of the new growth strategy as the capital and import intensity of durable goods was very high. This is reflected in the growing trade gap during the period in spite of fairly high growth rates of exports in rupee terms (Table 23.3). Particularly marked was the spurt in the import of capital goods – nearly 5.5 fold over the eighties. This was bound to have a deleterious effect on the domestic capital goods industry. On the other hand the policy of liberal imports of know-how and capital goods and over 5000 foreign collaborations approved between 1985-90 have hardly made any visible contribution to our technological capacity, while lot of obsolete foreign plants have been dumped in the country.

TABLE 23.2: Use-based Group Indices of Industrial Production (Base: 1980-81 = 100)

Industry Group	Weight	1981-82	1982-83	1983-84	1984-85	1985-86	1986-87	1987-88	1988-89*	1989-90
Basic Goods	39.42	110.9	118.7	125.7	139.7	149.2	163.0	172.2	189.2	199.4
		(10.9)	(7.0)	(6.0)	(11.1)	(6.8)	(9.2)	(5.6)	(9.9)	(5.4)
Capital Goods	16.43	106.7	110.6	123.5	127.2	140.7	166.3	192.8	206.2	252.3
		(6.7)	(3.7)	(11.7)	(3.0)	(10.6)	(18.2)	(15.9)	(7.0)	(22.4)
Intermediate Goods	20.51	103.7	104.6	114.9	126.1	135.5	141.5	148.3	165.4	172.5
		(3.7)	(1.0)	(9.8)	(9.7)	(7.5)	(4.4)	(4.8)	(11.5)	(4.3)
Consumer Goods	23.65	113.8	112.0	113.8	122.0	137.3	147.1	156.6	163.2	173.5
		(13.8)	(-1.6)	(1.6)	(7.2)	(12.5)	(7.1)	(6.5)	(4.2)	(6.3)
(a) Consumer Durables	2.55	110.9	121.0	140.5	170.8	202.8	241.2	260.1	291.2	296.1
		(10.9)	(9.1)	(16.1)	(12.6)	(18.7)	(18.9)	(7.8)	(12.0)	(1.7)
(b) Consumer Non-durables	21.10	114.1	110.9	110.5	116.1	129.4	135.7	144.1	147.7	158.7
		(14.1)	9(2.8)	(-0.4)	(5.1)	(11.5)	(4.9)	(6.2)	(2.5)	(7.5)

* Provisional.

Note: Figures within brackets indicate percentage change over the preceding year.

Source: Government of India, *Economic Survey 1990-91*, p.41.

TABLE 23.3: Key Indicators of India's Balance of Payment

(As per cent of GDP)

Year	Exports	Imports	Net Invisibles	Trade Balance	Current Account Balance
1980-81	4.8	9.2	3.2	-4.4	-1.2
1981-82	4.9	8.7	2.4	-3.8	-1.5
1982-83	5.1	8.4	2.0	-3.2	-1.3
1983-84	4.9	7.7	1.7	-2.8	-1.1
1984-85	5.2	8.1	1.7	-2.9	-1.2
Average 1980-85	5.0	8.4	2.2	-3.4	-1.3
1985-86	4.4	8.1	1.4	-3.7	-2.3
1986-87	4.5	7.7	1.2	-3.2	-2.0
1987-88	4.9	7.7	0.9	-2.8	-1.9
1988-89	5.3	8.9	0.8	-3.5	-2.7
1989-90	6.4	9.3	0.6	-2.9	-2.3
Average 1985-90	5.1	8.3	1.0	-3.2	-2.2

Source: Government of India, *Economic Survey 1990-91*, p.152.

The liberal import of foreign capital and technology also did not lead to a sizeable export growth, as the eyes of the foreign investors was on the large domestic market provided by India. In fact the share of engineering products in our total exports has declined in the eighties. The star performers on the export front have been traditional sectors like garments, leather goods, gems and jewellery, tea, etc.

The success of such a strategy of growth was predicated upon a large flow of foreign capital. The large deficit in the current account could be maintained initially due to net earning on invisible accounts. The situation in this respect, however, deteriorated continuously through out the decade (Table 23.3). The government then resorted to increased commercial borrowing on which high interest rates had to be paid raising the debt-service burden. India's external debt went on mounting rapidly to reach the figure of Rs. 1,20,000 crores including NRI deposits on 31st March, 1991. The debt service ratio also rose from 9.4 per cent in 1980-81 to around 21 per cent in 1990-91.

Thus the growth strategy followed during the eighties led to a gradual trapping of the Indian economy into the external debt trap as feared by several economists. Though government's own Economic Advisory Council had been drawing attention to the deteriorating situation of balance of payment no timely action was taken to correct the situation (EAC, 1989).

On the domestic front also the government resorted to soft options leading to growing fiscal imbalances. While government's current expenditure went up by leaps and bounds as a result of its policy of fiscal expansionism to boost the demand in the organised sector as discussed earlier, there was no determined effort to meet the increased expenditure by additional resource mobilization. Instead the government adopted the soft options of increased deficit financing and market borrowing at increasing costs (Table 23.4). The result was a creeping internal debt trap, with repayment of interest becoming the single largest item of the revenue budget. Throughout the decade revenue side of the budget has remained in deficit and market borrowings are being diverted to meet this deficit instead of going into planned investment.

Accompanying the high level of fiscal deficit has been the declining saving capacity of the government. Saving of the public sector have steadily declined from 4.5 per cent of GDP in 1981-82 to 1.7 per cent of GDP in 1989-90 (Table 23.5). In fact the government has remained a net dissaver continuously since 1983-84. These budgetary trends are reflected in the changing pattern of plan finances.

Since the seventies the contribution of balance from current revenues has remained negative, while the reliance on market borrowing and budgetory deficits has been increasing (Table 23.6).

TABLE 23.4: Various Measures of Deficit in Central Budget

(as per cent of GDP)

Year	Revenue Deficit	Budget Deficit	Monetised Deficit	Gross Fiscal Deficit
1975-76	—	0.5	0.3	4.1
1980-81	0.6	1.8	2.6	6.2
1981-82	0.1	0.9	2.0	5.4
1982-83	0.7	0.9	1.9	6.0
1983-84	1.2	0.7	1.9	6.3
1984-85	1.8	1.6	2.6	7.5
1985-86	2.2	2.0	2.4	8.3
1986-87	2.8	2.8	2.4	9.0
1987-88	2.7	1.7	2.0	8.1
1988-89	2.7	1.4	1.6	7.8
1989-90	2.7	2.4	3.1	8.0
1990-91 (RE)	3.4	4.1	3.0	8.4

Source: Economic Survey, 1990-91 and *1989-90*.

TABLE 23.5: Saving Investment Gap and Current Account Deficit

(As per cent of GDP)

Year	Public Sector			Private Sector			Current Account Deficit
	Saving	Investment*	Gap	Saving	Investment*	Gap	
1980-91	3.4	8.7	-5.3	17.8	12.3	5.5	-1.2
1981-82	4.5	10.5	-6.0	16.5	14.5	2.0	-1.5
1982-83	4.4	11.3	-6.9	14.7	11.6	3.1	-1.3
1983-84	3.3	9.8	-6.5	15.5	10.9	4.6	-1.1
1984-85	2.8	10.8	-8.0	15.4	10.3	5.1	-1.2
1985-86	3.2	11.1	-7.9	16.5	12.9	3.6	-2.3
1986-87	2.7	11.7	-9.0	15.6	11.4	4.2	-2.0
1987-88	2.2	10.4	-8.2	18.2	12.2	6.0	-1.9
1988-89	2.0	9.9	-7.9	19.2	14.0	5.2	-2.7
1989-90	1.7	10.7	-9.0	19.9	12.9	7.0	-2.3

Source: Government of India, *Economic Survey, 1990-91*.

Clearly the expansionary fiscal policy with increasing budgetary deficits and public borrowing could not be sustained in the long run as it was bound to lead the country to an internal debt trap. Economists of the country have been emphasising the need for correction in these fiscal imbalances, which have been there for quite some time. However, there was hardly any critical situation in this regard in the summer of 1991. It was only when a serious crunch in foreign exchange emerged and it had to run to multinational institutions to bale it out that the government perforce took measures to rectify the perilous course it was following, under outside pressure, thus compromising substantially its ability to take independent decisions on matters of economic policy.

TABLE 23.6: Pattern of Plan Financing

(As per cent of GDP)

Item	1971-76	1976-80	1980-85	1985-90
1. Balance from Current Revenues	-0.3	-1.2	-1.8	-4.9
2. Market Borrowings (Net)	0.8	1.5	2.1	1.8
3. Other Capital Receipts including Capital inflows	1.9	2.8	3.0	5.5
4. Budgetary Deficits	1.0	1.1	2.1	3.3
Total	4.2	5.3	6.4	7.8

Source: Taken from S. Guhan (1991), p.2002.

The Policy Response

To meet the 'economic crisis' the government announced two large doses of devaluation in quick succession. This was followed by a near total relaxation of the foreign trade regime. Soon after the government came out with its new industrial policy for de-regulation of the economy and the budget aimed at bringing down the fiscal deficit by a hefty margin. The sweep and the rapidity of the policy announcements were truly astonishing, which lend credence to the belief that these were dictated by the IMF to which the government had to run with a begging bowl. Of far reaching consequences the new policy package involves a sharp break from the past economic regime evolved over the planning period and poses a serious threat to the social and economic objectives being hitherto pursued. One has therefore to look not only at the short term impact of these policies on the economic variables but their long period implications for our developmental objectives.

The IMF-World Bank policy package of structural adjustment being imposed on the economy is based on a doctrinaire faith in the unhampered working of the market forces which requires a complete dismantling of the regulatory mechanism and opening up of the economy to foreign monopoly capital. The new direction that is sought to be given to the Indian economy is likely to have serious negative consequences for the objectives of self-reliance, employment generation, poverty removal, balanced regional development, etc.

The new policy package is based upon a number of questionable assumptions. Firstly, it is believed that any attempt to compress our imports will have serious consequences for our domestic growth and a bold export orientation to the economy has to be given to speed up the rate of growth and remove balance of payment disequilibrium. Secondly, it is argued that the competitiveness of Indian exports can be attained by sharp devaluation of the Indian rupee and upgrading the quality of its exports, which would require improving the efficiency of the Indian industry and its technological upgradation. Thirdly, it is hoped that inflow of foreign capital and technology can play a significant role in meeting the short term foreign exchange requirement of the Indian economy as well as in improving its competitiveness and efficiency and in giving the needed boost to exports.

Doubts have been expressed by several Indian economists about the correctness of these assumptions and the expected outcome of the policy measures adopted. The success of devaluation would depend upon the relative elasticity of demand for our imports and exports. The expected reduction in imports is unlikely in the liberal trade regime being introduced, while our exports are not price elastic and are handicapped by quota restrictions of the rich countries. The immediate result of the devaluation of the rupee has been to inflate our import bill and hike the debt service burden of our exports. The sudden and unregulated opening of the Indian economy to foreign capital and technology, being wooed with open arms, is bound to have a deleterious consequence on our domestic industries, so far developed in a sheltered market, particularly in the medium and the small scale sector. Moreover, the import of highly capital intensive foreign technology is likely to further worsen the employment situation. Given the overall shortage of international capital, the competing claims of countries in the eastern block and elsewhere and the prevailing political unstability in the country, the hope of a sizeable inflow of foreign capital is likely to be belied. Thus, the new liberal trade regime is more likely to worsen our balance of payment scenario rather than improve it in the short and the medium term, while having otherwise deleterious consequences on the domestic economy.

As regards the fiscal policy initiatives there is a consensus even among the critics of the government policy that the unhealthy trends visible in the government budgets in the recent years – rapid growth of non-developmental expenditure, mounting burden of direct and indirect subsidies, heavy reliance on public borrowing, large budgetary deficits, etc. need to be corrected and the fiscal deficits have to be brought down. However, what is controversial is how this fiscal balance is to be restored. In this context the overemphasis on bringing down the fiscal deficit, without paying attention to its structure, is misplaced. In the Indian case a moderate degree of deficit financing is desirable for maintaining the tempo of capital formation through budgetary mechanism. The structuralist assumptions that fiscal deficits have a proportionate relationship with inflation rate or current account deficits in balance of payment does not hold good in the Indian context (Rakshit 1991; Bhattacharya 1991). It does not, therefore, follow that by bringing down the fiscal deficit our current account deficit would go down or inflation would be arrested. In fact, the recent devaluation and upward revision of administered prices have pushed up the rate of inflation.

The focus of the fiscal reform policy should be on stepping up the rate of savings in the public sector by curtailing unnecessary non-developmental expenditure for which there is a fairly large scope and mobilizing additional resources by taxing the rural and the urban rich for financing the developmental expenditure. Unfortunately, in the 1991-92 budget the axe has fallen on the developmental expenditure, which is likely to be stagnant in real terms at best. The slowing down of investment on infrastructure is likely to adversely affect long-term growth prospect (Guhan, 1991). The ability of the government to keep under control its non-developmental expenditure seems to be doubtful, as its back tracking on fertiliser prices portends.

The retreat of the government on the front of the public sector, which has played a leading role in the process of economic development hitherto, is also basically related to the resource crunch the government is facing in the wake of the policy of fiscal indiscipline. Partial or total privatisation of the public sector is an ill-conceived policy in the Indian context, which compromises with the socio-economic objectives of Indian Planning. Similar would be the impact of the measures like abolition of the concept of monopoly houses altogether, removal of controls on location of industries and delicencing of industries over a wide front except for a small list of 18 industries.

It is true that the capacity of the Indian private capitalists to undertake large ventures has considerably increased over the years and the complex regulatory system evolved over the years had become in many respects dysfunctional besides leading to collosal corruption. In the light of these developments rethinking on the relative roles of the public and the private sectors and reform of the regulatory system were indeed called for. But the pendulum seems to have swung to the other extreme with talks of a market friendly approach which may ultimately lead to doing away with the plans altogether. It is extremely doubtful if the objectives of poverty alleviation, employment generation, reduction in economic disparities and self-reliance can be served effectively by a free enterprise system in our country.

Reorientation of Growth Strategy

As we have argued above the present problems of fiscal deficits and balance of payment are the inevitable consequences of the faculty growth strategy being followed since early eighties, which relied on raising the purchasing power of the people in the organized sector along with a policy of economic liberalization, which led to a process of industrial growth oriented to elite consumption with a high capital and import intensity. Unless there is a basic shift in the growth strategy these problems are likely to persist. The policy package of structural adjustment is based on assumptions which do not hold true in the Indian conditions and is likely to worsen the problems rather than solve them.

Growth with social justice has been the guiding objective of Indian planning. Today we are again witnessing primacy of growth objective irrespective of its composition and its consequences for social justice. Not only this the very notion of planned economic development has come under a serious cloud.

In fact, what we need today is a reorientation of our growth strategy towards a more balanced pattern of agricultural development, a greater concern for employment generation and focus on the production of wage goods as the Economic Advisory Council had forcefully argued in its 1989 report (EAC, 1989). Such a growth strategy requires a larger and not a lesser role of economic planning and public investment in infrastructure and other priority areas.

The vital question is whether the classes which have benefited most from the present growth strategy — big industrialists, rich farmers and the upper middle classes — would allow such a needed shift in our growth strategy, which may serve the interests of the masses.

REFERENCES

B.B. Bhattacharya (1991), 'Macro Imbalances, Stabilisation Programme and Union Budget', *Economic and Political Weekly*, Vol. 26, No. 4, August 24.

Economic Advisory Council (1989), *Report on the Current Economic Situation and Primary Areas for Action*, Government of India, New Delhi, December.

S. Guhan (1991), 'Adjustment in the 1991-92 Budget: Hard Headed or Soft Headed?', *Economic and Political Weekly*, Vol. 26, No. 34, August 24.

C.T. Kurien (1989), 'Indian Economy in the 1980s and on to the 1990s', *Economic and Political Weekly*, Vol. 24, No. 15, April 15.

Mihir Rakshit (1991), 'The Macro Economic Adjustment Programme: A Critique', *Economic and Political Weekly*, Vol. 26, No. 34, August 24.

24

RECENT CHANGES IN ECONOMIC POLICY: Issues and Prospects

ROHIT SHUKLA

Introduction

THE PROCESS of liberalisation of the Indian economy had been initiated in mid-eighties. It began as a desire to convert India into a modern, competitive and efficient economy. Intrinsically it was as a part of a process of westernising Indian society. All modern gadgets, for example, which are seen operative in a middle or upper middle-class household in a western society are now used in upper middle-class households living in urban India. Though proportion of these households is negligible, it is indeed surprising that their capacity to influence thinking of the decision-makers has been rather critical. Thus, colour TV, V.C.R., telephone, car (usually Maruti), washing machines and vacuum cleaners have kindled great passions in the bossoms of urban upper middle class people. This involved use of sizeable quantities of scarce resource like internal capital, foreign exchange, etc. It also introduced a certain amount of perversion in the priorities in the economy. Thus, housing, safe and enough drinking water, even community latrines in the villages, educational and hospital or medical facilities have failed to progress fast enough to meet needs of hundreds of millions even after four decades of planning.

The process of liberalisation which started somewhat imperceptibly in late 70s and became evident in the recent announcements, was instantly liked by many on various grounds. Some thought that it was helpful in cutting the obstinate, inefficient and, at times, corrupt bureaucracy to its proper size. Others believed in market economy as a panacea to the enduring problems of unemployment and low growth rate. This, they believed, will cut the Gordian knot and release the latent energy of the economy so as to boost it out of the gravitation pull of the 'Hindu growth rate'. All this was to be done while keeping the much vouchsafed paradigms of faith in Nehruism, Gandhism, Socialism, mixed economy and so on.

It is true that the planning process lacked both in focus and effort. However, true to the spirit of 'soft state', it went along well with the socio-political realities of the times. The economic philosophy remained a blurred vision trying to focus on highly divergent social philosophy; yet it remained an interesting vision.

The bureaucratic shackles, still others felt were the most oppressive and also self-defeating when it came to running of public sector. It is true that public sector incurred huge losses and failed in generating resources for further economic development. By and large, it did become a dead weight. However, the failure is not entirely ascribable to poor management quality. Nationalised banks, e.g., were required to serve the poor in the society by forcing to provide finance for certain beneficiaries under IRDP, etc., at a subsidised rate of interest of four per cent only. They were then asked to write-off debt up to Rs. 10,000. One can hardly expect any organisation to prove financial success while meeting such socio-political ends. There were many reasons for failure of public sector and to say that it, failed because of inefficiency or corruption would not be a clear statement of reality.

However, the structure of macro-economic relations which has established itself is hardly conducive to meet the rising needs of fast expanding population of the country. India shall have to come out of the prevailing quagmire of inefficiency, corruption and excessive controls. A good deal of thinking is called for in redefining the role and functions of state in economic matters.

The present day drift towards the 'market friendly' path is also influenced by the goings on in the Soviet Union and the erstwhile block of communist countries of east Europe. Many people read this as a 'death' of communism or socialism. The Soviet Union, which had inspired Socialistic pattern of society and planning in nascent India in the fifties has been dethroned from its pedestal now.

The moot question is: Is the world now headed towards a more promising future? Will all these policy changes like devaluation, opening up economy to the multinationals and others, etc., kindle new lamps in the huts and houses of millions of Indians? Will the new and emerging economic order usher in a just and harmonious comity of nations? The questions were hardly ever so relevant as they are today.

Answers to these questions are neither easy nor definitive. One can examine them in light of past experiences of policy formulations and changes in them in order to arrive at an informed judgement.

The Process of Liberalisation

The process of liberalisation had set in the late-seventies. Initially 24 industries were notified as delicenced industries. In certain industries, the limit of investment requiring licence was raised from Rs. 1 crore to Rs. 3 crores.

The process of liberalisation became a little speedy in 1980. An industrial policy statement was issued in 1980. This policy statement allowed an automatic growth in the installed capacity of industries at rate of 5 per cent per annum subject to a ceiling of 25 per cent in a given five-year plan period. This facility was applied to all industries covered under Appendix 1 of the industrial policy issued in 1973. Main ideas behind this were (a) better utilisation of installed capacity, (b) broad banding of certain industries so as to meet the changing market situation and (c) reduce physical controls.

Though the industries, in this way, were allowed some flexibility they yet suffered from too many controls. The genesis of these controls lied in our economic philosophy.

Economic Philosophy

The economic philosophy of the country since the days of independence and in some cases even before that was based in the international political and economic situation of the world. While the struggle for freedom in India was gathering momentum events in the world were rapidly changing the face of the world. In 1917, while still Soviet Union was in the thick of the first world war, the Bolshevik revolution took place. People, the world over, started looking at Soviet Union as an embodiment of new hope and faith. Many intellectuals thought of it as a 'new God'. Many thought that here was an example of how equality and progress could be combined together.

Not far removed from this date of 1917 came the great depression of 1929-33. It was believed that trade cycles were integral part of the capitalism; capitalism was considered an inherently inequatious, unsteady and even some times imperialist. Even in the free world following the strains of business cycles, people started having greater faith in the action of state. Thus instead of limiting the role of the state to police, law and order, defence etc. many thinkers wanted state to become an active partner in the process of economic development.

The second world war again exemplified the strength of socialist model. By the time second world war (1939-44) was over, entire eastern Europe became communist. Sun had already set on the British Empire. Many countries of Africa and Asia won independence during this phase.

During these days India had entered into the phase of intensive movement for independence. Gandhiji's call for *Swadeshi*, non-cooperation movement, and a general rejection of British rule was all round in the air. Leaders who were involved in the freedom struggle during those days and of these, those who continued to shape the destiny of the country after independence, were very much impressed by the events around them. In particular, Pandit Jawaharlal Nehru and V.K. Krishnamenon were keen to apply the Russian model to India in order to solve the deep rooted problems of this country.

Initial Phase of Economic-Policy

In the initial phase economic policy was governed by 'Socialistic pattern of society'. Socialism was in the air in congress party conventions since 1929, however, this philosophy was adopted at the Avadi session of the congress party. The period of first five-year plan was not very eventful in this regard. Since the second five-year plan relatively bigger investment, as a means of state interference was considered.

This thinking led to the system called 'mixed economy'. Under this system India was to have both private and public sectors. The public sector was expected to provide a model of how industrialisation aught to be done. Public sector units were to be ideal examples to technology use, service to the society, application of managerial skills and labour-management relations. Public sector was expected to capture 'commanding heights'; they were to guide private sector in evolving the socialistic pattern of society.

Industrial Policy Resolution 1956

As a part of this enthusiasm for socialism industrial policy resolution of 1956 was passed.

The industrial policy was a statement containing details regarding areas of operation of private and public sectors. The policy resolution, as is well-known, divided the areas of industrial activity into those reserved for public sector only, those in which both private and public sectors can operate and those where private sectors could operate exclusively. Though immediately after the independence the government had introduced the first industrial policy resolution of 1948 it could outline only the approach of industrial growth. It also contained a desire to achieve sustained increase in industrial production and also ensure its proper distribution.

The vision about society became more clear after the adoption of the constitution which had also embodied the socio-economic goals of the society. As a result of this, the industrial policy was revised comprehensively. It included three broad areas of operation so as to create a mixed economy in India. The industrial policy resolution of 1956 set before it, the objective of accelerated rate of economic growth and rapid industrialisation was considered an Engine of Economic growth. Because of this approach, public sector was given strategic importance and massive investment were continuously poured into the sector for almost 35-40 years. The policy resolution also made specific reservations for small scale sector, village and cottage industries sectors.

The industrial policy resolution was modified from time to time. The modifications included the emerging challenges of time. The policy was modified in 1973, 1977 and 1980. The process of liberalisation was in fact started from 1977; at that time 24 industries were delicenced. Investment limit requiring licences was also raised from Rs. 1 crore to Rs. 3 crores. Thus allowing more units to come up without passing through the lengthy procedure of licencing.

The industrial policy resolution of 1980 reflected a realisation that it was necessary to introduce competition atleast in the domestic market. As a sequel to this, measures were initiated so as to introduce greater liberalisation. Following this policy, units were allowed to expands their capacity automatically by 5 per cent per annum subject to a ceiling of 25 per cent in a given five-year plan period. This liberalisation was given to all industries falling under Appendix 1. This industrial policy also desired to allow greater technology upgradation and initiated a process of modernisation. It also wanted to make the export base of the economy more competitive and encourage private foreign investment in high-tech areas.

However, during Mr. Rajiv Gandhi's time, along with the initiation of the seventh five-year plan, measures were taken in more speedy succession. Broad-banding of industries was allowed, physical controls through licencing were reduced sizeably and some specific measures were also initiated for liberalisation in foreign trade. The idea behind this was to take advantage of the strength of the economy, which, as was thought by many, had become very remarkable. It was thought that country had achieved a high degree of self-reliance in most of the raw-materials, and intermediate goods. The country also had very large and technically competent man-power. The country had almost become self-reliant in many items that it produced. Some policy changes were introduced in 1985-86 during Mr. Rajiv Gandhi's Prime Ministership. With his dream of 21st century, and with the realisation regarding strength of the economy, it was thought that India ought to open-up in order to achieve the maximum advantage of growth and latest technology. It was felt that these measures had paid off well when growth rate in industry sector reached a figure of 8.5 per cent (average annual) during the seventh five-year plan period.

The earlier ideas of self-reliance, socialism, mixed economy and the entire inward looking stance, was not found fit for the day. While the government thought of achieving social and economic justice and remove poverty and unemployment, it also wanted to transform India into a modern prosperous and outward looking country.

Broad Banding

The process of liberalisation included some allowance for expansion in capacity of existing units without waiting for prior permission for such allowance. But beyond this, it was realised by the government that, certain industries, if allowed to enter into production lines of similar commodities the production cost would be reduced or the output could be managed in a more rational way and at an optimum rate. Considering this fact, certain industrial units were allowed to achieve expansion as well as limited diversification was also granted to them. It was thought that the product-mix which would be turned out by these units will be able to respond to the market demand in a more flexible fashion.

The first industry to be allowed broad banding was machine tools and this industry was given this permission in July 1983. In 1985 automobile industry and paper industry were also allowed this facility for broad banding. But the major step was taken in August 1988 when broad banding was allowed to all those units belonging to Appendix 1 of the industrial policy, i.e. those industries which were controlled even by MRTP and FERA regulations. Thus the process of liberalisation which started in a very halting fashion in 1976 starting gathering some momentum in eighties.

In particular the broad banding facility offered to MRTP units is more significant. In the earlier thinking of the government, monopoly was considered and evil only to be tolerated in the process of developing a socialistic pattern of society. It is evident that since 1988, the thinking was more on the lines of making economy more functional, viable and competitive; rather than worry about the normative aspects like redistribution and equity.

Re-endorsement of Capacities

The regime of controls started giving way with the process known as re-endorsement of capacities. This was one of the earlier measures in the direction of liberalisation. In October 1966, the government allowed increase in capacity up to a limit of 25 per cent without waiting for prior licence. However, even this step was circumscribed by a large number of conditions. Some of these were: (a) the unit will not be allowed to establish new plant or machinery, (b) the unit will not ask for any additional foreign exchange, and (c) this facility will be available only in those areas which were not reserved for the small scale sector. This amounted to only better utilisation of the existing capacity.

In October 1975 a similar treatment was allowed to other 29 units again with certain conditions. These units must not be either MRTP and FERA units, they must not establish new plant and machinery and the production should not fall into the area reserved for the small sector. The list of these units grew gradually as time passed by and the number of conditions became less stringent. That is why by August 1980 this flexibility was available to a large number of units and in particular, the condition regarding plant and machinery was dropped; that is, a unit can expand its capacity and it would be re-endorsed by the government even when it established either a new plant or added a few machines. Similarly, even the condition regarding foreign exchange was also dropped.

Price Controls

The economy also suffered from a large number of price controls which were imposed on the industrial sector as well. Price controls, in particular were used partly with the socialistic norm in mind. Partly it was necessary as Indian economy had become increasingly dichotomous. Instead of all avowed efforts at removal of poverty and in particular a use of the slogan of *garibi hatao* as a part of election strategy, the problem of poverty, unemployment and rural-urban dichotomy were strongly embedded in the Indian system. Control of prices was aimed at achieving some distributive justice as the poor and downtrodden, ought to provided with some basic necessities. Since it will not be possible for them to buy it at a competitive price some subsidy was to be provided to them. Along with the price controls the government also established a system of subsidy to be paid out to various groups. Subsidy on fertilisers amounted to more Rs. 4000 crores in 1991. Again there are subsidies on food, transport etc. Apart from this open subsidy, the economy is over-laden with hidden subsidies also. Higher education, most of the other services like railways, post etc. are also considered to be subsidised.

The government, thus entered into an unenviable situation of hidden and open subsidies, price controls and fixing of prices of certain items by administrative orders. In case of cement e.g., the price control continued up to 1982 when some partial decontrol was introduced. It was totally decontrolled only in 1989. Aluminium was decontrolled again in 1989. Prices of bulk drugs were controlled since 1963 by the Bureau of Industrial Cost and Prices (BICP). In case of fertiliser industry, the prices reflect some amount of control along with subsidies. In case of certain non-ferrous metals detailed monthly announcement are made by the Minerals and Metals Trading Corporation (MMTC). Prices of energy are yet controlled, so are the prices of steel. Prices even of essential commodities like sugar are indirectly controlled by method of monthly releases. Though indeed, the ratio of levy to non-levy sugar has been continuously decreased since 1973-74. It has been reduced from 70 per cent (1973-74) to 45 per cent (1988-89).

The combined weight of all administered prices in the wholesale prices index (base (1981-82) is as high as 23.35 per cent. If one considers the indirect effect also, like that of maneuvering the prices of sugar, the total weight of administered prices comes to 25.11 per cent which is more than one quarter of the total. Thus, the government can influence the price level as well as structure of prices by taking administrative decision. That is, why Mr. S.S. Marathe, Ex-Secretary in the Ministry of Industry writes, ". . .the earlier approach to price controls was based on the assumption that it is economically necessary and administratively feasible to operate an extensive and integrated system of controls consisting of price control, tentative allocation, import restrictions, and quotas for importers and, also the use of fiscal mechanism. There were little, if any, attempts to view the price controls and rationing, as temporary devices of transitional character until the demand and supply were in better balance". [Regulations and Development, SAGE (1986) p. 237]

Liberalisation in Trade

The policy of trade liberalisation had also been initiated earlier in the late seventies. Though direct control mechanism on imports continued, it was customary to announce import tariff in the budget. Since the tariff rates and structure were changed in budgets keeping emergent exigencies in mind, it also created uncertainties in the trade and industry circles. The first change towards stabilising foreign trade policy was initiated in 1985-86. Up to 1984-85 the trade policy was announced every year but beginning with 1985 a policy was announced for a three year period (1985-88), as recommended by the Abid Hussain Committee. This measure provided some stability in the approach. It was thought that industrial houses can plan their approaches in a more stable policy environment. This measure of announcing three yearly trade policy was repeated for the period 1988-91. However, on April 1, 1990 another policy was announced.

Within the framework of economic philosophy prevailing at that time, it was felt that India should go for self-reliance and gradually develop into a nation which is the least reliant on foreign technology imports. This objective itself is debatable, in essence as it is wrong to assume of technology as a given parametre. In a world which is taking leaps and bounds in science and technology, manufacturing technology can hardly remain constant. Since the developed world can invest larger amounts of the GDP in research and development (R and D), their capacity to innovate is always going to remain a few steps ahead of the developing world. The problem becomes more acute for country like India even amongst the developing world, because India suffers from problems of poverty, unemployment, illiteracy, insufficient development of infrastructure etc. The structure of economy that India is having, hardly provides for funds enough to achieve major break-through in manufacturing technology. As such India is destined to import technology for the foreseeable future. However, the policy of self-reliance and import substitution continued for years on end.

In this case again greater reliance was put on public sector. The so called 'failure' of public sector yet remains to be examined as there are many non-economic factors which have also contributed to mismanagement and insufficiencies. However, the fact remained that public sector could not deliver the goods. Performance of private sector also left much to be desired. In absence of enough investment in R and D and because of controls of imports, Indian manufacturing firms started becoming obsolete. In an over all environment of protection, because of the trade policy, some of the manufacturing units, did not feel compulsions of quality improvement, efficiency, etc.

In the process of liberalisation on this front in 1978-79 imports of capital goods was allowed for 13 industries among them were fertiliser, power, petrochemical, sugar, cement, etc. These industries were allowed to announce global tenders for their requirement of capital goods. Subsequent to this came liberalisation for the import of raw-materials and intermediate goods which can not be manufactured in India. A system of open general licence (OGL) was announced. In 1982-83, 100 items were added to this list; in 1983-84 another 144 items were added and in 1984-85 still another 149 items were added to the OGL. Along with raw-materials and intermediates more and more capital goods also started coming under OGL.

The Abid Hussain Committee (1985) was of the view that the trade policy should be liberalised so that Indian manufacturing can have more liberal access to imported technology. The Committee also opined that, even as a system of regulation, a shift away from quantitative controls and towards tariff controls was desirable. As the Indian industry adopted better and latest technology, it will lead to increase in output which again will lead to increasing export. This will offset the increased bill of imports. However, India did not have much flexibility on the front of increasing tariff as they were already higher as compared to some Asian neighbours like Pakistan, Bangladesh and China. This trade policy ultimately led to greater import intensity of Indian manufacturing. In some of the industries like picture-tubes for television, this was as high as 90 per cent. In case of telecommunications this was 70 per cent and in computer it was 60 per cent in 1990-91. In certain other industries like diamond, entire raw material was imported while in case of synthetic fibres the import content was 50 per cent of the total raw material component.

Decontrol of MRTP-FERA Companies

The Monopolies and Restrictive Trade Practice Act (MRTP) was passed in 1969. The idea behind enacting this was in line with the general economic philosophy of the country. It was thought that the monopoly houses will lead to greater inequality which again will generate more strife of the poor and downtrodden. The monopolies are never considered to be organising the resources in an optimum fashion. A monopoly succeeds because not so much of economic reasons but because of their non-economic measures. They hardly rely on competition, quality improvement, R and D etc. for their success. The history of U.S. economy is also exemplifying, this situation by its chapter on anti-trust act. With this objectives in mind, basically to see that the economic activity of a few does not result into concentration of economic power, the industrial policy changes in 1970 and 1973 provided for certain measure against monopolies in particular. The industrial policy of 1973 grouped certain industries as monopolies. These industries were considered to be core industries and were of great importance to the national economy. They also were industries having basic and strategic importance for the growth of the Indian economy. The list consisted of 19 groups of industries and were called Appendix 1 Industries under the 1973 Act. This list was reviewed and modified in April 1982. In fact the list was expanded to cover 33 groups of industries which are now called MRTP and FERA Companies (see Appendix 1).

New Initiatives

After the general election of June 1991 and the tragic death of Mr. Rajiv Gandhi during the electioneering, the government of Mr. P.V. Narsimha Rao came into power. The Government did not enjoy majority in the Lok Sabha. However, since the Congress Party emerged as the largest single party, it ventured into running the government. Mr. Manmohan Singh was inducted as the Finance Minister even though he was not an elected member of the house. It is to the credit of Mr. Manmohan Singh as a professional Economist, who held high offices in the national and international fora, that he was entrusted with the responsibility of organising financial matters of the country at a critical juncture. Mr. Manmohan Singh had a distinguished career as an academician, Deputy Chairman of Planning Commission and Governor of Reserve Bank of India. He also had an experience of working in the United Nation on South-South dialogue. He had to bring to bear all his experience and expertise in organising the financial matters of the country.

The present debate on economic situation is initiated after the large number of financial measures which will have far reaching implications. To some, the situation of country was almost like a crisis and the Narsimha Rao government had to act fast and comprehensively in all directions in order to bring the country out of its crisis situation. However, on the other side, people opined that there was no major crisis on the issues like agricultural development, manufacturing activity, internal trade, etc. It would be necessary in this light to examine the magnitude and implications of the crisis as perceived by some reflect upon the measures initiated by the Narsimha Rao government. Examining these measures in prospects and retrospect can allow one to visualise the possibility and danger which lay ahead in the closing decade of this millennium.

Nature of the Crisis

There is a general agreement that the economy was facing a serious crisis on the balance of payments front. In fact the balance of payments situation had started deteriorating in the eighties. There were days of late seventies when the economy had sizeable surplus on this front. Largely due to the policy of modernisation which incorporated import of new technology, the balance of payment situation started worsening. The current amount of deficit was only an average of Rs. 2,277 crores per annum between 1980 and 1985. It increased dramatically to an average figure of Rs. 7,771 crores between 1985-90.

The situation aggravated because of the Gulf War. The Gulf War has affected the economy in two ways: (a) repatriation from Indian workers in the Gulf region dried up almost entirely. The loss was sizeable as more than 150,000 workers were affected because of this, (b) import of crude petroleum became more expensive as well as uncertain. As domestic output of crude oil had been faltering because of political disturbances in Assam, import from Kuwait and Iraq became almost impossible. It is estimated that during 1990-91 import of POL products rose by as much as $ 2.2 b.

While imports increased as a result of the enthusiasm for modernising Indian economy, exports could not pick up largely as a result of the Gulf war. This started creating scepticism in the minds of NRI's who started withdrawing their deposits from India. The inflows of foreign exchange from NRI's stood at an average figure of Rs. 2,160 crores between 1987-88 and 1989-90, it came down to a trickle of just Rs. 210 crores in 1990-91.

All these led to fast depletion in foreign exchange coffers. By March 1986 India had a reserve of $ 6 b., which came down to nearly $ 3.30 b, by 1990. By May 1991, there was a further decline and the reserves stood at only $ 1.25 b. While, the IMF did sanction special loan facility amounting to $ 1.76 b. in January 1991 under the Compensation and Contingency Financing Facility (CCFF), the reserves could not pick up. All these led to a crisis situation as the credit rating of the country started going down.

While this view is based on the facts and there is no point in desagreeing with the facts, the moot question raised by some other Economists pertains to an over all view of the economy. The argument basically rests on the facts as indicated below:

(a) In the total world trade, share of India is only 0.56 per cent.
(b) The countries which talk of free market or competition in the market friendly situation, are not following the precepts when it comes to practicing them.
(c) The world trade is not picking up fast enough.
(d) The inward looking policies of the government followed up so far had already started paying dividend as a growth rate in the GDP had come out from 'Hindu rate' since the Sixth Five Year Plan.
(e) Even after granting that there was a crisis on the balance of payments front, the entire economy which is composed of sectors like agriculture, manufacturing and service, had been showing fairly high order of resilience.

(f) There also is a criticism that the government is following a 'bank fund' prescription and sacrificing its own self interest.

Measures Initiated

The market friendly approach to the economy consists of a number of measures which are introduced almost simultaneously in the economy. These measures basically aim at structural adjustments designed to reorient the macro-economic variables in a way which is termed as liberal. Since the measures are of far reaching implications leading to a programme of macro-economic adjustment, they require careful attention. The measures could be stated as follows:

Industrial Licensing: Further Derestricted

The industrial licencing policy which had become more acute in early seventies had been under pressure in the eighties. The system of industrial licensing is now restricted to 18 industries. The government announced a policy in this regard on 24th July 1991 which has virtually abolished the pressure of industrial licensing for almost all industries irrespective of the size and level of investment.

The 18 industries which yet fall under the perview of licensing, belong to five main categories, as follows:

(a) Industries of strategic importance and those important for security purpose,
(b) Industries necessary to be controlled from the angle of social-consideration,
(c) Industries which may pose serious danger to environment,
(d) Industries which are of hazardous nature,
(e) Industries which are producing items for the consumption of aristocratic sections of Indian society.

Though the list has now been brought down to 18 industries, prior to this only 27 industries or groups of industries were subjected to the system of licensing. Out of these 27 industries, some have been delicenced. They are, milk and malted food, vegetable oil and vanaspati and textile units operated by power, steel and steel-based products, non-ferrous metals and their products, ferro-alloys, telecom equipment, computer peripherals, micro-processors and industrial control instrumentation systems, fertilisers and some chemicals, etc.

New units entering into the economy need not take licences for this and old units need not take licences even while undertaking substantial expansion. The small scale sector units also need not take licences even while manufacturing some of these products.

All new industrial units will be availing the facility of broad-banding. They can produce various articles from the given plant and machinery without involving additional investment.

Location Restrictions

In the earlier system of licensing there were certain restrictions on location of units. The new policy does away with this, excepting the case of cities with population of one million and more. Again, industrial units other than the 18, yet falling under the licensing net, and which are non-polluting units such as diamond, electronics etc., can be located outside a periphery of 25 km even in case of cities of one million population and above.

In order to achieve greater decentralisation of industrial units, the government will promote infrastructural development, thereby making it more attractive for the industries to locate themselves away from big cities.

Public Sector

The recent policy change seems to be more eye-catching on the front of public sector units. There is a general feeling that public sector units have contributed in building up the economic-base of the country, and aided to the diversification of industries, while they have failed to generate enough surplus. Thus the ire against the public sector is that while the government has controlled more and more proportions of public and private savings for the development of public sector the net contribution from this sector has remained rather insignificant. With this type of thinking the role of public sector has now been limited to three broad areas as follows:

(1) Industrial units which are of strategic importance for the nation,
(2) Units which require high technology, and
(3) Units which are essential in the development of infrastructure.

The exclusive area of public sector activity has now been confined to eight aspects as follows:

(1) Arms and ammunition,
(2) Atomic energy,
(3) Petroleum oil,
(4) Mining of coal and lignite,
(5) Mining of copper lead, zinc, tin, molybdenum and wolfram,
(6) Mining of iron ore manganese ore, crome ore, gypsum, sulphur, gold and diamond,
(7) Mining of specific materials identified in the schedule of atomic energy order of 1973 and
(8) Railway transport.

It can be noted that many items which had been under the command of public sector are no more appearing in the above list. Thus, road and air transport, production of iron and steel, heavy industrial machinery, heavy electricals, ship-building, telephone and telephone cables, generation and distribution of power etc. are areas which will now be thrown open to the private sector.

Even in case of public sector units which are already existing, private participation is to be encouraged. Thus, the government equity in case of selected undertaking will be transferred to mutual funds. Presently the limit is kept at 20 per cent of existing equity of such units.

However, in case of the sick public sector units a clear policy statement is yet to emerge. Such chronically sick units are to be referred to the Board of Industrial and Financial Reconstruction (BIFR) or some other high power body in order to seek is revival. However, it is not clear whether the government will like to shut down all such units in case they don't come out of the sickness. The government has yet to spell cut its exit policy more clearly for sick and such other units. It may not be advisable to chop-off any unit in public sector which becomes sick.

MRTP Companies

In case of MRTP companies there is a remarkable change in government approach. The earlier efforts were at redefining the size of companies which would be considered MRTP. The emphasis on control and regulation of monopolies, so as to avoid unfair trade practices continued in order to control their dominant nature. However, many companies are now entirely out of the MRTP net.

Foreign Equity

Considering the fact that the recent crisis has its origin on the foreign exchange front, the government has shown special keenness to attract foreign investment. For this, the industrial policy has incorporated the following:

(a) The foreign investment can now be 51 per cent of the total equity of a company. The advantage is now available to the 33 industry groups under the MRTP-FERA list. The government intends to remove bottlenecks in the process of licencing, import, etc., so that other measures of industrial licencing policy can become more effective.
(b) The payment of dividend, repatriation etc. would be monitored by Reserve Bank of India with a view to ensuring that such units earn enough foreign exchange to compensate for such out-flow.
(c) It is thought that foreign equity proposals can be taken up independently of foreign technology agreements. However, in certain cases the foreign equity proposals will yet require prior clearance from government.
(d) While access to international markets is required by the 51 per cent equity holding foreign companies, they will be treated on par with the domestic trade houses in reference to the import-export policy of the government.
(e) In order to short-cut the procedural delay the government has decided to constitute a specially empowered board which will take up the approval of direct foreign investment in selected areas. They will also examine the possibility of attracting substantial foreign investment in high technology industries.

Electricity Generation

Generation of electricity had been under the control of the public sector. Distribution of power was also exclusively reserved for the public sector according to the Industrial Policy Resolution (1956). The new thinking has favoured both generation and distribution of power in the private sector. Considering the fact that requirement of power not only far exceeds its supply; but is also pivotal to the general economic development of the country, it is necessary to invest much larger resources in the power sector than it could be possible for the public sector to mobilise. Since the 8th Five Year Plan is on the anvil, it is necessary to introduce these changes with an early effect. The Union Cabinet has taken two important decisions in this light. They are:

(a) Permission is granted for 100 per cent foreign equity. Thus foreign multinationals, other companies or governments can directly set up exclusive power plants.
(b) The electricity (Supply) Act of 1948 is to be modified so that distribution of electricity does not become a bottleneck, once output picks up.

Foreign Trade

The government has initiated steps to introduce structural changes in the entire import-export policy. Basic objectives kept in sight for the purpose are:

(a) Export promotion,
(b) Import reduction, and
(c) Reduction or removal of licencing and introduction of automaticity.

With these objectives in mind certain measures are initiated which are as follows:

(1) The system of replenishment licences (REP) has been enlarged and liberalised.
(2) The REP rates are not only increased but they are also made uniform. The direction of the changes are as follows:

    (a) For exporters, the REP rate has been increased from 10 per cent to 20 per cent of foreign exchange earning, provided that they were obtaining imports through the schemes of advanced licences.
    (b) For certain items like diamonds, jewellery, handicrafts,

etc., which already had higher REP rates, will continue to benefit from these rates.

(c) REP rates will be different for the rupee currency area (RCA) and general currency area (GCA). In case of the former, imports against REP licences will now be permitted only from the RCA areas. However, up to 31st December 1991, strictly as a short-term measure, exporters to RCA may opt for the former REP rates for imports from hard currency areas. In case of GCA, the REP rates which earlier ranged between 5 to 20 per cent are now enhanced to 30 per cent as a uniform rate.

(3) The system of providing additional licences which were available to special export houses will now be merged with the REP licences.

(4) The government has suspended the system of compensatorv cash support (CCS).

(5) Certain imports are now permissible only against the REP licences. They are:

(a) OGL items which at present are merged, subject to the attestation by the D.G.T.D. It is proposed that such items could be imported only against REP licences.

(b) Some items which were unlisted under OGL are presently imported against special supplementary licences. These items are also now importable against REP licences.

(c) Items like raw materials, components, tools and spare parts, etc., which presently appear in the limited permissible list can also be imported, in future, against REP licences.

(d) The system of providing supplementary licences is withdrawn except for SSI units and certain other sectors sensitive to defence.

(e) As a measure of linking imports with exports and also reducing imports to the maximum possible extent, import of almost all items is linked with REP. A special committee known as a permanent review committee will be constituted for the purpose.

The REP licences are now to be called eximscrip and could be traded in the open market. Financial institutions can also be allowed to trade in this scrip.

Along with these policy changes, the government has introduced a system of decanalisation of imports. The Ministry of Commerce, along with other relevant bodies, will undertake a case by case review of items to be decanalised. The government has also decided to discontinue the system of providing import licences for all capital goods and raw materials.

While these measures are undertaken with a broad policy objective of opening up of the economy, some special measures are also contemplated. These measures are for necessary protection of small scale sector. Some life saving drugs and equipments will still be under the earlier system of protection. Such sectors will continue to have the facility of OGL imports under the old scheme of supplementary licences.

Money and Capital Market

On the front of money and banking, under the new environment a few measures are adopted. Apart from the measures like changes in the credit — deposit ratio, incremental cash-reserve ratio etc., announced by the Reserve Bank of India, there are certain changes which are of greater importance from the angle of macro variables. The most important among these is the change in the policy regarding interest rates. The government has been concerned about subsidies and the emergent structure in the system of interest rates also. It is felt that interest rates are on the lower side and hence there is a hidden subsidy in the use of capital. This leads to distortions such that the cost of capital as a resource is not reflecting its real value. Considering this, the Finance Minister Mr. Manmohan Singh mentioned in his budget speech ". . . . We can begin to relax the degree of intervention and impart a greater flexibility to the structure of interest rates. Reserve Bank of India has already taken an important step in this direction, by stipulating a floor rate of interest and providing freedom to commercial banks to charge interest rates above the floor level based on their perception of risk. The government proposes to extend similar freedom to term-lending financial institutions, where the minimum interest rate would be 15 per cent and these institutions would be free to charge an interest rate in accordance with their perception of the credit worthiness of borrowers" [Part (A), Para 15; 24th July, 1991].

"... Our ultimate objective is to achieve a significant reduction both in the nominal and the real interest rates. This would be possible if the rate of inflation is reduced significantly over the next three years".

With this new approach towards interest rates, the Reserve Bank of India had already announced an increase in the bank rate by one per cent age point; i.e., from 10 per cent to 11 per cent on July 4, 1991. This has been further raised by one percentage point, i.e. to 12 per cent on 8th October, 1991. Along with this, other interest rates for example, like those charged on commercial banks' deposit rates, lending rates and refinancial rates of Reserve Bank of India were also increased.

Rates on deposits as well as on the government schemes like Small Savings were also raised. Interest rates of the urban cooperative banks were also raised. The purpose behind the latest hike, i.e., the one effected on 8th October 1991, is to control the inflationary pressure which is being built for some specific purpose as the latest measures seek to freeze advances by scheduled commercial banks, on shares, for housing and consumer durables to the level as prevalent on the day of announcement.

Budgetary Measures

The measures discussed so far could be classified as non-budget announcements. These announcements were made by the concerned Ministries, Reserve Bank of India etc. The finance ministry itself had also undertaken a few other measures like devaluation of Indian rupee. The Reserve Bank and the Govt. of India also hypothecated gold with the Bank of England. In continuation of such measures, there were certain specific measures incorporated in the budget proposals. This could be briefly mentioned as follows:

(1) In case of black-money, the government announced a special scheme under which an individual can deposit his black-money with the National Housing Bank. Out of this, 40 per cent would be deducted and set apart as a special levy. The fund created out of this is to be used for financing housing schemes for the poor, particularly schemes of slum clearance in urban areas. The balance of 60 per cent of money is to be returned to the depositor. The depositor will not be asked any question as to the origin of this money; thus 60 per cent of such deposits could

become 'white'.

(2) In case of foreign exchange remittance coming to India, the entire amount can become tax-free. Even if it is received as a gift, no gift tax will be charged on this.

(3) Government sought to remove subsidies on fertilizers. The amount of subsidies had reached a level of nearly Rs. 4,000 crores in recent years. Since the government was forced to cut down on the deficits like budget deficit, fiscal deficit and revenue deficit, this could be achieved by first cutting on subsidies of either open or hidden form. Efforts to cut down the overall deficit are also reflected in tax efforts; as some new taxes, both of direct and indirect nature were introduced. Without going into details regarding the budget, one can observe the general line of thinking; which runs as follows:

(a) Control fiscal deficit to around 6.0 to 6.5 per cent of GDP so that inflationary pressures could be contained. The proportion of deficit is to be reduced gradually to a much lower limit so that the economy is freed from inflationary pressures.

(b) Provide much less support or even withdraw the support being provided currently, in the form of open or hidden subsidies. While on the one hand, this can help in generating an atmosphere of self-reliance, it can on the other hand, help in containing the budget deficit.

Ails of the Economy

Because of this wide ranging and remarkable changes which are introduced in the economy within a short time span of nearly 100 days of the rule of the new government, there are many claims and counter claims about the future course of economy. Inspite of all these discussions regarding the desirability or otherwise of the steps which are undertaken, there is a general feeling that these steps are irreversible. India can hardly go back to "Status quo Ante". The situation which prevailed in India before 1976 could also hardly be termed as ideal. Discretionary controls, rigid regulations, time consuming red-tappism, mistrust of foreign companies, and a wide-ranging control by the government in almost all spheres have led us to an economic regime of "quota-permit-licence Raj". The discretionary powers used by politician and bureaucracy resulted in wide spread corruption also. In this totality of the situation, the textbook economics of rationality, optimum resource allocation and utilisation, efficiency and competition could hardly become functional. This has resulted in wasteful resource allocation and undue protection to industries or industrial units or service sector, which, otherwise had a potential to perform much better if they were exposed to the competitive world as they developed.

While growth rate of industrial production increased, more remarkably in the later part of the planning i.e in the Sixth and Seventh Five Year Plans, however, the economy was infested with many unwanted bugs also.

Problem with the Structure of the Economy

While India is a labour surplus economy, an increasing amount of investment has been taking place in capital intensive units. The argument in this case was that in certain front-line industries, India should import latest technology. But this import of technology reduced labour absorption and displaced labour. While population continued to increase by leaps and bounds, capacity of industry to absorb such increases in the labour force did not keep pace with the fast-expanding labour force. Unemployment of skilled, semi-skilled as well as unskilled workers increased in absolute terms initially and thereafter as a proportion of the labour force also. On the other hand, in the organised sector, labour productivity did not increase fast enough because of the "soft State" approach of the government. In this situation the incremental capital output ratio (ICOR) worsened continuously. Thus while the transplanted latest technology flourished, capacity of Indian economy to make best use of it always remained very constrained. Sub-optimal use of capital resources arising out of administrative controls impinging on supply of raw-materials, availability of electricity and such other fiats of the government, resulted in additional drags on the ICOR.

Agricultural Situation

Agricultural situation of the country has become more and more dichotomous with development in agriculture. New technology which worked out as land augmenting system, helped in producing bumper harvest in irrigated areas. However, when it came to the issues like increasing growth rate of agriculture production in rain-fed or dry land farming areas, India really did not have much to offer. In the country as a whole, more than 60 per cent of the area is rain-fed or dry farm area. When there is less than sufficient rain-fall or when there is irregular rainfall, the crop out-turn is affected severely. This has made agriculture a risky business. That is, why it is said, "agriculture is a gamble in rain".

While agriculture has remained risky, efforts at increasing total country level output have been in the context of a large number of issues and actions emerging from the agriculture policy. Thus for example, the government has always taken a stand that agriculture needs to be subsidised, in use of certain inputs. Such open or hidden subsidies, as is well-known is given to fertilizers, irrigation waters, electricity etc. with a view to enhancing the rate of adoption of new technology.

In this context of subsidy is to be raised the problem of taxation of agriculture and terms of trade between industry and agriculture. In case of agricultural taxation, it is found that the wide-spread illiteracy of the farmers, absence of a system of maintaining accounts, high risk of agriculture, and very large number of farmers disbursed in so many lakhs of villages of the country, can make the task of taxing agriculture income really stupendous. Government has found in fact, the task of enforcing even minimum wages in agriculture, much beyond it capacity. It is only too well-known that agricultural labourers are hardly paid according to the minimum wages announced by the government from time to time. When even this single point action can not be handled in the farm sector, it will be obviously impossible to implement a system of taxation of agricultural incomes. Though the government has continued, at the state level, with the system of collecting land revenue and levying certain charges, imposition of agricultural income-tax has usually remained beyond its scope.

As agricultural inputs are subsidised and agriculture can not be expected to contribute to the national economy by way of direct agricultural income-tax, the government has adopted measures which can turn the terms of trade against agriculture and in favour of industry. Thus the agriculture sector, while buying industrial output, has to pay increasingly higher prices for industrial products where as products of the agriculture sector are priced at artificially low levels. By worsening terms of trade against agriculture and allowing industries to earn more profits, the government can hope to siphen-off a part of these profits by way of corporate taxation. Along with this, the process also nelps in mobilising resources for industry. This is in general line of thinking that in the early phase of development, agriculture sector has to release resources for the development of industry.

This type of thinking in regard to agriculture has led to the system of announcing lower floor and ceiling prices for some major agricultural commodities. The system of buffer stock and public distribution system, which are integral parts of the announcement of floor and ceiling prices, dampen agricultural prices as desired by the government.

In the new system of withdrawing subsidies the government shall have to think of its repercussions on the aspects like the policy of prices fixing, buffer stock and the distribution system. It is obvious that the change of stance can not be limited to fertiliser subsidies alone.

Service Sector

In the recent phase of faster economic growth since the Sixth Five Year Plan, it is observed that growth of the service sector has been phenomenal. Three important components of the service sector in the capital market, viz., banking, life and general insurance and mutual funds are entirely in the government sector. Besides, diverting sizeable amounts of public savings for investment in the public sector, the government also becomes the largest single employer.

When the market friendly approach is undertaken the labour productivity as such has to be increased. Indeed it is well-known that after all the labour productivity is dependent on units of capital which are invested per labour unit. However, it is already an accepted fact that India goods and commodities have to be made competitive in the world market as India shall have to enhance its exports sizeably. Thus, "shedding of Fear", has to take place; and this is going to be more on the side of labour than capital. This also is obvious as capital, is a scarce resources; because of this (and also because of the inflationary pressure), lending rates by the Schedule Commercial Banks have been raised by nearly 6 percentage points by recent announcements. Since productivity of capital is dependent on labour and as labour is in abundant supply the brunt of increase in productivity in making the goods more competitive has to be borne by no other resource than labour.

Prospects and Retrospects

The economic issues of the country are right now in the fore front of the nation's life. This is evident from the memorandum submitted to the government by more than 250 MPs and other eminent citizens regarding the Uruguay round of talks being conducted under the GATT. The MPs have expressed that if India succumbs to the pressures of the developed countries, it will be sacrificing its option regarding self-reliance and technology development. More serious than this according to them, is that India will also put at stake, its "political sovereignty". They feel that the foreign monopolies will exploit Indian labour and environmental resources to the detriment of the country and to the advantage of multinational monopolies.

In this light, one has to look at the entire procedure of "opening up" of the economy from the angle of political sovereignty and economic growth. It is obvious that the growthmanship will lend the country into deeper crisis.

Exit Policy

The most crucial point is regarding the exit policy as discussed earlier. Mr. Manmohan Singh has announced in the Fund Bank Meeting at Bangkok (October 16, 1991) that the sick public sector units will be closed down. Such an option is full of far reaching implications. While it is obvious that government could not shoulder the financial responsibility of loss making units *ad infinitum*, it has to adopt a gradual process of retrenchment as, unlike the western countries, India does not have a system of social security for unemployment benefits. Similarly, if the meaning of the exit policy is streched to the removal of employees, it will complicate the matter still further and add to the socio-political tensions in the country. It is indeed very doubtful if, in face of rising unemployment, rising rate of inflation and retrenchment; the government can maintain peace and political stability. Loss of peace and stability will be exorbitant cost to the society and the country can not bargain for growth at this cost.

Agriculture Sector

The agriculture sector is also going to come under serious stress. Removal of fertiliser subsidy to begin with, and then gradually removing other forms of subsidy, either direct or indirect; will lead to less than optimal utilisation of the newly emerging potential in the agriculture sector. In face of falling production, unemployment for this sector also is expected to mount. While it is already assured by the government that the prices of agricultural products will be raised in order to compensate for the withdrawal of various subsidies, the poor amongst the rural population will find in very difficult to sustain themselves. As, a large proportion of population is living below the poverty line, and when they find the prices of basic commodities going out of their reach while employment opportunities were not picking up, they can also lead to further social-political stress in the system. It should be remembered that the proportion of population below poverty line is put officially at 29 per cent. Though this percentage is contested; however, even by this figure, the absolute number is around 24 crore persons. The stress of development on this sector will be too heavy for continued peace.

Sequencing and Gradualness of Approach

The world development report (1991) talks of lesser pain if macro-economic adjustments are undertaken swiftly. The report cites experience of countries which have adopted gradualness (which, by their definition, is 'beyond two years)', as against this are examples of the countries which have undertaken swift measures. The world bank tries to argue that wherever the measures are swift the painful effects are much less. The economies also revive much faster if the measures are taken in a speedy way.

The approach of trying to compare country like India with small countries like Malaysia or Korea is a brave approach. Again, such comparisons lack in the perception of basic premises that "one can not jump in the same river twice". So, whatever happened in past can not be so easily considered replicable for the future. The world of yester years was a bipolar world and its dictates were much different. The present world is emerging as a G-7 hegemony where the objectives are no more those of development or providing assistance for development. The objectives are much more simple. The developed world is looking for markets, and the developing world has to serve the interests of the developed world. In the process, the developed world can be allowed to exploit the environmental resources which are otherwise a global heritage. This developed world is also to be allowed to exploit labour of the developing world in the name of improving labour productivity.

The Danger Signals

The new world economic order, which is emerging, has already sounded many danger signals. As a result of these policy measures intra and international economic inequality will increase. Hegemony of developed world will be deeply entrenched. There will be a large scale discontent amongst the people of the developing countries. Within any given nation this can give rise to political instability, starvation and large scale discontent. For example, if the Uruguay round of talks cultimate in carrying the brief of the developed world regarding the patents clause, in case of only one industry of India i.e., Drugs and Pharmaceutical, India will be required to pay out anything between $500 million to $ 1 b. as royalty to the developed world. As against this, the recent assurance from IMF and World Bank is for a loan of around $ 8 b. If the drugs and pharmaceutical industry is forced to pay such an amount of royalty it could not survive unless the prices of drugs and pharmaceutical products within the country are raised; according to some, this may be a monsterous rise of 500 per cent to 1000 per cent ! This will be catastrophic for the poor and ailing sections of the population. May be death rate in the country will also increase and life expectancy may be shortened. Such stories would be repeated in case of many other industries also with change in implications.

It is doubtful if these measures can lead to faster growth. In all probability, with rising prices of raw-materials, increasing rate of interest, etc., the cost of production will increase. When this is coupled with high rate of inflation, this will ultimately lead to a situation worse than stagflation.

A dim flicker of hope however, is in terms of how best the government can maintain peace and resolve the conflicts. It is also possible that if the developed world starts taking a more humane and helping approach, the debt of the developing world may be written-off to some extent. This can neutralise present impact of devaluation, which has raised the debt amount by the same proportion as devaluation. Discussions of Common-Wealth Heads of Governments and the outcome of South-South Dialogue are indicative of such approaches.

It remains to be closely watched as to how the events take shape in future course of actions. Presently, however, the dice is heavily loaded in favour of the hegemony of economic super-powers.

APPENDIX 1

GOVERNMENT'S EXPENDITURE

(*Rs. Crore*)

1	1991-92 Budget	1990-91 Revised	1990-91 Budget	1989-90 Actuals	1988-89 Actuals	1987-88 Actuals	1986-87 Actuals	1985-86 Actuals	1984-85 Actuals	1983-84 Actuals	1982-83 Actuals
	2	3	4	5	6	7	8	9	10	11	12
I. Non-Plan Expenditure	79697	76761	64514	64505	52960	44052	39920	32811	27026	21496	17774
(A) Interest payments	27450	21850	20850	17735	14278	11251	9246	7512	5974	4795	3938
(B) Defence	16350	15750	15750	14416	13341	11968	10477	7988	7061	5831	5021
(C) Subsidies	10395*	12121	10624	10677	7732	5980	5451	4796	4038	2749	2262
(1) Food	2600	2450	2200	2476	2200	2000	2000	1650	1101	835	711
(2) Fertilisers	4000	4400	4000	4601	3201	2164	1898	1924	1928	1042	603
(3) Export promotions	1224	2700	2316	2089	1386	962	785	603	518	463	477
(4) Other subsidies	1071	1071	2108	1511	945	854	768	619	491	409	471
(D) General services	6629	7186	5641	5283	4979	4388	3633	3C30	2051	2017	1680
of which											
Police	1758	1581	1394	1298	1132	980	819	631	520	429	363
(E) Social services	2046	1855	1891	1340	1293	1309	1206	877	669	547	412
(1) Education	758	720	664	536	474	608	499	328	242	223	209
(2) Health and family welfare	261	239	242	159	140	163	145	117	91	79	71
(3) Labour and employment	319	267	271	251	231	163	232	166	159	93	76
(4) Information and broadcasting	345	301	310	221	150	164	125	99	53	18	24
(5) Other social services	363	328	404	173	298	211	205	167	124	134	32

Contd.

APPENDIX 1 *Contd.*

1	2	3	4	5	6	7	8	9	10	11	12
(F) Economic services	2618	2640	2777	2792	1944	1894	1437	1361	1406	1034	1010
(1) Agriculture and allied services	391	404	427	381	261	243	164	243	265	177	21
(2) Energy, industry and minerals	821	959	748	1096	672	805	469	381	748	423	177
(3) Transport and communications	302	280	287	277	232	207	183	150	6	42	202
(4) Science, technology and environment	623	554	567	574	427	376	343	297	237	203	197
(5) Postal deficit	243	150	492	260	170	191	215	162	124	73	79
(6) Other economic services	481	443	256	464	352	263	278	290	150	189	334
(G) Expenditure on union territories without legislature	985	953	922	1098	725	437	556	413	321	284	253
(H) Grants to states and union territories	2613	2930	2986	2167	2186	1789	1714	1786	1027	879	824
(I) Other grants	181	222	190	123	124	139	114	81	89	90	78
(J) Loans and advances to state and union territories	6934	7356	56	5793	4293	3134	3722	4206	3272	1976	87
(K) Other loans	2077	2521	1645	1722	1107	905	1769	217	141	778	1964
(L) Non-plan capital expenditure	1176	1227	1182	1099	788	667	380	382	853	443	245
II. Plan Outlay	33725	29956	30192	28401	26151	24209	22996	19854	16606	14038	11913
(A) Budget support for central plan	19015	17594	17344	18159	16333	14458	15001	12791	11517	9220	7456
(1) Economic services	14517	14108	13721	14852	13073	11756	12809	10932	9784	7805	6424
(a) Agriculture and allied service	1813	1358	1546	1330	1275	1111	1375	1302	1086	1117	933
(b) Rural development	2702	2532	2664	2637	1753	1844	1360	706	729	383	244
(c) Irrigation and flood controls	267	186	224	191	209	158	114	58	74	47	54
(d) Industry and minerals	2412	2789	4438	2828	2846	3018	5074	4485	3918	3452	2439
(e) Energy	3083	3707	2146	4140	3575	2916	1566	1789	1514	995	1171
(f) Transport	2563	2313	2272	2419	2411	2015	2088	1602	1381	1144	1081
(g) Communications	92	111	-34	285	194	151	616	472	451	358	277
(h) Science, technology and environment	961	749	102	636	660	499	477	445	404	245	94
(i) General economic services	624	363	363	386	150	44	139	73	227	64	131

Contd.

APPENDIX 1 *Contd.*

1	2	3	4	5	6	7	8	9	10	11	12
(2) Social services	4473	3463	3605	3254	3202	2633	2134	1801	1593	1363	1012
(a) Education, arts and culture	1127	952	1001	902	1063	645	398	297	212	153	192
(b) Health and family welfare	1031	1040	950	864	872	750	728	690	637	552	211
(c) Water supply, sanitation, housing and urban development	1003	558	591	514	456	287	382	381	319	310	117
(d) Information and broadcasting	305	179	271	284	225	198	232	106	101	65	33
(e) Welfare of SC/ST and other backward classes	414	321	320	339	299	234	218	203	206	183	149
(f) Labour and labour welfare	95	49	85	30	20	15	15	10	12	7	298
(g) Social welfare and nutrition	478	364	387	321	267	504	161	114	106	93	0
(h) Others	0	0	0	0	0	0	0	0	0	0	12
(3) General services	25	23	18	53	58	69	58	58	140	52	20
(B) Central assistance for state plans	13428	11354	11778	9394	9082	8923	7079	6383	4554	4356	4043
(C) Central assistance for union territory plans	1282	1008	1070	848	736	828	916	680	535	462	414
III. Total Expenditure	113422	106717	94706	92906	79111	68261	62916	52665	43632	35534	29687
Defence expenditure as per cent of total expenditure	14.4	14.8	16.6	15.5	16.9	17.5	16.7	15.2	16.2	16.4	16.9
Plan outlay as per cent of total expenditure	29.7	28.1	31.9	30.6	33.1	35.5	36.5	37.7	38.1	39.5	40.1

* Includes debt relief to farmers Rs. 1500,

APPENDIX 2

CENTRAL GOVERNMENT'S DEBT

(Rs. crores)

Year	Internal	External
1982-83	46939 (26.4)	13682 (7.7)
1983-84	50263 (24.3)	15120 (7.3)
1984-85	58537 (25.4)	16637 (7.2)
1985-86	71039 (27.1)	18153 (6.9)
1986-87	86313 (29.4)	20299 (6.9)
1990-91*	151037	31851
1990-91**	151352	31831
1991-92*	171589	35122

Note * Budget estimate.
** Revised estimate.
All other years are actuals.
Figures in brackets are percentages of GDP at current prices.
Source: Economic Surveys.

25

EIGHTH PLAN AND INDUSTRIAL GROWTH: Trends and Constraints

P.C. JAIN

THE SEVENTH Plan (1985-90) is over. While a re-appraisal of the Plan is under way, in this paper an attempt has been made to assess the performance of the industrial economy during the Seventh Plan. Secondly, in a document on "Strategies for the Eighth Plan", as prepared by the Planning Commission, it has been emphasised that the economy must grow at an average rate of six per cent per annum. It is now realised that the agricultural sector may not be able to provide the necessary support in view of certain structural bottlenecks. Under the circumstances if the objective of six per cent overall growth has to be realised the industrial sector has to register 12 per cent rate of growth. It is felt that by the beginning of the Eighth Plan the industrial growth rate should be 10 per cent per annum. This paper also seeks to analyse some of the imperatives for the same.

The Seventh Plan growth target in the industrial sector was fixed at eight per cent per annum, based on 1970 series. In 1984-85, i.e. the last year of the Sixth Plan, there was a growth rate of 6.8 per cent with the manufacturing sector registering a growth rate of 5.7 per cent. In 1985-86 according to the 1970 Series, there was a decline in the overall growth rate of 6.3 per cent but the growth rate in the manufacturing sector at 6.1 per cent was higher than 1984-85 (Table 25.1).

Recently, a new series (1980-81 = 100) of Index for Industrial Production (IIP) was introduced. It was observed that, with new series, there was growth rate of 8.6 per cent in the industrial sector in 1984-85 and 8.7 per cent in 1985-86. The manufacturing sector, on the other hand, registered a growth rate of 9.7 per cent in 1985-86 as against eight per cent in 1984-85, which indicates a considerable improvement in production. During 1986-87, there was an overall slackening of growth, i.e. 7.5 per cent, and the manufacturing sector also registered an even lower growth rate, i.e. 7.2 per cent. This is significantly lower than the growth rate of 9.7 per cent in 1985-86 and 8.6 per cent in 1984-85. The trend during 1984-85 is, therefore, not very encouraging. The deceleration in industrial growth has taken place in spite of satisfactory performance of the infrastructure industries, namely, electricity, steel, coal, cement, and petroleum crude and refinery products. Electricity generation maintained a growth rate of over 10 per cent all along in spite of inadequate contribution of hydel generation. Production of coal, which had almost stagnated during 1985-86, increased by about nine per cent. Railway revenue traffic has also apparently increased by seven to eight per cent. However, compared to these, the rate of growth in the production of saleable steel and petroleum crude and refinery products were relatively lower.

TABLE 25.1: **Annual Growth Rates in Major Sectors of Industry**

Year (Weight)	Mining (11.46)	Manufacturing (77.11)	Electricity (11.43)	General (100.00)
1981-82	17.7	7.9	10.2	9.3
1982-83	12.4	1.4	5.7	3.2
1983-84	11.7	5.7	7.6	6.7
1984-85	8.8	8.0	12.0	8.6
1985-86	4.2	9.7	8.5	8.7
1986-87	6.2	9.3	10.3	9.1
1987-88	3.8	7.9	7.7	7.3
1988-89	7.9	8.7	9.5	8.7
1989-90	6.3	8.6	10.8	8.6
1990-91	3.5	9.2	8.6	8.4

Source: *Economic Survey*, 1990-91, p. 37.

Let us now observe the trends in some specific industries. The industries performing badly during 1986 were: sugar, cotton manufactures, caustic soda, synthetic rubber, cement, finished steel, steel structurals, zinc, ball and roller bearings, power-driven pumps, buses and trucks. While the rest of the industry registered an increase in production, the growth rate was not very high in several cases. Industrial with positive but low growth rate were: vanaspati, steel pipes and tubes, steel-casting, typewriter, sugar mill machinery, electric fans, passenger cars, jeeps and machine tools. However, the following industries have shown remarkable growth during 1986: jute manufactures, paper and paper products, newsprint, motor and two-wheeler tyres, footwear, fertiliser, petroleum products, hot metals, ferro-alloys, semi-finished steel, aluminium, copper cathode, lead, diesel engines, electric motors, power transformers, electric lamps, railway wagons, and two-wheelers. Industries which suffered stagnation during 1986 were: caustic soda, soda-ash, soaps, cement, steel structurals, steel casting, sewing machines, sugar-mill machinery, buses, trucks and bicycles.

From the above it is obvious that the momentum for high growth rate has yet to take place. Although there has been a significant growth in the letter of intents, industrial licences, registration with DGTD, etc., the actual level of investment has been much less than what it should have been.

The Planning Commission's own study in this regard shows that investment is not taking place at the desired rate. According to quick estimates released by CSO in January 1987, investment in the registered, manufacturing sector in 1985-86 is estimated at about Rs. 9,900 crores at 1984-85 prices. According to the Planning Commission, in the first year of the Seventh Plan there was a shortfall of about Rs. 1,100 crores in total investment. Further, much of the investment had taken place in the area of telecommunication, consumer electronics, petrochemicals and the automative sectors and not much of investment in the machine tools sector since May 1985. Thus, while production had not registered a significant growth, investment also lagged behind the desired level. What led to this situation of inadequate growth?

Barriers to Growth

No single factor fully explains slower economic growth rates or the present extent of industrial decline. To a considerable degree, contributing factors are related to one another in inconclusive ways and often interact with each other in an unpredictable manner. Some of them are:

High-cost Economy: A significant characteristic of Indian economy is the continuing rise in the capital cost. Decennial incremental capital-output ratio has increased from 2.79 per cent in 1960-61 to

4.49 per cent in 1970-71 and 6.22 per cent in 1980-81. Prices of capital goods are found to have increased at a much higher rate than in the developed countries. Between 1976 and 1985 they increased by 7.2 per cent per annum compound in India against 1.5 per cent in Australia, 1.39 per cent in West Germany, 1.1 per cent in Japan, 3.7 per cent in the Netherlands and 5.9 per cent in the USA. Investment cost per tonne of steel capacity increased from Rs. 1,100 in 1953-54 to Rs. 4,600 in 1974-75 and to Rs. 14,000 by 1983-84. In the case of fertilisers, investment cost per tonne increased from Rs. 1,180 in the early 1970 to Rs. 5,619 in the early 1980. Similar increases in certain other industries like cement, paper and paper board, sugar, tyres, tubes etc., during the same period were from Rs. 339 to Rs. 1,000; Rs. 2,558 to Rs. 7,269; Rs. 4,887 to Rs. 8,094 (late 70s); Rs. 1,917 to Rs. 5,457 and from Rs. 646 to Rs. 1,050 respectively.

One of the primary factors leading to such a tremendous increase in capital cost is the cost over-run due to delay in the execution of projects. During the period 1964-65 to 1969-70 the average over-run in the project cost was 19.7 per cent, during 1970-71 to 1974-75 it was 30.2 per cent and from 1965-66 to 1970-80 it was 20.7 per cent.

The problem can be viewed from another angle: with larger capital investments are, in fact, setting up comparatively smaller size units. To give some examples, a polyester cotton spinning plant in India is 20 per cent more costly than a similar plant in the UK. A polyester unit with 30,000 TPY capacity costs US $ 73 million investment in the USA whereas the 15,000 TPY capacity polyester plant in India entails an investment of US $ 70 million. Under the circumstances it is easy to understand why Indian industries are not competitive in the international market.

The high cost of investment and operation has been further compounded by lower productivity of the workers and lack of discipline which also contribute to a high incidence of breakdown and high cost of repair and maintenance. Between 1973 and 1980 gross value added per worker (at constant 1980 prices) increased by only 15.8 per cent as against 95.3 per cent in South Korea, 35.6 per cent in Singapore, 56.7 per cent in the U.K. and 26.1 per cent in Japan. During 1951-52 to 1975-76 productivity of Indian labour in the manufacturing sector increased by only 1.4 per cent per annum. On the other hand, in Taiwan labour productivity during 1976-77 and between 1960 and 1977 increased by 10.5 per cent and 11.5 per cent per annum respectively. In the Philippines, it increased by 3.6 per cent between

1956-57 and 1973-74 and in Singapore by the same percentage during 1970-77.

Faulty Perception: A serious barrier to growth faced by the industry relates to the general perception about the role of business and its character. This affects the industry in many ways. Although in the Seventh Plan the Government has recognised the role of the private sector in boosting industrial growth and accordingly liberalised various policies, problems arising from constraints such as slow implementation of these policies, heterogeneous rules and regulations, frequent inspections, dearth of finance, infrastructural bottlenecks, all of which can to a large extent be attributed to faulty perception, persist, whether it is finance or power or wagon allotment, preference is given to the predetermined priority sectors and industry does not fall in that sector. As a result it is always the residual resources that are left for industry.

Capacity Utilisation: The general level of capacity utilisation of the Indian manufacturing sector is not really great. The average for all industries came down from 85 per cent in 1970 to 77 per cent in 1986, indicating an enormous increase in idle capacity (Table 25.2).

The picture is all the more grim when we note that out of the 18 industry groups, only seven groups clocked capacity utilisation rates above 76.2 per cent for the 16-year period.

Industrial Sickness: The growing sickness is one of the most serious problem being faced by the industrial sector in India today. As at the end of December 1988, the total number of sick units in the portfolio of scheduled commercial banks stood at in the portfolio of scheduled commercial banks stood at 2,42,584 involving an outstanding bank credit of about Rs 7,705.3 crores.

Government Regulations: With a view to accelerating industrial growth, the Government has been announcing several measures. Apart from the liberalisation of industrial licencing from MRTP and Non-FERA companies, the measures include delicencing and broadbanding in number of industries, re-endorsement of capacity with reference to past production, minimum economic scales of operations in respect of certain industries, induction of modern technology and encouraging foreign financial and technical collaborations. Though industrial licencing is not required under the IDR Act, there are several other reference/procedures which are holding up industrial growth.

There is another category of industries where no licence is required. Non-MRTP/Non-FERA companies can move into and invest in urban areas up to Rs 15 crores and in backward areas up to Rs. 50 crores. But even here, there are: number of formalities to be observed. While the exemptions already made are a positive development and have spurred investment, MRTP and FERA companies which provide the thrust to industrialisation continue to be subjected to scrutiny at several points.

TABLE 25.2: Trend in Capacity Utilisation (1970-86)

Industry Group*	Rate of Capacity Utilisation %		
	1970	1986	1970-86
Beverage and Tobacco	105	86	97.8
Food Manufacturing	97	95	88.2
Petroleum Products	93	92	85.2
Chemical Products	84	85	79.9
Miscellaneous	109	58	79.6
Non-ferrous Products	90	94	79.3
Non-metal Mineral Products	84	85	76.1
Non-electrical Machinery	76	85	75.4
Transport Equipment	82	70	75.2
Textiles	75	68	73.5
Metal Products	82	97	72.5
Wood and Cork Products	100	71	70.8
Leather Footwear	83	57	70.5
Electrical Machinery	110	68	69.7
Paper Products	98	46	59.3
Ferrous Metals	59	61	58.3
Electricity	48	44	44.2
Leather and Fur Products	50	34	40.5
Average for Industries	85	77	76.2

* Ranked according to average capacity utilisation during 1970-86.

Apart from the MRTP/FERA angle, a project involving an investment of, say, Rs 50 crores, will necessitate, for example, permission for foreign collaboration and import of capital goods where required and permission from the Controller of Capital Issues if necessary from the State and Central Governments. The delicencing trend has introduced some element of flexibility and helped take specified industries and certain categories of companies outside the purview of industrial licencing, but that has not radically changed the picture because there are other procedures to be gone through before a unit is set up and becomes operational.

To get an idea about the extent of delays, the ASSOCHAM conducted a quick survey and contacted a number of companies to get to known their experiences. Some instances of the time taken are listed here.

Purpose	*Time*
Financial Institutions	4-10 months
Capital goods clearance for export	6-15 months
Environmental clearance: cases are still pending	3-18 months
State Electricity Boards: additional connection	2-3 months
Land acquisition	12-15 months
Company affairs: cases are pending	3-44 months
MRTP clearance: cases are still pending	2-44 months
Re-endorsement of additional capacity	6-24 months

Slump in Demand: Already industry has been facing a slump in demand in spite of the apparent growth of 7 per cent in 1986-87. Textile mills have been closed down while capacities in a number of industries like LCVs, scooters, refrigerators, fan, sewing machines, etc., are not adequately utilised. Though some industries have no doubt been expanding output there are others which were restricting it. In a sample of 152 industries, more than one-third had recorded negative growth.

Labour Productivity: Studies on labour productivity with the latest available data indicate poor productivity growth in India. The annual growth rate of labour productivity in India during 1960-61 to 1975-76 was 0.89 per cent. During a comparable period, labour productivity increased at an annual rate of 10.52 per cent in Taiwan; 11.20 per cent in Korea; and 3.6 per cent in the Philippines. A study revealed that the gap between labour productivity in India and Japan widened from 1: 2.8 in 1960 to 1: 7 in the late seventies, that between India and the USA from 1: 11 to 1: 12 and between India and Western Europe from 1: 4.3 to 1: 6.4.

In absolute terms also, labour productivity in different Indian industries is low as compared to that in similar industries abroad. For instance, in India, production of steel ingot per-man-year is 68 tonnes against 218 tonnes in the USA and 133 tonnes in Japan. Production of

Aluminium per-man-year is 30 tonnes in India as compared to 200 tonnes in the USA and 125 tonnes in Canada.

Lack of Infrastructural Support: While stressing the importance of a technological breakthrough for industrial growth, a matter that deserves attention is the development of infrastructrue, specially relating to energy, which is strategically important for industry. No doubt, of late we have brought about considerable improvement in power generation and production of coal. Still both the areas require to be looked into. There is vast scope for improving the plant load factor (PLF) of power units. About 65 per cent of the power generated comes from thermal units, which constitute 63 per cent of the aggregate installed capacity. But their PLF is still below the desired level of above 55 percent. In 1985-86 the all-India average PLF of the thermal units was 52.4 per cent, the highest ever achieved since 1980-81. The major reasons for low PLF are: equipment defects; defective maintenance and operation; declining quality of coal; lack of resources with State electricity boards for arranging spares/equipments in time; and inefficient management. The cost of power, and that of user industries, can be substantially reduced through effective measures to cut down transmission and distribution losses. In 1984-85, transmission and distribution losses accounted for 21.0 per cent of the power generation, reduction of which by about half, would have eliminated power shortage completely. It has been estimated that through a reduction in the transmission and distribution losses by one per cent, the cost of power could be reduced by Rs 78 crores (of 1984-85 prices and assumes cost of power at a rate of Rs 1.50 per unit). This means that the annual cost of power generation may be reduced by more than Rs 1,500 cores by conservative estimates as yearly transmission and distribution losses have been more than 20 per cent. Incidentally, this figure almost falls in with the cumulative loss of State electricity boards (Rs 1,424 crores up to March 31, 1984).

As regards coal, we have been facing a paradoxical situation in which despite the increasing pit-head stocks in coalmines, users are not able to get coal of the required quality. On an average, the ash content of coal affects productivity of blast furnaces of steel plants. It is estimated that one per cent increase in ash content reduces the production of hot metal by about three per cent. With the present quantum of ash content, the requirement of coking coal goes up to something like 800 to 900 kg per tonne of hot metal as against around 350 kg in Japan.

Lack of Adequate Modernisation and Technological Upgradation: The efficiency of our capital compares poorly with that of other countries. This indicates the poor technological progress by us. This is also reflected in the high incremental-capital-output-ratio (ICOR) in our country compared to that in many other countries. Again, looking at additional output per unit of investment, the figure in India is 15 per cent, compared to 22 per cent in Bangladesh, 28 per cent in Pakistan, 40 per cent in Indonesia and 35 per cent in Brazil. Though we have achieved remarkable success in sophisticated areas such as space programmes, atomic energy and oil exploration we have not taken adequate care to spread the fruits of science and technology to manufacturing areas as a whole. The credit we gain for our achievements in launching space satellites or in the field of atomic energy become meaningless to the masses if they are deprived of the basic necessities of life at minimum cost and at international quality standards. This is an urgent need to give priority to technological upgradation of industry which can help meet the basic needs of people in terms of basic goods and services.

While it is neither necessary nor possible to go into details, a few stray examples may explain the nature of the problem that arises due to technological backwardness, for instance, the consumption of energy in steel production in India is one of the highest input of energy per tonne of crude steel production. In India, it is 9.6, while in France it is 5.7, FRG 5.2, Italy 4.0, Netherlands 4.6, USA 6.0 and Japan 4.5 in terms of 106 kg calories. Notably, the inter-ministerial working group on utilisation and conservation of energy step up under the chairmanship of D.V. Kapoor indicated that a saving to the extent of 17.5 million tonnes of coal, 1.0 million tonnes of oil and 5,200 MW of electricity could result from energy conservation measures in the industrial sector. The report further indicated that an investment of Rs. 3,600 crores for implementing energy conservation measures in the industrial sector could save capital expenditure to the tune of Rs 5,780 cores on capacity build-up in the energy supplying sector by avoiding a recurring energy bill amounting to Rs 1,925 crores.

To take the case of aluminium industry, the latest technological advances in this industry have reduced power consumption per tonne of aluminium by anything between 13,000 KWT and 13,500 KWT. In India, power consumption per tonne of aluminium continues to be around 18,000 KWT. By making extensive changes in equipment design and process know-how, there are possibilities of reducing power consumption substantially, if not to the levels prevailing abroad. Even if we succeed in power consumption to the extent of 30,000 KWT per tonne of aluminium, this could reduce variable cost by Rs. 1,500 per tonne of aluminium, assuming a power tariff at 50 paise per unit.

The examples cited above indicate that there is ample scope to bring down per unit cost through changes in equipment design and process know-how. What is applicable in these few cases may be applied to industry as a whole. This essentially means modernization and upgradation of technology on a priority basis. Unfortunately, R&D efforts in India are far from satisfactory. This becomes evident from a look at the meagre R&D expenditure of around 0.7 per cent of GDP in India compared to 2.7 per cent in the USA, 2.0 per cent in Germany and 2.5 per cent in Japan.

Obviously, this was written much before the Eighth Plan took the final shape. Therefore, it is essential that, if not they wish proper though at plans updated, this part — SUGGESTIONS — be reviewed and amended as required, in the light of the July Budget also.

Suggestions

The following are some suggestions for bosting the industrial growth by, say, 10 per cent or more during the Eighth Plan period:

Concerted effort is required to tackle the problem of high cost. Attack on the cost has to begin with the capital goods sector so that the overall project cost comes down. Some specific suggestions are: encouraging the modernisation and technological upgradation of the indigenous capital goods sector at a cheaper cost; supply of steel and other core raw materials and inputs at international prices to the indigenous consumer goods manufacturers; lowering excise duty on capital goods; concessional rate of interest for the consumer goods industry; and creating scope for higher capacity utilisation by measures to ensure greater demand for the indigenously manufactured capital goods.

A second policy on administered prices with the objective to ensure that prices of administered items add to the competitiveness of Indian industry, is a need of the time. Steel, coal, power, fuel, aluminium and cement being the basic raw materials and inputs, greater care has to be taken towards monitoring the prices of such raw materials. The objective should be to ensure greater demand for such items, help to encourage greater production and economies of scale in these industries and thus reduce the cost of production.

. Through overhauling of the public sector undertakings engaged in the production of these items with a view to bringing down the overhead cost and rationalisation of expenditure through better managerial efficiency. Recourse to price increase as a measure to correct imbalances must be avoided as far as possible.

What is needed at the present stage is demand-oriented growth. A set of policy measures to encourage demand has to be initiated. The following suggestions need to be considered: development of rural economy through encouragement of small and village industries; development of the agriculture sector through diversification, larger technological inputs and also through price mechanism; while these two measures would generate tremendous purchasing power in the rural areas, there is also need for strengthening the rural marketing, infrastructure and also greater provisions of social infrastructure so that marketing activities can be strengthened in rural areas; stress on greater employment generation in the unorganised; sector and larger attention to such industries as housing construction, repairs, maintenance, etc.; a system of consumer credit for the consumer durables; and a mechanism to ensure that larger indigenous purchases take place out of the investment that are proposed to be made during the Plan period.

While it is necessary to reduce the cost of production and encourage greater demand for higher capacity utilisation it is also necessary to remove some important supply bottlenecks. Two such important bottlenecks are power shortage and labour problem. In onnection with these two, the following points need to be considered; increase in the plant load factor from the present level of 50 to 52 per cent to the accepted norm of 58 per cent; reduction in transmission and distribution losses, which is at present about 21.0 per cent, as against 5.2 per cent in Japan, 4.7 per cent in FRG, and 6.6 per cent in USA; increasing stress on hydel generation; improving cost efficiency of the power plant per MW of power has gone up from Rs 24 lakhs in the First Plan to Rs. 159 lakhs at the beginning of he Seventh Plan; need for change in the pattern of energy sales. The share of the industrial sector in total energy sales has gone down from 67.7 per cent in 1970-71 to 55.52 per cent in 1984-85; need for legislative support to improve the productivity of labour and better work ethos.

While the industry must improve the quality of the products, create quality awareness at all levels and introduce the quality circle concept. The Government must create: conducive environment for quality production. Some of the factors that need consideration are: purchase and price policy of the Government; the cost aspect, i.e. the cost of producing quality goods must not be prohibitive. Need for reviewing the fiscal policy *vis-a-vis* the production of quality goods; and commitment to quality on the part of the workers.

As has been pointed out by the Planning Commission, modernisation and technology upgradation must pay. In other words, such programmes have to be cost effective to be able to compete. Helpful fiscal policy support would go a long way in this direction. Necessary finances have to be provided and above all the capacity expansion that is likely to be generated as a result of modernisation and technology upgradation must be recognised. A significant step towards activising R&D activity would be the setting up of a technological bank to promote R&D in the private corporate sector. We must follow the example of South Korea, which has a Technological Bank to provide, among other services, venture capital for setting up risky ventures in high-tech areas. Canada went a step further in promoting technological changes through the creation of the Technological Transfer group of National Research Council of Canada. This group visits the industrial plants to identify the bottlenecks to production and assists in solving technological problems that their clients are eager to tackle. We, in India, would do well to emulate Canada's example.

The concept of large house dominance and its associated concepts, etc., need to be changed keeping in view the fact that such companies can play a very useful role in technological development and enhancing the competitiveness of the industry. As the Planning Commission's note has suggested, the total number of MRTP and FERA companies should be brought down to 200 to 300 and they may be assigned the task of giving leadership in frontier industries, technological sophistication, competitiveness and export promotion.

Similarly, the incensing limits may be raised and made selective depending upon the nature of technology, import level and size of investment. This will result in considerable saving of time spent in obtaining clearance. Further, as has been suggested by the Planning Commission, licencing should be simultaneously rather than sequential and all applications should be of a composite nature so that once a licence is issued there is automatic clearance of other things and the same time and cost over-run is minimised.

While the Government must continue to encourage development of small-scale units, it must be ensured that there is not too much fragmentation of capacity and creation of uneconomic units. After all, the question of economies of scale is also important for small-scale units. The definition of small-scale units needs to be reviewed to ensure that small-scale units being set up are viable and there is scope for modernisation and technological upgradation in the small-scale sector.

Finally, in order to help industry to meet the crisis of resources, there should be financial institutions in the private sector and such institutions, once permitted, should be allowed to compete with the public sector institutions. Also, the discrimination in favour of public sector undertakings in the matter of raising resources from the capital market, should be removed in the interest of at least the new entrepreneurs.

INDEX